Mapai in Israel:
political organisation and
government in a new society

Mapai in Israel: political organisation and government in a new society

PETER Y. MEDDING
Reader in Politics, Monash University, Melbourne

CAMBRIDGE
AT THE UNIVERSITY PRESS 1972

CAMBRIDGE UNIVERSITY PRESS
Cambridge, New York, Melbourne, Madrid, Cape Town, Singapore,
São Paulo, Delhi, Dubai, Tokyo, Mexico City

Cambridge University Press
The Edinburgh Building, Cambridge CB2 8RU, UK

Published in the United States of America by Cambridge University Press, New York

www.cambridge.org
Information on this title: www.cambridge.org/9780521144513

© Cambridge University Press 1972

First published 1972
First paperback printing 2010

A catalogue record for this publication is available from the British Library

Library of Congress Catalogue Card Number: 75-184900

ISBN 978-0-521-08492-5 Hardback
ISBN 978-0-521-14451-3 Paperback

FOR MY PARENTS

CONTENTS

PREFACE

This book seeks to explain how Mapai governed Israel from 1948 until 1969 when it became the major partner in the formation of the Israeli Labour Party. It analyses how Mapai's dominant role in Israeli society was first built up in Palestine prior to the establishment of the state, and how it successfully adapted itself to the changes that accompanied independent statehood after 1948. It is this pre-eminent role in Israeli society, and the characteristic and inter-connected patterns of organisation and processes of political decision making that accompanied it, which are our major concern.

In a work such as this the approach of the political scientist and the sociologist cannot convey the impact of the human miracle of the reestablishment of independent Jewish statehood after 2000 years of exile. On the other hand, the scholar who ignores it cannot comprehend and properly relate to his subject. Thus although it is acknowledged that the rebirth and development of Israel are its essential meaning, the reader will not find here the moving story of its various aspects: the process of settlement, immigration (legal and illegal), the horrendous persecution of European Jewry, self-defence and military prowess, economic progress, making the desert bloom, the ingathering of the exiles, the resuscitation of an ancient language, the flowering of a vibrant indigenous culture, the glorious resurgence of an ancient tradition and so forth. These, and many other aspects of Israel's rebirth, are triumphant examples of the power of human will, reason and emotion; in this particular case, they are generously mixed with the grandeur of the dream, with a prophetic and historic vision, with a deep-seated sense of justice and right, and with a stiff-necked determination.

These grand themes are not the substance of this book but the background against which it must be viewed. Our task is more modest; to examine and explain some of the fundamental political forms and processes within which this vision became a reality. It should also be noted that this book is not intended as a conventional and comprehensive history of Mapai. Many important events in the party, and in the state, and many important policies which the party initiated and put into practice are barely touched on, if at all. It sets out to explain the workings of Mapai rather than to chronicle its accomplishments.

This book represents the culmination of two research trips to Israel. The first was an extended stay from December 1964 until February 1966. The bulk of the research was carried out at this time, and it was later written up as my Ph.D. dissertation in the Department of Government at Harvard University. Financial assistance was generously provided by the Littauer Foundation in New York City and I am most grateful for their support without which the research would never have been undertaken and this book never written. The second research visit was made between January and March 1970. This served to complete the analysis of Mapai by covering events which occurred between 1965 and 1969, and led to Mapai formally ceasing to exist, and to the establishment of the Israeli Labour Party. This research visit was made possible by the financial support of the Australian Research Grants Committee, and the Memorial Foundation for Jewish Culture in New York, and their assistance is gratefully acknowledged.

I owe debts of gratitude to many people in Israel who assisted my research at various stages. This work would not have got off the ground had I not initially received the official recognition of Mr Reuven Barkat, the Secretary-General of Mapai. I am most grateful to him for this, and for permitting me to peruse party records, for making known his official recognition to many Mapai leaders I wished to interview, and not least for providing me with the assistance of Mr Mordechai Nesiyahu, Research Director of Bet Berl, and Mr Micha Harish, of the Department for International Contact at Mapai headquarters in Tel Aviv. I hereby wish to record my deepest thanks to them for giving freely and generously of their time and of their advice in guiding me through the labyrinth of Mapai, and in helping me to make the various arrangements and contacts that were essential for the pursuit of my research, and which in the faction-torn party at the time, were often extremely delicate, and complicated. My thanks for various forms of assistance and advice are also due to Mr David Golomb, at the time head of the Histadrut's Institute for Economic and Social Research, and to Mr Arye (Liova) Eliav, then head of Mapai's Organisation Department (and who in 1970 became Secretary-General of the Israeli Labour Party).

The bibliography at the back of this book indicates the main written sources of my research. A basic and important source was oral – interviews with a large cross-section of key Mapai figures who at various times occupied positions ranging from the highest in the land down to that of lowly local activist. Needless to say, I learnt a great deal from all these individuals, and I am grateful to them for the time they gave me in what were often extremely busy schedules. I assured them all that their anonymity would be protected, and often this was the condition of their agreement to be interviewed, and it is for this reason now that I do not mention them by name here. I have treated what they told me as primary evidence and after having checked it against other sources, I have, where necessary, simply incorporated it into the text without any acknowledgement of source. This is both because I believe that in studying a party a great deal of information must be gained in this fashion, by oral interview, and is not available in printed sources, and because I believe it would be of no further assistance to the reader to acknowledge the source as a Mapai official or leader who must remain anonymous. All interviews were conducted in Hebrew, and all translations of these, as of other Hebrew sources, are my own.

My thanks are also due to the staffs of the following institutions for their willing assistance; *Archion Haavoda*, the Histadrut Archives of the Jewish Labour Movement in Tel Aviv; the National Library at the Hebrew University; the Tel Aviv University Library, and the Widener Library, Harvard University.

The book or earlier versions of it have been read by the following scholars whose advice I acknowledge with thanks: Professor S. N. Eisenstadt, Dr Emanuel Gutmann, Professor Ben Halpern, Professor Nadav Safran, and Dr Jonathan Shapira.

I also wish to thank Mrs Joy Smith for her patience in typing a rather untidy manuscript, and Mr John Edquist for his sterling assistance with proof-reading–and with the index.

Last, but not least, I wish to express my deepest gratitude to my wife Ruth for her patience and understanding during the period of research and writing in Israel and Australia.

P.Y.M.

Melbourne
June 1971

1. THE PROBLEM AND THE SETTING

Among the new states established since 1945 Israel is something of an exception. It has avoided political instability, coups, internal violence, military takeover and general political decay: to the contrary it possesses a stable, effective, working, democratic political system enjoying widespread public support and legitimacy; the loyalty of citizens to the state is unquestioned; and its economic growth rate has been one of the highest in the world, putting its per capita income on a par with many modern Western European nations. All this has been achieved despite an under-developed economy at the outset, a population increase of over 200 per cent in the first fifteen years of its existence (with immigration accounting for two-thirds of that increase) and the need to defend its borders three times in twenty years. There are many possible explanations for Israel's success, but none would be satisfactory without close examination of the central role of Mapai.

What follows is a study of Mapai – the party that led the independence struggle prior to the establishment of the state, and all subsequent governments. It starts from the position that 'the distinctive institution of the modern polity...is the political party'.[1] Its centrality lies in the ability to direct and control governmental activities as well as organise mass support and participation. The political party is the major connecting link between governmental structures and social forces, and thus is among the key organisational structures that will enable a new state successfully to solve the political problems of independent sovereignty.

The major question which it seeks to answer is, how did Mapai, the governing party, cope with its various problems, including those of the new state? The general thesis of this study is that if Mapai had not been able to adapt itself to the changes brought about by political independence and a rapidly differentiating society with increasing and changing demands, it would not have been able to maintain its political dominance and retain political power. It seeks therefore to explain how Mapai organised to meet these specific changes whilst simultaneously fulfilling more general political party functions.

[1] Samuel P. Huntington, *Political Order in Changing Societies* (New Haven, 1968), p. 89.

1

Political parties and their functions

Political parties typically perform certain functions[2] in the polity and in society and it is with a brief analysis of these that we begin our study of Mapai. This is not intended as an exhaustive list of functions performed by political parties, but an effort to illuminate the operation of a particular party by investigating some of its most central and significant functions at three different levels – the party, the polity, and society.

In acting as connecting links between the social forces and governmental structures political parties facilitate and give expression to popular participation, organise public opinion, and communicate demands to the centres of government. In the polity they aim to control the executive and direct the government. Internally parties seek to secure solidary, material and ideal interests for members, and to ensure internal cohesion and organisational self-maintenance, which will enable the performance of their other functions. These functions are closely interrelated. Some interests of members, for example, cannot be gained without the party securing control of the government; but the party will not be able to win governmental control without popular support, while popular support might not be obtained without answering (or promising to answer) public demands. Similarly, continued control and ability to direct the government depend upon internal cohesion and organisational maintenance, and, deriving from this, capacity to make policy decisions; on the other hand, governmental control is a powerful incentive to continued organisational cohesion. These closely interrelated functions need to be spelled out more specifically so as to provide an analytical scheme within which to examine and explain the operation and organisation of Mapai.

Following the ideas of Friedrich[3] and Almond[4] we can list the major functions of political parties as follows: political recruitment; political socialisation; interest articulation; interest aggregation; leadership selection; providing for succession; rule or policy making; rule or policy application.

In new states the load that the governing party must bear in the performance of these functions is considerably increased due to their specific political problems. One problem, sometimes called nation-building,[5] is to gain legiti-

---

[2] The use of the term function raises many problems, an important one being the many varied ways in which the terms function, functional, and functionalist are commonly used. In the ensuing discussion therefore we shall be concerned with the most important political functions undertaken by political parties in the sense of roles or tasks, without any implications of functionality or dysfunctionality in relation to the political system as a whole, and without assuming interdependence as a mark of the system.

[3] C. J. Friedrich, *Man and His Government: An Empirical Theory of Politics* (New York, 1963), pp. 507–8.

[4] See the most recent statement in Gabriel A. Almond and G. Bingham Powell, Jr., *Comparative Politics: A Developmental Approach* (Boston, 1966), chs. 2–6.

[5] Almond and Powell, p. 35.

macy, support, obedience, compliance and loyalty on the part of the population, for the new system of government as well as for the new government.[6]
A second is state-building, which occurs when 'the political elite creates new
structures and organizations designed to "penetrate" the society, in order to
regulate behavior in it and draw a larger volume of resources from it'.[7]

Developing legitimacy, loyalty and obedience throws special emphasis, in
the first instance, upon the function of political socialisation. It also demands
the incorporation of new social forces which throw an extra load upon the
political recruitment, interest articulation and interest aggregation functions.
While legitimacy may be bestowed initially on the basis of the achievement
of independence, the governing party may convert this into popular support
for the system of government by widening participation, and by demonstrat-
ing effectiveness. Popular support may evaporate if the new party government
cannot rule effectively, cope with the various problems on its agenda, and
satisfy public demands and interest claims. Effectiveness itself depends greatly
upon the establishment of formal bureaucratic structures which by their
rationality and technical competence assist the political leadership to deal
with these problems.

Political independence is characterised by a vast expansion in available
political power resources which must be harnessed and integrated by the
party government through the establishment of a single national political
authority structure. Complex areas of political and societal responsibility are
for the first time handed over to the new party government, such as the
economy, defence, foreign affairs, education, health and welfare, the judiciary,
police power, and so forth, for which differentiated administrative structures
must be created. The new party government must also provide policy direction and administrative integration, by ensuring that the structures perform
the tasks for which they were set up and do not pull in contradictory directions.

The establishment, differentiation, institutionalisation and integration of
political structures are important aspects of the policy making and policy
application functions in the constitutional sphere, which governs relations
between political structures, of political structures to society, and norms of
behaviour within political structures. In older established polities by way of
contrast these have generally been finally settled in earlier times and can
usually be taken for granted. Similarly leadership selection and succession
may also become more prominent in new states because of their more problematic nature there.

Political parties are not alone in performing these functions, although they

[6] See Myron Weiner and Joseph LaPalombara, 'The Impact of Parties on Political
Development', in Joseph LaPalombara and Myron Weiner, eds., *Political Parties and
Political Development* (Princeton, 1966), p. 407.
[7] Almond and Powell, p. 35.

often play a central role. Thus they are shared with other societal bodies in a variety of combinations that differ from society to society. For example, political socialisation occurs within the family, the school, the religious group, and the ethnic affiliation, whilst specific political-role socialisation, i.e. political recruitment, is shared with the courts, interest groups, the bureaucracy and, in certain societies, the army. Interest articulation and interest aggregation are also shared with other political structures and groups. The political party generally plays a decidedly minor role in interest articulation, the bulk being undertaken by interest groups. Two aspects of interest articulation peculiar to it, however, may be highlighted. Ideological interest groups within political parties often use their influence within them to press for policies to which they are committed. The second is the interest of the party itself, its desire to gain and retain power, and arising from this its basic need to maintain organisational cohesion, as distinct from any purpose or value it seeks to achieve. Thus in decision making the effects that various alternative policies will have upon internal cohesion are often of the utmost significance.

Parties obviously play a major role in interest aggregation although the extent varies from system to system, depending mainly upon the roles of the legislature and the executive. One noteworthy aspect of this function is that it is served, not only by the formulation of policies but also by the selection of political leaders who represent certain interests. Their presence encourages involved groups to put their trust in the relevant institutions, as well as enabling them to promote particular policies. Interest aggregation may thus occur in the process of Cabinet formation, for example, or indeed in the formation of any executive or policy deciding group. This aspect of interest aggregation is especially relevant to the diffuse and symbolically-infused demands of ethnic groups whose claims for representation and visibility are often to be satisfied in this manner.

Within parties, the process of leadership selection is often difficult, and hotly contested. Party leadership confers a greater say in policy determination, the allocation of political resources and material benefits, and the selection of other key party personnel. It bestows prestige and deep internal gratification, and may also be used to achieve other desired values, such as economic security or social status. It is thus both a means and an end in itself.

Leadership selection may also be intimately bound up with policy making and policy application, and in structural terms with the control and direction of the government, including the bureaucracy. Party leadership may thus confer influence and control over some of the major political structures in a society. Parties share policy making and policy application with legislative and bureaucratic structures and important comparative lessons can be learned from the different ways in which these relationships are structured, and how parties share in them. Fairly obviously party–state relations in various societies contrast markedly, with a key variable being the relationship between party leaders and state leaders. Research into a governing political party such as Mapai must be directly and centrally concerned with it.

Clearly political parties perform crucial functions in most contemporary polities, and for this reason alone we ought to be interested in their internal organisation which, to a large degree, determines their external actions. Many possible aspects of internal party organisation and operation bear detailed analysis, as will be seen below, but the central question for investigation is its power relationships, upon which the performance of both its internal and external functions hinge. For these purposes power may be defined as participation in decision making. By examining decisions taken, one can ascertain how much, and how, power is exercised by either an individual or a group within a party. Such analysis also serves to reveal many of the complex and subtle forms of power and influence, particularly the two main forms: power based on coercive relationships, and power based upon the need for the leadership to gain the cooperation of the party followers, in short, power based upon consensus or agreement.[8]

Not all decisions made within a party in the course of its activities are equally important; some are trivial and others are of vital national significance. Parties decide upon tactics, finance, the minutiae of election campaigns, and the allocation of manpower and resources for day to day technical and administrative activities, as well as making decisions upon important policy, ideological and doctrinal matters, and electing leaders and representatives. To investigate all decisions would produce diminishing returns, and it therefore seems most fruitful to select the more important policy decisions. Similarly in view of the importance attached to popular support, a second major criterion are those decisions amenable to the greatest degree of rank and file participation, namely those relating to leadership selection.

A reasonable working hypothesis for research into power relations between leaders and followers is that leaders of political parties will neither dominate nor exploit, nor will they meekly follow. While in general leaders will have a more decisive say than followers, in certain important ways leaders will need to follow, or subject themselves, to various forms of veto. In particular, the more that leaders tailor their policy demands and initiatives to the expectations and views of their followers, the greater the likelihood that their leadership will be successful. To admit this, however, is also to accept it as a limitation on the power and authority of leaders wielded by their followers. The problem, therefore, is an empirical one. How much power is exercised by whom, and in what ways: how much reciprocal influence and mutual deference are there? Who initiates, who vetoes, who compromises, who backs down; how and why do they do so?

[8] This position is elaborated in Peter Y. Medding, 'A Framework for the Analysis of Power in Political Parties', *Political Studies*, 18 (1970), 1–17. The following paragraphs closely follow the concluding section of that article.

Participation, too, as a concept, needs further refinement and clarification. Our approach suggests that a variety of participatory roles are available to groups and individuals within parties. On policy matters these include direct and active participation; being consulted by decision makers; giving support to, showing compliance with or assisting in the implementation of decisions made elsewhere; being taken into consideration, or reckoned with by decision makers. In leadership selection they include the direct election of leaders; the election of delegates who either choose other leaders, or assist in policy making, or both.

A party's formal constitutional framework, and its social structure, also directly affect participation. The constitutional framework specifies the system of priorities which determines the validity and bindingness of party decisions. It makes provision for the establishment of institutions and defines the powers and authority which attach to them. It draws the lines of conflict within a party by laying down how issues are to be dealt with by various party institutions. Thus it defines the locus of sovereignty within a party to deal with cases of disagreement, in short, the arena where differences are finally settled. The party's constitutional framework determines who participates formally and how. It thus clarifies whose support must be gained and in which forum, and makes clear the formal steps that need to be taken in order to have decisions carried. It is also the constitutional structure which may vest formal authority in the rank and file by defining its role in elections and policy decisions.

Concentration solely upon the formal constitutional framework, however, may be misleading. For a more rounded and realistic assessment of party decision making its social structure must also be analysed, because this reveals who is available to participate and what they seek through their participation. Because a party may consist of a number of ideological, socio-economic, generational, regional, ethnic or religious groups, with their own outlooks, interests, and leaders and followers, to understand the process of party decision making their activities within the party's constitutional structure must be closely followed. And only by being aware of the subtleties and complexities of power relations, pointed out above, can these processes be correctly evaluated. These variables are closely related. Within a competitive system, the greater a party's social diversity, the greater its need to base decision making upon bargaining and discussion, and the greater the success of the various mechanisms of follower participation and influence over leaders.

The political and societal development of Palestine 1880–1948

New states and political parties are both the products of past historical developments, and for this reason they must be viewed against the background of the historical development of the society in which they have originated. This historical perspective facilitates comparative findings by enabling us to distinguish what is unique to a given society or set of historical circumstances, and, by implication, what is of wider significance. This section therefore deals with the societal and political development of Palestine and Israel. Our particular concern is the central role in this development of political parties, particularly Mapai.

The values, social structure and political institutions that characterised the Zionist attempt to reestablish an independent Jewish state in Palestine can be directly traced to the interaction between the ideological beliefs and aspirations of the Zionist–Socialist pioneers who entered Palestine in the period 1904–14, and the actual social, economic and political conditions which greeted them on their arrival. In 1900 there were some 50 000 Jews in Palestine, with the vast majority in the four holy cities of Jerusalem, Hebron, Safed and Tiberias, and some 4500 living in twenty-one agricultural colonies that had been established after 1870. In both types of settlement the main source of income was foreign capital; those in the former, mostly devoted to a pietistic life of prayer and religious study, lived directly on the proceeds of charity collected in other Jewish communities; while the new agricultural colonies, too, were supported by, and depended upon, Jewish philanthropy.[9] A Jewish proletariat hardly existed; the few workers there at the time had initiated an embryonic agricultural trade union, but this was rather weak, with agricultural workers mainly interested in becoming colonists.[10] Arab peasants provided the major source of labour. At this stage Palestine had the makings of a typical colonial structure: an economy owned and controlled by European settlers but dependent upon cheap native work. But there was one major difference. The colonists did not belong in nationality to the ruling power (the Ottoman Empire) which, in fact, was generally hostile to the growing Jewish settlement. On the other hand, there was nascent, but growing hostility towards the Jews on the part of the Arabs in Palestine (about 600 000 at the turn of the century) who owned most of the cultivable land. To establish Jewish settlement it was necessary for the Zionist authorities and the colonisers to purchase land from the Arabs.

Spurred by rising anti-semitism in Russia and imbued with Zionist–Socialist ideals, between 1904–14 some 35 000–40 000 Jews, later known as the Second Aliyah, came to Palestine with plans and hopes for national regeneration. Ideologically they strongly rejected and abhorred its colonial structure, its capitalist overtones, its dependence upon charity, philanthropy, and the exploitation of Arab labour. They argued that the mere purchase of land would not recreate an independent national existence; this would come

[9] M. Burstein, *Self-Government of the Jews in Palestine Since 1900* (Tel Aviv, 1934), pp. 4–6, 24–32.
[10] W. Preuss, *The Labour Movement in Israel* (Jerusalem, 1965), pp. 19–21.

about only on the basis of self-labour. These ideas were clearly expressed in
the writings of one of their foremost ideologues, A. D. Gordon.[11] This self-
selected elite of pioneers (*chalutzim*) were motivated, not by the conventional
revolutionary ideal of a violent seizure of power, but rather by the ideal of
personally creating a society and an independent, liberated nation from the
ground up. Thus they began by trying to become agricultural labourers, not
a particularly easy task for former students, middlemen, and the other urban
types of the European Jewish ghetto. They were shored up by the greatness
of their dream and their strong belief in the power of human will.

Voluntarism, then, was a major operative social ideal, stemming partly
from ideological beliefs and faith in human nature, and partly from the
political, economic and social vacuum which existed in Palestine at the time.
There was no coercive authority, no state, and no bureaucracy to undertake
this task or even assist in it. If anything was to be done in Palestine it would
have to be done by the pioneers themselves. Nor could they rely on the
assistance of the Jewish colons, whose preference for cheap Arab labour
aroused the resentment of the *chalutzim*. But more importantly, their inability
to find employment as agricultural labourers together with their socialist
ideals acted as midwives to proletarian self-help and eventually to new collective forms of social organisation, first in agriculture and later in industry,
which to this day constitute some of the distinctive characteristics of Israeli
society. The employment and labour problems were critical also to the long-
term interests and aspirations of the Zionist movement. It was futile to dream
of an ingathering of the exiles if the country could not support them economically. Industry, in its earliest infancy, was unable to provide the answer,
primarily because the same economic considerations operated there as in
agriculture, and cheaper Arab labour was preferred.

A solution was found in various forms of cooperative and collective effort.
Groups of workers banded together to form workers' settlements, some with
private plots as part-time supplements to agricultural work in the colonies,
others to undertake collective contract work for large-scale farmers. But the
most significant aspect of the collective solution was the move away from
settled areas to the deserted uncultivated lands to the north, in Galilee. Here
the collective movement reached take-off point, because it provided the
simultaneous answer to a number of problems. It provided employment,
avoided the exploitation of labour, enabled the population, reclamation and
resettlement of Palestine by the Jews, stimulated the flowering of an indigenous Hebrew culture, and most important of all, established a productive
agricultural base for Israeli society.

A basic feature of the political and societal development of Palestine were
the political parties. The Zionist pioneers of the Second Aliyah were not

[11] See the selections from A. D. Gordon, in A. Hertzberg, ed., *The Zionist Idea* (New
York, 1960), pp. 368–87.

individual Jews simply escaping from the persecution of Russia. They were members of Zionist–Socialist political parties who subscribed to particular coherent ideologies and who wished to put their ideological prescriptions into practice in Palestine, within the general framework of the Zionist endeavour. *The fact is that party pre-existed pioneering and all subsequent institutions.* In stressing, as we did above, what the pioneers had in common, we have obscured the issues that divided them, in the main, the ideological ordering of the reality which they encountered. And, as is often the case, differing ideologies gave rise to separate parties, and eventually to competing sets of institutional loyalties.

From the very beginning of the resettlement in Palestine, these parties, in keeping with their all-encompassing ideological view of life, sought to cater to the needs and interests of their members in many spheres. They produced separate journals and organised separate labour exchanges, soup kitchens, loan funds, cultural activities and agricultural collectives. They competed strenuously for converts and for the souls of unaffiliated immigrants. So pervasive was the belief in party and its necessity that even those who belonged to the non-party group did so, not because they negated the idea of party, but because they believed in one united party!

Increasing competition between the parties over control of the union of agricultural workers, the duplication of facilities and the waste of energy and resources in other areas created increasingly stronger pressures and demands for unity. Some progress was made in 1918 with the formation of the Achdut Haavoda party, and in 1920 with the establishment of the Histadrut. The Histadrut was founded to remove from the parties all functions except purely political ones. Thus it was formed by political parties, by way of contrast with Western countries, where trade unions set up the labour parties.

From the first, the Histadrut regarded itself as a microcosm of the future independent Jewish state; it was the 'state on the way'. Consequently, no sphere of activity was outside its domain. It catered for agricultural workers and trade unionists, set up a workers' bank, promoted varied forms of industrial activity, assumed educational functions, and founded its own newspaper. Its industrial activities were guided by autarchic principles and by the need to provide employment for the immigrants, rather than by economic rationality or profit motives. The emphasis was upon the needs of the nation as a whole.

In the Histadrut elections in the 1920s, conducted on the basis of proportional representation, Achdut Haavoda gained over 50 per cent of the votes, giving it control over its executive bodies, and over its ever-widening sphere of activities. This control was greatly increased when in 1930 it formed Mapai (*Mifleget Poaelei Eretz Yisrael* – The Palestinian Workers Party), by uniting with Hapoel Hatzair, which had consistently gained about 25 per cent of the votes. Thus not only was labour unity fast progressing, but in addition, executive unity and centralisation were largely in the hands of one political party, although under conditions of electoral competition with other parties, which formed the opposition.

But the labour sector was not the whole of the society. Palestinian society prior to the establishment of the state can be divided into three separate strata. The labour sector represented approximately 45 per cent of the population by the end of the 1930s, but carried more weight than this by virtue of its organisation, dedication, dynamism and ideals. Its leadership of the Jewish community further strengthened its position. The second was the religious sector, together with the old established Sephardi elements of Oriental extraction. The third stratum were the non-labour sectors; the shopkeepers, the merchants, the middlemen, the few industrialists and factory owners, many professionals, and large farm owners and orchardists. Most of these, with the exception of the last group, came from Poland in the 1920s or were refugees from Nazism in the 1930s.[12]

In the two decades prior to the establishment of the state the Jewish community in Palestine developed a fairly coherent and centralised political leadership within the framework of autonomy and self-government granted by the British Mandate. At first the functions of self-government were exercised with the acquiescence of the British, but in 1930 they gained legislative recognition. The Mandatory authorities were mainly concerned with ensuring law and order; they ran the police force, the postal and telegraph systems, the railroad and port facilities, and administered the civil and criminal courts, but left religious affairs in the hands of the religious authorities in each community. The Jewish community thus enjoyed fairly wide self-governing functions: the Elected Assembly and the National Council (its executive body) represented the Jews of Palestine before the British government in matters of civil and legal rights, and were responsible for economic activities, health facilities and, after 1931, education. The Jewish Agency Executive in Jerusalem, the local representative of the World Zionist Organisation, was given charge of all settlement activities, immigration, foreign affairs, education (until 1931), and defence.

By 1935, Mapai led all the main bodies of Palestinian Jewry. It welded the community together and brought about an important degree of coordination and unity. Not backed by the force of law it had to rely on the community's internal sources of authority. It therefore had to motivate and mobilise the community to cooperate voluntarily with its leaders and support their efforts, in short, to rule it largely by self-discipline.[13]

The Jewish community in Palestine developed this internal authority and

[12] See S. N. Eisenstadt, 'The Sociological Structure of the Jewish Community in Palestine', *Jewish Social Studies*, 10 (1948), 3–6.
[13] See A. Tartakower, 'The Making of Jewish Statehood in Palestine', *Jewish Social Studies*, 10 (1948), 209.

self-discipline from a number of sources. It derived partly from the leadership by the labour community which was characterised by self-discipline, voluntarism, and devotion to national goals. The rest of the community, too, were incorporated into the life and activities of the various national institutions, if only in a minor role. In some cases they shared the burdens and rewards of leadership which led to an internalisation of the goals, a commitment to the institutions, and the desire to continue to share their allocation of rewards and benefits. Of importance, too, in the incorporation of the disparate groups into one entity, was the existence of a competitive electoral system for the national executive and 'parliamentary' bodies, which attracted widespread registration and voting participation. The system was that of proportional representation, often a cause of splintering and excessive factionalism, but here it served the function of enabling the groups to unite and compete within one system which was recognised as legitimate. Eventually three major political blocs were established; labour, the religious groups, and the centre and right wing section. And within both the religious sector and the right wing there were strong and direct ties to the labour movement and commitment to its goals, as evidenced by the cooperation of Hapoel Hamizrachi, and the General Zionists. The right wing, middle class groups, despite their major economic contribution in terms of the inflow of capital and skills and despite their political successes at various municipal elections, never challenged labour supremacy.[14] The latter stood in direct contrast to the Revisionists who split from the Zionist movement and challenged the community's internal authority and self-discipline. It was militarily more activist about relations with the British Mandate and the Arabs, and held maximal territorial views. Furthermore, its attitude to socialism was such that most socialists seriously considered it to be proto-fascist. The Revisionists represented the major opposition group within the Jewish community.

External factors also contributed to internal unity, particularly the open hostility and sporadic violence of the Arabs, the inability of the British to guarantee the safety and security of the Jewish community, and the consequent Jewish concern with the clandestine organisation of self-defence. This emphasis on defence reinforced the leadership of collective agriculture. It was generally recognised that in the event of armed conflict the Jews would hold on to their territory only if it were settled. Thus it became a defence concern of top priority to establish collectives in isolated areas, so as to create a chain of Jewish settlement, and to set them up as semi-military outposts. Second, because of the need for clandestine military training the relatively isolated settlements provided natural locations for arms caches and training camps.

[14] On the reasons for their weakness see Dan Giladi, 'Private Enterprise, National Wealth and the Political Consolidation of the Right', in S. N. Eisenstadt, Ch. Adler, R. Bar-Joseph and R. Kahana, eds., *The Social Structure of Israel: A Collection of Readings and Research* (Jerusalem, 1966), pp. 85–97 (Hebrew).

Finally, because of their already high degree of self-discipline and dedication to the national cause, these settlements provided the first reservoir of officers and men for the Hagana, and its elite force, the Palmach. The labour movement too was greatly strengthened in its leadership position by its defence involvement. From 1925 onwards when the Histadrut established the Hagana it directed the defence activities. Only in 1945–7 did the Jewish Agency Executive take over and unify this defence structure (apart from the terrorists) which had grown considerably due to the Palestine community's involvement in World War II within the British Army, and its own internal development. At its head stood David Ben Gurion, a Mapai leader, Chairman of the Jewish Agency Executive and formerly Histadrut Secretary-General.

Beneath this overarching consensus about ultimate national goals and group cooperation in their achievement there existed a marked degree of institutional and ideological separatism and fragmentation. Political groups encompassed their members in major aspects of their political and social lives, and constituted what Neumann has termed 'parties of social integration'.[15] This separation divided the left from the right and in addition eventually separated the left into three major parties. Thus political parties typically had their own agricultural settlement networks, newspapers, housing schemes, youth and women's auxiliaries; whilst trade unions, health services and education, though slightly more unified, were still divided on left–right and sometimes party lines. In this situation ideological differences within, and between parties, and across the left–right axis were highly salient, intensely held, and bitterly fought out.

Of immense significance for the future was the fact that Mapai as the party at the head of this institutional arrangement learnt two important lessons that are not often learnt by dominant groups or parties within nationalist movements prior to independence. It gained experience in how to wield and exercise power in actual constructive, administrative and political situations; and at the same time it also learnt to share political power, both with other groups on the Left, and perhaps more importantly with groups on the Right. By gaining popular support inside Palestine and by acting as the stewards or guardians for World Jewry of the collective enterprise in Palestine, the political leadership there experienced important limitations upon political power.

The political elite in Palestine consisted of the leaders of the various national institutions, who represented the various political parties and their institutional offshoots. The highest values in the community were those of national service and dedication to the public interest over private goals and over private gain. Consequently it was widely felt, that those 'most active and most powerful in the realization of the main values and aspirations of

[15] S. Neumann, ed., *Modern Political Parties* (Chicago, 1956), p. 404.

Zionism should be the political leaders'.[16] As a result, most of the political influentials and officeholders were members of collective settlements, former agricultural workers in the colonies, ideologues and youth movement leaders. The influence of collective ideals was felt also in the great stress upon equality both in theory and in practice. The spirit of collective equality also extended to life styles; conscious efforts were made to emulate the simple and austere lives of the pioneers in matters of dress, consumer comforts and cultural tastes.

According to one Israeli writer:

The special ethos of pioneering – the strong emphasis on personal realisation, the egalitarian ideals, the tendency towards innovations, the increase in spontaneity, the societal concentration upon shared goals, the identification of individuals with collective activity guided by ideological decisions, the somewhat naïve optimism of the society's builders, the faith in the influence of decisions of will over social action and the consequent contempt for the 'sobriety of the experts', the drive for continuous progress, and the unique tension of a 'society under siege' – all left their mark upon the character of the Yishuv.[17]

A brief outline of the major changes in Israeli society after 1948

Independent statehood was one of three major changes in Israeli society after 1948, bringing about basic alterations in the social, institutional and value patterns that had characterised the Yishuv. The second derived from the tremendous immigration into the new state, particularly of newcomers from the traditional societies of neighbouring Asian and African countries, whose way of life, social organisation and value systems differed from those of European Jewry, and of Palestine. The third stemmed directly from the pursuit of industrialisation aimed at ensuring adequate means of employment and livelihood for the vastly increased population.

Independence and the creation of a state wielding coercive power brought simultaneous changes in both the institutional and value spheres. There was a steadily increasing tendency towards the formalisation, bureaucratisation and centralisation of political, social and economic activities. Relations previously informal, face to face, flexible, spontaneous and voluntaristic now became subject to more universal criteria and to more bureaucratic and rational standards. Ascriptive bases of recruitment have been steadily replaced by those of achievement.[18] Some degree of re-orientation in the dominant

[16] S. N. Eisenstadt, 'Israel', in A. M. Rose, ed., *The Institutions of Advanced Societies* (Minneapolis, 1958), p. 420.
[17] Dan Horowitz, 'The Differences Between a Chalutzic Society and a Normal Society', *Molad*, 146–7 (1960), 418.
[18] For an analysis of these processes as they have occurred throughout Israeli society see S. N. Eisenstadt, *Israeli Society* (London, 1968).

values has also taken place. In general, futuristic, selfless and collective devotion to national goals have tended to give way to immediate, individual and personal pursuit of instrumental ends.[19]

In the economic and social spheres, too, there has been a movement away from equality towards greater differentiation. The gap between the top and the bottom of the wages scale, for example, has widened since 1948 both in the civil service and in industry, and those at the top now earn relatively more than they did then. At the same time pressure has been applied by professional groups to further widen this differential in wage payments.

Economic modernisation has also entailed growing social differentiation. It has enabled the rise of new status groups with demands, expectations, values and needs of their own. Whereas in the pre-state era the autonomous existence of these fledgling groups was circumscribed by their relative insignificance and by the fact that, in the main, economic and social activities were valued to the extent that they contributed to national ideals and collective goals, after 1948 these groups and strata have begun to assert their independence. The new professional and executive groups have sought greater autonomy from the political sphere and demanded that achievement per se be recognised, that they be remunerated on this basis and judged by the universalistic and professional criteria of education, responsibility and expertise, and not by the collective considerations of the pre-state era.

These changes posed a critical problem for Mapai: its ability to adapt to the growing social and economic differentiation. If the party could integrate the new groups into its structure and mediate and resolve their problems internally it would become strengthened. On the other hand, if these groups could succeed in pressing their professional and economic demands as independent and autonomous interest groups outside the political party structure, the direct influence and power of Mapai would be weakened.

A major exogenous change affecting the Israeli political system since 1948 has been the entry of over a million migrants. Whereas in 1948 European Jews and their Israeli-born offspring accounted for nearly 90 per cent of the population, by 1962 42 per cent came from neighbouring underdeveloped areas. This migration wave has had a marked impact on many aspects of life in Israel, and has resulted in serious cultural, technological, educational, economic and social gaps and disparities. The basic problem is one of ethnic integration, and in this sphere failure might have led to major political disaffection and the steady rise of primordial, racial, and ethnic antagonisms. On the other hand, the integration of ethnic groups into the political system via the parties (provided that the parties were not sharply divided along ethnic lines), would make it easier to deal with ethnic needs, demands, and expectations.

---

[19] The extent and speed of ideological change in Israel, and the degree of decline of the dominant values in Israel, have been questioned by Alan Arian. *Ideological Change in Israel* (Cleveland, 1968).

Our later analysis will be concerned with how Mapai absorbed these various new groups, the products of socio-economic modernisation and differentiation, and immigration, and with how it directed the allocation of resources towards the satisfaction of their needs. In other words, how did it integrate them into the political system, and how did it integrate them into the party? The way in which the party had to adapt to the changes in society at large constitutes one of the recurrent themes in our analysis, whether it be the increasing socio-economic differentiation, the rapid bureaucratisation and increasing formalisation of political and social relations, the steady decline in ideological ferment, discussion and competition, the decreasing significance of formerly dominant groups, and the challenge of new ones, or the changes in the country's ethnic structure and cultural ethos. Only in so far as it was

Table 1.1 *Mapai membership figures 1930–64**

1930	6 000
1932	7 000
1935	9 000
1938	15 000
1941	19 782
1945	24 000
1946	31 000
1947	33 000
1948	41 000
1949	62 000
1950	91 000
1951	100 000
1952	129 000
1953	133 000
1954	144 000
1955	152 000
1956	154 000 (117 000) **
1957	159 000
1958	146 000
1959	172 000
1962	162 000
1964	196 000

* These figures have been compiled by the author on the basis of figures appearing in the party's official newspaper *Hapoel Hatzair*, the reports of the party's Secretariat and Membership Department, and figures personally supplied by the Chairman of the Membership Department in 1965.
** The sharp declines in the membership figures for 1956 and 1958 are statistical. In those years specific attempts were made to tally paid-up party membership rather than merely to add up the names on the lists, which produced an apparent decline in party membership. Thus the figure in brackets against the year 1956 represents those eligible to vote in the internal party elections of that year. On the other hand it should also be noted that an intensive membership drive took place prior to the internal elections in 1964, so that the figures in the Table for that year represent those eligible to vote. In that year approximately 15.5 per cent of the eligible voters in the Israeli electorate were members of Mapai.

able successfully to meet the demands imposed upon it by these changes could it retain power and exercise a directive influence over them.

The changing social bases of Mapai's membership
The changes in the wider society have been paralleled within Mapai. The vast numerical increase shown in Table 1.1 – over thirty-fold since 1930, ten-fold since 1940, five-fold since 1948, and two-fold since 1951 – closely follow the general population growth and the rapid development of the Histadrut in particular.

Especially striking is the period from 1947 to 1952 when Mapai gained some 100 000 members, three times as many as were members in 1947. The immigrant intake into Israel was also heaviest then with the arrival of over 700 000 newcomers. Similarly, the adult membership of the Histadrut (including workers' wives) increased by approximately 375 000 between 1947 and 1955. As the major party in both the government and the Histadrut, Mapai stood to gain members from the influx of migrants, provided that it encouraged membership and could convince newcomers to join it in preference to other parties. The rise in membership suggests that it did so rather successfully.

But the changes were not simply numerical. They also involved a radical reshuffling of the social bases of the party's membership. A party previously dominated ideologically and numerically by pioneering agricultural interests was transformed into one in which agricultural interests were insignificant in numbers and less influential in leadership and ideology, and one in which urban centres became dominant. Moreover, even within the party's agricultural sector changes occurred, as may be seen from Table 1.2.

Table 1.2 *Social bases of Mapai membership 1941–64 (percentages)*

	1941	1946	1950	1956	1962	1964
Agriculture						
Kibbutz	46.8	35.8	10.2	5.8	4.5	4.2
Moshav			9.3	9.4	7.7	7.4
Moshavot	18.3	15.4	14.4 ⎫		⎧ 15.4	
				84.8		
Cities	34.9	48.8	59.4 ⎭		⎩ 70.9	
5 largest cities						49.2
Development areas						14.7
Others						23.5
Sundries			6.4		1.5	1.0
N =	19 782	25 000	65 350	116 891	162 000	196 281

Not all the social differentiation within Mapai, however, is revealed in Table 1.2. It gives no indication, for example, of the widened occupational divisions, nor of those based upon ethnic origin, sex, religion and age, all of which became increasingly important after 1948.

While these distinctions existed within the party prior to 1948 they were rarely, if ever, expressed separately. Their interests were inchoate and subordinated to national and collective goals. The only interests with any degree of separate organisation within the party – agriculture and trade unionism – led the way in subordinating their particular interests to the collective demands of pioneering and Zionism–Socialism. These attitudes were directly reflected in the operation and organisation of the party as a whole, and especially in the way in which the party directed and controlled the network of institutions and groups that surrounded and supported it, and channelled them into collective and cooperative endeavour focused upon national needs.

This attitude was prominently expressed in the party's organisational ideology. From its inception in 1930, Mapai regarded itself as the vanguard of the Jewish renaissance in Palestine. In its role of pioneering vanguard it demanded, and received, devotion to collective needs and personal self-sacrifice from the vast majority of its members. It believed that its Zionist–Socialist ideal of creating a free working nation in Palestine could be fulfilled only through self-realisation and dedication to pioneering on the part of every individual member.

Greatly to facilitate its future expansion and diversification was the fact that in its membership outlook Mapai was from the outset highly aggregative rather than narrowly ideologically doctrinaire. Its only membership qualification was Histadrut membership. These limits were so broad that only a small proportion of the population, mainly larger employers, shopkeepers, and orchardists, were not eligible to join. In both belief and organisation it eschewed a narrow class outlook, as expressed in one of its key slogans, 'From Class to Nation'. This slogan incorporated its above-class orientation, the desire to provide the impetus and leadership that would weld all sections of the Jewish people into a classless nation and to encompass them in an inclusive and aggregative pioneering party. It is to its efforts in this sphere that we now turn.

PART ONE: PARTY AND SOCIETY:

THE INCORPORATION OF DIVERSE SOCIAL FORCES

INTRODUCTION

NON-COMPETITIVE AND COMPETITIVE PATTERNS OF ORGANISATIONAL PENETRATION AND CONTROL

Our concern in the next three chapters will be to examine the effect upon Mapai of these social changes. We shall investigate how Mapai coped with social differentiation; how it dealt with new social forces, with those recently risen in importance, and with well-integrated party groups possessing interests formerly subordinated to collective goals but later pressed as separate and self-oriented demands.

This analysis will be mainly concerned with the political party functions of recruitment, socialisation, interest articulation and interest aggregation, which are crucial to the gaining of electoral support and party control of government. Mapai's general aim was to gain assured, loyal and permanent support, although its tactics varied to suit the needs and qualities of particular groups. Despite flexibility in tactics a consistent organisational approach of institutional penetration and integration was pursued in Mapai's relations with these groups. Assured support for Mapai among organised interest groups was sought by capturing control of their executive bodies, and then coordinating their policies with those of the party. On occasion Mapai even organised the interest group's institutions in order to benefit from its support. Thus Mapai did not rely solely upon individual membership loyalty in its attempts to gain support but sought to surround itself with a network of supporting interest group institutions and executive bodies which provided more permanent and assured backing. Historically this pattern derived from the situation in the Yishuv described above, where such networks of affiliated or penetrated interest group institutions were established by all major parties. The question for Mapai after 1948 was the degree to which it was able to maintain this pattern, and the extent to which new groups could be fitted into it, or conversely did not cohere to it, forcing the party to adopt other tactics and methods to gain their support.

The theoretical argument of the first chapter emphasised that political parties seek public support by organising diverse social forces in order to control and direct government, and thereby to satisfy the material and ideal interests of party members and supporters. Public support at its simplest means gaining the votes of individuals at election time, at a more secure level it means gaining the support of whole interest groups and associations at election time mainly on the basis of favourable policies. A higher and still more assured level of party support involving a greater degree of recruitment is individual membership of the party and activity on its behalf, which renders electoral support a matter of course.

There are three basic types of non-competitive situation which ensure that high levels of secure support at the group and associational levels can be achieved by various degrees of organisational coordination through allowing only one party to play an effective role in the group. The first is complete organisational penetration and control by the party, so that the organisation is merely a front for the party, as in the communist front organisation model, and in the communist one-party state. In some groups the second type develops in the form of a pre-existing and deeply ingrained ideological identification and party commitment among group activists and leaders amounting to a marked degree of leadership and organisational penetration, plus widespread party identification among the rank-and-file members, but without formal organisational affiliation and control. Assured organisational support and almost unanimous individual backing for the party is nevertheless guaranteed. Finally a third non-competitive situation exists when a group or association affiliates formally as a body to a political party, or permits its members to join only one particular party.

Lower levels of secure and loyal support are to be gained in competitive situations, which exist when a number of parties compete for the control and direction of interest groups, or larger units such as trade union federations. The party gaining majority control via electoral competition wins crucial advantages in the ability to use the assistance, facilities, and executive bodies of the outside group for the purposes of gaining political support especially at national elections, but also between them. This affords a degree of organisational integration that may be consolidated by policies designed to keep the membership of the group satisfied with the party's conduct of affairs. It is also dependent upon the maximisation of individual party membership and activism within the outside group to ensure party control of its executive bodies at elections. This might be termed competitive penetration. Where a party successfully penetrates several such outside groups and associations its decision making bodies may face problems of interest aggregation and policy making due to their conflicting needs and demands.

Not all groups are subject to the same degree of political party competition and penetration. A group may be highly fragmented, or not organised for political or electoral competition, or organised in such a way that political party competition is not particularly relevant to its direct concerns. In such cases the party must place greater emphasis upon individual membership, recruitment and socialisation, and upon the mobilisation of more general policy or ideological commitments. This is limited competitive penetration.

In the following three chapters we shall show how Mapai successfully used these various approaches to integrate individuals and groups into the party. We shall see how it flexibly adapted itself to the varied institutional, organisational and individual situations of each of these groups, although we shall also be concerned with the limits of that flexibility.

2. AGRICULTURAL SETTLEMENTS: NON-COMPETITIVE ORGANISATIONAL PENETRATION

The kibbutzim
   The kibbutzim in Mapai during the Yishuv period

Until 1948 much of Mapai's leadership, vision and the embodiment of its most cherished ideals and aims were to be found in the agricultural sector, particularly in the kibbutz movement. In the 1930s, as we noted in Table 1.2, the kibbutz movement constituted the apex of an agricultural sector which accounted for over 60 per cent of the party's membership. Within that agricultural sector the kibbutz proportion totalled about six-tenths, with the remainder fairly evenly divided between the members of the moshavim and agricultural labourers in the small private agricultural villages and towns known as moshavot. The strength of the kibbutzim, however, lay more in their ideological primacy and organisational advantages than in their numerical weight.

Mapai was established as a pioneering Zionist–Socialist party, and in this sphere none excelled the highly prestigious kibbutzim. They reclaimed the land and settled it; used self-labour and exploited none; made demands upon themselves in the service of collective ideals; lived a life of strict economic equality; and carried a major defence burden. They were highly politicised, strongly aware of the political implications of their activities, and motivated by political goals. It is little wonder then that the kibbutzim assumed the leadership of Mapai, and the rest of the party seemed, at first, hardly more than an appendage of its kibbutz sector.

Party leadership further reinforced their ideological and numerical supremacy. In the 1930s and early 1940s the party's leaders were drawn directly from the kibbutzim or from the ranks of former kibbutz members or agricultural labourers, who had devoted themselves to full-time political activity on behalf of the party. Thus, in 1942, for example, five of the seven members of its active Inner Secretariat were in this category. In providing members and officials to represent the party in various political institutions, the kibbutzim exploited a crucial structural advantage; they could free members for political activity without undermining the collective's economic basis, which neither the moshavim nor individual urban families could afford to do. This gave Mapai reserves of ideologically trained and dedicated political activists ready to undertake party and Zionist tasks, with the financial burden often shared, or completely carried by the activists' collective settlements. The first signs of the weakening of the kibbutzim within Mapai arose from the party split in 1944 and the concurrent increase in urban party membership. The dissidents within Mapai in the late 1930s and early 1940s, while in the minority in the party, were mainly members of Hakibbutz Hameuchad, the country's largest kibbutz federation, where they commanded a majority, approaching 60 per cent. Known as *Siya Bet* (Faction B), they demanded recognition within Mapai as a separate faction. Later they sought the right, as a recognised minority faction, to veto majority decisions. Ideologically, the minority was more favourably inclined towards the Soviet Union and to Marxism, and in Zionist affairs it opposed partition of Palestine and immediate demands for a Jewish state. The majority at the party conference in 1942, led by David Ben Gurion, banned all internal factional activity. It believed that separate factions would inevitably seek ideological justifications for what were basically organisational, personal, or temperamental differences, which, unless curbed, would lead inexorably to a party split. The majority hoped to avert a split by banning factional activity, but failed. The minority maintained that the split was in fact brought about by the imposition of this ban by a personally antagonistic and politically aggressive majority.

The split in Mapai produced a major political realignment within the three major kibbutz federations. Prior to this Mapai encompassed two kibbutz federations, Hakibbutz Hameuchad and Chever Hakvutzot. The third, Hakibbutz Haartzi, was affiliated with Hashomer Hatzair. The secessionists from Mapai united in 1948 with the latter to form the marxist, pro-Soviet Mapam party. But the union was short and in 1954 they seceded from Mapam over the question of the Soviet Union and formed a separate party, Achdut Haavoda. With this the kibbutz movement became completely rearranged along party lines. Mapam was more or less synonomous with Hakibbutz Haartzi. Meanwhile the political and ideological differences between the Mapai and the Achdut Haavoda factions within Hakibbutz Hameuchad had become so bitter and violent that members of the two groups found it impossible to coexist within the same collective settlement. Collective settlement organisation is such that for orderly decision making and harmonious social life members must be of the same ideological persuasion. At the very least there must be preparedness to shelve political differences, so as to enable decision making to continue on the basis of direct democracy. Compromise is especially significant because economic, productive and work-assignment decisions are made collectively. Clearly defined ideological factions which act separately in all matters can quickly immobilise the life of the collective, as the inherent tendency in such situations is for the escalation of conflict on essentially economic and technical decisions through the infusion of ideology and ultimate values, making compromise well-nigh impossible.

Eventually those settlements with a clear majority of members of one party either drove out the members of the opposition and replaced them with members of their own party evicted elsewhere, or else the collective settlement and its property were divided between the contending groups into two autonomous settlements. Following this bitter division, the settlements in Hakibbutz Hameuchad which remained loyal to Mapai joined with Chever Hakvutzot to form a new federation, Ichud Hakvutzot V'hakibbutzim (referred to here as the Ichud), whilst the remaining settlements in Hakibbutz Hameuchad became the federation of Achdut Haavoda. By 1964, the Ichud numbered 76 settlements with 24 560 population (including children); Hakibbutz Haartzi had 74 settlements with 27 770 population; whilst in Hakibbutz Hameuchad there was a population of 22 297 in 58 settlements.[1]

The split in Hakibbutz Hameuchad took place in an atmosphere of immense bitterness and even violence which ended lifelong friendships and even split families. For those concerned it was a highly traumatic and searing psychological experience, and as well it left its mark on the political behaviour and activities of the Ichud kibbutzim. It was particularly disturbing to them in view of the high goals which they had set themselves – their desire to live a collective life embodying ideals of equality, self-labour, social justice and national service, and to be an example of self-sacrifice and dedication for the nation as a whole.

In the Yishuv the kibbutzim were fortunate that their direct and immediate economic interests – the consolidation and development of their agricultural activities – were regarded as central to Zionist and national concern. Consequently no special claims needed to be made, and no particular demands pressed, for their interests were supported as part of the national and Zionist effort. Thus the primacy of collective agriculture's needs was recognised and a major proportion of Zionist resources invested in it without typical pressure-group activity on its part. The kibbutzim, furthermore, did not view their function or role in terms of economic interest. To the contrary, they saw themselves as standing above material concerns; they were self-abnegating pioneers, pursuing collective and national goals and elevated human social values.

Independence, population growth, and the need for the rapid development of an industrial economy side by side with agricultural self-sufficiency, made it clear that the path of the kibbutz, however highly esteemed ideologically, was one for a self-selected minority of pioneers. It could never serve as a mass ideal; it was, at best, a partial, not a total solution. Large-scale solutions were to be found only in socio-economic modernisation, specifically in industrialisation and in technological progress. In economic terms this meant that collective agriculture, previously not the only, but the main, and relatively unchallenged recipient of scarce national resources and assistance, now met

---

[1] *Statistical Abstract of Israel* (Jerusalem: Central Bureau of Statistics), 16, (1965), p. 31.

severe competition in their allocation. It could no longer be widely accorded almost automatic priority over other economic demands; it now had to compete on more even terms with cooperative and private agriculture; and with industry in all its facets, large and small. What was previously accorded collective agriculture as of right now had to be fought for among a plethora of competing interest groups by the utilisation of various pressure-group tactics. Special assistance accorded collective agriculture in the Yishuv period seemed less justified and more open to challenge when continued into the state, and more like a privilege than a right.

For the kibbutzim within Mapai two aspects of these changes were central: the need to press economic interests competitively – to act as an economic interest group; and the need to assess the relevance of kibbutzic values to a society undergoing industrialisation and social diversification. These problems are closely interrelated. It was not just that economic interest and ideological interest, synonomous in the Yishuv, diverged in the state, implying that economic interests, to be achieved, had to be pressed separately. It was also that pressing them separately involved the kibbutzim in an internal ideological conflict that had to be resolved.

Central to their ideology was self-abnegation – standing above sectional, selfish, and particular economic interests for the sake of collective ends. To fight for their material interests, they either had to adapt ideologically, or fight for them in such a way that the ideological contradiction was muted. In fact, they did both; they generally conducted their pressure-group activity out of public view, so that the contradiction was rarely openly displayed; and they found ideological justifications for their pressure-group activity.

The significance of the Ichud's ideological stance in its economic activities is further emphasised by the Ichud's self-image. Even while acting successfully as an economic interest group in pursuit of particular interests, it saw itself in a completely different light. It believed that it was cast in the role of moral teacher, guide and ideological goal-setter:

> Our party, in its very essence, is intended to fulfil a mission, and not to satisfy the selfish interests of pressure groups...The function of the kibbutz within the party is to assist it in the fulfilment of its goal. The kibbutz is not an economic interest within the party, but is the expression of the party's vision; it is an instrument in its hand for the realisation of its social goals.[2]

Such views cannot alter the fact that the kibbutzim had economic interests to protect and did so rather successfully. They should, however, make us aware of the special way in which the Ichud united economic interests and ideological interests.

[2] A. Ofir, *Iggeret*, 28.6.1956. [Dates for newspaper references given thus throughout, i.e. 28 June.]

Economic interests

The agricultural interests of the Ichud kibbutzim are widely spread and so are the sources of its agricultural income, thus freeing it from dependence upon one or two products for the major part of its income. Its greatest income earner in 1961/2, poultry, accounted for only about 14.5 per cent of its agricultural income, while another six commodities (milk, deciduous fruit, bananas, cotton, eggs and cattle meat) each produced between 9.5 per cent and 12.6 per cent of its agricultural income.[3] Further diversification of its sources of income came from a rapidly growing programme of industrialisation; by 1960 the Ichud ran forty industrial undertakings, and sixty-one guest houses and convalescent homes, together employing 2235 workers with a gross output of IL34 995 000 and a gross product of IL15 902 000.[4] The decision to industrialise was not an easy one for the Ichud to take. To the extent that labour was not available within the kibbutz, it had to be found outside. But to hire labour outside meant severe moral, social and ideological problems for the Ichud, which was founded upon belief in the supreme and ultimate value of self-labour and on the negation of the exploitation of the labour of others.

What then were the Ichud's economic interests and how were they pressed? In the most general terms, its economic interest was to improve its economic position and status, both absolutely and relatively. All agricultural producers, kibbutz, moshav and private, share a common interest in maintaining prices and in stabilising farm income, particularly with regard to dairy produce, poultry, eggs, meat and vegetables which, after a period of expansion and high incomes, 1948–55, met severe problems and declining income after that as supply exceeded demand. Agricultural problems were further intensified by simultaneously increased industrial wages, which increased the cost of agricultural inputs. Farmers sought and received subsidies aimed at maintaining prices in the event of oversupply, linked to production quotas enforced by rationing water, land and credit. Nevertheless from 1955 to 1964 the index of prices received by farmers did not keep up with costs over the whole period even after it had already been adjusted to include all the subsidies and price supports paid to farmers in the period under review.[5] Where such general interests of agriculture were concerned, all sections and groups within the agricultural sector tended to pull together. Similarly, agriculture generally opposed increased urban income and consumption if rural income and consumption did not also rise commensurately. In these areas Mapai kibbutzim

---

[3] These figures are based upon the tables in the *Statistical Abstract of Israel* (pp. 376–396) and those in the Histadrut annual volume, *Shnaton Hahistadrut*, 5724 (Tel Aviv, 1964), p. 444.
[4] R. Kahana and A. Einhorn, eds., *The Social Structure of Israel: A Statistical Collection* (Jerusalem, 1966), p. 25 (Hebrew); *Shnaton Hahistadrut*, p. 444.
[5] *Statistical Abstract of Israel*, p. 286.

and moshavim agreed with Mapam and Achdut Haavoda kibbutzim and private agriculture. But in the distribution of the gains or allowances made to agriculture this unity broke down. The scarcity of land and water in Israel engenders competition, especially between kibbutzim and moshavim, as each section attempts to increase its proportion of these resources. General policies designed to assist one type of farm, for instance large-scale kibbutz collectives, often meant less resources for other farm types, such as the small-scale family moshav farm.

The Ichud rarely voiced its economic and agricultural interests publicly. To the extent that it did it appeared to subordinate economic needs to ideological goals and ideals. Its economic demands were rarely put in economic terms. Its inherited power position generally enabled demands to be pressed quietly via its extensive ministerial, parliamentary and bureaucratic 'access'. (In this it was supported by the kibbutz sections in Mapam and Achdut Haavoda.) In the periods 1950–9 and 1964–7 either the Minister of Agriculture or the Deputy Minister were members of the Ichud, as were many senior officials in the Ministry. (Only after 1956 were senior officials of moshav background appointed, and in the period 1959–64 for the first time was the Minister, Mr Dayan, of moshav background.) Furthermore, the proportion of members of Knesset of kibbutz background during the same period oscillated between 15 and 20 per cent, with a similar proportion in the Mapai delegation itself, most of whom were well represented in the Knesset's Finance and Economic Committees. A significant exception to the practice of the Ichud of conducting its pressure group activities out of the public eye occurred in 1964 after the resignation of Mr Dayan, when the Ichud openly called on Mr Eshkol, the Prime Minister, to give this position to its nominee (Mr Chaim Gvati, the former secretary of the Ichud and a former Director-General of the Ministry of Agriculture), in preference to a rival moshav candidate.

Its stance stemmed partly from ideological disinclination and conflicts with its self-image. Generally the Ichud was somewhat uneasy about making demands upon the state for price subsidies which would improve its standard of living, rather than have demands made upon it for the benefit of the rest of society, as in the pre-state days. While it supported price subsidies out of economic necessity and to stabilise prices, and out of just recompense to farmers,[6] it preferred to reserve its public pronouncements and pressure for the more general ideological and social values it wished to promote. Thus both publicly and in its own self-image the protection of economic interests took second place behind the promotion of moral values. But at the same time an essential condition of this was the marked degree to which its economic interests were in fact successfully pressed.

[6] See, for example, the speech of Aharon Yadlin, *Report 9th Mapai Conference, 2nd Session*, 1960, p. 78.

Ideological interests

The Ichud, by way of contrast, was quite unselfconsciously and publicly vocal in its response to the economic demands of other groups in Israeli society, and in the party. In stating the case for agriculture its spokesmen took care to avoid creating divisions between agriculture and urban workers which it regarded as two closely connected sections of the labour movement, and they strongly criticised the moshavim who pressed the case for agriculture by attacking urban workers for not working hard enough.[7] This emphasis upon the unity of labour formed an important part of its ideological outlook. It saw itself as the 'spinal cord of the state and Mapai', or as another leading member of the Ichud argued at a Mapai Conference:

> The greatest problem facing the state is how to ensure that its very founda-
> tion, labour agricultural settlement, will rest upon a human and social
> bearer, that is not liable to change or decline, but will be permanently fixed
> as the human foundation of the state, both economically and in terms of
> its social character.[8]

The kibbutz movement within Mapai also took strong exception upon ideological grounds to certain aspects of urban life and social differentiation. Concomitant with its emphasis upon unity it opposed wide wage disparities between different sections of the working population. In addition the ideological implications and justifications which accompanied such wage claims were vehemently rejected. Concentration upon material benefits and financial remuneration, to its way of thinking, constituted a major symptom and cause of the decline and loss of true pioneering values and the rejection of social and human equality.

The Ichud's capacity to press its economic demands successfully, and its ability to make its ideological viewpoint widely heard, were both dependent upon its organisational relationship with Mapai. This was particularly true following the decline in public acceptance of the collective ideology after the establishment of the state, and the steady growth of competing economic pressure groups both inside and outside Mapai making significant economic demands. Merely declaring them in public without any party connection would have been useless. These two aspects were closely connected: the more the Ichud could convince the party of the correctness of its values and ideology the easier it was for it to gain positions of power and access within the party.

Organisational relationships

The potential strength and influence of the Ichud within the party organisation were always greater than its numbers. They derived from its early ideo-

[7] S. Lavi, *Report 8th Mapai Conference*, 1956, p. 113; and E. Shoshani, *ibid.* p. 291.
[8] M. Mandel, *Report 8th Mapai Conference, 2nd Session*, 1958, p. 65.

logical and organisational role in the party, from the residue of ideological aspirations that continued in currency within the party, and from the ability of the kibbutz economy to free members for party service without endangering its economic and organisational stability. This last factor was relevant both to long-term service in the Knesset, the Histadrut, the civil service and the party bureaucracy, where few members were involved, and to short-term services, such as election campaigns where kibbutz volunteers and transport facilities were widely used to assist the party effort.[9]

After 1948, when the state had to establish structures overnight to cope with the governmental, bureaucratic, legal, diplomatic and military problems of independence, as well as the onrush of migration, it was greatly assisted in the supply of functionaries by the kibbutz movement in general, and by Mapai kibbutzim in particular. Their contribution was made even more significant by the absence of a career civil service or even of a corps of professionally trained administrators. Having had some experience in the pre-state days either in the kibbutz, the party, the Jewish Agency or the Histadrut, members of Mapai kibbutzim were quickly moved into central roles in the rapidly expanding administrative machineries of the state, the Histadrut and the Jewish Agency, as a stop-gap measure, and in this way they were able to influence policy execution and place their stamp upon the developments going on around them.[10] Thus in 1951 some 300 members of Ichud kibbutzim were engaged in various activities on behalf of Mapai, and the Ichud called for a doubling of this figure.[11] But by the middle of the 1960s, however, the situation had altered greatly, partly due to the establishment of a career civil service, and to the solution of many problems, and partly to greater

[9] According to Emmanuel Gutmann, between 10 and 20 per cent of total campaign expenditure is spent on election day itself, in addition to substantial voluntary services. See 'Israel', *Journal of Politics*, 25 (1963), 703–17. In fact the kibbutz federations call upon the established kibbutzim in particular to free 6 per cent of their members for activity outside their own kibbutz, either for the party or the federation itself, e.g. recruiting members overseas or assisting less developed kibbutzim, or for running its own administrative machinery. See E. Kanovsky, *The Economy of the Israeli Kibbutz* (Cambridge, Mass., 1963), p. 28. The extent of such non-paid voluntary activity can be gauged from the fact that it averaged 10 labour-days per member for kibbutzim established after 1947, 12 labour-days in those established 1935–47, and 15 labour-days per member in those set up prior to 1935, more in fact than is devoted to the internal administration of the kibbutzim themselves. It has even been suggested that they account for the difference between profit and loss in many kibbutzim. Paid political activities bring income to the kibbutz at least as great as the person would contribute if he worked on the kibbutz economy, but more importantly they bring long-term political advantages not easily reckoned in monetary terms. See Kanovsky, pp. 114–15.

[10] *Haaretz*, 30.3.1951.

[11] *Davar*, 5.10.1951. This figure probably does not include those in the state civil service. The extent of this support can be gauged from the fact that it has been estimated that one-eighth of the veteran membership left their kibbutzim during 1948–53 for permanent service in these fields. These, of course, would represent only a part of the total number of kibbutz members involved in these activities; see Kanovsky, p. 22.

unwillingness of the kibbutzim to free members for party service. It was also due to greater competition from other pressure groups for representative and symbolic positions of power for their own members. The degree of this decline in kibbutz activity on behalf of Mapai can be gauged from the fact that in 1964 there were only fifteen kibbutz members engaged full time in tasks on behalf of the party.[12]

The decline in intensity of activist involvement in party activities was a symptom of a general decline in intensity of Ichud relationships with the party. This could be seen in a fall in overall membership proportions, but its most characteristic expression was the development among the younger kibbutz members of marked demonstrative apathy towards the party, as well as disinterest in politics in general. Thus by the mid-1950s only about 43 per cent of kibbutz adults were party members (as compared with over 75 per cent in the early 1940s), and in some of the Ichud kibbutzim there was not even an organised party branch.[13] Ichud membership in the party followed a pendulum pattern. After intensive recruiting campaigns prior to Mapai Conferences these proportions were periodically raised only to fall again immediately after. For example, in 1956 the membership was boosted to about 50 per cent; again in 1964 it was raised from about 33 per cent to over 50 per cent, totalling just over 8350.[14] The low level of party membership in the Ichud kibbutzim was to some extent counterbalanced by the fact that Mapai received between 90 and 95 per cent of the votes cast in Ichud kibbutzim at national elections.

The Ichud was after 1951 keenly aware of the differences between its relationship with Mapai and those of the other kibbutz movements to Achdut Haavoda and Mapam, particularly the latter. These it regarded as kibbutz parties, and their settlements as party kibbutzim. Mapai, by way of contrast, was a national party representing varied interests and views. The kibbutz in the other parties acted as the party's vanguard, and within its ranks enforced complete allegiance to the party line, with all other views more or less formally proscribed. Similarly, the whole kibbutz was formally constituted as the local party branch.

The position in the Ichud kibbutzim was far less formalised. Members who wished to join Mapai had to do so individually, rather than belonging automatically through collective affiliation to the party. Mapai members within a particular kibbutz then came together to constitute the local party branch, but its organisation varied in different kibbutzim. In some there was no organised party activity at all; in others, the party members chose their own

[12] Y. Yizreeli, *Hapoel Hatzair*, 23.7.1963. Although it is not clear that the figures of the two periods are strictly comparable, or certain which posts are included each time, the disparity is wide enough to provide ample support for the contention made.
[13] *Iggeret*, 28.6.1956.
[14] These figures are based on party membership records together with those of kibbutz spokesmen and party leaders.

local branch executive, while in some the executive bodies of the kibbutz organised party activities.[15]

The sporadic nature of local branch organisation in the Ichud kibbutzim stemmed directly from differences between their functions and those of local party branches in Israeli politics. The local party branches of Mapai outside the kibbutzim actively recruited new members, and socialised them into its ways. They also sought to increase general support for the party in the surrounding areas so as to increase its vote at election time. This function was hardly relevant to Ichud kibbutzim where over 90 per cent of the voters already preferred Mapai.

The second major function which local Mapai branches in urban areas fulfilled was that of representing the party on municipal and Histadrut institutions. It was the task of the branch to coordinate all the activities of its representatives in the various bodies and to ensure that the national policy of the party was applied locally. This function did not apply at all to the party branches in the kibbutzim. Attempts to institute it would have been strenuously rejected and opposed by kibbutz members who regarded the kibbutz as a higher form of social institution than the party. According to one leading member of the Ichud, 'it would never enter anyone's mind to think that the local branch in the kibbutz should decide, for example, upon the membership line-up of the kibbutz institutions or ratify their work'.[16] Yet this is precisely what local party branches did within their spheres of activity.

Thus the main functions of the local Mapai branches in the kibbutzim were: to be a framework for ideological and political discussions in matters beyond the concern of kibbutz institutions; to instil political party consciousness in non-party members and especially the younger generation; to assist near-by branches organisationally and culturally; and to develop opinions on internal party questions, eventually to be brought before wider party bodies. None of these functions, even if carried out to the full, demanded strong or permanent local organisation on the kibbutz, and in fact many of them could be carried on informally within the close-knit structure of collective living in an autonomous community where the vast majority supported Mapai anyhow. As compared with urban branches, neither competing social forces and interests nor competing party structures interfered with the direct and informal communication of the party's message or with the mobilisation of activists to carry out its tasks, and consequently local branch organisation remained weak and informal.

Until 1958 the organisational relationships of the Ichud with Mapai presented few complications. The Ichud was the kibbutz movement of Mapai, a situation which needed little definition or clarification. Individual kibbutz members affiliated directly with one of the thirteen territorial regions into

[15] C. Gvati, *Iggeret*, 17.5.1961.
[16] Y. Yizreeli, *Iggeret*, 18.10.1962.

which Mapai was nationally divided. There was no formal connection with Mapai of the Ichud as a federation.

It was at first hoped in the Ichud that the participation of its members in many local branches would help to spread its moral and political message throughout the party. But in fact the reverse occurred and the Ichud found that its potential influence had been dissipated. Power and influence in the mass party that Mapai had become were determined by numerical strength and internal coalition formation within branches and regions, and not on an ideological or value basis as the Ichud had hoped. It soon realised that without unified and separate representation its influence would decline even further.

The new party constitution of 1958 conferred upon the major settlement movements within the party the status of separate regions, on a par with the other territorial regions, each consisting of its settlements alone. It was hoped that this exact representation of membership strength would maximise their influence. But the establishment of an Ichud region raised new problems of the political self-identification and activity of these kibbutzim within Mapai.

Mapai leaders in the Ichud sought to continue and maintain the widespread identification with and loyalty to Mapai, and to increase kibbutz influence within the party. But they were not prepared to do this if their political activity threatened the unity of the individual collectives, or the unity of the Ichud as a kibbutz federation. It therefore had to ensure that the individual kibbutzim or the Ichud's executive institutions did not become political battlegrounds, which might eventually split the collectives or the federation along political lines. But this was no easy task given the Ichud's aim of maximising its political influence, which demanded political organisation and discussion, and where, inevitably, political differences arose. The Ichud met this problem by adopting specific methods, tactics and organisational forms which were intended to ensure that political differences were not pressed too far.

One tactic was the opposite of ideological collectivism. In cases where its leaders and members were not in unanimous agreement, the Ichud generally refrained from taking majority decisions and from binding its delegates on party institutions to follow any particular line. Instead it gave them freedom to decide according to their own personal views. Taking binding majority decisions, the Ichud feared, might lead to divisive political conflict within the kibbutzim. It therefore preferred to allow delegates freedom of action even if this meant the weakening of its own position and strength as an interest group. Pressure groups generally tend to avoid issues which threaten their internal cohesion or the loss of membership support, but by way of contrast with the Ichud, they take majority decisions on issues and bind their delegates and representatives to behave accordingly.[17] This distinction stems from a basic difference in comparative social structures. The Ichud and its settlements constituted a system of mutually reinforcing loyalties. A wedge driven

[17] D. B. Truman, *The Governmental Process* (New York, 1952), ch. 6.

in at any point rapidly could have escalated into an issue of high principle and resulted in bitter internal conflict destroying the communal social structure and cooperative existence. Pressure groups, on the other hand, usually form part of a system of cross-cutting cleavages and overlapping memberships which allow conflict to be isolated. Paradoxically, then, the very strength of the Ichud, which derived from unity and unanimity of purpose and world-view, also constituted the major source of organisational weakness, because of the potential dangers inherent in its structure.

A second method adopted by the Ichud to avoid the dangers of splitting the collective communities was consciously and consistently to separate the governing bodies of the Ichud from those of the Mapai region within it, while still preserving enough connection to make it clear that the Ichud was the kibbutz movement of Mapai. There was, importantly, no formal connection: the Ichud institutions were separate from the Mapai region institutions. Thus political decisions were those of the Mapai region, that is, of the organisation of Mapai members within the Ichud, and not of the Ichud itself, which in times of crisis stood above the conflict and could not be held responsible for them. This isolation of conflict proved successful during various periods of internal party crisis between 1960 and 1965. For nearly three years after the party split of 1965 there were two party regions within the Ichud – Mapai and Rafi – with the former enjoying the support of about 80 per cent of the Ichud's membership, which again demonstrated the value of that tactic for the maintenance of the internal cohesion of the Ichud as a kibbutz federation.

Despite the absence of formal political ties there was not a complete separation between the institutions of the Ichud and those of the Mapai region. This was hardly possible given the marked degree of Ichud leadership and membership support for Mapai. Moreover, the Ichud as a close-knit federation of collectives did not wish to ignore completely an important aspect of the activities that went on within its boundaries, and sought some degree of control over the Mapai region institutions and their political activities, without any formal responsibility for them. Finally it was aware that a complete divorce of Ichud and Mapai region institutions might develop into competing centres of power and decision. A compromise solution finally adopted was for delegates of the Mapai branches in the kibbutzim to elect executive bodies which were chosen en bloc from a list of candidates drawn up by the Ichud Secretariat to represent a wide cross-section of the Ichud's Mapai membership. Thus the Mapai members within the Ichud were closely guided by Ichud bodies in choosing a political leadership, which had to work in close cooperation with both Mapai headquarters and with the Ichud's institutions.

These political problems and experience of the Ichud illustrate the difficulties of incorporating close-knit collective communities in competitive political parties. There seem to be two radically different methods. In one the collective community as a whole rigidly enforces conformity from the top via ideological collectivism – a line is adopted and all must follow it. This solution is suited to doctrinaire parties and collective communities, and allows little deviation or freedom of discussion. The cohesion of the collective is maintained by the rigidity of the enforced conformity, though this very rigidity makes a split inevitable once the line is questioned by a large enough group. The other alternative entails the separation and isolation of political activities from other collective activities to forestall and avoid politically-based conflict. For historical, ideological and temperamental reasons the Ichud was not interested in the solution of ideological collectivism; it preferred open, democratic and free political discussion and decision making. The price it paid to maintain this was to weaken its bargaining position within Mapai by refusing to bind delegates to adhere to majority decisions, except on issues of basic kibbutz concern when it had unanimous support. Otherwise it placed the future and unity of the collective above political power within Mapai, and at the same time maximised freedom of political discussion.

The overall picture of the organisational relationships between Mapai and the Ichud kibbutzim was one of non-competitive penetration of the Ichud by Mapai without formal organisational control or affiliation. It was achieved by shared ideological outlooks cemented by close political relationships at both leadership and membership levels, and a degree of organisational coordination. Some of its disadvantages for the kibbutzim were advantages for Mapai as a whole. The kibbutzim through their internal processes of socialisation guaranteed secure Mapai identification and voting support. This was reinforced by party organisational structure and activities within the Ichud, and by the Ichud's leaders, often Mapai leaders as well. Moreover, it provided Mapai with a cadre of loyal activists, largely motivated by ideals of volunteering and service to the general interests of the party, rather than seeking to convert this to the special and particular advantage of the kibbutzim within Mapai.[18]

While the kibbutz became weaker as the arbiter of social and moral values in the party and the state, it did not react in an extremist or doctrinaire manner. It tended more to nostalgia, regret and even apathy, rather than towards extremist ideological or political claims. Moreover, the Ichud emphasised the unity of the social forces comprising the party, and if it was opposed ideologically to the claims of some groups within the party it was without rancour or bitterness and without causing public embarrassment to Mapai. Overall its stance towards the party was an integrative and aggregative one: it did not adopt positions or act in ways that made it difficult for the party to integrate other groups or meet their demands, or act in an extreme or disintegrative manner in pursuit of its own claims. Its desire for internal freedom of political discussion was maintained in its attitude to other groups in the party.

18 See the discussions on this question in Iggeret, 10.5.1956, 28.6.1956.

In short, Mapai could count on the Ichud to give it secure and unquestioned support, and in a manner emphasising consensus and compromise. Non-competitive penetration and identification thus worked to the mutual advantage of Mapai and the Ichud.

The moshavim

Moshavim are cooperatives of small family farms, with a lesser degree of collective organisation and a narrower range of collective decisions than the kibbutzim. Nevertheless, the success of their social and economic organisation also depends upon a high degree of trust and close cooperation between settlers in many spheres of life, which would be made impossible by deeply felt political differences, and by intense or regular political competition. Although less likely than in the kibbutzim to be ideologically generated, such political conflict could mean the dissolution of the cooperative, and a split in the moshav federation, Tnuat Hamoshavim. Tnuat Hamoshavim therefore adopted the same basic stance as the Ichud kibbutzim: non-competitive, non-formal organisational penetration by Mapai as a political party. The movement as a whole was closely linked with Mapai, through historical connections and continued overlapping leadership and large-scale membership identification gained on an individual basis. While there was no test of Mapai membership for moshav membership, nor was the cooperative federation as a whole formally affiliated with the party, nevertheless the organisation of Mapai activities in the settlements was supported and promoted. That of other parties, on the other hand, was formally banned, not by the individual decisions of the settlements, but by the general rules of the federation. There was thus a high degree of identification without formal organisational affiliation: Tnuat Hamoshavim was Mapai's moshav federation; Mapai was the party to which Tnuat Hamoshavim was loyal.

The level of secure political support in the moshavim was generally lower than in the kibbutzim, despite the similarity in the enclosed, one-party environment. The moshavim were also distinguished by a lower degree of ideological commitment. More specifically they had to contend with problems of political loyalty and identification, and of ensuring secure support for Mapai, arising from their recruitment policies. Most of their new settlers after 1948 were not self-selected, with pre-existing ideological and political party commitments, but were immigrants sent to moshavim by the state authorities as part of the country's immigrant absorption programme, and were characterised by ethnic and religious commitments which cut across political identity. Thus to make the new moshav membership secure and loyal Mapai supporters raised significant questions of political recruitment and political socialisation.

The moshavim as a consequence of their numerical growth increased in prominence, whilst at the same time their economic problems multiplied. Together these changes generated a problem of interest articulation: how and through whom could their interests be pursued; how could they influence agricultural policy in their direction?

The moshav movement in Palestine before 1948

The first moshavism in Palestine were founded in 1921 by members of Hapoel Hatzair who were dissatisfied with life in the early kibbutzim. In rebelling against the rigid collectivism of Degania and other early kibbutzim, men like Eliezer Yaffe and Shmuel Dayan sought to create a new form of settlement which would allow greater scope and initiative for the individual and for individual family life.

The break from the kibbutz was not easy and gave rise to a rivalry accentuated in the 1930s and 1940s by competition for the allocation of scarce land for settlement. The moshav movement was regarded by the kibbutzim as having strayed ideologically by having diluted the elevated social goals of strictly collective settlement.[19] Within both Mapai and the Yishuv as a whole the moshav movement lagged behind the kibbutzim in importance, visibility and overall strength. In the continuous struggle for scarce settlement resources the kibbutz movement had the advantage; its leaders were more important politically and defence considerations coupled with the lower establishment costs of kibbutzim promoted this process further. Thus between 1922 and 1945 the kibbutzim grew from 19 settlements with a population of 1190 to 116 settlements with 37 400 settlers, compared with 8 settlements and 860 population in 1922, and 63 settlements and 18 000 population in 1945 for the moshavim.[20]

A further important reason for their lesser political significance lay in the organisation of the moshavim. Their family farm structure restricted members' time almost entirely to their farms, and to mutual assistance. Each member was himself directly responsible for his own financial obligations and his income was largely determined by the amount of labour invested by the family in the farm unit. Moshav members were thus less likely to be available for full-time or even part-time political activities.

The moshavim within Mapai represented about 10 per cent of the party in the 1940s (compared with nearly 40 per cent for the kibbutzim). The top party leadership included very few moshav representatives. The moshavim

---

[19] According to one account Achdut Haavoda considered the moshav 'as a suitable pattern for farmers, property owners and white collar class employees'. Kibbutz members described those who left as 'members of the family who were going over to a repugnant cult'. Cited in H. Viteles, A History of the Co-operative Movement in Israel (7 vols., London, 1968), Book Four, p. 35.

[20] Quoted in J. Ben-David, 'The Kibbutz and the Moshav', in J. Ben-David, ed., Agricultural Planning and Village Community in Israel (UNESCO, 1964), p. 50.

generally accepted the kibbutzim as spokesmen for those on the land, putting aside their differences in the common struggle for national independence, and emphasising their unity with them. As with the kibbutzim, in the period before the establishment of the state Mapai could count on the moshav movement for undivided support, achieved upon the basis of identification with the ideals involved.[21] Their self-image was that of a partner in the national struggle rather than of its leader.

Political developments in the moshavim after 1948

Their growth after 1948 made the moshavim more conscious of their potential political importance and less ready to accept second place. By 1964 there were 367 moshavim with a total population of 123 709. There were 216 settlements affiliated with Tnuat Hamoshavim, with about 75 000 settlers. In the 53 settlements established before 1948 there were 18 345 settlers, and in the 163 set up after 1948, the population was 56 549. Demographically these two populations differed by country of origin. Almost all the settlers in the veteran moshavim were of European background, while about two-thirds of those in the new moshavim were immigrants from countries of the Middle East and North Africa. Thus by 1964 over half the total population in Tnuat Hamoshavim was of non-European origin.

Mapai membership within the settlements of Tnuat Hamoshavim rose steadily, from 6174 in 1950 (9.2 per cent of party membership) of whom two-thirds were from veteran settlements, to 10 707 in 1956, reaching a peak of 14 600 in 1964, following a strenuous recruiting campaign prior to the party's 10th National Conference. The increase in absolute numbers masks a relative decline to 7.4 per cent in the moshav's proportion of party membership, representing about 38 per cent of the adults in the moshavim. At the Knesset elections in 1959 and 1961 Mapai was supported by just over 70 per cent of the voters in Tnuat Hamoshavim. The lower membership proportion and the lesser support for Mapai in the moshavim as compared with the Ichud kibbutzim indicate their less secure political and ideological commitment. On the other hand, their support for Mapai was numerically twice as great, providing Mapai with about 23 000 votes as compared with about 11 000 in the Ichud.

New moshavim: the problem of political socialisation

The members of the veteran moshavim were, in the main, motivated by ideological visions of becoming independent self-labouring farmers. They

---

[21] Y. Zohar, 'The Party in the Moshavim and its Problems', *Tlamim* (February 1954), 36 (Hebrew); see also G. Yaacovi, 'The Hityashvut and its Public Stance', *Tlamim* (April 1958), 20–4.

simultaneously served the goal of national independence. By the middle of the 1950s they had generally reached a fairly high standard of living compared with most other Israelis. Even if overshadowed by the kibbutzim, the veteran moshavim, nevertheless, formed part of the country's political and ideological elite, and were culturally fully integrated into the society of the Yishuv. Their internal government was democratic, with widespread internal participation and relatively friction-free.

The new moshavim settled by immigrants from Middle Eastern and North African countries present a significant contrast. Their economic position during the 1950s was very poor. Almost none of the settlers had been farmers before immigration. The intense ideological commitments of pioneering and Zionist–Socialist forms of land settlement were quite foreign to them. Internally, many immigrant moshavim were ridden by factionalism based upon traditional clan loyalties and rivalries which made difficult the establishment of stable communal institutions, and also interfered with economic and agricultural productivity. Immigrant moshavim were thus often faced with severe obstacles in developing some of the basic requirements of successful moshav living, such as voluntary cooperation and mutual aid cemented together by reciprocal trust.

Mapai dominance in the major administrative agencies dealing with immigrant absorption underlined the party's major political problem with regard to these settlements, whether it could gain and retain their support. It was understood that in the moshav the immigrant settler would acquire a party orientation as well as developing loyalty to the state. The task that Tnuat Hamoshavim and Mapai set themselves was to ensure that this would mean support for Mapai. Initial loyalty was made possible by the system of placing immigrants directly in a politically committed settlement federation. Here the resident instructors and other officials, formally the salaried representatives of the Settlement Department of the Jewish Agency, were drawn from veteran settlements of Tnuat Hamoshavim and were members of Mapai. This was made possible by agreement between the political parties, whereby the settlements were permanently assigned to settlement federations (and therefore parties) before the settlers arrived, which left settlers no opportunity of defining the political orientation and commitments of their settlement, even at some future date. (Individual settlers, on the other hand, could move to other settlement federations.) It was hoped that in this situation settlers in Tnuat Hamoshavim would recognise the practical advantages of political cooperation with Mapai, which controlled the Histadrut (and especially its health facilities in the moshav), the Jewish Agency and the government. Support for Mapai was further enhanced by the absence of competing and conflicting sources of political information and service provision which resulted from this system.

This system differed significantly from that of the Yishuv. Before 1948 scarce material resources were also allocated by agreement among political parties, but settlers were recruited by education and ideological persuasion. After 1948 settlers came 'from ship to village' and were allotted to settlement federations and therefore to political parties by a political agreement sanctioned by the state and institutionalised in the administration of the Jewish Agency. The element of free party choice was often entirely absent. In some periods after 1948 greater freedom of choice and flexibility existed, when immigrants were recruited both outside and inside Israel by representatives of the political parties and the moshav federations, rather than being sent directly to villages without any choice on their part. But even this element of freedom of choice ceased once initial settlement had taken place.

Initial recruitment was only part of Mapai's problem, the other part being that of maintaining the party identity of the new settlers, which meant more long-term political socialisation. In the absence of ideological commitment and pre-existing loyalty to Mapai, political socialisation and continued support rested heavily upon the functions of interest articulation within, and interest aggregation by Mapai in meeting the demands and needs of the moshavim. Despite the formal establishment of a one-party, non-competitive moshav situation in which all formal contact with opposition parties was banned, Tnuat Hamoshavim was unable to prevent members themselves making contact with, and developing loyalties to rival parties. That between 25 and 29 per cent of settlers in Tnuat Hamoshavim did not vote for Mapai in the 1959 and 1961 elections illustrates the degree to which opposing loyalties developed and the fragility of the Mapai political identity in the new moshavim. A permanent source of rival party support in the immigrant moshavim were the religiously observant members, many of whom were naturally attracted to the religious parties, and they represented the majority of the non-Mapai voters. The fragility of Mapai identification in the moshavim as compared with the Mapai kibbutzim suggests that a one-party non-competitive political environment alone cannot ensure loyal party support, and that this needs to be reinforced by other methods. One method, adopted by Tnuat Hamoshavim, was convincing the settlers that the party represented their interests.

Economic interests and their pursuit

Having separate internal constituencies did not weaken the internal cohesion of Tnuat Hamoshavim vis à vis competing groups. Common agricultural interests overshadowed the other differences between the veteran and the immigrant moshavim. Tnuat Hamoshavim sought to obtain for all of its settlements the greatest possible proportion of scarce agricultural resources by influencing policy making in a manner designed to promote the specific needs and propensities of their farms. In the long run it sought to create an adequate standard of living for members and to further the economic consolidation of the moshavim. Market conditions after 1948 combined with the structural inability of family farms profitably to produce certain crops, such as field crops, led to specialisation in some areas, and almost complete non-participation in others. Thus by 1963 Tnuat Hamoshavim produced 62 per cent of the country's milk, 53 per cent of its cattle meat, 60 per cent of its eggs, 65 per cent of its vegetables and 50 per cent of its sugar beet.[22] These products alone gave Tnuat Hamoshavim approximately 23 per cent of the value of Israel's agricultural production for that year (as compared with 32.7 per cent for the agricultural output of all kibbutzim).[23]

Tnuat Hamoshavim saw its interests as being in direct conflict with those of the kibbutzim. While the latter moved into the more rapidly expanding and under-developed sections of agriculture, moshavim were concentrated in sections facing severe crises of over-production. Attempts to curtail such production in the moshavim were looked on as preference for the kibbutz and its interests at the expense of the moshavim, particularly as they were linked to allocations of credit, water, and land. The moshavim argued that they would put credit to better use and that its allocation to kibbutzim simply meant less for them.[24] Conflict and competition between the moshavim and kibbutzim over agricultural policy and its implementation occurred at many levels, extending from the top policy planning strata of Cabinet, the Ministry of Agriculture, and the Settlement Department of the Jewish Agency, right down to the local planning and administering authorities. This had the advantage of allowing interests to be pressed locally and centrally by the party-affiliated agricultural instructors. While for the party this had the beneficial result of cementing the immigrant settlers' loyalty to it, it provided the latter with access to the political system which they would otherwise have lacked. In this situation individual moshavim, first through their instructors, and later through their own leaders, quickly learnt to play off the Jewish Agency, the government, Mapai, Tnuat Hamoshavim, and the Histadrut, and departments within each, against the other. According to Weingrod such tactics were common.[25] In such activities the Settlement Department of Mapai took a leading role, coordinating and mediating between various groups and interests, and seeking solutions suited to the overall interests of the party.

Many of the concrete economic demands of Tnuat Hamoshavim were satisfied, for example tax concessions for immigrant moshavim gained by the direct application of pressure through Tnuat Hamoshavim's Knesset members. The moshavim were also active in seeking protection against competitive imports. Most important of all was the growing subsidisation of dairy,

[22] *Shnaton Hahistadrut*, 5724, pp. 463–6.
[23] Based on figures in *Statistical Abstract of Israel*, and Kanovsky, p. 151.
[24] For representative moshav expressions of dissatisfaction with this state of affairs see Yaacovi, 20–4 and A. Assaf, 'The Controversy over the Ministry of Agriculture'. *Tlamim* (January 1956), 5–7. See also Viteles, Book Two, pp. 675–8, 713–14.
[25] A. Weingrod, *Reluctant Pioneers* (Ithaca, 1966), pp. 87–98.

poultry and vegetable production. Subsidies grew from IL 6.7 million in 1954 to 41.9 million in 1958, and to 124.1 million in 1964. (In that year subsidies for vegetables, milk, meat and eggs represented over 75 per cent of total product subsidies.) The moshavim were highly dependent on this subsidy income. In 1959, for example, subsidies in established moshavim accounted for about 35 per cent of net income, and in the new moshavim for 52 per cent of net income.[26]

The moshav movement also strongly differentiated itself from urban workers and their representatives within Mapai, and saw its interests threatened and damaged by their wage demands. This was particularly evident in the mid-1950s when the moshavim were struggling economically. This controversy erupted in 1956 at the 8th National Conference of Mapai. The moshavim took the offensive, seeking the abolition of the policy of automatic cost of living adjustments, and the pegging of the basic wage at its current level. Their arguments were economic, psychological and political. Economically, higher wages were inflationary, were not matched by increased productivity, and resulted in higher agricultural input costs. Psychologically they expressed a marked sense of relative deprivation and injustice based upon the comparative ease of city life and the harshness of rural living, heightened by their contribution to national defence, immigrant absorption and land reclamation.[27]

Politically they argued that this situation was dangerous as it would produce a rift between the members of these settlements and Mapai, unless their interests were met, and all the value of initial political recruitment and socialisation would be lost.[28] These considerations directed the attention of Tnuat Hamoshavim to organised action as a politico-economic pressure group within Mapai and outside it, epitomised in its struggle for increased political representation.

This struggle had many manifestations, but after the middle of the 1950s it was concentrated on the Ministry of Agriculture, particularly the portfolio and the senior administrative positions. Tnuat Hamoshavim aimed to free agricultural decision making from being a 'kibbutz monopoly', making relations between the two movements rather strained.[29] It was indignant at the continuation of the past subordination for which there was no longer any justification. It believed that the Ichud was more favourably disposed towards the kibbutzim of other parties than to Mapai moshavim. This was clearly expressed in the policies of the Ichud-controlled Ministry which discriminated against small-scale family farming. Control of the Ministry of Agriculture was also symbolically important to curtail the sense of relative deprivation

[26] *Bank of Israel Annual Report*, 1961 (Jerusalem, 1962), pp. 183–5.
[27] Shmuel Dayan, *Report 8th Mapai Conference*, 1956, pp. 98–101.
[28] Sh. Shoresh, *Report 9th Mapai Conference, 2nd session*, 1960, p. 61.
[29] Yaacovi, 20–4.

and to show members that their interests were being taken care of by those who understood them.

Just before and after the Knesset elections of 1955 Tnuat Hamoshavim put pressure on the Prime Minister to appoint the Minister of Agriculture and some senior administrators from the moshavim. But their representations initially went unheeded. A leading member of the Ichud (Kadish Luz) became Minister of Agriculture, the Deputy Minister was a kibbutz member from Achdut Haavoda, and both the Director-General and his deputy were also kibbutz members. To underline their deep dissatisfaction the four Mapai Knesset members from Tnuat Hamoshavim threatened to resign and then remained demonstratively absent from parliamentary sessions and party meetings for about six weeks. This pressure, well publicised in the press, finally brought results: two leaders of Tnuat Hamoshavim, Ami Assaf and Shmuel Dayan, were received by Prime Minister Ben Gurion and Finance Minister Eshkol and assured that the situation would be remedied.

These assurances were fulfilled with the appointment in 1958 of a new Director-General nominated by Tnuat Hamoshavim, which regarded it as only the first step. Final victory came in 1959, with the appointment of Moshe Dayan as Minister of Agriculture. Following his appointment a number of other moshav nominees were recruited into the higher levels of the Ministry. By the time Dayan resigned in 1964 a precedent of rotation of the Ministry between the two Mapai settlement federations had been established, as well as continued representation at the higher levels of the Ministry.

In keeping with this policy of applying maximum pressure upon centres of decision making the Knesset representatives of Tnuat Hamoshavim made a particular point of being elected to the major economic policy committees, the Finance Committee and the Economic Committee. In their Knesset activities relating to economic and agricultural policy they worked in direct coordination with the Secretariat of Tnuat Hamoshavim, which bound them to follow an agreed line in intra-party faction discussions, Knesset debates, in parliamentary committees and in individual discussions with ministers and officials.[30]

These activities of Tnuat Hamoshavim reflect an approach to interest group representation which, for example, contrasts directly with the British approach. The latter system is based upon an independent, autonomous career civil service, where impartial and disinterested administrators take decisions and advise politicians with regard to policy, and where the various interest groups make demands, appear as clients, as suppliers of basic information, or as members of joint civil service–interest group consultative committees. The moshav approach, made possible by parliamentary legitimation of party control of the upper levels of civil service, is satisfied with nothing less than the direct involvement of interested groups in, and their direct control of, key

[30] Y. Korn, 'Our Representation in the Knesset', *Tlamim* (April 1960), 48.

decision making positions having direct relevance to their interests. The latter are protected, not by the impartiality of the bureaucrat, but by his being a member of their own group, naturally having their interests at heart.

Political organisation

Pressure group activity of the type undertaken by Tnuat Hamoshavim depends for its success upon internal cohesion and a marked degree of formal organisation. Conversely, cohesive organisation would allow Mapai to gain maximum political support from this settlement federation. Ever conscious of the need to organise as a pressure group, Tnuat Hamoshavim was the main force promoting the Mapai system of regional organisation for settlement federations introduced in 1958. Its special economic, agricultural, and socio-organisational interests, it believed, could be satisfactorily represented and dealt with only if it spoke with one united voice within Mapai. Moreover, regional organisation manned by members of Tnuat Hamoshavim was promoted as a means of protecting and maintaining the political identity of the individual villages as the sole preserve of the party. Moshavim would be shielded from the pressure of other parties seeking entry into settlements for their officials and speakers by the argument that the settlements were open politically only to members of Tnuat Hamoshavim.[31]

Membership of Mapai, as in the kibbutzim, was individual, with members in each moshav forming the local Mapai branch with its own committee. This committee was directly linked with two bodies; the Moshav region, and the Settlement Department at Mapai headquarters in Tel Aviv, which organised and coordinated Mapai activities in the two settlement federations. Although there was a marked degree of leadership overlap on these two bodies, they were functionally distinct. The Settlement Department represented Mapai headquarters in microcosm; it conducted Mapai political activity within the settlement federations which in urban areas were shared by a number of departments: membership, dues collection, information, and organisation. The moshav region, on the other hand, was the organisation of Mapai members in the moshavim, selecting representatives, putting forward views, and organising its influence within the party. The Department, while serving both federations, concentrated more on Tnuat Hamoshavim and was staffed mainly by personnel drawn from its settlements. Numbers were partly responsible – there were 74 Ichud kibbutzim, compared with 216 moshavim – but the main reason lay in the absence in the moshavim of the ideological commitment of kibbutz members, and their relatively fragile Mapai identification, which demanded greater effort and activity.

Until the Mapai split in 1965, Tnuat Hamoshavim as a body was

[31] A. Ben Aryeh, 'The Status of Tnuat Hamoshavim in the Party', *Hapoel Hatzair*, 15.10.1957.

completely loyal to Mapai, and unlike the kibbutzim had no history or bitter experience of internal ideological conflict leading to settlement splits. Tnuat Hamoshavim faced an entirely new and potentially dangerous situation with the split in Mapai, which forced it to take steps to ensure its unity and cohesion as a settlement federation. In this it did not adopt the tactic of the Ichud kibbutzim of isolating the federation from politics and of permitting for a time the existence of two organised party regions within its ranks. Because Tnuat Hamoshavim began from a vulnerable position, with only about 70 per cent of the voters supporting Mapai before the split it was less able to afford organised opposition within its ranks, even if from a separatist Mapai group. It therefore took formal steps to maintain its non-competitive organisational penetration and identification by strongly reiterating its refusal to permit any organised non-Mapai activity within its settlements:

> It is easy to take a liberal and tolerant position and to declare that in the moshav, as in every other place in Israel, there is freedom of opinion and freedom of political organisation. At the same time it must be emphasised that this approach stands in direct opposition to the unity, cohesion and special situation of the moshav...this is conscious extremism, based on the recognition that it is necessary to prefer the cohesion of the moshav to every other need, even that of the political affiliation of every member of the moshav...In addition, the moshavim need a political ally which will enable them to exist...and in the past this connection was with Mapai. Such close connection cannot exist with two rival parties.[32]

Thus Tnuat Hamoshavim remained a Mapai preserve. Although some members of Rafi were active in its leadership, the unity of the moshav movement was not challenged by the escalation of this division nor was the non-competitive situation seriously questioned. Neither the minority nor the majority were willing to push matters to a point that endangered the cohesion of the moshav federation. At the 1965 Knesset elections Rafi received 22.2 per cent of the votes in the moshavim compared with 55.1 per cent for the Mapai–Achdut Haavoda Alignment. Had the Alignment received less than 50 per cent of the votes it is doubtful whether it would have been possible for long to ban the formal activity of other parties, and the non-competitive situation would in all likelihood have given way to a competitive, or coalition arrangement, or possibly to the kibbutz solution of the isolation of political activity and its separation from the governing bodies of the moshav federation. The loss of a Mapai majority would almost certainly have exposed the individual settlements to internal party conflict. One of the major advantages of the non-competitive situation, and widespread support for one party, was that politics and party differences were kept out of the internal government and decisions of the individual settlements which could be made on functional and personal lines. Internal party conflict might well have split settlements, in

[32] Sh. Shoresh, *Davar*, 10.12.1965.

addition to intruding a factor into their elections and decision making that was in most cases irrelevant to the questions at issue. The more that political party affiliation was a test for internal support, the more likely were mutual cooperation and trust to break down and with it the unity and cohesion of the moshav.

But, as we noted above, in many settlements unity and cohesion were already challenged by ethnic differences and conflicts. Here the Mapai region institutions played an important role in ethnic integration and therefore of interest aggregation. Relations between European and Oriental settlers seem to have been remarkably free of tension, and the leadership took special care to ensure that political problems of representation and power did not act as a catalyst in increasing ethnic competitiveness. Specific steps taken to avoid these problems included ensuring widespread non-European membership in the moshav bloc's delegates to the Mapai Conference (about half of the 269 delegates in 1964); strong representation in the moshav region's Knesset team (50 per cent and the Deputy Minister of Agriculture in 1965); and electing these moshav candidates for the Knesset in the Region Council from a 'balanced ticket' prepared by the Region Secretariat.

The overall picture of political representation suggests the conscious use of political recruitment and leadership selection for symbolic as well as material and interest purposes. Personnel selection and representation, together with the meeting of interest demands, thus played a significant role in the continued integration into Mapai of the moshav movement despite the radical changes that overtook it after 1948. While Tnuat Hamoshavim showed itself to be flexible and adaptable in this sphere, one of the most important elements in creating its capacity for such a response was its incorporation into Mapai and its ability to exploit the non-competitive organisational penetration that Mapai moshav leaders had previously established and maintained.

3. INDUSTRIAL WORKERS, ARTISANS AND PROFESSIONALS: COMPETITIVE PENETRATION

Competitive organisational penetration and control

We turn now to three occupational groups which between them constituted nearly 90 per cent of the party's membership – industrial workers, artisans and professionals. They live in competitive urban environments, where each person must fend for himself and his family. While their interests are furthered by various organisational frameworks, these individuals do not enjoy the protective security and social support of collective and cooperative environments. They are thus subject to the various cross pressures and competitive influences of the surrounding society, and, most importantly from our viewpoint, competitive political influences. In seeking to gain the support of these individuals and groups Mapai competed with other political parties and influences. On the other hand, success among these numerically significant groups was vital because it determined Mapai's overall political strength.

Unlike the situation of the kibbutzim and moshavim, which are unique to Israel, there was nothing unique about the competitive urban political situation. What distinguishes Israel from other countries, however, was the manner in which functional and occupational aspirations, aims and organisational forms were related to the party system, as symbolised in that unique institution, the Histadrut, the focus of competitive penetration.

Competitive organisational penetration was a major mechanism of political recruitment and socialisation, facilitating Mapai's efforts to integrate and incorporate diverse social forces into its structure and to aggregate their interests. Its main feature was the way in which Mapai sought control of functional and occupational organisations in order to gain secure political support and to impose a degree of political direction over their activities. Mapai's penetration was made possible because its members and activists in these bodies won electoral control against the competition of other political parties bent on the same end. The condition upon which it was based, therefore, was the formal and recognised participation of political parties in the internal electoral processes of these associations, and continued party competition on their executive bodies between elections.

Competitive organisational penetration in which national political parties fought for control of occupational executive bodies had the advantage for Mapai, the successful party, of minimising the strength of sources of influence outside the party. Rather these were brought within the party structure where, it was hoped, the welding influence of common party loyalty and aspirations would facilitate smooth and efficient policy making. It thus prevented the politicisation of functional and occupational demands that might have arisen had Mapai lost control of these bodies. Penetration and control of occupational and functional organisations by more than one political party would have infused functional and occupational policies with party interests and exacerbated differences, thereby rendering policy making much more difficult.

Industrial workers

Rapid immigration into Israel after 1948, and marked economic growth and expansion, together produced important changes in the country's social structure which had profound effects upon Mapai's membership structure. There was an absolute increase in the number of wage and salary earners in industrial and service occupations in both the private and public sectors, and a growing occupational differentiation to cope with the demands of a rapidly expanding economy in an increasingly complex technological era. These processes radically altered the structure of Histadrut membership as is revealed in Tables 3.1 and 3.2.

Table 3.1 *Membership of Histadrut branch unions 1944–63**

Trade union	1944	1950	1963
Agricultural workers	30 000	50 000	92 000
Clerical workers	7 500	42 663	90 000
Building and public works	7 040	29 094	88 000
General industrial workers	1 070	1 981	15 000
Metal workers	6 210	12 187	53 000
Food industry	3 645	5 774	15 000
Textiles, clothing, leather	2 360	3 352	25 000
Transportation	3 490	9 654	30 000
Woodworkers	1 280	3 245	10 000
Health workers, doctors, nurses	3 500	6 000	13 000
Engineers, technicians	806	1 928	11 500
Printing, paper	940	1 487	4 500
Seamen	—	—	4 500
Diamond workers	—	612	2 500
Teachers	965	2 181	17 000
Liberal professions, social workers, pharmacists, laboratory technicians, etc.	1 956	3 224	13 000

* Based on Preuss, p. 160. His figures are estimates only.

Of the Histadrut's membership organised in unions in 1963, 37.2 per cent were to be found in clerical and liberal professional unions and 62.8 per cent

Table 3.2 *Histadrut membership by occupational position* (in percentages)*

Employed in	1947	1955	1961
Agriculture	28.6	21.2	18.5
Industry and building	32.2	27.1	29.1
Education, offices and services	32.9	36.4	40.1
Unskilled workers	6.3	15.3	12.3
	100.0	100.0	100.0

* Based on Preuss, p. 160.

in manual workers' unions.[1] By this time the Histadrut's membership included approximately 90 per cent of the nation's employees.[2] Together with non-employed wives (permitted to join the Histadrut by virtue of their husband's membership), the adult population of the Histadrut (excluding members of collectives in both town and country) was in the vicinity of 800 000 in 1964. Moreover, in 1963, 1 690 000 people including women and children were members of the Histadrut Sick Fund (Kupat Cholim) which provided mutual health services, and they represented nearly 70 per cent of the country's total population.[3]

These dramatic changes in the party's main reservoir of potential members and supporters created a major problem of incorporation for Mapai which in the early 1940s comprised only about one-third city dwellers, mostly industrial and construction workers. Previously it had coped with small numbers of urban members employed in industrial occupations, and had retained its power with a predominantly agricultural base. Under the new conditions this would no longer be sufficient: to retain power it would have to make significant headway in terms of membership and support among the masses of urban industrial workers. In short, it had to integrate and incorporate them into the party. By the mid 1950s 55 per cent of Mapai members were employed in industry, crafts, transport, and the free professions, and another 14 per cent in various administrative positions,[4] which suggests that it successfully met this challenge. Our major task in this chapter is to describe and explain how it did so.

Grass roots penetration: the workplace

The basic cell of Histadrut organisation in almost every workplace in Israel, even the very smallest, is the Vaad Ovdim, the Workers Committee, usually elected every year or every two years by secret ballot among the employees. The potential political power of the Workers Committee, and, consequently

[1] Preuss, p. 161.   [2] Ibid. p. 151.   [3] *Shnaton Hahistadrut*, p. 364.
[4] S. Rolbant, *Mapai: The Israel Labour Party* (Tel Aviv, 1956), pp. 21–2.

the reason for political party interest in its members, particularly the Secretary (in large companies a full-time employee of the Workers Committee at the company's expense, in others, only part-time), derives from their constant and intimate contact with the workers in pursuit of their functions. Basically, these can be divided into two categories; those which are directly connected with the process of production and labour relations in the plant; and cultural, fraternal and social assistance activities.

The committee must agree to, or acquiesce in, management decisions to dismiss permanent workers, and takes an active role in promotions (and consequently in salary increases). In the sphere of social services most Workers Committees secure loans and other forms of financial assistance for workers, which are the most important direct instrumental benefit available to the committee. Decisions in this sphere are not subject to specific Histadrut regulations and are entirely at the discretion of the Workers Committee. Such loans can thus be used as political rewards, sanctions or incentives. Membership of the committee, is, itself, an important channel of occupational mobility. A significant proportion of its members, particularly secretaries, have moved into the ranks of management, especially in personnel work, thus benefiting from their specialised experience. Members of the committee, and the secretary, in particular, also undertake significant general service and advice functions, a form of counselling, social work and problem solving for employees, especially new immigrants.[5]

They also provide opinion leadership and act as centres of influence within the work place. Mapai's task is to convert this political potential into some form of political support such as party affiliation, or votes in Histadrut and Knesset elections. They aim, therefore, to achieve a majority of members on the Workers Committee, and thereby secure the position of Secretary. Once this is achieved, to obtain the desired political support, members of Workers Committees need not withhold services from non-party members, but can call upon debts and obligations which workers owe for services. Similarly, workers hopeful of gaining assistance and the favour of the committee may join the party and work for it, or make the committee's party members aware of their support. The establishment of such a network of reciprocal obligation and mutual benefit represents the conversion of trade union functions and social assistance into political advantages for the officials' political party.

This process is institutionalised in Workers Committee elections. In keeping with Histadrut practice most are chosen on a political basis with the rival parties presenting lists of candidates, either directly or indirectly. There may also be non-party lists, and in addition party lists often take occupational considerations into account, but the basic element remains the political party criterion. The first past the post system which is used in conjunction with

[5] See F. Zweig, 'The Jewish Trade Union Movement in Israel', *The Jewish Journal of Sociology*, 1 (1959), 38.

these lists of party nominees tends to produce committees with either a very large or complete majority for the leading party. The few available figures illustrate this trend clearly. In 1952 there were ninety-five workplaces in Israel employing between 200 and 500 workers, totalling 55 000 altogether. In twenty-one workplaces the committee was entirely Mapai in composition, in fifty-three there was a Mapai majority, in two the committee was entirely Mapam, whilst in only fifteen committees neither Mapai nor Mapam had a majority. Altogether Mapam was represented in only forty-seven of these ninety-five committees[6] at a time when it commanded the support of over 30 per cent of the total Histadrut population. In Haifa in 1959, in the eighty-one committees in the largest workplaces representing 30 000 workers, sixty-three were entirely Mapai in composition, while the other eighteen had decisive Mapai majorities.[7] Overall in 1965 Mapai clearly controlled the majority of the 10 000 Workers Committees in Israel.[8]

The party's task was facilitated by these direct and familiar channels of communication to the mass of workers via well-known party members and activists in the plants themselves to whom workers were often indebted. This enabled it to dispense with the many officials and organisers needed to transmit the party's message. Such access was particularly valuable at election time when Mapai members of the Workers Committees actively sought support for Mapai, on a direct, informal and personal basis, either at the plant, or by visiting the workers' homes. Small informal home gatherings to which workers were invited became increasingly common Israeli electioneering techniques. Here workers met leading party members and officials, and possibly even Cabinet ministers. Workers were also assisted in the completion of formal procedures making them eligible to vote.

Middle-level trade union activities

The direct and uninterrupted communication between Mapai institutions and its political activists in Workers Committees was further reinforced by the trade union structures which intervened between the Workers Committees and the central national executive bodies of the Histadrut. Mapai also controlled the intermediary bodies; the local Labour Councils, the local unions and the national unions. The result was greater capacity to form a united and coherent industrial policy and to have it communicated to the workers. It also meant the absence of conflicting policies and actions which could have arisen had the various sections of the trade union movement been politically in different hands.

Overall the local and national unions played an insignificant role at the grassroots level, with workers often unaware of their existence. Zweig

[6] *Minutes Mapai Central Committee*, 19.10.1952.   [7] *Haaretz*, 24.2.1959.
[8] *Minutes 10th Mapai Conference*, 1965, p. 12 (mimeo).

reported that he often found that 'in a small or medium-sized factory the Secretary of the Workers Committee does not know to which union he actually belongs as it does not matter very much to him, and his contact with the national union is only casual'.[9] By way of contrast, supervision of the Workers Committees by the local Labour Councils was regular and direct. The member of the Council responsible for that trade union paid regular visits to the plant, and discussed problems with the secretary of the Workers Committeee. He also supervised the elections and gave his final authorisation to the results. Where the responsible Labour Council official was also a member of Mapai, as he was in the vast majority of cases, the possibilities of co-ordinated party policy and action were extended, although it often gave rise to a conflict between local industrial militancy and the greater moderation of the more central structures.[10]

Industrial interests: ideological and material

Industrial labour in Israel also suffered somewhat from the decline in the public acceptance of the predominant pioneering ideology of the pre-state era. Previously manual labour was accorded an evaluation second only to agri-cultural pioneering. Many labourers were engaged in the direct upbuilding of the land, on roads, in building construction, and in essential services and industries. Workers no longer appear to be direct contributors of indispensable voluntary effort to the development of the state. What previously demanded moral idealism is now largely determined by state and Histadrut action and by economic incentives. Industrial workers with regular claims for higher wages, cost of living adjustments and, in general, for a higher standard of living now appear as a group seeking its own advancement, comfort and economic self-interest, which, although legitimate in themselves, do not elevate them ideologically.

Following these changes industrial workers and their representatives regarded their main interest as the need to maintain and if possible improve the standard of living of workers, and to provide social security. Consequently they strongly rejected attempts to alter the existing basis of wage remunera-tion, and, likewise, suggestions that lowering wages or keeping them steady would lead to a rise in productivity. They returned to this point again and again, but the closest their representative spokesmen came to clothing this in ideological garb was the oft-repeated statement that the workers were 'the section that engages in actual productive work', or the 'constructive and producing section'.[11] For the most part they were content to reject the various assertions that held workers responsible for the problems of Israel's economic situation.[12] Similarly they refused to accept the views of those (usually mem-bers of collective agricultural settlements) who held trade unionists responsible

[9] Zweig p. 39.   [10] Ibid.
[11] B. Z. Feurman, Report 8th Mapai Conference, 1956, p. 166.   [12] Y. Almogi, ibid. p. 119.

for having divided 'the camp into an organisation of self-interested on the one side, and an organisation of those who are concerned about the general interest and its future, on the other'.[18] In response to the demands of the moshavim for no wage increases, spokesmen for industrial labour demanded a greater say in fixing agricultural prices, so as to keep them down in the consumers' interests.[14]

Organisational relationships

Of particular note in this context was the absence of an internal administrative department within Mapai headquarters to deal with trade union affairs. This was a striking exception: we saw above the crucial role played by the Settlement Department in relation to agricultural interests and below we shall examine similar vital functions carried out on behalf of many other groups. Things were not always this way. Prior to 1948 Mapai had an extremely active Trade Union Department, but this gradually declined in significance, and was formally abolished at the 1956 Conference. After that Mapai relied upon its elected and appointed representatives within the Histadrut (chosen to carry out administrative and policy making duties on behalf of all Histadrut members irrespective of party affiliation) to undertake the task of protecting its political interests and promoting its views among Histadrut members. Its members in positions of responsibility within the Histadrut were expected to turn to the appropriate party body for consultation and direction. From here the party's view was brought to the Histadrut and implemented without the need for further intervention or mediation by a special department for the coordination of all trade union activities. Thus at the highest level of Histadrut decision making on matters of national importance, for example wages policy decisions or a major country-wide strike, the leading and responsible Mapai Histadrut officials usually dealt directly with the party's highest decision making bodies.

An administrative department specifically to direct these manifold purposes, activities, and policies was more suited to Mapai before 1948, when there were few internal differences about the aims and objectives of Histadrut policy, and more general agreement on principles. With the social diversification of the party after 1948, the growing differentiation and conflict of economic interests, and the questioning of the old ideological principles governing economic reward, and with the complicated relationships between Mapai economic ministers, Mapai Histadrut leaders and Mapai party leaders, it was obvious that matters of this kind would have to be settled at the highest echelons of the party, and that such a department was redundant. The immense growth of Histadrut activity, moreover, made the task of co-ordinating it within any one department almost impossible.

---

[18] A. Arad, ibid. p. 166.   [14] Ibid.

The ability to rely upon the party's representatives in the Histadrut to look after its interests at the top levels, and to carry out its policies, is a significant indication of the success of Mapai's approach of competitive penetration and control. By penetrating the trade union bodies through the activities of their Mapai activists, Mapai was able to direct and coordinate their policies in line with what it perceived to be its interests, and those of its members. At the same time it exploited this controlling position to extract increased party membership and support that extended beyond the trade union sphere into the realm of national politics. In this context the salient fact is that at Knesset elections Mapai consistently polled best in those areas of greatest Histadrut concentration, where Histadrut membership was at its highest, and Histadrut organisation and worker control at its best. In short, the stronger the Histadrut, the stronger Mapai, because of its successful competitive organisational penetration and control.

Independent artisans and craftsmen

This group includes independent artisans and craftsmen in textiles and clothing, leather and plastics, metal, food, paper, printing, building, wood and furniture, chemicals and services. Most were either self-employed or employed very few workers in small-scale establishments. Our analysis deals with their attempts to gain the support of Mapai in the furtherance of their economic interests and conversely Mapai's systematic efforts to secure their confidence and votes. In 1955 there were 22 000 establishments of small independent artisans and craftsmen, employing some 43 000 hired workers.[15] By 1964 there were 35 000 such establishments employing 45 000 hired workers. They provided the income of some 100 000 families in 1964, which represented 50 per cent of the independent sector of the population. Half were engaged in the production of goods and the other half in the provision of services.[16]

The 1951 Mapai Constitution specifically stated that 'membership of the party is conditional upon membership of the Histadrut'.[17] Thus independent artisans who employed others (unlike professionals) were excluded from Mapai membership. Their removal of this obstacle represents a remarkably smooth and successful process of integration, beginning with Mapai support for their policy demands and ending in their admission to party membership.

The changing place of artisans in Israeli society

Before 1948 artisans were not generally regarded as belonging to the employed classes: some were actually employers, while their life and work styles suggested that they had capitalist aspirations and ambitions. Moreover, the

---

[15] Y. Yagol, *Changes in the Jewish Labour Movement* (Tel Aviv, 1958), p. 145 (Hebrew).
[16] *Internal Report*, Mapai Department for Artisans and Cooperatives, 11 (August 1964). (mimeo).
[17] *Mapai 1951 Constitution*, ch. 4, cl. 1.

Zionist–Socialist revolt against the life of European Jewry was in many ways specifically directed against the petty-bourgeois, lower middle class urban Jew. No state could be built if its members aspired to petty-bourgeois occupations, and so the pioneers emphasised the sanctity of physical labour and membership of the working class. Small independent artisans clearly did not fit the picture of the ideal type of the Zionist–Socialist vision.

With the establishment of the state these matters appeared in somewhat different perspective. Mapai became responsible for the state and its economic advancement, and the major address for groups seeking to further and advance their economic interests. Groups which for ideological reasons were ignored in the Yishuv era had to be taken into consideration in terms of their contribution to the state's economy, and of the social welfare of those dependent upon them for their income. It soon became apparent that for economic reasons there was a great need for small independent artisans and craftsmen to assist larger industry. As this economic contribution became clear, ideological opposition gradually subsided, and even turned into support. This process passed through two distinct phases, firstly, recognition by the government; and secondly, recognition by Mapai followed by their formal incorporation into the ranks of the leading Zionist–Socialist party.

Governmental response

Part of the artisans' eventual success derived from the limited nature of their demands. Artisans' claims were specifically economic, within the capacity of the economy, and promised to result directly in greater productivity and efficiency. They were not directly linked with the claims of other sections and thus did not involve the economy in any chain reaction. Politically this made the conquest of artisans and craftsmen by Mapai easier to achieve, because it alone could deliver the economic goods demanded.

The first major step taken by the Israeli government in assisting artisans and craftsmen in their economic pursuits was the establishment of the *Bank Limlacha*, the Artisans Bank, for the purpose of providing loans and credit. It was set up after the 1955 national elections following representations to the Prime Minister, Mr Ben Gurion, and the Minister of Finance, Mr Eshkol, by Mapai members of the *Hitachdut Baalei Mlacha*, the Artisans Association. This step, regarded by the artisans as a most progressive and encouraging move, gained for Mapai as a political party much support and goodwill among them.[18]

Subsequently called upon by artisans, Mapai further strengthened the artisans' sector by increasing the artisans' share of the Ministry of Trade and Commerce's development budget; facilitating artisan representation in institutions; assisting with new buildings, workshops, tools and equipment; encourag-

[18] I. Spivak, *Report 9th Mapai Conference, 1956*, p. 196.

ing exports; and lightening the income tax burden.[19] This, naturally, gained for it secure and loyal support among this segment of the population.

Formal admission to Mapai membership

The second stage occurred at the Mapai Conference in 1960. Artisans and craftsmen employing small numbers of workmen were, for the first time, formally permitted to join the party, with the condition of Histadrut membership being specifically waived. Because the decision involved the requirement of Histadrut membership it was not merely a formal decision, but called into question ideological criteria and involved consideration of the nature of Mapai as a political party. Discussion revolved around the extent to which Mapai was still a strict class party after the establishment of the state. Thus the admission of artisans and craftsmen into Mapai symbolised the process of change which overtook the party after 1948.

The Minister of Trade and Commerce, Mr P. Sapir, the Mapai minister most closely associated with artisans, and their major patron, suggested that the Conference authorise 'the Central Committee to accept artisans and craftsmen into the party on an individual basis'.[20] Opposition on ideological grounds came from Mr Zev Onn, head of the Histadrut's economic enterprises and a leading member of the Ichud. Artisan membership would blur Mapai's labour image and dull its pioneering content. It might also prove to be inhibiting for members in the same branch as their employers.[21] A compromise wording spelling out certain conditions under which artisans might be admitted to the party was eventually put before the Conference. It permitted membership to artisans 'who accept the party's way'.[22] In proposing it Mr Meir Argov, M.K., chairman of the Conference Standing Committee, emphasised that 'artisanship and craftsmanship are as sacred as labour'. Mr Argov could find no justification for refusing membership to a group which already supported Mapai politically, particularly as professionals employing labour were fit for membership.[23]

Just prior to the vote the Prime Minister, Mr Ben Gurion, intervened to lend his authority and strong support to the admission of artisans and craftsmen whom he praised 'as part of the working and productive class in Israel'.[24] The compromise resolution gained a clear majority, and artisans and craftsmen who employed others were for the first time officially permitted to join Mapai.

Organisational penetration and control

Formal admission facilitated the organisation of artisans and craftsmen within

---

[19] Ibid.   [20] Report 9th Mapai Conference, 2nd Session, 1960, p. 138.
[21] Ibid.   [22] Ibid. p. 140.   [23] Ibid.   [24] Ibid. p. 141.

the party and enabled Mapai to extend further its influence within their ranks by organisational penetration and control, and by continued policy assistance. While this process had begun earlier in the 1950s with the activities of Mapai's economic ministers, formal admission led to its institutionalisation and its extension via the Department for Artisans at Mapai headquarters. This department sought the support and loyalty of artisans and craftsmen through activity within the local and central bodies of the Artisans Association, and by representing their economic interests to Cabinet and the ministries. It was further assisted by Mapai control of the artisans' major source of credit, the Artisans Bank.

By 1962 there were about 3000 artisans and craftsmen in Mapai and in 1964 there were 4150 members, about one-third of the membership of the Artisans Association. A membership drive immediately after added another 2000 members.[25] After 1964 they constituted a recognised electoral sector of the party Conference, electing over thirty delegates in that year. Similarly 150 were elected to the executive bodies of local party branches. They represented the party on the municipal councils of Tel Aviv, Haifa and Jerusalem, and two smaller cities. In 1959 Mapai gave a secure place on its Knesset list to Mr Joseph Fisher, Chairman of the Artisans Association, which he retained in 1961 and 1965. In the Knesset he served on the major economic committees.

Control of the Artisans Association fell into Mapai's hands after it realised the electoral potential of this group and decided to organise within it to gain its votes. It thus succeeded in transforming a highly divided, factionalised and splintered organisation with little real power and low membership into the second largest trade association in the country – highly organised, disciplined, and with a rapidly increasing and interested membership. For example, Mapai was instrumental in the democratic reorganisation of the Artisans Association in 1960 which created closer ties between its central and local executive bodies. In that year's elections Mapai was supported by over 75 per cent of its members which gave it overwhelming control of all its decision making bodies.[26]

Mapai organisational control existed also at the local level. By 1960 it had won power in the local executive bodies of the Association in most places, and in 1964 finally gained control of Jerusalem, the only major city till then beyond its net. Altogether the Artisans Association had 39 branches and parallel with each of these the department established an artisans' cell within the relevant Mapai party branch. Through these cells it extended its control down to the grassroots.

In conjunction with the central bodies of the Artisans Association the department established, equipped and staffed the local branch offices of the

[25] *From Conference to Conference* (Tel Aviv, 1964), p. 45.
[26] *Internal Report* (March–June 1963).

Association, and later set up clubs and halls for recreational, cultural and social activities. Thus organisational control at the top was reinforced and strengthened by the direct involvement of the department in local social and organisational matters. It was further facilitated by having the same individuals serve as local and regional organisers for both the Artisans Association and the Mapai department. Mapai's political advantages in terms of organisational penetration and control are obvious.

But it was the combined ability of the Department and the Artisans Association to secure and further the group's economic demands and needs that continued and reinforced this loyalty and affiliation gained through such social and organisational activity. Artisans' rather limited economic demands were successfully met *outside* the party's formal decision making bodies through direct consultation between representatives of artisans' interests and ministers and civil servants. The common party membership and preexisting political consensus were emphasised and exploited in order to facilitate this consultative decision making process. In many instances the department, as the central forum for intra-party consultations, not only initiated issue discussion, but was itself the actual decision making body, through coordination of the responsible and relevant decision makers among Mapai ministers, Knesset members, civil servants, Artisans Bank officials and so forth.

This process emerges clearly in an analysis of both the personnel making such decisions and of the demands made and policies adopted under the aegis of the department. There were regular consultations and discussions in the Department in which, apart from department officials and its Chairman, Mr Shraga Netzer, regular participants included Mr Pinchas Sapir, the Minister of Trade and Commerce (and, after May 1963, the Minister of Finance as well), Mr Y. Gil, the Director of the Section for Artisans and Members of Cooperatives in the Ministry of Trade and Commerce, the Director of the Artisans Bank, the Director of the Government Corporation for the Development of Artisanship, leading officials of the Artisans Association, and their member of Knesset, Mr Fisher.[27] Where necessary other officials referred to as 'our fellow party members' were called in to the Mapai Department for consultation, discussion and policy decision. A typical case was the discussion of the tax burdens of artisans. The department dealt with the problems 'in a combined discussion between our fellow party members in the Income Tax Authority and our fellow party members in the Central Committee of the Artisans Association'.[28]

This Mapai Department recognised and lauded the important role played by civil service departments in strengthening the political control by Mapai of trade associations set up to further sectional economic interests. According to one of its directors this was one of their expected functions:

[27] Ibid.   [28] Ibid.

Parallel with the Department in Mapai headquarters there exists a Section for Artisans and Co-operatives in the Ministry of Commerce and Industry which from the financial and economic aspects complements these institutions and organisations[29] and strengthens the position of our fellow party members in the executive bodies of the Artisans Association.[30]
In this respect the Department attributed much of its success to the work of Mapai ministers.[31]

The Department was unconcerned about possible negative implications of decision making processes which utilised political affiliations in meeting the interest demands of a specific group. On the contrary, it was the duty of these Mapai ministers and officials who owed their positions to the party to concern themselves with the problems of their fellow party members and to deal with them directly regardless of their own official governmental or civil service position.

This approach, however, did not always lead to departmental direction of the Minister and civil servants; while on some occasions the Department more or less imposed its will upon an unwilling minister or official, on others the latter refused to take suggested actions. In both types of situation matters were generally decided on the basis of discussion and consultation ending in mutual agreement or compromise.

An analysis of the various policy discussions and decisions in the early 1960s reveals that they were mostly concerned with the standing economic concerns of artisans such as sources of credit and finance, new buildings, equipment and tools, foreign exchange, and the alleviation of taxation burdens. Once agreement was reached among the participants in these discussions, the Department shepherded the policies through the various institutions where further action was needed, for example the Knesset, and its Finance and Economic Committees. Significantly, issues were brought to the legislative committees only after the Minister's agreement had been secured, thus ensuring their acceptance. The practice of first achieving ministerial approval contrasts directly with that of Mapai's Settlement Department, and particularly its vocal moshav section, which usually brought demands and requests for subsidies directly to the Knesset Committees via their representatives on them. In these instances the Mapai Settlement Department attempted to use the Knesset Finance Committee as a lever to exert maximum pressure on the Minister of Finance. In the case of artisans the public application of pressure was avoided by prior agreement between the Minister and the Department.

While serving to connect the party to artisans and their specific problems, the organisational structures erected around the Department and the Artisans Association enabled Mapai to get its general message across and facilitated the mobilisation of support among this group for unpopular or sudden policy

[29] That is the Bank, the Government Corporation, the Association, and the Department.
[30] *Ibid.*   [31] *Ibid.*

changes. A good case in point was the devaluation of 1962, which forced artisans and craftsmen to pay more for imported goods without enjoying the benefits of the export advantages. The Department mobilised immediate support for this move within the central bodies of the Association and from here it passed down to the regional and local level.

Mapai's successful competitive organisational penetration and control of the Artisans Association facilitated economic interest aggregation and policy making. It was able to use its dominant position to encourage and convince a constituent interest group to tailor and withhold particular needs and demands in the light of more general party and national considerations.

Mapai's organisational penetration and control was based, not only upon success in competitive situations within artisans' organisations, but also upon the party's reorganisation of the previously moribund Artisans Association. This process initiated by loyal Mapai activists already within the Association, together with the ensuing process of policy support and membership incorporation, demonstrates the party's flexibility and organisational adaptability. It not only took over a functional group outside its usual scope and reservoir of support, but also bent long-established and hallowed ideological principles governing conditions of membership fully to incorporate it within Mapai.

Professionals and intelligentsia

There are some general problems of definition of these groups. If restricted to the major independent professions with university qualifications – doctors, lawyers, dentists, scientists, engineers, architects, university teachers, secondary school teachers, and other graduates in the social sciences and humanities – this would constitute a group of some 20 000 in Israel in the mid-1960s. This would rise to about 100 000 if primary school teachers, actors and artists, nurses, pharmacists, laboratory technicians, accountants, etc., were also included. Most of the subsequent discussion deals mainly with the first group which, since 1956, has been organised in the Histadrut's Department for Professional Employees (as distinct from the Trade Union Department). Mapai in its organisational structure also followed this division. Nevertheless even after this distribution some blurred edges remain; for example, secondary school teachers, who were regarded by the Histadrut as part of the General Teachers Union affiliated with the Trade Union Department and denied the right of separate formal organisation under the Professional Employees Department.

Professionals before and after 1948

In the pre-state era the status of professionals varied. Generally speaking, intellectual pursuits, university education and professional expertise were disvalued. The pioneering ethos of the country's major political movement was based upon a revolt against such occupations as being unnecessary and unproductive, and not suited to producing a normal occupational pyramid. This did not, however, extend into outright anti-intellectualism. On the contrary, the ideal type was the individual who had given up intellectual and professional occupations in the service of building up the national home, but who, nevertheless, remained cultured.

Not all professional occupations, however, were downgraded. Medicine and teaching were regarded as essential for the progress of the national aspirations of independence, and became part of the ethos of pioneering.[32] Lawyers, on the other hand, were especially disvalued because of their connection with the source of law and formal authority in Palestine, the British Mandate.[33] In general, those professions which proved essential to the fulfilment of the Zionist–Socialist and national aspirations were positively valued by virtue of their connection with these ideals. The independent and legitimate interests and inherent prestige evaluation of the professions were almost completely submerged, although there were some indications that emphasis on professional standards was getting stronger particularly among doctors and teachers.[34]

The establishment of independent statehood brought a reversal of these attitudes. The state bureaucracies were in need of advanced professional and technical skills to carry out the many new tasks among the vastly increased population. Industrial, technological and military development brought to the fore professional groups less significant before 1948, such as engineers and scientists. The legal profession, moreover, gained in importance and prestige from its connections with the legislative and judicial framework of the independent state. Teachers and doctors, too, became more significant as a result of the country's health and educational problems.

Professionals increasingly sought recognition of the legitimacy of their demands as well as increased material rewards, both symbolised in the struggle for greater wage differentials. Wage differentials imply higher valuation of achievement and contribution and are therefore commonly regarded as indicators of social status and prestige. Professionals also justified their demands for greater remuneration in terms of their way of life, self-expectations and internalised needs to provide higher education for their children. These demands created ideological problems in Israel with its background of egalitarianism, and its history of a low valuation of professional work and higher valuation of manual labour. The problem was complicated further by the realities of the wage remuneration system operating in Israel in the early part of the 1950s. During this period the relative position of higher-paid workers declined as inflation increased, and, for example, the salary ratio between the

[32] Yagol, p. 134.   [33] Eisenstadt, *Israeli Society*, p. 177.   [34] Yagol, p. 134.

highest and lowest grades in government service narrowed. Moreover, in absolute terms professionals earned less than a number of privileged manual groups, particularly dock workers and members of bus cooperatives who had successfully exploited their bargaining position.

The period after 1954 was thus punctuated by a series of strikes and strike threats by various professional groups, and characterised by extremely poor relations between them and the Histadrut's Trade Union section. It culminated in the establishment outside the Histadrut structure of a loosely organised Academic Coordinating Committee, to fight for academic and professional salary demands.

These circumstances placed Mapai in a somewhat unfavourable position in its relations with academic and professional groups. Direct conflict between professionals and non-professionals made it virtually impossible for Mapai to satisfy the demands of both groups. Its representation of industrial and agricultural workers, its historical experience and its ideological preferences did not augur well for professional claims. Moreover, strong support for professional claims could seriously challenge the basic unity of all employees (as distinct from employers) on which the Histadrut was founded, and undermine Histadrut authority over the numerically more significant non-professionals. Apart from ideological and economic considerations Mapai had to take care not to destroy the mass basis of its electoral support, the foundation on which its national and Histadrut power rested. On the other hand, as the party responsible for the direction of the government it simply could not afford to ignore this problem either. Thus, the interests and demands of professionals created serious problems for Mapai's interest aggregation and policy making capabilities, and cast into doubt its ability to recruit and make available for leadership selection members and representatives from these strategically important groups in Israeli society.

Problems of incorporating professionals within Mapai

The nature of employed professionals' ties with politics and political parties, and therefore of the possibilities of Mapai organisation among them, presents a significant contrast with non-professionals. Because of their greater inclination towards ideological and intellectual commitments in politics, their integration into the country's social life and culture, and their income, which by Israeli standards was relatively high, professionals were not available for the methods of organisation which predominated among manual and industrial workers. Yet standing in the way of an intellectual or ideological commitment of professionals to Mapai were preexisting commitments to professional values and standards which were not directly connected with politics. While not necessarily in conflict with party and political commitments, they competed with the party for the interest and attention of the professional. Thus professional ties were far less directly connected with political action than trade union activity among industrial workers.

Mapai sought the support of professionals despite these problems and difficulties, and their low potential voting strength, for a number of reasons. The Histadrut to which it was unreservedly committed aspired to be the general representative organisation of all employed persons in Israel, and aimed to include a group as important as professionals within it. Second, Mapai was not prepared simply to hand them over to other parties, which would add a partisan political dimension to already complex economic and social questions. This formed part of its general approach to interest aggregation, of encompassing many groups within the party despite the internal complications, and of attempting to solve problems within the party framework where common party loyalties and consensus could be brought to bear.

Equally important was Mapai's recognition, stemming from its leadership role in society and government, of the special quality of the professional contribution to a modern technological society. It believed that not only did the state need to harness the abilities of this group, but that the party also had to do this. Mapai leaders feared that without professionals within it, both the party and the state would be left directionless and leaderless.[35] In return, Mapai could offer professionals the inducements and attractions of the party in power, dominant in the areas of decision making relevant to their claims and interests, despite the competing interests of other groups within the party.

But Mapai was limited in what it could offer. It sought the support of these groups for the reasons outlined above, but in exchange was unwilling to offer the kind of return that parties typically offer for such support, that is, the promotion of their interests. In the case of Mapai's relations with academic and professional groups the opposite seems to have occurred. Mapai tried to incorporate these groups in order to tailor, curtail and hold down their demands, and to adjust them against both the interests of the other groups within the party and the objective realities of the Israeli economic situation. Its capacity to perform this task successfully depended upon its ability to create an ideological viewpoint of egalitarianism and narrow wage differentials among the professional and academic groups so as to encourage them to exercise a marked degree of self-restraint in their demands, and on its ability to manage the economy in such a way as to ensure that inflation would not continually erode wage differentials agreed upon. None of these was easy, and in fact Mapai did not fully succeed in any of these objectives. As a result it continually lost support among academics and professionals and its degree of successful competitive organisational penetration and control declined. This was seen in the loss of control of the executive organs of the various

---

[35] Louis Pincus, 'The Egghead and the Israeli Labour Movement', *Israel Seen From Within* (September 1958), 8.

professional unions such as the Engineers Union, to groups and factions committed to occupational goals rather than to rival political parties, and later in its marked inability to convince its representatives in these committees to follow the party as distinct from their professional interests, for example, in the prevention of militant strike action. Membership of Mapai came to be regarded by professionals outside it not as an advantage deriving from close connection with the ruling party, but as a disqualification which tended to weaken commitment to professional interests. Torn in two different directions Mapai professionals often, if not invariably, opted for professional and occupational solidarity.

Limited organisational penetration

In 1956 both Mapai and the Histadrut set up departments and organisational structures to deal with the problems of academics and professionals. The Professional Workers Department at Mapai headquarters worked through an organisation which it set up for this purpose, known as *Irgun Haakedemaim Chavrei Mapai Veohadeha*, The Association of Mapai Professionals. By 1964 it numbered 6500 members, of whom 3500 were actual party members, with the rest in the category of sympathisers.

The activity of these groups proceeded along both regional and occupational lines. The professional cells in each major region elected local and national professional executive bodies. Similarly regional and national cross-professional bodies were also elected, headed by a national secretariat which chose the director of the Department for Professional Workers, subject to the ratification of the Mapai Secretariat.

The Department and the Association were mainly concerned with the status of the professional worker and his representation within various institutions – securing adequate professional standards; establishing links with the Histadrut and exploring the possibilities of a general professional confederation; and protecting the principle of wage differentials. Mapai's difficulties in making policies to cope with the problems and demands of the professional sector were clearly apparent in the workings of the Department, which could not act as a policy initiator or planner. It accepted the fact that in most instances professionals had ceased to believe in Mapai's ability to solve their problems or its willingness to accede to their demands. Because Mapai itself adopted no clear policy towards their demands, Mapai professionals felt free to press their occupational claims as strongly as possible, even against the party's wishes. Thus the Department and the Association were generally unable to prevent them going out on strike. Its officials recognised that often professionals played a double game, extracting what they could from and through Mapai by virtue of their party membership, but at the same time willing to join anti-Histadrut and anti-Mapai action in pursuit of occupational goals. The Department was caught in the middle; the party had no clear policy for which the Department could gain support among professionals; and because of the relative numerical insignificance of professionals within the party, and their almost complete absence from leadership positions, the Department itself was not strong enough to formulate such a policy for the party. It therefore concentrated on cementing the loyalty of Mapai professionals through other major policy areas where it could make Mapai's achievements and policies attractive to them, such as defence and foreign policy. The appeal was to professionals at an intellectual level to convince them of the correctness of Mapai's general approach to major national problems, and thereby gain their support despite the relative non-satisfaction of basic economic demands. Securing policy support at an intellectual level served as a counter-balance to the inability to supply instrumental needs, and as a compensation for the limited degree of competitive organisational penetration and control.

The Department also acted in a mediating role during strikes and other professional crises, and attempted to find a middle path between the party and the professionals, using its good offices to bring together Mapai members of the executives of the professional bodies with the relevant ministers, civil servants, and Histadrut officials. In a few cases, as in the Engineers Strike in 1962, the Department was instrumental in assisting the party's Secretary-General in his mediation. But in most other cases Mapai's professionals either accepted the view of their more militant professional colleagues, or were powerless to do anything against the militant majority within the professional union executive. Nowhere was the absence of successful competitive organisational penetration and control more noticeable in its effects upon Mapai's capacity for interest aggregation and policy making.

Mapai professionals were not highly represented in the party's central decision making bodies, or its Knesset and Histadrut lists. The Department's efforts did not effect any major improvement. This had important implications in the policy field. Professional interests and policy demands were not pressed within Mapai with the direct pressure that characterised other sections (agriculture, industrial workers, artisans), nor were professionals in a position directly to combat opposing viewpoints within party decision making bodies. Their non-representation on the bodies where decisions about their interests were made led to expressions of feelings of isolation and alienation by spokesmen for Mapai professionals. They often contrasted their increasing importance in the technological and scientific development of Israel with their treatment in Mapai where they felt that they were regarded with suspicion, and as 'second class citizens', 'strangers', and 'barely tolerated guests'.[36]

Nevertheless, the party seems to have done remarkably well in retaining

[36] For examples see *Report 8th Mapai Conference, 1956*, pp. 197–8, 342–3; and *Report 8th Mapai Conference, 2nd Session, 1958*, pp. 58, 71.

the loyalties of some 6500 professionals when it was not able to give its direct support to their demands, and contained within it groups and leaders strongly opposed to them. At the same time it must be noted that their situation improved after 1955 and that in the last resort it was the agreement of Mapai, as government, despite internal party opposition, that permitted and sanctioned these gains, even if under intense pressure from the professional groups.

Professional groups and their incorporation within Mapai demonstrate in a negative sense the value to Mapai of successful organisational penetration and control for interest aggregation and policy making. Moreover, it illustrates that when interest aggregation and policy making failed or were severely limited, the party's capacities for membership recruitment and leadership selection among professionals were likewise curtailed. On the other hand, Mapai showed flexibility and adaptability in appealing to the general intellectual commitments of professionals, in order to gain general policy support, despite economic policy differences.

The foregoing analysis has demonstrated that Mapai utilised three different patterns of competitive organisational penetration and control in its efforts to incorporate diverse social groups into the party and secure and maintain their assured support. The more successful examples are those relating to industrial workers and artisans. Only limited success was achieved among professionals where competing occupational values made the party's task more difficult. It is interesting to note the way in which instrumental advantages, policy promises and activities, general party commitments, party membership, and electoral success within the organisations to be penetrated, were combined differently by Mapai in each of the three cases. Among industrial workers, instrumental advantages, party membership, electoral success, policy satisfaction, and ideological commitments all played their part in their successful incorporation within Mapai, and in its continued control of the Histadrut. For artisans, policy achievements and formal incorporation into the party membership were the main methods. Amongst professionals only limited policy success, and limited party membership were achieved, but further headway was made by the mobilisation of general ideal commitments.

4. ETHNICITY, SEX, RELIGION AND AGE: CROSS-CUTTING CLEAVAGES AND ATTENUATED PENETRATION

Horizontal and vertical bases of differentiation

Our concern to date has been with socio-economic groups and interests within Mapai. While these groups shared common values and aspirations within the overarching consensus of Mapai affiliation, their memberships did not overlap. They thus constituted horizontal cleavages. Our concern in this chapter is with vertical cleavages based upon ethnicity, sex, religious belief, and age, which cross-cut the horizontal. Furthermore, these vertical divisions themselves tended to overlap. Thus each vertical division also contained within it elements of other vertical cleavages. For example, in the cleavage based upon age, epitomised in the party's leadership struggle, within both the veteran and youthful leadership groups those of European origin combined with those of Oriental origin. Similarly, women were present on both sides of this generational struggle. Again within the horizontal divisions, members of kibbutzim and moshavim, workers, trade union officials, professionals, and artisans were divided on generational lines, as well as on ethnic, sexual and religious lines. Horizontal divisions, being closely related to economic interest, were more directly associated with specific demands and identifiable policy making bodies. As we saw, these groups generally played a major role in interest aggregation and policy making on behalf of Mapai. The vertical divisions, by way of contrast, were characterised by highly generalised, diffuse, and symbolic demands for the representation of members of their groups within centres of decision making and by the relative absence of specific and concrete policy demands.

A number of factors attenuated the process of party penetration of these groups, making it less direct and less successful than among the horizontal divisions. Nevertheless limited party penetration of these groups involving their partial incorporation into the party, and its ability to rely on them for secure and loyal support was achieved. In turn they gained separate and specific forms of organisation, administration and representation within it. But the process never went as far as it did among the economic groups.

This attenuated penetration derived, in the main, from the cross-cutting nature of these loyalties and the character of their demands. In many cases their demands and interests were diffuse, symbolic, and highly generalised, which made them particularly difficult to aggregate. Moreover the organisa-

66

tional structures needed for penetration and control were either non-existent as in the case of youth, weak as in the case of ethnic groups and women, or already penetrated by other parties, as in the case of religion.

Ethnic groups

Ethnic groups in Israeli society

The society in Palestine and Israel into which came the immigrants from the traditional societies in Arab and North African countries was predominantly European in its social and cultural environment and political and economic organisation. Even in the religious sphere, despite common beliefs and practices, the Ashkenasi tradition of the Europeans differed in style, outlook, temper and mood from the Sephardi and Yemenite traditions of the newcomers. The majority of these immigrants were unfamiliar with European ways and manners.

The initial cultural and technological gaps became perpetuated in Israel through the economic and educational spheres. Oriental immigrants were concentrated at the lower levels of the income ladder, and had larger families. Similarly the proportion of Oriental immigrants receiving tertiary and secondary education was extremely small.[1] Thus ethnic and class cleavage tend to overlap: educated, well-off, upwardly mobile Europeans occupied most elite positions in politics, economics, administration, and the cultural sphere, and uneducated, poor, non-mobile Orientals occupied the lower positions in these spheres. Added to these were various popular negative stereotypes on both sides. This situation created resentments, disaffection, and claims of discrimination and deprivation by the non-European sectors of the population.

Yet cultural and ethnic conflict in Israeli politics and society were relatively limited. This has been due to the overriding unity and consensus on national security, and to a marked absolute improvement in the economic position of non-Europeans despite a relative decline. Moreover, there has been a concerted effort by the authorities to correct the inequities of the system.

These ethnic groups made economic, educational, and social demands, and demands for representation and access, which served both material and symbolic purposes. The latter, predominantly political demands, are particularly significant for subordinated ethnic groups because the prestige and visibility of the political positions gained can assure others 'of symbolic

[1] See A. Weingrod, *Israel: Group Relations in a New Society* (London, 1965), pp. 49–58 for a brief analysis and discussion of these figures. See for a more detailed analysis and presentation of the basic statistics on which most subsequent work has been based, G. Hanoch, 'Wage Differentials in Israel', in *Fifth Report of the Falk Project For Economic Research in Israel* (Jerusalem, 1961), pp. 39–130. See also R. Bar Yoseph and D. Padan, 'The Oriental Communities in the Class Structure of Israel', *Molad*, 195–6 (1964), 504–16 (Hebrew).

recognition of the group with implied estimation of its worth and dignity'.[2] It thus serves to counteract the ethnic group's own acceptance of low status and of societally imposed negative stereotypes.

Political incorporation of ethnic groups

Mapai set out to satisfy the political demands by integrating the Oriental migrants into the political system and making them participants rather than mere objects of policy decisions. The concept of *Mizug Galuyot*, the intermixing and fusion of the exiles, or, put in other terms, national integration, was at the forefront of its concerns both as party and as the leading force in the government. It was also strongly reinforced by the Zionist call for the ingathering of Jews from all over the world, which constituted the official doctrine and ideology of the state.

In seeking the support of immigrants Mapai enjoyed advantages over the other parties, deriving from the bureaucratically administered, centralised, and party-controlled process of immigration absorption after 1948.[3] In the agencies dealing with the problem of immigrant absorption, immigrants came into contact with officials who were party men, playing the dual roles of official and party recruiter, indoctrinator, and socialiser. Although most parties shared in this division, Mapai, the majority party, had the greatest number of officials, and occupied the controlling and decisive positions at all points of recruitment. Party control also applied to employment, housing, health services, trade unionism, and in general to the provision of most of the significant instrumental needs and demands of the new immigrants. Thus in many ways the power and ability of Mapai to fulfil the promises it made, and to meet their instrumental demands was continually highlighted. Loyal Mapai bureaucrats and officials sometimes tied the provision of such services to the possession of a party membership card. Or else, those with instrumental demands came to believe, rightly or wrongly, that a party card would entitle them to preference. On the other hand, officials in their role as party activists often recruited new members without tying this to their official position. In other instances, particularly in outlying areas, government officials implicitly connected Mapai with the government or the state.[4]

[2] R. Lane, *Political Life* (Glencoe, Ill., 1959), p. 252.
[3] S. N. Eisenstadt, *The Absorption of Immigrants* (London, 1954), *passim*.
[4] For example, the use of Mapai premises for the carrying on of official business, the use of the back of Mapai 'how to vote cards' as official governmental paper for sending notices re registration to vote, the public candidature in Mapai internal elections of leading local taxation officials, and local custodians in control of abandoned property and housing and responsible for its reallocation. For examples of such practices that were the subject of Ministerial enquiries after being raised by opposition parties in the Knesset see *Divrei Haknesset*, vol. IX, 2073–87, 26.6.1951; vol. XVIII, 1297–8, 28.1.1955. At no time did Mapai ministers condone these practices; they were normally quite embarrassed by such actions of their local activists and gave orders to cease them immediately.

The membership effects of this are quite clear. After 1948 Mapai accepted into its ranks large numbers from Oriental countries. By 1954 their proportion was 27 per cent, in 1956 30 per cent and by 1962 it had risen to 45 per cent, which was approximately the Oriental proportion of Israel's population.[5] Thus by 1965 there were in the vicinity of 90 000 Mapai members of Oriental origin, as compared with, at the most, a few thousand in 1948.

Organisational integration

Mapai's aims of integrating non-European ethnic immigrants within its ranks were carried out in a number of separate steps. Its first task was to direct them into the Histadrut. This was crucial, as we saw above, because it laid the basis for successful organisational penetration and control, which would secure for it a secure reservoir of members and supporters. Mapai also sought to become a major channel of direct immigrant political socialisation by providing basic information and understanding of the Israeli environment, via publications in foreign languages, as well as in Hebrew, and by organising foreign language political meetings addressed by ethnic leaders. Mapai quickly recognised the importance of ethnic leaders in the political socialisation of the immigrants, and in assisting them to articulate their interests. These activities were pursued by specific party programmes and courses aimed at preparing new immigrant leadership groups to fill the leadership gap within ethnic communities resulting from the decline of traditional authority figures and structures.

To carry out these tasks Mapai set up more permanent organisational structures consisting of special departments, or sections of the Organisation Department at Mapai headquarters, based on country of origin. These ethnic administrative frameworks employed ethnic leaders who sought to encourage widespread party membership and participation by ethnic groups at the local level. Thus after 1948 various departments and sections were set up for the largest immigrant groups. Despite various attempts to abolish them, in 1965 separate Yemenite, North African and Iraqi departments still existed.

The development of these central ethnic organisational frameworks (with their local representatives) facilitated and promoted the further development of ethnic interest groups within the party. It gained access to political leaders and resources and provided a central focus for the activities of the groups vis à vis their own memberships. Most important of all, this structure was not financed by the groups themselves but by the party. It also enabled the further development and training of group leadership through participation in party affairs.

This organisational structure helped to fit ethnic groups and ethnic group

[5] The figures for 1954 are from *Davar*, 30.7.1954; for 1956, from Rolbant, p. 22; and for 1962 from *Hapoel Hatzair*, 5.6.1962.

representation into the pattern of interest group representation typical of
Mapai. It also gave rise to an attenuated and loose form of organisational
penetration which was used to secure and increase party support among the
various ethnic groups. In Israel in the mid-1960s there were altogether over
thirty associations of immigrants from various countries of Asia, Africa, and
Europe. Generally representing immigrants from a particular country or
region (e.g. the Association of North African Immigrants), they were concerned with the political, economic, and civic representation of members,
rather than with religious needs, which, by way of contrast, traditional ethnic
communities had done before 1948.[6] Mapai participation in the election of
their leaderships provided it with some degree of influence and control in
many immigrant associations, including the largest (Iraq, North Africa, and
Rumania). For the sake of ethnic unity these bodies generally gave space in
their journals to the views of a number of parties, but Mapai's position was
such that the executive bodies often directly urged their members to vote for
Mapai. A well-known example was the call by the Council of Sephardi and
Oriental Communities to all non-Europeans in 1961 to support Mapai.[7] To
coordinate its activities Mapai established a Section for Immigrant Associations at its headquarters. This section advised immigrant associations through
the Mapai members of their executive bodies on dealings with public
authorities in all matters of immigrant absorption. It thus followed the pattern
adopted by Mapai in other spheres, of making use of the fact that 'fellow
party members' occupied positions of responsibility in the relevant administrative hierarchies.[8]

The Mapai Knesset members of non-European ethnic origins were deeply
and centrally involved in the activities of these departments. This work was
deemed by them to be of prime significance owing to their belief (shared by
the members of their groups) in the importance of personal connections for
getting things done in Israeli bureaucracies. Few members of these ethnic
groups held positions of authority and responsibility at the middle and upper
levels of decision making and administration. Between the top few parliamentarians and the group mass there was a marked gap in political power,
responsibility and knowledge. The importance of ethnic M.K.s in this context
went beyond the symbolic. In their own view and that of the ethnic departments, these M.K.s performed vital functions in the integration of immigrants
which could not be performed by others. They understood the immigrants,
and had an immediate, and relatively direct and personal interest in the
solution of their problems. They could thus overcome the difficulties arising
from the lack of personal connection, and hoped to achieve results by super-
imposing another and more disciplined form of loyalty and obligation over

[6] Walter P. Zenner, 'Sephardic Communal Organizations in Israel', *Middle East Journal*,
21 (1967), 173–93.
[7] *Ibid.*   [8] *From Conference to Conference*, p. 25.

officials, that of Mapai membership. Having such departments and utilising the services of ethnic M.K.s partly assured members of the ethnic groups that officials would feel obliged to grant them equal treatment.

By way of direct contrast with, say, the Mapai Department for Artisans, the Mapai departments for ethnic groups and their parliamentarians in particular, specifically concerned themselves not with matters of policy but with individual cases. They spent a large proportion of their time attempting to solve the problems of individuals and families. Matters dealt with were usually routine, involving the mundane and practical aspects of human existence, such as housing, employment, bank credit, and family problems, intergenerational conflicts, educational advancement. Overall they constituted a party-organised and financed social welfare agency which guided, instructed, educated and personally intervened on behalf of ethnic clients.

Specific mobilisation functions within their own ethnic groups were undertaken by the ethnic departments at election times as part of Mapai's general electoral effort. They were particularly active prior to internal Mapai elections, seeking to increase their paid-up party memberships, and the number of candidates they could elect to various party bodies. The party also recruited and developed a continuous stream of ethnic leaders in political training centres, such as *Bet Berl*, and subsequently placed them in important local administrative posts. Thus in effect Mapai provided leadership continuity and succession for groups which were faced with an authority crisis. The political careers of many Mapai ethnic activists followed a pattern beginning in a party training centre followed by a steady rise in importance in local administrative posts culminating in the position of either mayor, or Secretary of the Labour Council, while one or two went on from there to the Knesset.

Representation

The relative proportion of ethnic representation rose steadily after 1948. Moreover, ethnic representation was highest at the lowest level but decreased steadily as the importance of the institution increased. Thus Oriental immigrants constituted 12 per cent of the delegates to the party Conference in 1950, and 33 per cent by 1956, and continued to increase after this. In 1960 19 per cent of Mapai's Central Committee were of Oriental origin, and by the mid-1960s this had increased to just under 30 per cent. On the other hand in the party Secretariat the Oriental proportion was usually two or three out of more than thirty. In the Knesset it oscillated between 12 and 20 per cent of Mapai's representatives. There was usually at least one minister of non-European origin, and after the early 1960s there were two. Similarly there was usually one on the Histadrut's Central Executive Committee of seventeen members.

An important mechanism for assisting Oriental immigrants to obtain representation at Mapai Conferences was the reserving of a minimum proportion of places in all local and regional delegations to the Conference. It was first instituted at the elections for the 7th Conference in 1950, when their guaranteed minimum proportion in the major urban areas was 14 per cent, but was dropped prior to the 10th Conference.[9] Similarly in 1958 ethnic representatives pressed for a reserved proportion of places for Orientals for the party's Knesset list. After discussion they accepted an assurance that 'the list of candidates will ensure fitting representation of non-Europeans'.[10]

In sum, Mapai's relations with Oriental groups in Israel represents a successful example of the incorporation of a new social force within what was previously a predominantly European party in outlook and membership. It was an incorporation and integration, moreover, that in numerical terms secured major electoral support by meeting demands for representation, and by intensively pursuing policies designed to improve their socio-economic situation.

Women

Women have common interests with their menfolk in the major socio-economic, educational, religious, generational, and ethnic divisions within the society. Consequently in Western societies, both despite and because of legal and economic equality, women generally play a secondary role in politics and public life; they tend to be less interested in politics, less likely to participate actively and less concerned about its outcomes than are men.[11]

Equality between the sexes was also held high in the pioneering ideology of the Yishuv. Women, particularly those in the agricultural settlements, were treated like men with regard to work and communal duties. It was further underlined by the example of leading women political activists who achieved important positions both before and after 1948, most notably Mrs Golda Meir (formerly Myerson), who at various times was Secretary-General of the Histadrut, Secretary-General of Mapai, Israeli Ambassador to Moscow, Minister of Labour, Foreign Minister, and elected Prime Minister in 1969.

Organisational penetration

Women are integrated into formal organisational structures, mainly within the broad framework of the Histadrut rather than having independent structures. Many Israeli women are members of the Histadrut; 309 000 in 1959 and 417 000 in 1964. They were organised in Tnuat Hapoalot, the Women Workers Movement, which comprised three main sections; one each for

[9] Hador, 15.3.1950; Mapai Electoral Constitution approved by the Central Committee, 22.3.1964, and 28.5.1964.
[10] Report 8th Mapai Conference, 2nd Session, 1958, pp. 239–49.   [11] Lane, pp. 209–16.

working women (122 500 in 1964), those in Labour Settlements (39 500) and those at home (260 000). At the elections to its governing bodies held in conjunction with Histadrut elections Mapai generally received over two-thirds of the votes, a proportion well in excess of its general Histadrut vote.

A major reason for Mapai's success among Histadrut women can be found in its organisational penetration and control of Histadrut activity among women. Some occurred in conjunction with the Histadrut's Trade Union Department (also Mapai controlled) in such spheres as employment training, and wage negotiations. But the main focus of Histadrut women's activity was in the domestic and residential sphere, and here the Women Workers Council operated through a special organisation known as Irgun Imahot Ovdot, the Organisation of Working Mothers. By 1964 it had eighty-four branches in cities, towns and development areas, devoted to educational and social welfare work. Thus its contacts with the mothers whose children it served were mainly instrumental, and centred around scarce and valued facilities and resources that would otherwise not have been available.

The Women Workers Council employed some 1920 officials in 1965, in political, administrative, clerical and educational tasks. From Mapai's point of view they were available to influence women voters, and were significant because of the wide contact that their institutional and instrumental activities afforded them. Particularly important in this political mobilisation network were the fourteen full-time organisers of the Secretariat of the Women Workers Council (mostly Mapai), and the larger team of some 110 regional and local officials of the Organisation of Working Mothers who directed most of the grassroots activities.

This provided Mapai with a cadre of paid activists able to use their official positions to promote the interests of the party. It complemented their activities by setting up a Women's Department at Mapai headquarters in 1955, to secure votes for Mapai at elections, although between elections it was relatively inactive. The Department was neither concerned with policy making nor policy initiatives, nor with the coordination of the activities of Mapai's women representatives in the Knesset, Histadrut or municipalities.

By way of contrast with other departments which directed and coordinated highly conscious party members and activists in increasing the party's overall strength through organisational penetration and control, the Women's Department sought to boost party consciousness among the women who were already active in a particular sphere through their party connection, but whose party involvement was secondary in importance. Many women activists within the Organisation of Working Mothers generally known to be Mapai members were not up to date in their party membership, had not taken out membership cards, and were not eligible to vote in intra-party elections. With other departments, organisational penetration and control were a means of extending party influence; here the reverse occurred. Control of external activities (education, social welfare and culture) were drawn upon in order to strengthen the party connections of those involved. The Department first had to make active party members out of activists representing it outside, whose party commitments were submerged beneath their general interests and activities. Only then could Mapai gain the electoral support of the clientele of the various Histadrut activities for women.

Representation

Whereas women constituted about half of the Israeli population their proportion within Mapai was always considerably smaller. In 1954 they made up about 27 per cent of the party, and by 1964 this figure had risen to 30 per cent.[12] This meant that there were nearly 40 000 women members in 1954 and about 57 000 in 1964. The Department was also instrumental in increasing the number of women within party institutions. Thus about 600 women members in 1956 and 900 in 1964 held various party elective positions. (Many of these also represented Mapai in other institutions.) Women made up about 10 per cent of the delegates to the 8th Conference in 1956 and 11 per cent (257 delegates) in 1965. There were regularly between five and seven women in Mapai's Knesset team (about 12–17 per cent).[13] This representation was the subject of fairly regular debate within the party, and women unsuccessfully applied pressure on a number of occasions to increase the proportions of their representation in these various bodies. As one of their spokeswomen put it, 'a party that closes its eyes to women and courts them only prior to elections will end up losing them on election day'.[14]

As with ethnic groups formal guarantees of a fixed proportion of places for women (for example 10 per cent at the Conference) were instituted. But unlike ethnic groups, who agreed to the dropping of this provision, women activists insisted on keeping it. Similarly Mapai women activists attempted to get formal guarantees of a minimum quota of Knesset seats in 1958, and rejected the general provision of 'fitting representation' that ethnic groups accepted. Instead they demanded 25 per cent of the places in line with their proportion of party membership. The male-dominated Conference overwhelmingly rejected this claim, while retaining the general provision for 'fitting representation'.[15]

The overall pattern of Mapai organisational penetration among women's associations suggests that its weakness derived from lower political interest and consciousness among women, forcing the party to devote its efforts to instilling party consciousness in its activists in outside organisations. While

[12] Women's Department Report, *From Conference to Conference*, pp. 27–8; and *Davar*, 30.8.1954.
[13] These figures are based on my own calculations.
[14] E. Herlitz, *Report 9th Mapai Conference, 3rd Session*, 1963, pp. 198–9.
[15] *Report 8th Mapai Conference, 2nd Session*, 1958, pp. 239–44.

this did not prevent the mobilisation of electoral support among wider groups of women, it gave rise only to marginal degrees of interest articulation by women, and to little specific involvement in policy making and policy application.

Religious groups

Religion as a legitimately recognised basis of organisation and as a focus of policy concern was only marginally significant for Mapai after 1948, although more so than in the previous period. Prior to 1948 there were three main attitudes to religion within Mapai: opposition, bordering on the militant; neutrality and tolerance; and a positive attitude without religious observance, manifesting nostalgia for traditional culture and values. Religious and traditional circles, for their part, regarded the labour movement as freethinkers who had thrown off traditional values and practices and were engaged in stamping out the heritage of centuries. This picture was reinforced by the Yishuv's federative institutional structure. The religious community established a number of religious parties which sought to further religious observance and traditional education. It set up an institutional network to cater for its interests, including economic, trade union, and settlement structures, in addition to specifically religious ones. Because of Mapai's need for political support the religious parties made gains in the religious sphere in return for backing Mapai in other spheres.

After 1948 religious arrangements previously established in political party agreements or as unwritten conventions, as well as those about which the British had made formal regulations, became part of the new legislative system of the state. This led to controversy and marked disagreement from the very outset. For example, no agreement was reached on a written state constitution because of the refusal of the religious groups to accept anything except Jewish law as the constitution of the state. Nevertheless, on some matters agreement was reached and in the main this reflected an acceptance of the pattern of the pre-state period; Sabbath as the official day of rest and widespread restrictions on public activity and transport: adherence to dietary laws in public institutions; the establishment of a state religious education network within the Ministry of Education at the primary level; and official state recognition of the authority of rabbis and rabbinical courts in matters of personal status. A major element in reaching agreement on these measures was the inability of Mapai to form a stable coalition without the religious parties.

Religion as a basis of solidarity and organisation within Mapai differed from all the social forces we have encountered above in one major respect; in this sphere Mapai competed with rival political parties specifically organised around this factor. Moreover, because of its coalition needs, Mapai's policies, interests and influence were severely limited. The ministries and bureaucracies dealing with these matters were the closely guarded preserve of the religious parties, which removed one of the major advantages Mapai enjoyed in other areas.

Religion became an internal Mapai problem with specific policy, organisational and representational demands following the immigration of traditional Jews from Oriental countries. An important demand, particularly of those settled in moshavim, was for the provision of religious facilities. Mapai could have adopted any one of a number of attitudes towards these religious demands. It could have done what the religious parties had urged all along – make religious belief and observance the criterion of allocation to settlements. Religious immigrants would then have been handed over to the religious parties, who claimed that they could best look after their spiritual and educational needs. Mapai rejected these claims of the religious parties for political reasons and insisted on the proportional allocation according to political party strength.

Once the immigrants were settled Mapai had to decide about making provision for meeting their religious needs. It could have assumed that there would be a decline in religious observance as part of the process of acculturation, and done nothing, or it could actively have attempted to combat their religious beliefs and observances, as did some individual instructors.[16] Or it could simply have done nothing about meeting their religious demands on the premise that religion was a private matter. But this would have served to increase the pressure from the religious parties offering to provide such facilities, and went against the predominant pattern of settlement. Another possible approach, the one eventually adopted by Mapai, was recognition of the legitimacy of these religious demands and willingness to meet them by helping to provide religious needs. It was followed by the establishment of an organisational framework to cope with these problems.

Organisation

The first organisational moves took place, not surprisingly, within Tnuat Hamoshavim, which set up a department to cope with the religious needs of its settlers in conjunction with the Religious Department of the Histadrut. Its main task was to look after the sixty-five moshavim with some 10 000 settlers which were officially recognised as religious moshavim, although it also catered to the religious needs of other moshavim as well. Once religion was recognised as a legitimate demand to be met by party-affiliated, and party-penetrated and controlled bodies, it was only a matter of time before attempts were made to organise a religious section within Mapai itself. In addition, some urban Mapai religious activists desired special provision for

16 See Viteles, Book Four, pp. 174–80.

religious representation because religious members were often precluded from participating in party affairs that took place on the Sabbath.

Factors such as these led in 1959 to the establishment, by some religious party activists, of Mapai Religious Circles, to present their point of view on religious questions. The group had three main aims: to set up a Religious Department at Mapai headquarters; to provide some form of religious education for Mapai members that was not controlled by the National Religious Party; and to convince Mapai to wrest rabbinical institutions and personnel and the municipal Religious Councils out of NRP dependency, made more powerful and concrete by that party's control of the Ministry of Religious Affairs.

Part of the Mapai leadership strongly opposed both the establishment of this group and its aims. Some felt that in general Mapai ought to give unequivocal support to the state-secular education system, rather than contemplate any form of independent religious educational system. This opposition formed part of a general inclination not to upset Mapai's religious coalition partners. Thus while the Department which could serve to mobilise electoral support among observant Jews was finally conceded, the other issues never made much headway.

The Department's main activities were to maintain administrative and political contact with the local Religious Councils, on which Mapai's share was 30 per cent as compared with that of the religious parties of 60 per cent. The Department worked in close cooperation with the Histadrut Religious Department in the provision of religious needs in both rural and urban areas, and in this was particularly active at election time, not only in meeting such needs, but also in general campaigning to mobilise support for Mapai. In the areas of policy making, and of achieving recognised interest group representation in Mapai institutions, on the other hand, the Department made little headway. Despite its avowed aims of having a say in policy formulation in religious matters within Mapai it had no policy making functions to exercise because Mapai had almost no policies with regard to religious matters, leaving them almost entirely to its religious coalition partners.

Its weakness in these two crucial areas was symptomatic of a much broader problem, that of Mapai's place within the religious sector. It is an interesting example of the problems that ensue in the absence of organisational penetration and control. Mapai did not enjoy the support of major rabbinical or lay religious personalities. Nor was it a force within the organised sections of religious Jewry as a whole, which generally followed their religious leaders and parties. In addition it had almost no leverage in any of the major religious institutions. Even though the Orthodox community was split between three major parties and a group of militantly religious, best described as anti-state, these groups were at one in their opposition to Mapai, and other non-religious parties, as secularising, irreligious, or anti-religious forces. Apart from the 10 000 or so settlers in the religious moshavim of Mapai, the Mapai Department dealt with and represented a relatively unorganised force, consisting mainly of individuals spread throughout the country. In the highly authoritative, militant and well-organised context of Israel's religious community, with its rabbinical, bureaucratic and educational structures solidly controlled by the religious parties, particularly the NRP, through the Ministry of Religious Affairs, the religious section of the Ministry of Education, and the hierarchical structure of the Chief Rabbinate and the rabbinical court system, the Mapai religious section paled into insignificance. Under these conditions, and given Mapai's own strong internal competition for the allocation of scarce resources and representative positions, it is little wonder that it exercised little real control or influence in these matters.

Youth

Whilst the sex differentiation within Mapai was obvious, the dividing line for youth was the subject of controversy. Similarly, while separate organisational structures were freely granted to women, these same demands by youth met constant opposition. This situation is symptomatic of the absence of clear political interest on the part of youth as a group. As Lane has pointed out, the social and socio-psychological demands and needs of youth in stable and institutionalised political systems are characteristically fulfilled outside the political arena.[17] In addition, the specific claims of Mapai's youth aroused bitter historical memories of the party split in 1942–4 which began as a call to youth, vigour and freshness in thought, and ended in the development of a rigidly disciplined faction seeking control of the party. Many Mapai leaders were therefore suspicious of any separate organisational structure for youth, for this carried within it the seeds of incipient factionalism and the dangers of another split.

Youth had always occupied an important place in the social structure of the Yishuv because of its close connections with the pioneering ethos and movement, and in many important ways youth movements were the very backbone of the Zionist reconstruction in Palestine. Mapai had various affiliated youth movements, both for those under 18 and for those over 18. For our present purposes the most important for those over 18 was *Mishmeret Hatzeira*, the Young Guard, founded in the early 1940s by individuals like Katznelson and Golomb (two of the most important Mapai leaders of that period) to prevent further loss to the party of talented youth.

The Young Guard decreased in significance after the firm stabilisation of Mapai power in the new state. By the early 1950s most of its leading members were well into their thirties and outside the scope of organised youth activities. Moreover, many had already begun to establish themselves in careers in

[17] Lane, pp. 216–19.

the army, the bureaucracy, parliamentary and other political institutions, and in the Histadrut. Mapai's problem was what to do with the next generation, those in their late teens and their twenties. This was a problem of political recruitment and political socialisation: how could it attract them into political activity and gain their support? How could it continue and maintain the loyalty that for some had been engendered in Mapai-affiliated movements for adolescent youth? In particular, it had to cope with the general decline in interest in politics and political parties among youth as compared with their pre-state equivalents who had been readily mobilised in the manifold defence and voluntary pioneering tasks.

Compared with the pre-1948 era there was nothing specific that the party wanted young people to do. In theory they ought to have had the same tasks and duties as other party members. But some of the older party leaders were apprehensive that if the younger party members were treated in this way and not given specific tasks to perform factionalism would inevitably develop, and this was reinforced by events in the early 1950s when controversial pro-posals for internal party reform and 'renewal' together with demands for democratisation had been put forward by former leading members of the Young Guard.

But to lose the important electoral support of youth was no solution either, and in the long run seemed to be the worst of all evils. Mapai therefore set up an organisation to attract the support of young voters in the 1955 elections, called *Mateh Dor Hatzair*, the Young Generation Staff. The choice of name is highly significant because of its emphasis upon capacity to get things done, and upon speed, efficiency, clearly defined goals and lines of authority. It was hoped that this approach would prove especially attractive to youth who shared the common experience of service in Israel's armed forces, and a generational emphasis upon 'getting things done' as opposed to the supposedly wasteful, inefficient, abstract theorising of the older generation.

After the elections in July 1955 the Mapai Secretariat agreed to grant this group a degree of organisational permanence in the form of a Young Genera-tion Secretariat. It also drew up plans and programmes for this body to follow, in which the major concern was with voluntary activity among the immi-grants, in the Negev and other new settlements. It reinforced this pioneering image by mobilising a number of members of the younger generation from kibbutzim and moshavim to serve in full-time administrative posts. But this organisational structure, designed to channel the energies of youth into nationally useful and politically non-sensitive areas of pioneering and immi-grant integration, did not divert leading party youth from critical attitudes towards party organisation, methods, and the emphasis on abstract ideology.

The party Secretariat therefore disbanded this framework and substituted a looser form of organisation, still with the hope of channelling the activities of the younger generation into 'defined areas'. In addition to volunteering work of various kinds, the main innovation was the establishment of ideological circles. The Mapai Secretariat's agreement to allow the members of the younger generation formally to discuss ideological matters gained it the approval of the latter. There were, however, very different views of what this entailed: for the party leadership and the older generation 'their task was to arouse in the youth and the members of the young generation a spiritual link to the foundation values of the society and of socialism and to sharpen the sense of partnership between the state and the people'.[18] For the younger generation's leaders it meant freedom of ideological discussion, freedom to criticise basic values and accepted formulae, freedom to suggest reforms, and freedom to suggest new methods of coping with new challenges and new problems. Consequently conflict was imminent and almost unavoidable.

From 1956 until the early part of the 1960s the conflict was considerably sharpened by the entry into active Mapai political affairs of Moshe Dayan, formerly Chief of Staff, and Shimon Peres, the Director-General of the Ministry of Defence. Not only did they have prestige and stature not enjoyed by other young generation activists, resulting from their defence exploits, they were also close to Ben Gurion, widely regarded as his proteges, and his models of what the new generation of Israeli leadership should be like. Their entry into the fray heralded a general challenge to the veteran leadership and its ideological values which completely overshadowed the organisational problems of the young generation. Nevertheless, despite the high level at which these issues were fought out, it manifested itself in the organisational sphere as well. The party leadership opposing youthful incursion assumed that any form of organisation for youth would serve merely as a disciplined administrative basis of support for their claims and was therefore to be opposed.

Thus during this period conflict occurred over the limits the young generation were to observe in their ideological discussions; whether the ideological circles should be organised solely on a local basis, or on a national scale; if local, how far were they to be autonomous, and how far subject to the local party administrative authorities, invariably controlled by the older generation. At all times the veteran party leadership favoured the alternatives that restricted the autonomy of the organisational structures of the younger generation, maximised local and central control over them, and granted the least possibility of developing an organisationally based permanence.

The early 1960s was a period of relative calm and during this time the younger generation was granted the degree of organisational permanence and national authority it had so long sought by the establishment of a department in Mapai headquarters. By the end of 1964 it organised some 18 000 young people aged between 18 and 30. Of these 3000 were in ideological, intellectual study and discussion circles. The other 15 000, most of whom had little more than primary education, were organised for social activities. While never

[18] Y. Kesse (Party Secretary-General), *Report 8th Mapai Conference*, 1956, p. 255.

completely happy about this, the Department kept up its function of entertaining young people because these activities represented important potential sources for new members; in other words, they were significant avenues for political recruitment; and secondly, because this would provide further opportunities for political socialisation by serious educational and informational activities within the framework set up for social and entertainment purposes. While it was recognised that attachment to the party for entertainment purposes was likely to be transitory for young people, it was hoped that the latter would cement party loyalty and commitment, and lead to more secure support.

The problems of Mapai and its youth highlight the questions of political recruitment and socialisation undertaken directly by the party without the benefit of any organisational penetration and control. Unable to avail itself of the facilities and executive bodies of other associations to which Mapai's potential supporters were committed on other grounds, it had to attempt to appeal directly to youth and incorporate them immediately into the party without the benefit of the mediation afforded by organisational penetration. (This does not include those already incorporated through other commitments, e.g. the Histadrut, agricultural settlements and so on.) But, as we saw, direct incorporation involving the establishment of separate organisational structures was regarded with apprehension because it threatened to spill over into conflict over leadership selection and succession, that could (and did) threaten organisational cohesion and maintenance. In fact for Mapai's younger generation, interest articulation, leadership selection and succession were intimately bound up together, as we shall see in later chapters.

INTRODUCTION

Part one dealt with how Mapai incorporated many of the diverse social forces that comprised Israeli society. The relationship was reciprocal: these social forces had interests which they wished the party to promote; the party needed their electoral support. But these interests were not pressed in a vacuum. To the contrary, they were mediated by the party's organisational structures. To aggregate the raw interests the party had to maintain an institutional structure that would allow these conflicting interests to be pressed, and policy preferences and decisions arrived at.

The same organisational structure also recruited and integrated the individual party member, socialised him to the party's demands upon him, and facilitated his participation in its affairs. It sought power through electoral campaigning, and directed the various institutional structures in which this was achieved. Thus the party's organisational structure was central in connecting its constituent social forces with governmental institutions, and the party membership with party, governmental, municipal, and Histadrut leaders. It was of crucial importance in interest aggregation, leadership selection, and in the direction of governmental structures via policy making and application. It was thus strategically situated to cope with the party's internal and external functions, and joined the two together in a coherent manner.

The role of organisational structures in facilitating participation can be further elaborated. Parties (or their members, representatives, institutions, and bureaucratic structures) make decisions on many issues ranging from the insignificant and trivial to momentous decisions of national scope and impact. Members participate in these decisions in different ways. As we explained in chapter one, a central concern of this book is with the various forms of participation and decision making. These interlocking processes of participation and decision making are best examined if separated structurally. In point of fact, the same individuals within the party may simultaneously share different relationships with each other in separate institutional involvements. For example, in Mapai, the party rank and file was divided geographically and connected to the party via local branch and regional structures. Members had certain rights and duties of participation and decision making in internal party affairs, for example they elected their own committees and executive bodies to administer the activities of the local branch. They also performed duties on behalf of the party in the local municipal and Histadrut institutions which Mapai controlled. Thus they had to organise to represent the party on these bodies. This raises a whole set of questions about the nature of local institutional relationships between rank and file members, local party institutions and the other local institutions.

But, more generally, the local situation raises a number of questions that are of wider import than the question of local institutional relationships – those of representativeness, responsiveness, the degree and nature of rank and file participation in decision making, and the organisational and technical imperatives of efficiency, and coherent coordination and control. It also calls into focus the problem of constitutionality – how far and to what degree the party representatives and institutions follow the rules and regulations laid down in the party constitution and how far these allow for rank and file participation. Finally the nature of the institution to which the party member is chosen as representative or delegate must also be considered. For example, a member may be chosen to head the party's list for municipal elections and become mayor. This raises other questions of responsibility and representation – how far and to what degree is he responsible to the electorate which voted him into office? How far does this conflict with his duties and obligations as a party member to party institutions and the party members that initially put his candidature forward?

But the local party member participates in party affairs not only at the local level for local party institutions and for local government institutions. He is first and foremost a member of a national party. Thus he participates in elections for national party institutions. This, too, raises important questions about the relationships of the party member to these institutions, and their members and leaders – how they are chosen; the role played by the average member; how these bodies relate to each other; where and how issues are initiated, discussed and finally decided.

Examining this decision making network only in relation to the party itself and its internal relations, however, illuminates only one of its major dimensions. The national party is primarily interested in the pursuit of national power, and in the Israeli context this includes both the parliamentary and Histadrut spheres. Here, too, the same questions arise, in addition to further complex problems of the coordination of the major decision making bodies, such as the Mapai Cabinet Ministers, and the Mapai members of the Histadrut's Central Executive Committee. The answers to these questions will also largely determine the answers to some of the earlier questions. Thus the relations of these coordinating bodies to the party rank and file in terms of responsiveness and participation are directly involved, as is the familiar question of the relationship between the extra-parliamentary institutions and the parliamentary representatives. One must also be aware of the possibility that bodies and groups not recognised in the party constitution may have developed, and influenced the formally stated constitutional processes. Party machines are a familiar phenomenon and we must therefore seek out and assess the operation of such informal groupings within Mapai, and their effects.

5. INDIVIDUAL MEMBERSHIP, BRANCH ORGANISATION AND LOCAL REPRESENTATIVE INSTITUTIONS

The party before 1948: the participant ethos

After 1948 Mapai's local branch organisation found it easier to attract members than to give them a sense of participation in party affairs. This situation contrasted markedly with conditions between 1930 and 1948. Prior to 1948 the party developed a highly participant ethos in theory, and a marked sense of participation in practice, facilitated by its small size and the relatively narrow range of decisions in which the party was involved. Because of the concentration in dispersed agricultural settlements most party branches were rather small, although as time went on the proportion of members in the bigger cities increased rather rapidly from a third in 1941 to about a half by 1946. The largest branch was in Tel Aviv, where in 1942 there were 3500–4000 members in one central branch.[1]

Contact between leaders and followers in the 1930s tended to be based upon personal acquaintance, and was informal, direct and fairly regular. Party leaders visited party branches throughout the country to discuss the vital issues with the rank and file, particularly during periods of crisis such as the party split. Direct contact with party leaders as well as actual participation in decisions created a sense of intimacy and warmth within the party, a feeling of equal partnership in a gemeinschaft-like fellowship. Informality, and the absence of clearly defined or written rules of party organisation and procedure were the norm.[2] Thus, for example, the party did not get written rules until the pressure of the imminent split in 1942 forced it to adopt formal criteria of what was to be permitted in the party, and what was to be proscribed. Even then, the rules adopted were a mere skeleton of the procedures needed to run a party.

From its foundation in 1930 Mapai had operated without a written constitution on the basis of the unification agreement which specified that all institutions be manned on a parity basis by the two uniting parties, Hapoel Hatzair and Achdut Haavoda. The absence of a written constitution was particularly suited to, and characteristic of, the party ethos of the period. In fact the party at that time, and even later, prided itself on the absence of

---

[1] B. Tal (Chairman, Organisation Department), *Report 8th Mapai Conference, 1956*, pp. 260–4.
[2] M. Argov, 'Some of the Party's Organisational Problems', *Hapoel Hatzair*, 18.7.1950.

formal constitutional rules, and on its political flexibility.[3] Formal constitutions and self-realisation and fulfilment were at opposite poles, and for some, inversely related.

The sense of participation of followers in Mapai was heightened by their sharing goals and an acute sense of national mission with the party's leaders. There were many actual decisions in which they did not fully participate (and by 1947 complaints of this were becoming increasingly common)[4] but for much of the period these were hardly noticed due to the powerful effects of the dominant ideology and the concerted efforts to achieve its goals. All were committed to them and cooperated in seeking to bring them about. This common aspiration and striving was capped by those who personally fulfilled the moral prescriptions of *chalutziut*, volunteering and pioneering.

The impact of independence upon the participant ethos:
the growth of formal organisation

With the establishment of the state this situation altered appreciably. The party underwent a tremendous growth in membership so that by the early 1950s the party branches in Tel Aviv and in Haifa were each individually bigger than the whole party had been prior to 1948. This led to a proliferation in the number of units, at the sub-branch, branch and later the regional levels, causing marked organisational problems. The numerical increase together with the processes of bureaucratisation and formalisation of procedures and institutions within both the state and society that accompanied the achievement of statehood destroyed much of the sense of intimacy and personal contact with leaders that had characterised the party previously. Party leaders were often too busy to concern themselves with the kind of widespread informal contact that they had undertaken before, and what direct contact they did have reached few of the party's 100 000 members. This was particularly true of the party's top leaders who were charged with ministerial and parliamentary responsibilities and with a widely increased domain of decisions. What the individual member noticed was the sudden formalisation of relations with leaders, the loss of contact, the erection of barriers in what had been direct and informal relationships, his distance from the centres of decision and administration, particularly if the policies were of national significance. Above all, much of the sense of participation was lost: the participant had become, in the main, an observer.

Independence served to reinforce this feeling. Gone was the ideological sense of participation, the chalutzic tension, the call for volunteering and pioneering; there were now state agencies to carry out most of the tasks that had previously called for self-realisation. Many members, particularly those

---

[3] R. Bash, 'An Improved Way of Life for the Party', *Hapoel Hatzair*, 6.8.1956.
[4] For example see M. Baram, 'Towards The Party Conference', *Hapoel Hatzair*, 11.4.1946.

who had been active before 1948, found it difficult to adjust, and voiced their dissatisfaction in no uncertain terms. They complained at the absence of discussion, and at the growth of social distance between senior government officials and party members, apparent in distinctions of dress and approach and in the absence of the former from branch meetings because they were thought to be too busy attending diplomatic receptions.[5] The formality which had replaced the intimacy and warmth of the past was not appreciated.[6]

Certain sections of the party leadership were also concerned at the social distance that had begun to characterise relations within the party, and particularly those manifestations of conspicuous consumption that had suddenly become perquisites of office-holding in ministerial, civil service and Histadrut positions, and which greatly contributed to the development of social barriers within Mapai. Thus the party Control Commission established in 1950 spent much of its time between 1951 and 1956 in the role of 'moral conscience' of the party, exhorting party leaders and officials to show an example to the nation of simplicity and austerity in social and official life, and to reject those material conveniences and luxuries of various kinds, which were regarded in other countries as necessities for the execution of official duties.[7]

The social role of the local party branch also changed radically. Previously the activities in the party branch embraced much of the member's social life, and were his major source of information and guidance in political and social affairs. His employment, friendships, cultural interests, and leisure hours were all deeply influenced by his party membership focused on the local branch. Attempts were also made to encourage the member to live in politically homogeneous Histadrut housing developments. In addition, he read the Histadrut newspaper, Davar, which because of Mapai's control of that body was in reality a Mapai paper, and subscribed also to one of the party journals, such as Hapoel Hatzair. A Mapai member could, if he so desired, live his life in a completely party-circumscribed environment, hardly coming into major political contact with outsiders, and barely subject to competing political influences or conflicting sources of information. While instrumental in developing and maintaining party loyalty and in reinforcing the member's readiness to commit himself to achieving the party's goals, it also gave rise to a heightened political intensity.

Much of this was broken down by the social diversification that followed the achievement of statehood; the development of state, party-neutral activity in many spheres; the establishment of an impartial government radio service, the growth of an independent widely read popular evening press, the loss of

[5] N. Ziv-Av, 'Faults and their Correctives', Hapoel Hatzair, 2.1.1951.
[6] See S. Avizemer, 'Repairing the Party House', Hapoel Hatzair, 30.1.1951; and also R. Bash, 'An Improved Way of Life for the Party', Hapoel Hatzair, 6.8.1956.
[7] See Report of Control Commission, 1950–1956 (Tel Aviv, 1956), pp. 36–44; and O. Porat (Secretary, Control Commission), Report 8th Mapai Conference, 1956, pp. 217–32, for full details of its various activities.

contact of the individual member with the branch, and the emergence of independent centres of socio-economic and professional interest. Party membership came to mean less to the average party member, was of less significance in determining his life pattern, and the party, consequently, commanded fewer of his loyalties. This represented a partial decline in the degree of social integration which was a major distinguishing characteristic of Mapai (and other Israeli parties).[8] As a result, party activity became the preserve of a much smaller proportion of the party membership, and was more than ever before confined to the activists, who constituted far less than 10 per cent of the members in the larger branches.[9]

These changes highlighted two basic problems which the party had to meet and solve: the problem of organisation at the local level – how were the smaller individual units to be joined to the party structure, how were their activities to be organised and coordinated, and what functions were they to fulfil?; and the problems of membership participation – how were the individual members to participate in these tasks, what other functions were they to fulfil, and in general what was to be their role within the party branch?

The problem of local organisation: the constitutional provisions

The tremendous numerical increase in the party brought a two-fold change in organisational structures; first, the marked growth in membership in existing branches, and second, the opening of new branches all over the country. Including the branches in the kibbutzim and the moshavim, by the middle of the 1950s the party was organised in over 400 individual branches. Similarly Tel Aviv and Haifa, which prior to 1948 were each organised in one single branch, had grown to twenty-five and thirty-six sub-branches respectively. An analysis of party branches in 1964 (excluding those in agricultural settlements) showed that there were thirty-seven branches with less than 500 members, seventeen branches numbering from 500 to 1000 (totalling 11 000 members), twenty-two branches with over 1000 members (totalling 45 000) and the five larger branches in the cities of Tel Aviv, Haifa, Jerusalem, Ramat Gan and Petach Tikva (each subdivided into smaller sub-units) together totalling 80 000.[10]

The numerical increase led to demands for reorganisation. It was clear from the organisational chaos which set in after 1948 that the previous system of central control and contact whereby Mapai central headquarters through its

[8] On the concept of 'parties of integration' see S. Neumann, 'Towards a Comparative Study of Political Parties', in S. Neumann, ed., *Modern Political Parties* (Chicago, 1956), p. 404.
[9] On the general changes in the nature of party membership see A. Ofer, 'The Chosen Must be Elected', *Hapoel Hatzair*, 18.7.1957.
[10] Benzion Weisman (Director of the Organisation Department), 'Some of the Party's Organisational Problems', *Hapoel Hatzair*, 10.3.1964.

Organisation Department kept in direct contact with each individual branch on all matters was not functioning well.[11] The first attempt took place in 1950–1 by introducing various forms of decentralisation.

The constitutional responsibilities of the local branches fell into two distinct categories, the internal party functions, and the external political and representative ones, where each branch was responsible for its own activities. The sub-branches individually carried out most of their internal political functions – organisation, membership recruitment, the collection of membership dues, local propaganda, relations with local Histadrut institutions and contact with the local social groupings such as youth, immigrants and ethnic groups. As regards the party's central organisational structure, they conducted elections for delegates to the Conference, were meant to 'discuss fundamental questions', and to pass conclusions up the party hierarchy.[12] Sub-branches were to be established in large cities or towns and to number between 250 and 2000 members, organised in existing residential districts, with the member being obliged to join the sub-branch closest to his home. Each sub-branch elected executive bodies consisting of a committee, which chose a secretariat and a secretary (usually a paid part-time worker).

Each sub-branch committee also elected its representatives to the Branch Council, which consisted of 60 per cent sub-branch representatives and 40 per cent local trade union party cell representatives. The Branch Council, which met every three months, elected a Branch Secretariat to convene fortnightly. The latter chose a secretary, usually a full-time paid official, especially in the larger branches. Branch boundaries were identical with local government ones.[13] Later constitutional provisions adopted in 1956, 1958, 1960, 1963 and 1964, introduced further detailed provisions concerning the powers and functions of branches and their institutions without altering this basic structure.

Further clarification was also introduced into relations between the local branch executive bodies and external representative institutions. Branch Councils were to elect Mapai's candidates for the local Histadrut and municipal institutions. The party's factions in these bodies chose the party's representatives on municipal and Histadrut committees in conjunction with the Branch Secretariat; and were expected collectively to 'discuss and decide on all matters on the agenda of these institutions', except in 'fundamental questions' or where the faction was divided, which came to the Branch Council for decision. They were to report on their activities to the Branch Council and Secretariat every six months, and to a general meeting of branch members annually.[14] There were also detailed provisions about local party trade union organisation.[15]

[11] Organisation Department Report, in *Report of Mapai Central Committee to the 8th Conference*, p. 34.   [12] *Mapai 1951 Constitution*, ch. 7.
[13] *Ibid.* ch. 11.   [14] *Mapai 1956 Constitution* (amended), ch. 9.   [15] *Ibid.* ch. 11.

Central control and coordination of local affairs: the experiment with regions

In order to cope with the task of coordination, the 1951 Council, devoted to constitutional matters, decided after much preliminary discussion that further decentralisation was needed, and called for the establishment of *Machozot*, regional administrative areas. The task of dividing the country into these regions was left to the party Secretariat, which decided upon thirteen territorial regions on a geographic basis to incorporate all party branches within the given area, including those in the relevant kibbutzim and moshavim. The three larger cities of Tel Aviv, Jerusalem and Haifa each constituted separate regions, as did the areas surrounding the cities of Petach Tikva, Bnei Brak and Ramat Gan. Each region was governed by a Regional Council of up to 121 members, made up of representatives of the constituent branches in proportion to their numbers, and elected by the Branch Council. It was to meet at least once in three months and chose a Regional Secretariat of not more than seventeen members. The Regional Secretary, on the other hand, was appointed by the Organisation Department, to whom he was responsible. It was hoped that this system would enable the Region's executive officers and secretariat to maintain almost daily contact with the constituent branches, whilst its various bodies would enable local activists to meet together to discuss party problems. Similarly it was expected that this would strengthen the Organisation Department's control. It was also believed that decentralisation would lead to greater integration of the party by enabling and encouraging older and pre-state members to come into contact with immigrants, youth and members of ethnic groups, in the context of common party activity. In particular it was thought that kibbutz members would prove ideal examples in this integration and socialisation process.[16]

These Regions were completely abandoned at the 1963 Conference, and organisational contact reverted back to the system in operation prior to 1951, the direct contact of each of the eighty party branches with the Organisation Department in Tel Aviv. A number of factors contributed to this reversal. The settlement movements, the Ichud, and Tnuat Hamoshavim withdrew from this geographical arrangement in 1957 and were recognised as Regions in themselves (see chapter two). Their withdrawal considerably weakened the Regions' command of experienced personnel while underlining the basic problem of regional organisation, the lack of clearly defined function and scope, combined with the absence of any institutionally based source of power and authority. The Regions were an artificial creation caught between the real centres of power in Mapai, the municipal and Labour Council-connected local branches with jobs, budgets and clearly defined areas of authority, the national Mapai institutions and administrative departments, and the socio-economically based centres of influence concentrated around the settlement

[16] *Mapai 1956 Constitution*, ch. 7, section 3.

movements, the Histadrut industrial and cooperative complex, and its trade union and social service agencies.[17] In the context of Israeli politics this doomed them to failure.

Party reorganisation and participation

It is difficult to know exactly how far the party reorganisation actually assisted individual participation in party activity. For example, a survey in 1963 showed that only 55 per cent of party members paid their affiliation fees regularly, on time and were up to date when the study was made.[18] On the other hand, the proportion voting in internal party elections was quite high; in 1964 the average turnout for the elections to the Conference and Branch Councils was 72 per cent, ranging from 67 to 86 per cent,[19] this figure being representative of those for other internal elections in the period 1948–65. There was also ample scope for activists; there were many positions to be filled in internal party bodies and in representing Mapai outside, which according to one estimate were held by over 70 000 Mapai members,[20] although many of these did not demand a substantial amount of activity on the part of the position holders.

Dissatisfaction with the role of the individual member in the regular activities of the party branches was constant. Party journals and reports registered continued criticism of apathy, the lack of opportunity for participation, the absence of discussions, ideological clarification, and policy consultation. The feeling was often expressed that except at election times the branches were 'dead', that members discovered more from newspapers about party affairs than from the branch institutions, that less than 10 per cent of members participated regularly or actively, that control of party branches was concentrated in the hands of a few activists, and that decisions were made within a small top leadership.[21] The 1960 Conference decided unanimously to solve this problem by making it an immediate organisational aim to 'maintain an uninterrupted process of bringing the party's problems before the mass of members in the branches and of giving suitable expression to their reactions'.[22] But the gap between resolution and implementation was wide, and little, if anything, came out of it.[23]

Facilitating rank and file participation prior to the decisions of the party's authoritative institutions was made more difficult by the lack of specific

---

[17] See A. Ben Tzila, 'New Organisational Forms', *Hapoel Hatzair*, 16.11.1954.
[18] *Hapoel Hatzair*, 25.2.1964.
[19] *Internal Report of Mapai Organisation Department*, 'Lessons for the 1965 Elections' (mimeo, n.d.).
[20] *Haaretz*, 6.7.1962.
[21] See *Report of Party Control Commission, 1956–1960*, p. 22.
[22] *Report 9th Mapai Conference, 2nd Session*, 1963, p. 129.
[23] *Report of Party Control Commission, 1960–1964*, pp. 38–9.

procedures or constitutional provisions for bringing issues to the branches and
their views back to the Central Committee or Secretariat. Even more detri-
mental to effective branch discussion was the fact that branch and regional
delegates in national party bodies such as the Central Committee, the Secretariat and the Conference, were not obliged to give systematic reports to their
branches of the activities of these institutions, and their part in them. This
resulted in feelings of political inefficacy on the part of potential activists
who doubted whether views expressed in the branches would carry any
influence at the centre, even if passed on.[24] On the other hand, there is a little
evidence that in some branches the membership was actively involved in, and
derived satisfaction from branch activities and discussions of ideological problems and national issues.[25]

External representative functions: control of local government and Histadrut institutions

The constitutional provisions intended that the branch operate as a unit
under the direction and control of its institutions. The party's representatives
in the municipal and Histadrut bodies were chosen by it and expected to be
responsible to it; this is seen clearly, for example, in the demand for consultation, and the acceptance of the decision of branch bodies in cases of major
importance, or where the party faction was divided. At all events, the party
was expected to control the policies of its representatives and through them
the activities of the bodies on which they sat, and it was to do this through
the Branch Councils and Secretariats. In point of fact, the experience of the
period 1948–65 suggests the opposite. *The party institutions, rather than
controlling, were controlled by the party's representatives in the outside
institutions.* Instead of acting as the independent arbiters and mediators in
matters of policy difference, or disagreement, the party institutions became
the forum within which the competing factions fought out their differences
and settled them, at best, by a vote. More usually they provided a rubber
stamp for the actions of the dominant group, and served as an instrument
assisting the dominance of party institutions by a particular group. In other
words, the party institutions were hardly an independent centre of power, as
envisaged, but, in most cases, were subject to the control of other competing
centres of power.

There were three basic centres of power in the local branches each capable
of either paralysing branch activities or, more usually, of gaining control of
the branch institutions; namely, the trade union and Histadrut group; the
municipal affairs group; and the ethnic groups within the branch. Control of
the branch institutions was essential for maintaining a group's position in the

[24] See, for example, Raanan Weitz, *Report 8th Mapai Conference, 1956*, p. 339.
[25] *Report 8th Mapai Conference, 1956*, pp. 133–4.

outside institutions, for the same party bodies that chose candidates for these positions had the power to revoke these mandates. On the other hand, the loss of these positions was particularly damaging to local political leaders because with them went the control of political appointments, and other instrumental benefits for distribution among followers within the branch, whose support was needed for success in internal Mapai elections, and for the retention of control between elections. The relationship was reciprocal: branch control provided positions of institutional power; institutional power positions provided resources that facilitated further branch control.

Histadrut affairs

The relation of party to local trade union affairs was always rather vague, except for the choice of secretary and the major executive positions in local Labour Councils. Thus constitutional provisions for the establishment of Mapai Trade Union Councils were not introduced until October 1963 and even these did not specify any functions for them. An official report at the end of 1964 suggested their functions were not understood, and overlapped with Histadrut and workplace affairs.[26]

Clearly defining the scope and role of the party's local branch operation in trade union affairs was difficult because local Histadrut institutions were part of the central Histadrut hierarchy and bureaucratic apparatus, and therefore directly subject to it in the administration and execution of policies. On the other hand, the local party branch was responsible for providing personnel for the key local positions in the representative bodies some of whom were full-time, salaried officials. The latter were highly influential in the choice of salaried Histadrut officials at the lower levels, for all local Histadrut institutions. As a result there developed in many Mapai branches throughout the country a cohesive group within the party branch centred around the trade union and other Histadrut institutions. This was almost always led by the secretary of the local Labour Council, who could usually rely on the support of other local Labour Council representatives and of the many clerks and officials in the various Histadrut bureaucracies.

Municipal affairs

The second major centre of power developed around the municipal institutions. The mayors of cities, towns and regions together with the majorities in their councils enjoy statutory powers of administration which enable them to appoint various salaried officials at all levels in the municipal bureaucracy. As with the Histadrut, the key municipal positions themselves carried full-time salaries, apart from the power and authority to provide other jobs. And,

[26] *Report of Party Control Commission, 1960–1964*, p. 40.

of course, the larger the municipal administration, the more jobs to be filled. Unlike the Histadrut, part of a national hierarchy, the local municipal institutions remained fairly autonomous and independent in their activities and decisions in the limited area of authority granted to them by legislation and supervised in the most general way by the Ministry of the Interior. They administered services in education, health and sanitation, social welfare, water, road maintenance and public parks. They were thus able to provide employment of all kinds and at many levels of skill to supporters or potential supporters within the party branch. Moreover councils granted licences and concessions for the establishment of various types of small business, and these, too, were available as rewards for support.

Ethnicity and ethnic conflict

The third major centre of power within local Mapai branches was that of ethnic solidarity. Although relevant for Mapai throughout the country, it was particularly crucial in the development towns with very large concentrations of non-European ethnic groups which constituted a majority of their Mapai members. After 1958 serious inter-ethnic political conflicts occurred in many Mapai branches which, in places like Beer Sheba, Ashdod, Ashkelon, Dimona, and Kiryat Gat led to the mid-term replacement by the local branches of municipal and Histadrut leaders, the paralysis of local government, splits in party branches and the expulsion of leading individuals.

In some cases ethnicity became so important that it provided the major form of organisational basis of the local branch. This was the case in Beer Sheba, for example, where the Mapai constitution's residential criterion for sub-branch membership was completely replaced by the existence of seven ethnic circles. All the party institutions were constituted according to an ethnic key, as were the various forms of representation within the party, as well as the representation of the party in outside institutions.[27] This situation arose out of Mapai's need to gain the support of immigrant groups and ethnic leaders for its electoral success. To gain their support Mapai had to promise and supply various instrumental and symbolic rewards. At this stage the groups and their leaders were able to make demands upon the party with the implied or explicit threat of withdrawal of support, to which in many cases, the party acceded, although in others it did not. Thus there were many instances of ethnic groups making such demands, being rebuffed, leaving the party, fighting local elections on ethnic tickets, getting soundly beaten, and often returning to the party.[28]

[27] R. Zamir, *Beer Sheba 1958–9: Social Processes in a Development Town* (The Sociology Department, Kaplan School, Hebrew University) Researches in Sociology, 3 (1964), p. 50 (Hebrew).
[28] Examples of this occurred in many places. A typical case in Beer Sheba is reported in Zamir, p. 44.

Under the pressure of these various social forces three basic patterns of branch politics emerged. In the older, established branches, the dominant tendency was towards the development of unitary control of the branch by the majority, which while representing many groups was in a position to completely exclude disfavoured minorities from participation in decision making. The second pattern was that of recurrent ethnic conflict. The third was of inter-institutional conflict with, or without, an ethnic component.

Unitary control by entrenched veteran groups

In the older established areas where the proportion of Europeans was much higher, and, where control of party life at the top was firmly in the hands of veterans with long histories of party service, a characteristic pattern emerged in the running of the party branch and in its relations with the local municipal and Histadrut institutions. This was the pattern of unitary branch control, in which a single group or person effectively directed the activities of the branch and controlled the branch institutions. While not actually determining the policies and operations of the local institutions, such as the municipality or the Histadrut (unless of course the major figure occupied the leading position in one of these institutions) the group controlling the local party was able to exercise a decisive voice in appointments and nominations to these positions. Rather than the divided authority and competing centres of power which characterised the newer branches, in the older established ones the Histadrut and the municipal factions and leaders often formed one cohesive and united group, or else were both in turn controlled by another group, the dominant power in the party branch. Where the Histadrut and municipal factions formed a cohesive group it is clear that they could between them easily control the party branch, provided they remained united and limited competition between them. It could also be expected that over a period of time the two would coalesce into one group. There was also always the possibility of the maintenance of two separate groups competing within limits, but overall adopting a stance of steady cooperation, particularly against disfavoured outsiders. The case of the unified branch, best described as the development of unified party machines, is the most important because it describes the situation in the two largest branches in the country, Tel Aviv and Haifa. (They are examined in detail in chapter eight.)

Ethnic conflict

The most common ethnic demands were to be given representative positions, or positions of bureaucratic significance. These positions combined symbolic rewards with the capacity to distribute instrumental benefits, including other such positions. Conflicts and competition over such demands were so common that they were the very stuff of local Mapai activity; and often they became so fierce that they either split or paralysed branches. It is instructive briefly to examine a number of case histories of Mapai branches in development areas which provide some characteristic examples of ethnic problems.

One study demonstrated the power of the Secretary of the Labour Council, who successfully recommended candidates for various positions. More than once this enabled him to satisfy the demands of ethnic leaders or others when this seemed to him to be politically desirable. He recommended candidates for positions in the local factory, the local council, the branch of a new bank, the Histadrut institutions, and the Mapai branch. It is not surprising that nearly all the officials in the town – in the local council, the administration of the immigrant transit camp, the Histadrut, and the Labour Exchange – were members of Mapai.[29]

The Beer Sheba study reported that according to one of their leaders, the Iraqis 'demanded the post of executive officer of the Labour Exchange for one of our ethnic group, and after a protracted battle we got it...We began to supervise the employment queue at the exchange...Our committee became stronger and the institutions saw that it was impossible not to accept its demands...Everything that was gained by the Iraqi group was gained through conflict'. Overall few Iraqis were unemployed, and its housing and social welfare problems had been solved. They also held central positions in the various local institutions – deputy mayor of the city, director of the municipality's social welfare department, secretary of the local Building Workers Union, and head medical attendant in the local Kupat Cholim.[30]

Inter-institutional conflict: non-ethnic and ethnic

Inter-institutional conflict without an ethnic basis consisted mainly in the clash of interest between the representatives of the Histadrut and the municipality. It also occurred between various individual institutions as well, such as the labour exchanges, Kupat Cholim, municipal departments, and local branches of governmental departments. Conflict was often intensely personal, deriving from the desire of an individual leader in one of these institutions to become the undisputed local leader, or to use his local position as a springboard for further political advancement. The end result of these conflicts was usually the same; the division of the branch into two warring factions, one centred around the municipal institutions and the other around the Histadrut, each seeking to capture control of the local branch, by using its institutional position and the distribution of instrumental benefits to gather supporters in the elections for Mapai branch institutions. The typical Mapai internal

[29] C. Weil, *Communal Problems in an Immigrant Settlement* (Department of Sociology, Kaplan School, Hebrew University), Researches in Sociology, 2 (1957), pp. 21–2 (Hebrew).   [30] Zamir, p. 38.

election was fought out between two tickets of candidates, one representing municipal workers and officials, and the other representing Histadrut activists, with little opportunity for independents to gain election. Voting support was achieved by mobilising workers in the various institutional complexes to vote for their own candidates, and institutional pressure was applied to ensure this. Often there was no contact between the dominant and the minority groups; the majority took decisions in a small circle prior to, or instead of, at the meetings of branch institutions, and, in general, the branch became paralysed.

The 1963 Conference attempted to obviate the problems that had arisen from the increasingly common practice of the head of a local municipal or Histadrut authority installing members of the branch secretariat in official salaried positions in the municipality or the Labour Council in order to ensure a majority on the party body.[31] One far-reaching suggestion was that no employee of any local institution could be a member of a branch secretariat; a second suggestion limited the proportion of such officials on branch secretariats to 40 per cent. Both suggestions were opposed by the Conference Standing Committee, however, and were lost.[32]

Inter-institutional conflict focused around leading personalities was made more complicated, explosive and dangerous by the intrusion of ethnic conflict. A common tactic of ethnic group recognition in Mapai was to divide positions of institutional authority among different ethnic groups. Thus municipal–Histadrut conflict became intensified when the institutions were led by members of conflicting ethnic groups. As they struggled for control of the branch, or attempted to overturn a previous ethnic modus vivendi, some of these conflicts bordered on the racial. The ethnic component made co-operation and compromise even more difficult because issues involved questions of group prestige and identity. A similar end-result occurred when one group, firmly in control of the party branch and the outside representative institutions, was challenged by an insurgent group on ethnic grounds. A third case typically occurred when a Mapai municipal representative left the party, on the grounds of ethnic grievance, thereby undermining Mapai's narrow coalition majority. Although the party sent the individual to the municipality as its representative, it could not revoke his electoral mandate.

The general and damaging consequences to the party of such actions in various towns and cities in Israel after 1958 caused the party a great deal of concern. In more than a few instances such conflicts cost Mapai its coalition majority, deprived it of the instrumental advantages of office, and often led to a loss of local and national prestige. Another typical consequence was for a local branch secretariat to depose a mayor in mid-term by a vote of no-confidence, thus bringing down the whole coalition. In such cases Mapai central institutions were forced to intervene to make peace in the local branches, and to maintain Mapai control. On some such occasions the party

[31] *Report 9th Mapai Conference, 3rd Session, 1963*, p. 180.   [32] *Ibid*. p. 213.

paid a heavy price, being forced publicly to come to terms with the very individuals causing these problems. Between 1959 and 1964 there were twenty such major crises and ten Mapai mayors were removed from office.[33] Neither the local party nor central bodies were happy with this situation. Thus on the initiative of the party's Municipal Department, the 1963 Conference removed the right of local branches to displace mayors in mid-term by putting such matters under the control of Mapai central bodies.[34]

Growing central control and direction: the Municipal Department

The general picture, then, in contrast with the aims of the decentralising organisational and constitutional changes of the early 1950s, was of growing central control and intervention in local affairs. This tendency is exemplified in the expanding activities of the party's Municipal Department situated in Tel Aviv. The Municipal Department at first had more limited functions. It was initially established in 1954, prior to the municipal elections of July 1955, to assist the party in its pre- and post-election tactics, particularly the establishment of municipal coalitions. In 1955 these negotiations resulted in Mapai receiving the position of mayor (and with it control of the coalition and the administration) in 13 out of 17 cities, and 43 out of 57 local councils. After that it maintained this pre-eminent position; in 1964, for example, it controlled 20 out of 24 Jewish cities, and 47 out of the 62 Jewish local councils. In the latter year some 500 party members were elected to these councils and another 1000 or more to various municipal committees.[35]

Over the years the department concentrated increasingly upon acting as 'fire brigade' in cases of local conflagration, and less upon general municipal policy or coalition agreements at the national level. It developed a number of ad hoc rules and practices in dealing with local problems. It was actively involved in the choice of Mapai mayoral candidates. It often found suitable candidates, particularly when relations between the factions in a local branch made it essential that an outsider be chosen. Generally, if the party list for municipal elections passed the Branch Council without a hitch, the branch merely reported it to the Department, but if there were disagreements and problems at the branch level the Department stepped in to arrange a compromise and to quieten things down. The Department assisted local branches if coalition problems arose, when it would meet with parallel bodies in other parties to iron out local issues. In its dealings with crisis-ridden branches it intervened directly in conjunction with the Organisation Department.

The Department also developed two other important areas of activity. It

[33] See Report of the Head of Municipal Department in *From Conference to Conference*, pp. 48–53.
[34] *Mapai 1956 Constitution* (amended), ch. 9, clause 3.
[35] Report, *Municipal Department*, p. 48.

participated in policy making in municipal affairs through close cooperation with Mapai members of Knesset, and in particular its representatives on two Knesset Committees, *Vaadat Hapnim*, the Interior Committee, and *Vaadat Hachuka, Chok U'mishpat*, the Constitutional, Legislative, and Judicial Committee. In these matters it was aided by the fact that Mapai's M.K.s on these and other committees, and some Ministers, were actively involved in the work of the Department. As might be expected, many important Mapai figures in the world of municipal government, including the mayors of Tel Aviv, Haifa, Jerusalem, Herzlia, Dimona, Kfar Saba, Petach Tikva, and the heads of a number of smaller local councils, were also active in its work. Thus the Department was uniquely informed in municipal affairs and therefore able to keep a watchful eye on all legislation affecting municipal affairs and to initiate proposals and amendments. It also had access to parliamentary channels to have these discussed, and, in all likelihood, passed, by the relevant bodies.[36] The involvement in its operation of those in charge of municipal affairs throughout the country ensured that the laws or amendments it approved were unlikely to meet with opposition or obstruction at the local level.

The Mapai Municipal Department was also actively involved in representing the interests of Mapai's municipal office bearers in the development towns. It believed that there was a need for it to support their efforts to gain the allocation of resources for the development of their towns from the relevant government ministries whose attention to local requests was regarded as unsatisfactory. Thus the Department assisted their claims for housing, immigrants, educational facilities, and health services. Its officials emphasised that despite excellent relations with Mapai ministers and bureaucrats they were not always successful in achieving their clients' demands.

The Department thus performed a significant role in the political socialisation of local leaders. By bringing them into contact with ministers and officials it enabled them to learn the conventions and procedures to be observed, and to acquire the invaluable resource of personal acquaintance and recognition.

[36] *Ibid.*

6. NATIONAL REPRESENTATIVE DECISION MAKING INSTITUTIONS: THE CONFERENCE, COUNCIL AND CENTRAL COMMITTEE

Representation, efficiency and constitutionality

In the development of Mapai's central decision making institutions after 1948 certain basic problems and trends recurred, and we shall therefore begin with a brief theoretical overview and analysis before turning to a detailed study of these institutions themselves. The bodies we are mainly concerned with in this analysis are the Conference (*Veida*), Council (*Moetza*), and the Central Committee (*Merkaz*), the Secretariat (*Mazkirut*), the Political Committee (*Vaada Medinit*, or *Vaada Politit*) and the Leadership Bureau (*Lishka*). The first general problem lay in the conflict between demands for greater representation and those for greater efficiency and capacity in decision making. With the increased social diversification of the party, the growing multiplication of demands, and the rapid rise in awareness of group identity and interests, pressures were built up for their inclusion in the party's decision making structures. The result was a steady increase in size in all these major institutions after 1948 as each group was accorded its demands. Mapai's typical response to these constant demands for greater representation was simply to increase the size of the institutions. This was especially so with the Central Committee and the Secretariat. But these demands for representation in the context of the broad general powers and functions of these bodies brought seriously into question their efficiency and capacity to make decisions.

The demands of efficiency were met in various ways. There was both a de jure and de facto division of functions, and a degree of specialisation. The Central Committee met monthly, which confined it to limited discussion of a limited number of issues. Other issues were handled by the responsible bodies; for example, by the parliamentary faction, or by the faction in the Histadrut, sometimes after general policy guidelines had been set. Matters came to the Central Committee at the end of a long process of discussion and deliberation, rather than at the beginning. The detailed process of deliberation often took place in the Secretariat, or in specialised small sub-committees set up by the Secretariat or the Central Committee. The trend towards smaller bodies or ad hoc committees or even permanent specialised sub-committees facilitated efficient decision making, but when this trend became obvious, cries for representation were again loudly raised and the whole process repeated. To prevent this cyclical process Mapai occasionally set up limited bodies of the very top leaders who enjoyed considerable power and authority within the party. They met the requirements of efficiency, could have their decisions accepted, and because of their limited high-level membership could forestall further demands for widespread representation.

But the increasing use of such bodies gave rise to a number of other problems. The first of these was the problem of constitutionality. Should the party's written constitution always be strictly adhered to, or could it be broken or simply ignored for the sake of political convenience and in the interests of political flexibility? In most cases, Mapai with its history and tradition of unwritten constitutions and of pride in its ability to produce politically flexible responses to changing situations opted for the latter. This meant that the party did not feel itself bound to adhere rigidly to written constitutional demands or rules if it would prove politically inconvenient or embarrassing to do so, or if the simplest solution was simply to ignore the written rules. The reports of the party's Control Commission, one of whose major tasks was to report regularly to the Secretariat and the Conference on how the party was living up to its constitutional provisions, were replete with criticism and complaints about the party's nonfulfilment of its constitution. Conferences were not called on time, elections for various bodies were not held, those that were held were often subject to major irregularities, seriously infringing constitutional requirements, party institutions of a fixed size were simply inflated to cater for further demands for representation, and bodies with no constitutional standing carried out important functions conferred by the constitution on other bodies.

The multiplicity of decision making bodies raised another significant general problem for Mapai in its institutional development, the clear demarcation and delineation of power and authority, and, flowing from this, the question of coordination. It also necessitated the existence of commonly agreed upon and understood rules about the way in which decisions were to be taken, about institutional involvement in the issues, and the manner in which disagreements within institutions, and more importantly, disputes between institutions and decision making bodies were to be settled.

The Conference

The party constitution adopted at the Council in March 1951 carried on the predominant practice of Mapai during the period of the Yishuv, to elect a Conference every three years, normally to convene once in three years. It did not specify how these elections were to be conducted; this was left to the party institutions to arrange. Despite lack of specific provisions the general practice that representatives be chosen in both the branches and trade union cells was always adhered to, and finally laid down in the party's Electoral

Constitution adopted in 1964 by the Central Committee. Before that the party institutions specified prior to each Conference how many delegates were to be elected in relation to the number of members eligible to vote: thus in 1946 one delegate was chosen for every fifty eligible city voters and one delegate for every forty rural voters.[1] Later the proportion was one delegate for every 100 eligible voters. The number of delegates thus reached was then divided up among the branches according to their numerical strength, with special provisions to enable the representation of smaller branches. In areas with a Histadrut membership of more than 8000, the quota of delegates was divided into two groups; one of 60 per cent elected from branch lists and one of 40 per cent from trade union lists, with each member exercising two votes, one for each list.[2] (In earlier years this proportion was restricted to the three largest cities only and was divided equally between the two.)

The 1951 constitution did not say anything about the electoral system to be adopted in choosing these delegates; it seems to have been taken for granted that the previous method would be continued, and it was only in 1956 that the constitution stated that 'elections were to be direct, personal and secret'.[3] That is to say, the voter directly elected the delegates by indicating the names of the individual candidates he preferred (and not by supporting a ticket or any other en bloc procedure, as in Knesset and most other Israeli elections).

The 1951 constitution did not specify the power or authority of the Conference, but this was remedied in 1956 with the opening pronouncement that 'the supreme institution of the party is the national Conference'.[4] As such, there was nothing, in theory, that it could not do in party affairs, but meeting, at most, yearly, its effective powers were severely limited. In 1951 it was assumed that the Conference would meet once in three years; in 1956 this became an election for the Conference every two years, with the Conference meeting every year; whilst from 1963 onwards the Conference was to be elected every four years and to meet at two-yearly intervals.[5]

The Conference was charged with a number of specific tasks, the most important being the election of other decision making bodies, namely the Council, till 1956, and the Central Committee, after that date. For the Council, the Standing Committee proposed a complete list filling all available places for ratification en bloc by the Conference. One-third of the Central Committee members were chosen in this manner, while the other two-thirds were elected directly by the Conference delegates organised in Regions in proportion to their numerical strength.[6]

[1] *Hapoel Hatzair* 15.3.1946, and 22.3.1946.
[2] *Mapai 1956 Constitution* (amended), ch. 6, clause 12a.
[3] *Ibid.* ch. 1, clause 3.   [4] *Ibid.* ch. 1, clause 1.
[5] *Mapai 1951 Constitution*, ch. 1, clause 1; *Mapai 1956 Constitution*, ch. 1, clause 2, 5a; *Mapai 1956 Constitution* (amended), ch. 1, clause 2.
[6] *Mapai 1951 Constitution*, ch. 1, clause 2; *Mapai 1956 Constitution*, ch. 2, clause 2.

The constitution attempted to encourage rank and file participation by instructing the Secretariat to publish the agenda at least three months prior to the Conference. Branch institutions were expected to organise local discussions on these topics and to pass on their views and suggestions to the Secretariat. The right was also reserved for them to suggest additional topics for discussion, as well as draft resolutions for Conference decisions.[7]

Table 6.1 shows the number of delegates attending Conferences and the frequency of Conference sessions for the period 1930–65.

Table 6.1. *Frequency of Mapai conferences and number of elected delegates*

Conference	Year	Number of delegates
1st	1930	280
2nd	1932	147
3rd	1935	187
4th	1938	388
5th (3 sessions)	1941–2	388
6th	1946	616
7th	1950	1474
8th (2 sessions)	1956, 1958	1074*
9th (3 sessions)	1959, 1960, 1963	1963
10th	1965	2241

* To this must be added another 130 members of the Central Committee who were automatically delegates.

These formal requirements and theoretical possibilities must be supplemented by a close examination of the realities of the situation.

There was a common saying in Mapai that the more supreme a particular party body, the less authoritative it was.[8] If this is true it will be more applicable to the Conference than to any other party institution, and therefore it provides a useful focus around which to discuss the realities of the situation. This problem is not one restricted to Mapai alone; it relates to the general question of the possible influence of rank and file opinion and action on party leaderships, which is relevant to many political parties.[9]

The rule that constitutional supremacy and real power and authority were inversely related is partially correct in the sense that a body that met as infrequently as the Mapai Conference could not exercise direct and constant power and influence over party decisions. Infrequent meeting does not, on the other hand, prevent the setting of general guidelines of policy for a number of years. In point of fact, however, the discussion at Mapai Confer-

[7] *Mapai 1951 Constitution*, ch. 1, clause 9.
[8] See, for example, M. Baram, 'Towards the Party Conference', *Hapoel Hatzair*, 11.4.1946 for an early formulation of this position.
[9] For a theoretical analysis of this question see Medding, 'A Framework for The Analysis of Power in Political Parties', *passim*.

ences was mainly of the most general kind, with little relation between the actual discussions and the resolutions that were passed at the end. The constitutional demand for local branch pre-discussion was met prior to the 1960 and 1963 Conferences, but there is no evidence of any effect upon delegates or upon the content of discussions and decisions, and they produced no suggestions for discussion or resolution that were taken up at the Conference. Mapai Conferences, therefore, tended to serve two basic functions. The first was that of a mass demonstration of party strength, a way of showing the flag to the nation, to the opposition parties, and not least of all to the party faithful. Second, they provided an opportunity for representatives of each of the party's many and varied interests to speak out publicly on matters of deep and immediate concern to them, irrespective of whether these were on the agenda or not. They were thus a significant forum for the articulation of interests and for bringing to the attention of party leaders problems, demands and needs that their spokesmen felt had been neglected.

The rule is also correct in relation to the organisation of the Conference, particularly with regard to the power of the outgoing Secretariat to 'prepare' a Conference. Its power was such that it could exercise decisive influence and control over all matters that were brought before the Conference and over the manner in which they were presented to it, covering the content, substance and form of matters and resolutions to be discussed. The constitution laid down that the Central Committee should, before each session, set up a Preparation Committee, consisting of two-thirds from the local branches and one-third appointed by the Central Committee. The Secretariat and the party's Organisation Department or any group controlling them could easily secure a majority on this committee. If it could fill most of the one-third quota to be appointed en bloc by the Central Committee at the suggestion of the Secretariat and the Organisation Department (via an Appointments Committee), it needed only a little more than one-sixth of the delegates from the local branches to gain a majority. Moreover, it could also secure the key position of chairman. In actual fact, relations between the Organisation Department and many local branches were such that it regularly achieved far more than that minimum, thus giving the outgoing Secretariat control of the Preparation Committee.

Control of the Preparation Committee meant a marked degree of control over all proceedings of the Party Conference. It prepared all the resolutions for the Conference, beginning to work weeks and even months before each Conference, and in the days immediately prior to the Conference itself it would meet daily. It worked in close cooperation with the Secretariat, thoroughly discussing the matters on the agenda and attempting to formulate these as decisions or resolutions that could be voted upon. It often divided into sub-committees – the constitution obliged it to set up an Appointments Sub-Committee to select the central candidates for the Central Committee prior to their presentation to Conference – and it sometimes coopted sub-committees. This happened in 1956 when a Committee of Eleven earlier set up by the Secretariat to discuss economic policy was coopted as the economic sub-committee of the Preparation Committee when it was decided that economic policy was to be a major item on the Conference agenda.

At the beginning of the Conference the Preparation Committee became known as the *Vaada Matmedet*, the Standing Committeee, and was approved en bloc as such by the Conference. No resolution could come before the Conference unless it had first passed through the Standing Committee, which attempted to reach agreement on resolutions or policy decisions and to present them to the Conference as unanimous decisions. Where it was divided it brought the majority view to the Conference as its recommendation together with such minority amendments as were suggested. A debate ensued and the Conference then had to vote and decide.

Much of the real debate and discussion at Conferences took place in the Standing Committee, not only because matters could not be brought for decision to the floor of the Conference without its prior discussion and recommendation, but also because many matters brought to the Conference as agreed resolutions of the Standing Committee were never discussed by the Conference. Moreover, only on rare occasions were the recommendations of the Standing Committee rejected; usually they were unopposed and passed unanimously. The rare defeats occurred when the Standing Committee itself was divided. A further basic factor facilitating Standing Committee control of Conference was control of the Standing Committee and Conference by the party machine (to be analysed in detail in chapter eight).

For all these reasons the argument that because it was theoretically supreme the Conference was weak in power has a marked degree of validity. Before discounting it completely, however, one must consider the factors operating in the other direction which emphasised its power and importance. Despite these effects of organisation, preparation, and control of delegates, the Conference was, in some ways, powerful, and in a number of areas proved itself to be supreme in actuality.

The very existence of the Conference acted as a lever of pressure. Concessions to dissent, and compromises, were made in order to ensure that the Conference as a whole would give its assent. Wherever there were conflicting viewpoints on matters of importance the tendency in the Standing Committee was to try and reach a formula that both sides could agree upon so that the Conference would be able to demonstrate the unity of the party by giving its unanimous assent. While this imposed probably greater pressure on the minority to compromise for the sake of party unity, it also involved the need for the majority to take significant steps in the direction of the minority in order to make it possible for the latter to withdraw or accept the offered compromise. This pressure towards compromise and unanimous assent was reinforced by the bitter historical experience of the party split in the 1940s, which provided a constant reminder of the dangers of pushing issues too far and refusing to compromise. The notion that issues could be debated and decided by a genuine majority vote were rather foreign to Mapai; in its place unanimity or something approaching it had to be achieved before a matter was put to the vote. A good example of this approach in the policy area occurred in the debate over economic policy in 1956. On the wages question, government ministers and Histadrut leaders were sharply divided. Rather than have the Conference decide the issue then and there as a reflection of the will of the party, a very general middle of the road policy was enunciated, and the matter thrown back to the Central Committee for further discussion.

Even more important was the fact that despite the most careful control and preparation, the Standing Committee's recommendations had to be voted upon by the Conference, which then retained the possibility of rejecting them. Not only was this a possibility which in itself was powerful enough to induce compromises in order to ensure majority support, there were occasions on which the Standing Committee was defeated on the floor of the Conference. This occurred in 1956, over constitutional issues, when it was defeated over the question of the size of the Central Committee, over the inception date of the division of delegates for the Central Committee between the central list and the branches, and over a technical aspect of secret elections.[10]

The theory that constitutional supremacy was inversely related to real power suffers from a basic error in its implicit assumption that what the majority at Conference gained by bloc organisation did not reflect the 'real' or 'true' state of affairs. There is no evidence to suggest that a majority of the party favoured views that were defeated or were not even put forward, nor any to suggest that even a majority of Conference delegates favoured a defeated point of view. To maintain this claim in the absence of such evidence is to adopt the untenable position of accepting an assumption for which not only is there no evidence, but with regard to which the only evidence is directly to the contrary. It rests upon supposed knowledge of the 'real' interests and the 'true' views of the majority, which for some reason it did not express, but which were in direct opposition to the decisions taken. Moreover, the argument of minority control of the Conference is self-defeating. Issue conflicts could be won only by organisation and with the support of the majority of delegates at the Conference. Thus all that is being said is that the majority controlled the Conference.

But at the same time, the question of the nature of this majority must be made clear, even if the fact that it is a majority cannot be disregarded. In any theory of consensual decision making the ideal situation is for delegates to be democratically elected in such a way that there can be no question that the election process provides as exact a reflection of rank and file will and opinion

10 *Report 8th Mapai Conference*, 1956, pp. 90–1, 399.

as is attainable, and that they have ample opportunity to make themselves acquainted with and discuss the issues put before them for deliberation. If they can get the views of their electors on these issues, it would be even better. After due consideration of the pros and cons of the issue, each delegate votes as an individual according to what he conceives to be the best interests of the party, without group pressure, or the influence of any particular faction or interest with which he is affiliated or which has any power over him in relation to career, promotion, job, livelihood and so forth.

This is, of course, a highly idealised, Rousseauian conception of individualist participation in decision making, which takes little account of political realities. The first step towards taking account of political realities is to recognise that representatives have interests to protect, further and promote, that these inevitably exercise a great deal of influence on their thinking and views, that they may have been elected because they could be relied upon to represent these interests and that group leaders will mobilise the opinions of these delegates by organising among them to ensure their support on given issues. All these represent political realities which 'impinge' upon the individualistic 'freedom' of the representative or decision maker. But his 'freedom' may be further impinged upon, its existence may become questionable, and he may even become 'captive'. This occurs when, through control over life chances, particularly economic existence and opportunities for political promotion, an individual or group can determine who is elected, and direct the behaviour and actions of the delegate or representative. It is in this light that the position of the majority support gained at Mapai Conferences must be examined. The two main Mapai branches, Tel Aviv and Haifa, fit this description, as we shall see below; each was controlled by an individual or small group in this manner, and generally voted monolithically. The same applied to other large major urban branches, and together they constituted a majority. This is where the problem of assessment arises: while for victory at Conference a majority was needed, and in that sense the argument is self-defeating, what arouses uneasiness is that the majority was nearly always constituted in the same manner, of the same groups. Had there been changing majorities each time the position would have been entirely different, but it is the solidarity and stability of the majority which raises doubts.

But with all this said, in the absence of evidence to the contrary, there is no reason to assume that the majority, however constituted and constructed by the party machine, did not represent the views of the majority of the delegates or the party. It is entirely possible and, indeed, likely, that the machine majority enjoyed its success precisely because it reflected the party, and precisely represented its attitudes and interests. In other words, in the absence of strong evidence to suggest that a 'free' vote would have been otherwise, we must either accept the majority decision at Conference as the view of the party majority, or else sceptically argue that we do not know what a 'free' majority of party delegates would have decided in a 'free' vote.

Most important of all in assessing the power of Mapai's Conference is that it was the locus of final sovereignty within the party. It was here within Mapai that an end was put to all argument, and after a Conference decision a dissenting group could either seek another session of the Conference to reverse the decision; or accept it and keep quiet; or leave the party. Thus the two major power struggles within Mapai, the 1942 and 1965 splits, were finally decided at Conference, with the dissenters in both cases refusing to accept the decision of the majority in backing the incumbent leadership on a number of substantive questions at issue between them.

Overall, then, the Conference, if looked at in terms of constant policy maker and superviser, or as policy maker on the wide range of issues facing Mapai as a party, was clearly not of the greatest importance. If, on the other hand, looked at as a locus of final sovereignty in constitutional matters, in personnel and leadership struggles and in the outlining and approving of the general lines of policy in some areas within which other policies were formulated and into which they had to be fitted, it was clearly of major significance. Thus rather than direct it ratified, and rather than initiate it took final decisions. The initiation and the earlier stages of decision were taken elsewhere and it is to these institutions we now turn.

The Council

The 1951 constitution made it a function of the Conference to choose a Council which was 'the supreme institution in the party between Conferences'. Its members were to be elected 'bearing in mind the make-up of the party', and they were to meet at least once in six months. The Council at its first sitting after the Conference was to elect the Central Committee. Prior to its meeting branches were expected to discuss the topics on its agenda and to pass on their opinions to the central institutions. Once a year the party's central institutions were to report to it on all their activities.[11]

The 1950 Conference chose a Council of 405 members, using the traditional method of a sub-committee of the Standing Committee acting as an Appointments Committee, preparing a list of those that it recommended for the Council and having these approved en bloc by the Conference. This body met six times between August 1950 and 1954 when it met for the last time. The general feeling was that with a Central Committee meeting monthly there was little need for such a body and consequently it was eliminated in the 1956 constitution.

The Central Committee

Constitutionally the Mapai Central Committee was the 'supreme body' in

11 *Mapai 1951 Constitution*, ch. 1, clause 4.

the party between Councils and after these were abandoned, it became the 'supreme body' between Conferences.[12] The 1951 constitution defined its general function as 'discussing and deciding on all the party's fundamental questions' but this was omitted from later constitutions, with the designation of 'supreme body' apparently sufficing.[13] It was expected to meet once a month, and was charged with the task of electing the Secretary-General of the party, the Secretariat, and when it existed, the Political Committee.[14] Later amendments to the 1956 Constitution also gave the Central Committee a role to play in the choice of Mapai candidates for the Ministry and Prime Minister, and for the Mapai members of the Histadrut's Central Executive Committee (see chapter nine).

As with the Conference one must carefully distinguish between constitutional requirements and prescriptions and the actualities of behaviour and practice. The increased membership of the party generated pressure for greater representation on the Central Committee and over the years it grew in size. Before 1950 it numbered 101 members, in the period 1950–6, 130 members, and from 1960 onwards 256 members. A number of attempts were made to limit the size of the Central Committee, the most important of which was at the 8th Conference when an initial vote limited it to 123 members. This was reversed within hours and the number increased to 180 and to 196 a few days later. All suggested limitations were based on the need to improve efficiency and increase capacity for taking decisions. The assumption was that for a Central Committee to perform the role assigned to it by the constitution, to be an actual decision maker, to be more than formally supreme, to initiate discussion on issues, carry out the main stages of discussion within its ranks, and have the final say, it would have to be limited in size. A large body simply could not be called together often enough and would prove too unwieldy to perform these roles. On the other hand, the major arguments in favour of enlarging the Central Committee were based upon the need for representation; the party, it was stressed, was socially diverse and composed of a multitude of interests that had to be accommodated if the Central Committee was to be able to lay claim to the wide authority conferred on it by the constitution. Thus to enlarge it was to deprive it of power; to limit it in size was to rob it of legitimacy and authority. As is obvious, the arguments in favour of representation were successful and its critics claimed that this did deprive it of decision making capacity. In particular, it was argued that increased size would force the making of decisions into smaller bodies, which, constitutionally, did not possess such powers.

Capacity to make decisions, however, is not solely a function of size. It is also a function of the way in which the decision making process is conducted,

[12] *Mapai 1951 Constitution*, ch. 1, clause 5; *Mapai 1956 Constitution*, ch. 2, clause 1.
[13] *Mapai 1951 Constitution*, ch. 1, clause 5.
[14] *Mapai 1956 Constitution*, ch. 2, clauses 3, 5.

whether the body involved has an opportunity to exercise its powers, how issues are presented to it, for example, whether options are open or have been foreclosed by prior discussion in other party bodies. If it is to be argued, as some have, that the Central Committee did not exercise its constitutional powers over decision making, the reason is not to be found in any failure to meet. On this score it completely fulfilled its constitutional requirements; in the period 1950–6 114 meetings were held, averaging one every three weeks, whereas from 1960 to 1964 58 meetings took place, on the average just under one a month. (On the other hand, attendance left much to be desired; in the first period the average present was about 75 members of a possible total of 130; whilst in the second the average was about 125 out of a possible 256.)[15]

To assess the role of the Central Committee one must look primarily at the range of topics considered, the decisions taken, its part in them, and, by implication, what the Central Committee did not do. Such an assessment, of course, will rest heavily upon the view taken about the functions that the Central Committee was meant to fulfil. For those starting from the assumption that the Central Committee should have discussed all important matters, it was a dismal failure. For those who believed that it should take decisions on issues, not merely register those made elsewhere, it was no more than a debating forum and a sounding-board for delegates present. Moreover, decisions seemed to have been 'cut and dried' before debate in the Central Committee: although in theory it had the right to reverse any policy recommendations of the Secretariat it never did so.[16] Nevertheless, these are extreme views and a more correct analysis of the role of the Central Committee would be somewhat more balanced. In certain important matters it acted decisively. In others, it was instrumental in crystallising viewpoints and creating consensus and compromise between disagreeing groups.

Because it was theoretically capable of dealing with anything, the range of matters dealt with by the Central Committee was rather wide. That is not to say, of course, that it dealt with everything. There were vast areas that it did not even touch upon, including, in particular, much of the legislation passed through the Knesset under Mapai's auspices, which was mainly left to Mapai's Parliamentary Party and ministers. If we analyse the list of topics dealt with by the Central Committee since 1950 it is immediately apparent, on the other hand, that certain matters were dealt with extensively in the Central Committee and decided there. The most important of these were wages policy decisions, usually discussed annually, and economic policy in general; ratification of the choice of ministers and candidates for the party's Knesset list; discussion of reports from the Mapai Parliamentary Party, the election of the Secretary-General and Secretariat of the party, and of various appointment

[15] See *Report Party Control Commission*, 1950–1956, p. 8, and 1960–1964, p. 25.
[16] *Davar*, 11.11.1964.

committees; discussion of internal party conflict, organisational problems and programmes for Knesset and Histadrut elections. These matters were regularly discussed at its meetings but in addition it often dealt with others. Thus its importance lay in the fact that it could be, and often was, called in to decide matters about which other party bodies were unable or unwilling to reach a final decision.

The main role of the Central Committee seems to have been in settling differences in cases of marked interest conflict between different sections of the party, or between the party's representatives in the Cabinet and the Histadrut's Central Executive Committee. Again, the Central Committee was called in to add its authority to decisions that other party bodies, generally the Secretariat, were unwilling to proceed with on their own. This might have been because the Secretariat itself was divided and unable to reach a decision without enforcing a majority viewpoint upon a considerable minority, or because the issue was regarded as being too large or important to be handled without some degree of ratification or approval by the Central Committee. Classic examples of these kinds of matters were decisions relating to the agreement of the Israeli government to accept reparations from Germany, of Mapai to enter into a coalition with the General Zionists, and the education debate of 1951–3. In each case the Parliamentary Party and the Cabinet first achieved Central Committee support for its approach. In the case of education, the Central Committee took a policy line which brought the government down, and it was only after it partially reversed itself that the coalition was reconstituted. Similarly in the case of the Lavon Affair, Lavon's removal from the post of Secretary-General of the Histadrut was finally decided by a packed and dramatic meeting of the Central Committee, the last in a series, after many meetings of the other party bodies as well. The Alignment with Achdut Haavoda was first approved in 1964 by the Central Committee prior to being brought to the Conference. Another major example was the 1952 choice of the Mapai candidate for President of the State of Israel, when Mr Ben Zvi was chosen over Mr Sprinzak by the Central Committee after a lengthy debate. The next President, Mr Shazar, was chosen unopposed by the Central Committee in 1963.

The overall assessment of the Central Committee, then, must reflect a balance between these conflicting factors. Although the constitution nowhere specified what it could not discuss, on the other hand, it laid down only a limited range of subjects with which it had to deal. The result was that there were many important matters that the Central Committee simply did not get a chance to tackle. Decisions about its agenda were made by the party Secretary-General and the Secretariat. The Central Committee was not autonomous in this sphere and there existed no procedures by which it could ensure that particular matters were brought before it for deliberation, although in the early period after 1948 it was customary for Central Committee meetings to open with a question period which enabled members to raise any matters they wished. But even this did not assist in bringing to the Central Committee for discussion matters that had already been decided elsewhere and acted upon. Thus, for example, the Political Committee of 1950–6 was expected to discuss matters that demanded secrecy, speed and careful preparation, following which its decisions, according to the constitution, were to be brought to the Central Committee. In fact, of 135 separate matters dealt with, only 19 were brought before it.[17] In addition, the Central Committee usually had before it a recommendation of the Secretariat, which it almost invariably ratified or approved, so that here too, it demonstrated little evidence of independence or autonomy. This was especially true in the case of nominations to other bodies which were brought to the Central Committee en bloc after being drawn up by an Appointments Committee. Apart from the virtual inability of a large institution to undo the careful work of a small committee in such a delicate area, the approval of the Central Committee was generally greatly facilitated by the very large bloc vote, if not majority, enjoyed by the party machine on the Central Committee.

This does not mean that the Central Committee was completely without power and importance. The fact is, as we pointed out above, that the custom developed of regularly bringing certain matters to the Central Committee and once this occurred it had the power and authority to alter, amend, reject or approve them as it saw fit. The fact that in many cases it merely ratified or approved decisions taken in other party bodies does, however, complicate the analysis. We can either assume that it agreed with the decision made elsewhere, or otherwise would have done something about it, or else that it 'really' disagreed but was 'captive'. As in the case of the Conference, while plausible, there is little evidence to support the latter conclusion. A reasonable middle position is that there were many issues which had already been finally decided elsewhere (and sometimes acted upon), and on which the Central Committee was called so that it could be informed, or act as a rubber stamp to legitimise something agreed upon elsewhere. In short, despite its constitutional powers, the reality was such that it was either not expected to decide or in such a position that its disagreement was too late to be effective. This arose from the fact that for reasons of efficiency, policy initiation and the detailed process of policy deliberation usually did not take place within the Central Committee. Issues usually reached it after ample discussion elsewhere, when viewpoints had been crystallised, and some agreement already reached.

The importance of the Central Committee was most clearly evident in those matters in which the final decision was made by it. As a general rule it was called into action when agreement could not be reached in other party

[17] *Report Party Control Commission, 1950–1956*, p. 9.

institutions, or reached only at great cost. Short of the Conference, the Central Committee, in such instances, became the party's authoritative decision making institution. Similarly, even when agreement was reached in other bodies on matters involving radical policy changes the Central Committee was called in to lend greater weight or authority to the decision. Moreover, it influenced decision making by virtue of its mere existence; it exerted considerable pressure upon the various contending parties at the Secretariat level to settle their differences so as to present the Central Committee with a clear policy recommendation. Conversely a group in the minority on the Secretariat could maintain its opposition in the hope of achieving a majority on the Central Committee. In a certain sense, then, the importance of the Central Committee lay, not in what it did, but in what it could do, and this will be seen in greater detail when actual decision making processes are examined in later chapters.

In conclusion, it seems evident that the large party bodies meeting infrequently did not generally undertake the initiation, detailed discussion and deliberation, and the final decision; nor did they do this even for a small and limited range of important issues. Mostly this was done in smaller executive bodies and at higher levels of the party's leadership. The function of bodies like Conference and the Central Committee was to give recognition to, and legitimate and authoritative registration of, majorities and compromises agreed on elsewhere. But this is not to say that they were entirely powerless, or mere rubber stamps wielded automatically and reflexively. As we took pains to point out above, there were a number of crucial issues, policies and decisions which were made by the Conference and the Central Committee, and which were regarded as the party's authoritative decisions, and we specified those conditions which maximised their power and authority in certain decisions.

The questions of representation and responsiveness in relation to the party rank and file are highly complex. Party rank and file organised in local branches had little impact on Conference and Central Committee decisions, either in initiation, in consultation or in the expression of views and opinions. But as we pointed out in our theoretical analysis in chapter one, representativeness, responsiveness, and participation cannot be measured mechanically. The party did not consist only of rank and file members and leaders; and these divisions were cross-cut by important social groupings, forces and interests. In this sense, these bodies were highly representative; Mapai went to great pains to ensure that all its diverse social forces were adequately represented on these bodies, and if the party was forgetful, these groups were ever ready to remind it. But here too, as above, the question of how the representation of social forces was achieved must be further examined. Nor should efficiency and representation be regarded as mutually exclusive: even smaller bodies with executive functions can attempt to meet the requirements of representativeness, as we shall discover in the next chapter. In general, we must recognise that an individualistic, Rousseauian approach to a party like Mapai, which in its patterns of incorporation of diverse social forces was explicitly geared to group, interest, and organisational penetration and control, will produce analysis based upon normative presumptions that distort realities.

7. NATIONAL EXECUTIVE INSTITUTIONS

Introductory

As we have just seen, the Mapai Conference and Central Committee possessed differing degrees of ultimate authority, and intermittently exercised powers of direction, ratification and approval. Ultimate authority, however, cannot be regarded as the sum total of effective power, because it does not include such basic functions as the initiation and immediate taking of policy decisions, on which these ultimate authorities were never consulted. There were a number of bodies in Mapai which decided matters of importance without resorting to consultation with the 'supreme bodies', particularly the Secretariat, the Political Committee, the Leadership Bureau, and *Chaveireinu*.[1] Formally they were responsible to the Central Committee and Conference, were chosen by them to initiate and suggest policy decisions, and were responsible for the execution of party policy. Whilst general lines of policy and important matters of principle, should, theoretically, have received the approval of the 'supreme bodies', widespread powers in many spheres gravitated towards or were delegated to the party's smaller executive bodies. Thus not all aspects of party policy and decision making came to the attention of the larger bodies. Significantly, where the smaller executive bodies reached agreement on policy, the matter was unlikely to proceed further in the party's decision making institutions. Ability to agree on policy and tactics, then, increased their effective power and control.

The development of the executive structure 1948–50:
the relations of party and government

With the establishment of the state in 1948 the Mapai leadership recognised that the role of the party institutions had radically altered, and that increased societal responsibilities had to be accepted. A major question was the relationship of the party institutions to the Mapai controlled government. During the period of the Yishuv Mapai had developed attitudes and practices promoting the primacy of the party institutions; its representatives and leaders were

---

[1] In translation this would be rendered 'Our fellow party members'. Loosely translated, it is the 'Top Leadership', but because of the unwieldiness of the term in English, we shall use the Hebrew.

delegates of the party, as evidenced in their choice by party institutions and by the directives the party gave them, and which they often sought. Moreover, the parties' federative arrangements in the political institutions of the Yishuv emphasised the centrality of their internal political institutions, and in particular, conferred political responsibility on parties rather than on leaders as individuals.

The establishment of an independent state increased the problems of coordination and direction for the party institutions, arising from the development of new legislative and administrative structures and from the growth of those already existent, such as the Histadrut. Differences between party leaders and representatives in state and Histadrut bodies needed resolution by the party institutions which chose those representatives. There was also the question of priority. Before 1948 parties were hardly less important than the Yishuv's institutions. Whilst statehood increased the importance of political functions, it simultaneously downgraded that of the individual political parties. Popular democratic elections implied notions of responsibility to the whole electorate; and Cabinet government, those of responsibility to Parliament, independent of responsibilities to the party that chose candidates and ministers. The question was: how would Mapai adapt to this situation? How far would it continue actively to direct its representatives in state bodies? In other words, what status were its ministers and parliamentarians to have vis à vis party institutions? How far could they act independently and how far were they to be subject to control?

These were not merely theoretical questions, posed by political scientists studying the party from without. The party itself was fully aware of their dimensions as Secretary-General Iserson (later Onn) told the Central Committee in September 1948:

> Immediately after the 15th of May the problem of the connection of the party with its members in the government, the Histadrut, and the Executive of the Jewish Agency arose. Every one of us understands that the situation of the party during the Mandatory Government differs from its situation today when every action the government undertakes, the party, as a party responsible for its members, is responsible for. This problem has intensified...We must find a regular and stable method of connection, mutual inspiration and reciprocal influence between our members in the government and the top party institutions.[2]

Before 1948 the party bodies with effective power were the Party Executive, the Secretariat and a Political Committee of thirteen members. The Party Executive of fourteen members included the members of the party's full-time administrative staff and met at least once or twice weekly, whereas the Secretariat with forty members met less frequently. Effective powers of initiation and decision rested in the hands of the Party Executive, but

[2] *Minutes Mapai Central Committee*, 21.9.1948.

important matters of principle and policy were usually passed on to the Secretariat for final discussion and decision. For example, just before and after the establishment of the state, the Secretariat discussed the composition and operation of the Provisional Council and approved the inter-party agreements on these which the Mapai representatives on the Executive of the Jewish Agency and on the National Council had made. The Secretariat also set up a committee to choose Mapai's candidates for the first ministry (for the approval of the Central Committee), and it discussed many issues of government policy to be put by Mapai ministers.

The Party Executive ran internal party organisational and administrative affairs, and coordinated the decision making process. Thus it sent some matters to the Secretariat with a recommended course of action, and others without. Within a week of the establishment of the state the Party Executive took the initiative in trying to work out a satisfactory arrangement connecting party institutions with Mapai's ministers in the Provisional Government. Two basic proposals developed: the Secretariat suggested that Mapai members on the Provisional Council should meet regularly with Mapai ministers; and a joint meeting of the Party Executive with the ministers decided upon further regular weekly joint meetings.

Thus initially the party (through the Party Executive) sought regular contact with its ministers in Cabinet, without subjecting them to constant control or direction. Nevertheless the Party Executive attempted to maximise its influence over them by assiduously upholding the arrangements for regular meetings. According to party Secretary-General Aranne the Prime Minister had complained that 'Your meetings have driven me dizzy', and another minister, 'that the Party Executive is destroying the ministry through too many meetings'.[3]

These initial arrangements had a decisive influence upon the institutional structure of the state and the role of political parties within it. As the major party in the new government it was up to Mapai to provide the state with an example of party–state relations. It was conceivable, given the history and institutional arrangements of the Yishuv, that parties might become even more elevated in importance than before, and that some form of one-party regime might have eventuated as occurred in other newly independent states. In point of fact, the predominant trend became one of limited depoliticisation; political party became less significant, and increasing party-neutral, bureaucratic state agencies took over many activities formerly run by political parties on particularist lines. A major reason was the Mapai leadership's emphatic belief in the need for an independent set of state institutions standing above particularistic, sectional, political parties. It followed that the party's representatives in state institutions had to be granted a marked degree of independence, and ample scope for decision making. It would be contradictory to

[3] *Ibid.* 4.8.1949.

uphold the independence and significance of state institutions and simultaneously to bind their leaders constantly to seek the decisions of party bodies before acting. (This is to say nothing of the problems of efficiency of decision making and the question of unnecessary duplication.) Thus from the outset Mapai gave due recognition to the demands of democratic electoral responsibility and to parliamentary and cabinet responsibility, without completely removing itself from its role of policy leader, goal-setter, and institutional coordinator.

Although changes later took place, as we shall presently note, the initial relationships between party institutions and government were based upon a set of principles and practices that remained substantially unaltered throughout the period 1948–65. The four basic elements subsumed in them set the pattern for the party and through it for the political system as a whole. There was, first, a clear division of authority; Cabinet ministers were not solely the representatives and delegates of the party, they owed responsibility to Cabinet, parliament, and the electorate, and consequently they had to be given considerable freedom of action to enable them to initiate, decide and implement policies in the state sphere, without constant or specific supervision or direction. On the other hand, they were not given complete freedom of action. Thus the second basic element was that under certain conditions party institutions would exercise a significant influence, for example, if there were differences of opinion within the ministry, or between the ministry and Mapai's Histadrut leaders, or if it was not clear which forum should decide a particular matter. In these circumstances matters were brought to the Party Executive for joint decision. While the party took the view, in principle, that because the minister was the party's delegate all matters within a minister's jurisdiction (except defence) were fitting subjects for party discussion, nevertheless, a conscious attempt was made to limit such intervention. It was thought unnecessary for party institutions to 'follow ministers around like shadows', as one leading actor in these events put it to the author. The third basic element was the general role of the party institutions as arbitrators and coordinators of Mapai's widespread activities and representatives. Fourth, the intention was for the Party Executive to represent the party and its interests in such dealing with ministers. But it could do this only if it was not dominated by a large ministerial membership. Thus in the first Party Executive after the establishment of the state, the Prime Minister was the only minister chosen. Whether the absence of ministers served to strengthen the Party Executive is a different matter; in fact, it made it an unequal rival to the more powerful ministry, and eventually, as we shall discover, the opposite tack was adopted.

Problems of coordination, 1950–4

These institutional arrangements between the Party Executive and the Secretariat continued until the Conference of August 1950 when a new organisational framework was approved. The Secretariat was abolished but a Party Executive consisting of the heads of the central administrative departments, plus Mapai's four representatives on the Histadrut's Central Executive Committee, was retained. There was also a party Executive Committee of five members. The Party Executive was expected to deal with the routine party operations, and the Executive Committee to act as the top executive body. To these was added a Political Committee. Significantly its members were: the seven Mapai ministers, its representatives on the Jewish Agency Executive, the Knesset Speaker, its members on the Knesset's Foreign Affairs and Security Committee, the Secretary-General of the Histadrut, and the five members of the party's Executive Committee. This marked the first time that Mapai established a committee specifically combining its leading representatives in the most important institutions in the state. Such an approach was constantly to recur in the subsequent period.

This arrangement lasted only until a new constitution of the party was adopted at the Council of March 1951. According to this constitution the party's executive bodies were to consist of a Secretariat, a Party Executive and a Political Committee. The Political Committee was to discuss 'questions of domestic or foreign policy that demanded speedy decision or needed to be prepared before they could be brought to the Central Committee for decision', and 'was to present its decisions to the Central Committee'. The Secretariat was to 'direct and coordinate the day to day activities of the party and prepare the agenda of the Central Committee, the Political Committee and the Party Executive'. The Party Executive was to 'discuss and decide on day to day questions that demand combined discussions of the heads of departments and their members'.[4] It is immediately apparent that by this stage the party's central institutional structure which consisted of six separate bodies was top heavy. Within months the Party Executive disappeared and the Secretariat took over its functions. Thus the major executive bodies of the party from the end of 1951 to 1954, coinciding with the period in which Meir Argov was Secretary-General of Mapai, were the Secretariat and the Political Committee.

These bodies acted in coordinating roles, with the Secretariat also carrying on the administration of the party. The new Secretariat elected in November 1951 consisted of eight members including the Prime Minister, one other Minister, the Secretary-General of the Histadrut, the party Secretary-General, and four key party officials. It met weekly and enjoyed a wide scope of operation. A consistent consultative approach to the conduct of policy dis-

[4] *Mapai 1951 Constitution*, ch. 1, clauses 6, 7, 8.

cussions and decisions was adopted, whereby it did not seek to gather information about problems and make decisions independently, but rather dealt with them jointly with Mapai's representatives in the relevant institutions. As Mr Argov told the Central Committee, 'in every matter we invite our fellow party members in the institution involved, we hear their views – and in no small measure are influenced by them – and reach a decision'.[5]

Where the Secretariat felt that it lacked authority it referred problems to the Political Committee which was constituted as before, but such occasions were more the exception than the rule. For example, in the six months after this arrangement began in November 1951 some eighty-six matters were discussed by the Secretariat but only fifteen of these were referred to the Political Committee.[6] In most cases the Political Committee acted as an alternative to the Central Committee rather than as a preparatory body as the constitution had intended; of some 135 issues it discussed in the period 1950–1956, only nineteen were brought to the Central Committee. The Political Committee mainly concerned itself with coalition arrangements and negotiations, personnel changes in the Mapai ministry, relations with other political parties, Cabinet crises, and important issues of policy which involved radical changes, or had generated great opposition or were particularly delicate, for example the acceptance of reparations from Germany, the transfer of education to the state, wages policy, food rationing, economic policy in general, as well as foreign policy and defence matters. It was not the subject matter of an issue that was decisive in determining whether it came before the Political Committee, but rather the degree of difficulty involved in reaching a decision, its delicateness for whatever reason, and the degree of need for secrecy prior to its resolution. Thus aspects of major policy about which there was widespread agreement might not have been brought to it, whereas relatively insignificant and temporary problems of municipal affairs which were politically embarrassing to the party were.

The period from November 1951 to March 1954 was characterised by fairly close cooperation and good relations between these institutions, and between the party institutions, on the one hand, and parliamentarians and ministers, on the other. There is no evidence of any sharp differentiation between them or of any conflict based upon the rights or duties of the respective party or parliamentary groupings. There seems to have been an atmosphere of joint participation in a common enterprise on behalf of the party. Thus ministers frequently brought issues of parliamentary concern to the party institutions for decision. In the discussions it was rarely possible to discern a united ministerial stand opposing that of the party officials. At times matters were decided according to the 'sense of the meeting' and at others they were put to a vote. When the Political Committee was deeply divided, as on the question

[5] *Minutes Mapai Central Committee*, 26.6.1952.
[6] *Report, Party Control Commission*, 1950–1956, p. 9.

of whether to enter into a Cabinet coalition with the right-wing General Zionists, which was a matter of basic principle, the issue was referred to the Central Committee for a more authoritative decision. It is interesting to note that although the Political Committee had voted on the issue, it decided not to inform the Central Committee of its decision, or how its members voted so as to enable the latter body to make a completely open decision.[7] Similarly, the Secretariat took the view that it could refer discussion of parliamentary questions to the Political Committee, but this power was used fairly sparingly, and it is probably for this reason that there was no resentment on the part of the parliamentary faction when it occurred.[8] The general approach of the Secretariat was to act as a body protecting the legitimate interests of the various party institutions and to determine within which institution particular decisions should be taken so as to ensure that they would not be taken by a small group of three or four individuals.[9]

The development of a non-constitutional top executive body: Chaveireinu 1954–6

Early in 1954 three events radically altered these relationships. Ben Gurion resigned from the position of Prime Minister and withdrew to a Negev retreat, although it was widely understood that his retirement was not permanent. Thus in accepting his intention to resign, the Central Committee declared that it regarded it as temporary, and that even during his absence from the government the party would continue to regard Ben Gurion as its leader and guide. It felt assured that 'the day is not far off when Ben Gurion will return to his role in the cabinet.[10] Ben Gurion's retirement to the Negev, partly motivated by a desire to groom other leaders and to make it clear that he was neither indispensable nor irreplaceable, and thereby strengthen democratic succession, had unintended deleterious consequences for the maintenance of the authority of the party institutions and their ability to take decisions in formally constituted meetings. This resulted from the practice of party and government officials of making regular trips down to the Negev to consult with Ben Gurion, in a more or less informal manner. This served to set in relief the fact that party institutions during the period 1948–53 derived much of their authority and power from Ben Gurion's participation in them. Thus these informal but decisive consultations in the Negev with ministers, party officials and close followers represented a downgrading of the authority of party institutions.

A second basic change took place with the election of a new Secretariat of nineteen members in March 1954. The enlargement of the Secretariat was indicative of the steadily increasing pressure for the representation of diverse

[7] *Minutes Mapai Central Committee*, 22.9.1951.
[8] Ibid. 26.6.1952.   [9] Ibid.   [10] *Davar*, 12.11.1953.

groups and interests and in addition to ministers, parliamentarians, Histadrut and party officials, room was now specifically made for representatives of the party branches in Tel Aviv, Haifa and Jerusalem, and of women, younger members, ethnic groups, kibbutzim, moshavim, and workers in smaller agricultural towns (moshavot).[11] The position of party Secretary-General, vacated by Argov immediately after the election of the new Secretariat, was filled jointly by Raphael Bash and Yona Kesse, who had long been involved in party affairs at the administrative level. In this position, however, they lacked the strength of their predecessors, Aranne and Argov, who had both been members of the Mapai parliamentary party. Thus their relative weakness vis à vis other leading party personalities also contributed to the decline in the significance of the party institutions after 1954.

The third basic change came when Prime Minister Sharett began to assemble an informal body known as *Chaveireinu*, which consisted of the Mapai ministers together with the Secretary-General of the Histadrut, meeting to discuss either ministerial and parliamentary matters, or those demanding close coordination with the Histadrut. A number of factors brought about its establishment. First, enlarging the Secretariat had robbed it of the capacity to fulfil the role that it had played earlier. Secondly, Sharett did not enjoy the unquestioned charismatic authority of Ben Gurion, and thus *Chaveireinu* represented a form of collective leadership, strengthening the Prime Minister and the whole leadership after the retirement of Ben Gurion. Finally, a number of particularly delicate security problems arose after July 1954 involving Mapai members of Cabinet, which could not be brought either to the party's Secretariat or Political Committee. The issues were so secret that they had to be kept strictly within small, mainly ministerial circles and thus *Chaveireinu* was given added impetus.

When Ben Gurion resumed the Prime Ministership in November 1955 he continued the practice of using *Chaveireinu* to assist in the process of decision making, but with its utility proven it began to spread its functions into many other areas as well. Thus it served as the basic forum for the discussion of the conflict between Ben Gurion and Sharett over foreign policy and also became involved in internal party matters and reorganisation which, by the middle of 1956, were a national issue. In short, *Chaveireinu* had assumed many of the functions of the Secretariat and the Political Committee; it had become the party's top executive body, making important and crucial decisions. Thus in March 1956 Kesse resigned from his post in protest against the fact that vital party decisions had been taken outside the legitimate party institutions.[12] And as party Secretary-General Bash told the Conference this problem had assumed major proportions:

> . . .some matters demand secrecy and silence. There are issues that necessitate discussion and decision in central and narrowly constituted bodies.

[11] *Ibid.* 25.3.1954.   [12] *Haaretz*, 12.3.1956.

And there is a need to make a careful distinction between matters that are brought to the attention, and made the responsibility of an authoritative leadership, and those that the whole movement can and must give its opinion upon...The boundaries between these two types have become blurred in recent years. And among the reasons for this – and not the least important – is the fact that members of the recognised party leadership, whose public-moral authority and movement status are challenged by none, identify themselves in too great measure with the whole leadership. From here derives the negative phenomenon that a whole string of crucial matters were discussed amongst these members and not in the legitimate and elected party institutions. Matters have reached the stage where the central institutions have been emptied of their content over the years.[18]

Thus by mid-1956 Mapai's institutional structure only partially fulfilled the constitution's provisions, while the legitimate and elected institutions had been replaced and supplemented by informal institutions with great authority and prestige but no constitutional standing. In so far as the Secretariat and the Political Committee were operative, they were effective, and relations between parliamentarians, ministers, and party officials were, by and large, good. The problem was that many important issues were decided elsewhere, or brought to the constitutional bodies only if *Chaveireinu* thought it necessary.

The Yosephtal era: attempted constitutional executive reorganisation 1956–9

The 8th Conference of Mapai in 1956 attempted to alter this institutional set-up. The new constitution abolished the Political Committee and handed over its powers to the Secretariat. In line with these expanded powers the Secretariat was given new organisational form. It was divided into an Inner Secretariat and the Secretariat and given a number of sub-committees, one for foreign affairs and defence.[14] It was hoped that the abolition of the Political Committee, the handing over of its powers to the Secretariat, more stream-lined organisation, the formation of the Inner Secretariat to act as an executive body, and the delegation of functions in major policy areas to specialist sub-committees would increase the power of the Secretariat and contribute to the efficiency of its decision making. None of this, however, touched upon the more basic problem of the Secretariat, the challenge to its authority deriving from the existence and operation of *Chaveireinu*. But to question the operation of this body was openly to challenge the personal authority of Ben Gurion, and there were few in the party who were prepared to do this.

Immediately after the 1956 Conference the Mapai Central Committee elected Dr Giora Yosephtal as Secretary-General. His election was highly significant from a number of points of view. This was the first time that

18 *Report 8th Mapai Conference, 1956*, p. 242.
14 *Mapai 1956 Constitution*, ch. 3, clauses 1–5.

Mapai had chosen a Secretary-General from outside the ranks of those who were mainly involved in internal party work and administration. At the time of his election he was Treasurer of the Jewish Agency, a major national bureaucratic position because of its direct connection with immigrant absorption and with the establishment of new agricultural settlements. In point of fact the party specifically attempted to raise the status of the post of party Secretary-General by giving it to a person who had achieved high stature in some other leading institutional framework.[15] Dr Yosephtal's election was significant for another reason. The 8th Conference had been held in the shadow of a strenuous conflict between the veteran party functionaries associated with the dominant party machine, and the insurgent younger forces commonly known as the *Zeirim*. Dr Yosephtal was in his early forties and although not a leading figure in the youthful opposition was clearly identified with it. Moreover, he enjoyed close and good relations with Ben Gurion, and his election was partly due to Ben Gurion's direct intervention on his behalf.

Dr Yosephtal set about to try and infuse life and efficient administration into the Mapai party apparatus. He began by replacing most of the previous heads of Mapai departments, mainly veterans directly associated with the party machine, with younger men who had gained administrative experience in the various state, Jewish Agency, and Histadrut bureaucracies. This directly challenged the party machine, which reacted strongly, and thus his period as Mapai Secretary-General was characterised by constant conflict. Whilst Yosephtal succeeded in inducing many younger people to take over the party's administrative departments, the party machine was not exactly a defeated element. The head of the key Organisation Department remained one of its leading members, and it succeeded in blocking the appointment of one of the *Zeirim* to this position.[16] In general the party administrative structure became the scene of an intense battle between the veterans and the youth for positions of power.

Yosephtal attempted radically to improve the capacity of Mapai's institutions to make decisions. He firmly believed that to make these bodies too large was to rob them of any real power and he therefore consistently opposed all claims for greater representation. As the constitution had not specified the number of members of the Secretariat or the Inner Secretariat Yosephtal fought to have these as limited as possible. He ended up with a Secretariat of thirty-five members, in addition to all Mapai ministers, deputy ministers, the Knesset speaker, and the chairman of the Jewish Agency Executive, who were to be invited in an advisory capacity, so that the effective total was over fifty members. The principle of functional, interest, and regional representation established earlier was maintained with a number of noteworthy additions – the intelligentsia, new moshavim, and a number of large party branches.[17]

[15] See *Report 8th Mapai Conference, 1956*, pp. 404–5.
[16] *Haaretz*, 11.5.1958.   [17] *Ibid.* 24.9.1956.

Yosephtal's plan was for the Inner Secretariat to take over the general political functions of the Political Committee and for a series of sub-committees – foreign affairs and security, economic, municipal, etc. – to carry out the detailed policy planning and discussion functions formerly exercised by the Secretariat. The latter would be called in when the detailed deliberations had been completed and there was a specific policy formulation to consider. This derived from Yosephtal's general administrative approach, involving clear divisions of functions, and emphasising efficiency:

> We need many institutions each of which is able to decide a problem in a specific sphere, e.g. economic affairs, foreign policy, organisational questions, municipal problems etc., and not one institution with the authority to decide everything, and not a hierarchy of institutions each one of which discusses a question after a more limited body has already discussed it...A hierarchy of institutions is needed only for basic decisions important in the long term. The second condition is institutions limited in their membership...A Secretariat of 35 and in practice of 50 members, and a Central Committee of nearly 200 members are not able to run the day to day affairs of the party but only to decide general and basic questions. Such institutions necessitate the establishment of more limited institutions and in a certain sense liquidate themselves.[18]

The vacuum created by the abolition of the Political Committee and the decline in power of the Secretariat was filled by *Chaveireinu*, which during Yosephtal's term as Secretary-General reached the zenith of its authority. It consisted in this period of Mapai's ministers, the Secretary-General of the party and the Secretary-General of the Histadrut, and some of Ben Gurion's personal assistants. It was called by Ben Gurion and the list of invitees was fixed by him. On occasion, if the topic demanded, others were invited to participate in some discussions; for example, Mapai's members on the Knesset Finance Committee were present in 1958 to discuss the proposed budget.[19] *Chaveireinu* took over the role of the decisive policy initiator and coordinator, and all major policy proposals or changes had to get its approval. Thus major changes in Solel Boneh and its total reorganisation were first approved by *Chaveireinu* in 1958 after being brought to it by Histadrut Secretary-General Lavon, before they were discussed in the party's constitutional institutions.[20] But just at the end of Dr Yosephtal's tenure, the efficiency and capability of *Chaveireinu* was called into question when Lavon stopped participating, and, it became clear that *Chaveireinu* without the Secretary-General of the Histadrut could not coordinate in matters involving the Histadrut.

[18] *Report 8th Mapai Conference, 2nd Session, 1958*, p. 28.
[19] *Haaretz*, 2.12.1958.
[20] *Ibid.* ,0.10.1958.

The Almogi era: the attempt to reestablish the Secretariat as executive and coordinating body

With the resounding Mapai success in the Knesset elections of November 1959 and Yosephtal's entry into the Cabinet, Yoseph Almogi was elected on 31 December 1959 as the new Secretary-General. Almost from the first his style and approach were noticeably different from those of his predecessor. Almogi had been trained in the Haifa party machine and had never been associated with the *Zeirim*, as had Yosephtal. He was therefore immediately able to establish rapport with the dominant party machine which did not fear him as an insurgent, or as a reformer likely to challenge its power and authority. Long associated with a machine, Almogi knew that the only way to beat it was to join it, and this he did. His first public pronouncement after assuming office was to announce that he would not be making any major personnel changes in Mapai headquarters,[21] which would leave the party machine solidly entrenched in the key administrative departments under its control.

Almogi opposed Yosephtal's views and practices with regard to institutional organisation. He supported the view that numbers were not decisive in determining the way in which institutions worked. As he put it rather pithily, 'I know members who support the idea of limited numbers, who think to themselves that the very best institution is a committee of three members one of whom is sick and the other of whom is overseas. This in their view is a model democracy'.[22] The issues and questions dealt with and the way the institution was run determined for him capacity for making decisions. He disapproved of the emptying of the content of the Secretariat, of its infrequent meetings, and the ineffectiveness of the Inner Secretariat. He also served notice that *Chaveireinu* would have to be limited in scope and function and possibly in membership. In his opinion an active Secretariat could prevent any faction, group, or members from emptying the Secretariat of its content.[23] Therefore he proposed that the Secretariat and the Central Committee should discuss all matters except defence and similar political questions.[24]

His general approach, therefore, stood in direct opposition to that of his predecessor and his attempts to institute his ideas signified a distinct reorientation in Mapai's institutional structure and decision making processes. This was apparent in the way the new Secretariat was constituted. This body of thirty-one members apart from the Secretary-General included, for the first time, all nine Mapai ministers. Altogether there were twenty members of Knesset, four members of the Histadrut's Central Executive Committee including the Secretary-General of the Histadrut, and the head of its Trade Union

[21] *Davar*, 15.1.1960.
[22] Y. Almogi, *Report 9th Mapai Conference, 2nd Session*, 1960, p. 44.
[23] *Ibid*. p. 49.   [24] *Ibid*. p. 45.

Department, the chairman of the Jewish Agency Executive, and representatives of various groups and interests – Tel Aviv, Haifa, Jerusalem, Beer Sheba,
kibbutzim, moshavim, moshavot, municipal government, artisans, ethnic
groups, women members, local Labour Councils, *Zeirim*, the party machine
and intellectuals. For the first time the Mapai Secretariat now contained the
party's leading representatives in all major institutions within the state, and
consequently enjoyed prestige and power which would enable it to act as the
party's top decision making body. It thus reasserted its position vis à vis
Chaveireinu, and in fact was intended to take over many of the functions of
coordination, direction and initiative which the latter had assumed over the
previous five or six years.

The need for the Secretariat to play the active role envisaged by Mr Almogi
was accentuated by the virtual paralysis of *Chaveireinu* following Mr
Lavon's boycott of its meetings. Whilst Mapai's ministers, known as *Sareinu*,
now met to discuss matters directly related to their parliamentary and Cabinet
functions, *Chaveireinu* virtually ceased to exist. Yet a top-level body capable
of making authoritative decisions, particularly if these involved both the
government and the Histadrut, was clearly needed. This was a problem of
major proportions for the party because strong and serious disagreement and
lack of cooperation between the Histadrut and the government would have
unpleasant consequences for Mapai and seriously threaten its capacity to rule.
This need was made more urgent by the extremely strained personal relations
between Dayan, who was now Minister of Agriculture, and Peres, now
Deputy Minister of Defence, on the one hand, and Lavon on the other.

Matters quickly came to a head in Mapai institutions. Lavon complained
to the Secretariat that the powers and authority of the Histadrut in almost all
spheres of its work had been infringed by Mapai ministers who had decided
policies of crucial importance to the working population and the Histadrut
without bothering to consult its governing bodies and without seeking their
views.[25] This conflict forced the Secretariat to decide the general question of
where such matters would be settled: which body would carry out the task of
coordinating or arbitrating between the Histadrut and the government.

In the initial discussion three suggestions were put forward. One was that
the Secretariat should perform this function, a second that it should be done
by a special ad hoc body to be elected, and the third that it should be the
party's *Vaada Kalkalit*, its Economic Committee. The Secretariat decided to
retain the task of coordination for itself. It also charged the Secretary-General
of Mapai with the duty of ensuring smooth cooperation and coordination
between the government and the Histadrut on a day to day basis and to
bring to the Secretariat those matters on which agreement could not be
reached.[26] In point of fact this decision proved rather academic. With the
development of the Lavon Affair (see below) almost all else was overshadowed

[25] *Davar*, 19.6.1960; *Haaretz*, 19.6.1960.   [26] *Ibid.*

and there was little done in the way of coordination. Moreover, Almogi resigned in November 1961 to enter the Cabinet. Nevertheless something of his administrative contribution remained in the fact that *Sareinu* met regularly on a weekly basis from about the beginning of 1960 onwards to discuss important parliamentary questions.[27] From the middle of 1961 *Chaveireinu*, too, met at regular intervals for discussions on matters affecting both the Histadrut and the government; mainly to clarify views and to develop compromise and agreement rather than to take definite decisions by voting.

The Leadership Bureau

The Secretariat itself, with more than thirty members, soon ran into problems of efficient decision making, and it thus elected a smaller body with no constitutional status to provide it with direction and initiative. This was the *Lishka*, the Leadership Bureau, and in establishing it, the Secretariat, like so many of its predecessors, abdicated much of its own authority. Thus while *Sareinu* looked after the parliamentary sphere, and *Chaveireinu* the task of coordination between the Histadrut and the government, the Leadership Bureau was entrusted with exercising effective power and the functions of executive leadership in the sphere of major intra-party matters, and over party policy in representative bodies that did not fall into either of the previous two categories. Because Mapai was rent with bitter intra-party conflict during the period after the establishment of the Leadership Bureau, eventually it came to play a decisive role in intra-party affairs.

The establishment of the Leadership Bureau signified lack of confidence in the Secretariat's ability to act as an efficient executive body capable of holding full and frank discussions and of reaching authoritative decisions. A reason often given by party leaders for its establishment was that the Secretariat was too large for this, that there were too many press leaks about its deliberations, many of which misrepresented the facts.[28] A typical example of this loss of faith in the party's top executive body is the reply given by Secretary-General Barkat to a leading member of the Secretariat who asked why it had not even been consulted over an agreement between Mapai and the National Religious Party on the elections to the Religious Councils, in which Mapai agreed to allow the NRP to have a majority of 55 per cent of the delegates. Barkat replied that the Leadership Bureau had thought this matter too sensitive and complicated for the Secretariat, and that it had dealt with it itself in conjunction with the Parliamentary Party Executive, Mapai's members of the Knesset's Interior Committee, and some members of the party's committee on religious affairs.[29]

The number of members consulted in this and similar situations makes it

[27] *Davar*, 24.2.1960, 10.11.1960, 28.8.1861, 4.12.1964; *Haaretz*, 6.9.1963, 20.5.1964.
[28] *Hapoel Hatzair*, 4.6.1963.   [29] *Davar*, 10.3.1963.

clear that numbers and the problems of secrecy were not the major criteria – but a concern for a compact, cohesive executive body capable of giving leadership and direction and exercising initiative, and of efficiently conducting intra-party policy discussion. Rather than engage in time-consuming and arduous discussions in relatively large and representative bodies like the Secretariat, the path of consultation by a narrow, top and prestigious executive with the parties involved, was preferred. Nor could the advantages of a compact and cohesive executive body be ignored under the conditions of intense internal party conflict. Narrow, informal bodies could more easily than large, representative bodies, either ignore, isolate or override the internal critics.

The Leadership Bureau was set up at the end of 1962 with a narrow membership and with rather wide powers. It consisted of six members, Eshkol (Minister of Finance), Becker (Secretary-General of the Histadrut), Dayan (Minister of Agriculture), Barkat, Netzer, and Yeshayahu, M.K. Empowered to choose a seventh member, it selected Abba Choushi (Mayor of Haifa). It was given broad general powers of action and decision, but was instructed to bring these to the Secretariat for ratification. The Secretariat, despite its right of ratification, exercised little control over the Leadership Bureau, in fact, the evidence points in the other direction, to the control of the Secretariat by the Leadership Bureau; its decisions were automatically ratified, and many, as we saw, were not even brought for ratification.

A major contributing factor hastening this development was the intensification of the internal party struggle following the assumption of the Prime Ministership by Eshkol in June 1963 and the steady progress towards Alignment with Achdut Haavoda, which met with the bitter opposition of Ben Gurion and his supporters, including Dayan. The Leadership Bureau became the spearhead of the Eshkol forces, promoting the Alignment and opposing Ben Gurion's demand for a reopening of the Lavon Affair, a task made easier by Dayan's resignation from it in July 1963. As organisational and policy matters converged in a major internal party conflict, the Leadership Bureau emerged as the supreme and unchallenged decision making body of the party majority, and therefore of the party itself.

The ambiguous status of the Leadership Bureau – its non-constitutional position and its high degree of effective power and leadership within Mapai – were highlighted by its critics and brought into the open at the 10th Mapai Conference early in 1965. The party Control Commission, charged with ensuring Mapai's adherence to its constitution, raised the matter in its report to the Conference. It recognised that the Leadership Bureau was 'a vital organisational necessity, which demands that it be accorded significance greatly different from that given to any other committee, permanent or temporary'. But it suggested that its functions, powers, and relationship with the Central Committee be clearly defined in the party Constitution.[30]

[30] *Report Party Control Commission, 1960–1964*, p. 31.

The Conference did not give adequate consideration to this question, being overshadowed by the great debate between Eshkol and Ben Gurion. Nevertheless it passed the following resolution without debate:

> The party Secretariat, with the knowledge of the Central Committee, will choose a Leadership Bureau with the task of examining problems of special importance to the party, and to deal with current matters, in order to bring them to the attention of the party's authoritative institutions, the Central Committee or the Secretariat, for clarification and decision. The Leadership Bureau will not adopt resolutions or take firm decisions in matters of principle or in matters that according to the party Constitution and practice fall within the authority of the party's supreme institutions without being authorised to do so by these bodies.[31]

In other words, the party's supreme bodies could abdicate their power and authority to the Leadership Bureau if they wished. But this was not the major problem, which was the question of organisational strategy. Once a body as prestigious and inherently authoritative as the Leadership Bureau decides on a course of action or a policy, which is then brought to the Secretariat or the Central Committee for discussion, in most cases the outcome is a foregone conclusion. It is virtually impossible for the latter bodies to overturn such a decision, and the scope within which they can bring influence to bear is greatly reduced. This was, in fact, the whole point of the resolution: that the Leadership Bureau was in effect taking important decisions, both on matters referred to it by the other bodies, and on those on which it exercised its own leadership initiative. In both cases, when the matter eventually came before the Secretariat (or the Central Committee) it was usually as a crystal-lised and specific policy approach which left the Secretariat little to do or say.

Conclusions

Surveying the development of the Mapai national executive institutions over the whole period after 1948, and particularly the tendency for a top informal leadership group to recur in various different forms, despite a number of constitutional attempts to prevent it, leads to a number of more general concluding observations.

There occurred over the period a clear separation between administrative staff and those on bodies setting party policy. In the early stages the former were heavily represented on these bodies. But later the administrative proportion, while not completely eradicated, fell dramatically, and that of leading politicians and Mapai representatives in major institutions rose perceptibly. If we compare the composition of the top bodies at the very beginning and the end of the period this change is clearly evident. This corresponds with a subtle change in role of the party executive institutions from direction and

[31] *Minutes 10th Mapai Conference, 1965.*

control to coordination, arbitration, and conflict resolution, and the granting of greater independence to representatives where no differences of opinion or conflict appeared. The doctrine of primacy of party served both situations equally well in so far as it was never interpreted to mean specific attempts to control, direct or coerce Mapai ministers. It was generally used to get ministers and other Mapai representatives to discuss problems and issues when party decision making bodies or administrative departments felt that matters needed attention. In some instances ministers developed steady relations with party bodies, in others, the nature of certain issues made it obvious that ministers would involve the party in the decision making process.

An important distinction ought to be made between *Chaveireinu*, at its peak, and the Leadership Bureau. While neither was anywhere recognised in the party constitution, and to that extent were similar, and while both acted as the top party executive body, the basic difference was that the Leadership Bureau was formally established by a Secretariat decision. *Chaveireinu*, on the other hand, drew most of its authority from the prestige of its members, and most importantly from the personal authority of Mr Ben Gurion as Prime Minister. It was even further reinforced by the fact that in the party constitution there existed no formal position of Party Leader. This was partly against the party tradition with its socialist emphasis upon collective leadership and the non-recognition of individuals, and also partly due to the fact that during Ben Gurion's time there was no need for such formality as there was no question who the party leader was. The absence of such formal recognition increased the power of the person in that position in so far as formal acknowledgement would have spelled limitations by specifying clearly the roles, functions, powers and authority of the party leader, and would have based it upon some form of internal party election procedure. To the extent that Ben Gurion occupied the position in his own right his wide personal authority was reinforced by its being unspecified. At the same time, the fact that he was Prime Minister and that all Mapai ministers were members of *Chaveireinu* together with a few other leading representatives (for example the Secretary-General of the Histadrut) reinforced the power of Mapai's elected representatives over party institutions and detracted from the degree of coordination or control that constitutionally recognised party bodies exercised over the party's representatives.

Another important personal element in the conduct of these bodies suggests some limitations on their effectiveness, despite their small size, informality, and the top-level nature of their members. That is, these bodies could not work if their members did not try to make them work, and the conditions for their success depended upon mutual cooperation and trust at the *personal* level. When personal differences arose in these informal bodies they could not easily be contained. Lavon's departure from *Chaveireinu*, as we saw, paralysed that body and temporarily left it basically an all-ministerial coordinating body known as *Sareinu* and concerned with parliamentary affairs.

This personal element in both cases supports the proposition that formality rather than informality promotes efficiency. To the extent that personal conflicts and lack of trust make far less impact on formally constituted bodies, this is indubitably true. That is to say the level at which personal trust is significant is more quickly reached in informal than in formal bodies, and that the latter in their working are not so dependent upon the agreement of the participants to make them work, although there comes a stage in all bodies where lack of mutual trust and confidence, and agreement to make them work, becomes relevant to efficiency and continued existence.

This is of course precisely the case for formal bodies – their non-dependence upon personal criteria. Instead they are endowed in political parties with certain forms of legitimacy which promote their efficiency. In democratic political parties legitimacy will be derived from a representative formal electoral process which reflects rank and file intentions and is not subject to the suspicion that individuals have manipulated it for personal reasons. It is reinforced by effective operation and efficient results. But this was precisely what Mapai in its internal procedures did not cater for. The constitution (for reasons we will go into below) did not establish such direct and representative election procedures. Because, amongst other reasons, the party did not have a legitimate election procedure for formal executive bodies it suffered from all the problems of personal authority and informality that we have examined in this chapter. Formal legitimate electoral procedures would have helped to reinstate and reinforce constitutional authority, rather than personal authority.

To take this analysis further we must examine the party's electoral procedures and the influences of various groups upon them, particularly the development of the party machine, the relations between the party and major representative institutions (the Knesset and the Histadrut), and the actual decision making process as it occurred in a number of major substantive policy areas. It is to these we turn in the succeeding chapters.

8 THE PARTY MACHINE

The theory of the political machine

Our discussion in the last three chapters has been concerned mainly with the party's constitutional decision making bodies, and with those that developed from them, or within them. We must now turn our attention to a set of relationships existing *behind* these other institutions, which constituted the party machines, and we will examine their existence in Mapai in relation to general theories of the rise and development of such phenomena. The political machine has been defined as 'a party organization that depends crucially upon inducements that are both *specific* and material'.[1] Specific, in contrast to general, inducements, are offered to some and withheld from others; material refers to money and other objects to which value attaches, in contrast to such non-material inducements as satisfaction deriving from power, prestige, or enlarged participation.[2] While not restricted to specific and material inducements, its emphasis upon them, and the reliability of its control over behaviour deriving from them characterise the 'machine', and account for its name.

The machine is basically apolitical; it is interested mainly in controlling and distributing income (or the sources of income) to its workers and supporters, and is little concerned with questions of political principle, which Brogan called 'political indifferentism'.[3] Its existence depends upon its ability to control votes, which it can achieve only where individuals place no value upon them, or more upon what the machine offers in exchange for their votes. This can occur only if the voter is indifferent to issues, principles or candidates, and therefore can easily be induced to put his vote at the machine's disposal. This is most true of party primaries and the lower level of internal party elections, which is especially fortunate for the political machine. These elections are the most crucial for the machine because party officials are chosen there. Moreover, they are the easiest to gain control of, because there is a lower turnout and therefore less votes to be controlled, and they are conducted less in the spotlight of public scrutiny. As Banfield and Wilson put it aptly, 'the minor offices are the ones essential to control of the party

---

[1] Edward C. Banfield and James Q. Wilson, *City Politics* (Cambridge: Mass., 1963), p. 115. Emphasis in original.
[2] *Ibid.*   [3] Quoted *ibid.* p. 116.

machinery, and this, of course, is half the battle in the short run, and the whole of it in the long run'.

In our theoretical analysis of power relations in political parties in chapter one we briefly contrasted two models, which were termed coercive and consensual power.[5] The political machine represents a paradigm case of coercive power which stands at the opposite pole to consensual power based upon decisions being made following an exhaustive, rational discussion process in which compromises are arrived at and agreements are reached on the merits of the issues themselves. The political machine maximises coercion and minimises free discussion. By making representatives and sub-leaders subservient to, and bound by, their political superiors, it destroys much of the political authority that radiates upward representing the rank and file, and being responsive to their demands. If decision makers feel that they will lose not only the satisfactions, gratifications, and prestige of office holding, but also their present livelihood, as well as all chances of political promotion and advancement, by deviating from the orders and dictates of their machine superiors who control their chances of reelection, then most claims to representativeness and responsiveness have been destroyed. This has different implications according to whether the person so controlled is an internal party official or representative, or an external party representative. Thus parties commonly bind parliamentary representatives to accept the discipline of their ministers, and conversely ministers, to accept that of the parliamentary caucus, or parliamentarians and ministers, to accept that of party executive bodies. But generally these pressures and acts of discipline are formalised and performed by constitutionally elected party bodies. In the machine situation, by way of contrast, party politicians, office holders and representatives owe their promotions and their continued incumbency to groups in the party which are neither formally elected, nor constitutionally authorised, nor clearly identifiable. The latter base their power upon their control of specific and material inducements which directly affect either the office holders, or the voters who elect them. Thus in analysing the machine and its control of office holders we must be sensitive to two separate variables: the method and manner of their election; and the degree to which their subsequent behaviour is controlled, particularly their participation in decision making.

There is another major aspect of the machine – the needs it meets and the functions it fulfils. Merton[6] has written the classic piece on the functions of the political machine. His fundamental general point is that political machines exist and flourish because they fulfil functions which at the time are not

---

[4] *Ibid.* p. 117.

[5] These are elaborated in full in Medding, A Framework For the Analysis of Power in Political Parties'.

[6] R. K. Merton, 'The Latent Functions of the Machine', in *Social Theory and Social Structure* (Glencoe, III., 1957), pp. 71–81.

adequately fulfilled by other existing patterns and structures. Thus when the electorate is either not enlightened or not alert, and when there are large numbers of offices to be filled, machines will develop to fill them. This may be because there are no satisfactory methods or structures of election, or because the citizenry is not willing to invest the effort to make them work. Thus the basic function fulfilled by political machines is to 'organise, centralise, and maintain in good working condition scattered fragments of power', which are dispersed through the political organisation.

Thus the political machine is a mechanism for the centralisation of political power, which is essential for political parties seeking to connect social forces with, and direct, governmental structures. This centralisation of political power and organisation enables the machine to satisfy the needs of diverse sub-groups within the society, which are not adequately satisfied by legally devised and culturally approved social structures. This was particularly evident in the United States with regard to the new immigrants having different ethnic origins to the dominant groups and cultures. The political machines provided personalised and humanised political participation and personal assistance. Thus not only were specific and material inducements offered and accepted, but important social support was rendered in the early stages of immigrant settlement. In this manner the political machines integrated newcomers into politics and served as alternative channels for social mobility.

Mapai in its early development concentrated upon gaining national independence and creating the new Zionist–Socialist society. As a democratic socialist party it emphasised the individual participation of members in policy discussion and policy decision, and the importance of ideological criteria of judgement. It is therefore somewhat surprising that a party cast and moulded in this tradition should develop structures that we have defined as political machines. But as Ostrogorski put it so graphically, '[a] population may, so to speak, go to bed with an Organization and wake up with a Machine'.[7] But surprising or not, the foregoing analysis makes us ask why and how did the machines in Mapai develop, what forms did they take, what functions did they fulfil? It is to answer these questions at both the local and national level that we now turn.

The Tel Aviv branch machine

The origins of the dominant group in Tel Aviv, the Gush (a Hebrew word meaning 'bloc'), led by Mr Shraga Netzer, lay in the party split of the mid-1940s. One of the earliest conflicts with the breakaways was the Tel Aviv Labour Council elections in 1944. Mapai greatly feared this first test of her

[7] M. Ostrogorski, Democracy and the Organization of Political Parties, S. M. Lipset, ed. (2 vols., New York, 1964), vol. 2, p. 215.

popularity after the split, particularly the possibility that it might lose control of the Histadrut institutions in Tel Aviv. To combat this possibility, Mapai in Tel Aviv organised what became known as *Siya Gimmel* (Faction C). Its members led by Shraga Netzer and his wife Devora, Golda Meir (then Myerson) and Mordechai Namir, carried out a full-scale campaign of personal contact with Tel Aviv party members in their homes, at their places of employment and in their neighbourhoods. Six important consequences for understanding the *Gush* followed from the resultant Mapai victory in these elections. Firstly, Mapai retained control of the Tel Aviv Labour Council and the local Histadrut institutions with all the instrumental and material benefits and advantages that such control conferred. Second, the group around *Siya Gimmel* and its leaders were left in complete control of the Tel Aviv Mapai branch. Third, because of this, they were in a crucially important position to influence and determine the allocation of jobs in the local Histadrut institutions, which further strengthened their positions within the branch. Fourth, as a result of their efforts they had welded themselves under the impact of an outside enemy into a self-conscious and cohesive leadership group. Fifth, the top party leaders who were concerned with foreign policy and defence matters, such as Ben Gurion and Sharett, were extremely grateful to them for having saved the party from a difficult situation. Sixth, the group had strengthened its contact with the rank and file in the branches and in the Workers Committees in the work-places; it possessed unmediated and direct knowledge of their problems and capacities, and was in a position to assess their potential for leadership and sub-leadership positions and their suitability and reliability for various appointments and elective positions. (It must be remembered that at the time the Tel Aviv branch of Mapai numbered only some 3500 to 4000 members.)

The Tel Aviv Mapai branch emphasised direct and intimate contact with rank and file members in their neighbourhoods and in the workplaces, and built up a network of contacts with a reliable and trusted sub-elite connecting the masses with the branch leadership. This chain of communication later became central in enforcing *Gush* control of the branch. Promotion and ascent to leadership positions was often a long and slow process, based upon long apprenticeship, and more importantly, upon having proved oneself reliable by beginning at the bottom and slowly building up a chain of personal contact. This process was exemplified in the personal career of Netzer himself. Netzer began in Tel Aviv as a building worker and later moved to permanent employment in the municipality's sanitation department. In this position he became a representative of the workers at the local level, and later became a representative of Tel Aviv municipal employees on its Labour Council, and represented them in dealings with the municipality, in those days controlled by the General Zionists. He moved up from there to become a Mapai representative on various Histadrut bodies, mainly in the cooperative field, and eventually the national Histadrut Executive Committeee. All this time he was active in the Mapai Tel Aviv branch, and was constantly willing to help and assist those with problems. He prided himself on his personal contacts with the mass of workers and, in particular, on his close personal connections with local leaders, as well as those that he had developed through Tel Aviv Labour Council activity in the workplaces. Through his Histadrut and Tel Aviv branch work, where he was a member of its executive bodies (and later of Mapai central bodies), he was in a key position to act as a middleman. He knew the top leaders of the party and the Histadrut, and had accrued political debts which he could call on them to repay. As well he had developed widespread institutional connections both through the party and the Histadrut. What is more he was interested in calling in his political debts, not directly on his own behalf, but to help others, to help the rank and file member who needed assistance, to aid the local sub-leader who wanted something for his local devotees, to reward local sub-leaders for loyal party service. Much of his strength lay in his self-abnegation, in the willingness to devote endless time and effort to develop connections with others by helping in the solution of their problems and the satisfaction of their needs, the constant desire to remain in the background, the conscious refraining from seeking high office or personal publicity, and the ability to busy himself with what others regarded as dull, mundane and unexciting tasks. These qualities also served to reinforce the power base that he slowly built up over the years. They gave him a reputation for devotion to the small man, and to others in general, and for doing work on behalf of party members that party leaders recognised and wished to reward. At the same time he won unquestioning loyalty and devotion from below.

This policy and approach was consciously applied with the great influx of population and party members in Tel Aviv after 1948. As much of this was of non-European ethnic origin the contact with leaders and sub-leaders of this community was strengthened; older sub-leaders and contacts within these communities made earlier were now in a position to be developed. Sub-leaders were promoted, rank and file became sub-leaders and in the general proliferation of tasks and branches many advances were to be made, and many rewards handed out to the faithful, or to promising new immigrants anxious to avail themselves of political channels of mobility in Israeli society. This was true of all sections of the party in Tel Aviv; of immigrants and veterans, of Europeans and non-Europeans.

This occurred whilst the state was trying to cope with the problems of independence and with the tremendous immigrant influx. For Netzer and the Mapai branch in Tel Aviv this had three important results. First, with the growth and development of the various bureaucracies the party was called on to provide individuals to fill positions. Thus many party leaders and activists in Tel Aviv went into these posts, leaving control of the day to day branch work even more in the hands of those who remained, such as Netzer. Moreover, many leading branch members went into top government, ministerial, Knesset, civil service, Histadrut and Jewish Agency positions which not only left little time for branch work but also attracted their career orientations and aspirations. Machine control was thus facilitated by the moving elsewhere of politically prestigious individuals who by virtue of their status and achievements were in a position to challenge the machine or to block it should they so decide. Second, because so many positions had to be filled someone had to allocate them, and thus the person or group able to advise on these appointments, and to recommend candidates was in a position to derive political advantages. In Tel Aviv, the group centred around Netzer took to this task most diligently. Thus Golda Meir complained to the Mapai Central Committee in 1949 that not enough was being done for immigrants in Tel Aviv because 'the Tel Aviv branch are completely involved in whether yet another member can be got into the governmental administrative apparatus ...The Tel Aviv branch struggles for this, and the most important thing as far as it is concerned is how many members will get into this ministry or that'.[8]

The advantages Netzer derived are clear; by rewarding friends or by getting jobs for potential allies he not only extended his personal network of connections into the ministries but at the same time strengthened his ability to satisfy the wants and needs of the rank and file and the party sub-leaders, through the governmental bureaucracy. Moreover, by being responsible for their rise in political and administrative life, he was in a position to have them as political allies should the need arise. This was especially true at the middle levels, particularly in view of his reputation for good relations with the party's top leaders.

These developments in Tel Aviv immediately after 1948 attracted little public comment or notice. The state, the party and political leaders were engrossed in the more major tasks confronting them. Their main concern in the Tel Aviv branch was in election campaigns. As it turned out, the Mapai Tel Aviv branch performed these tasks more than satisfactorily, providing the party with many new members and with the numerical foundations of its national success.

Between 1951 and 1954 the Tel Aviv branch reorganised to meet the new constitutional requirements of decentralisation and the establishment of sub-branches. The party branch secretary, at that time still directly appointed by the central Mapai institutions, was Yoseph Yizreeli, a leading kibbutz member. When Yizreeli resigned to return to his kibbutz, the central party institutions decided to appoint as a replacement Mr Abraham Ofer, one of the most outspoken and vocal of the younger members, who, in the early 1950s, had publicly criticised the party and called for widespread democratisa-

8 *Minutes Mapai Central Committee*, 11.11.1949.

tion and for the renewal of ideological discussion (see below). Ofer's appointment brought the *Gush* into the open, and was the catalyst for its conscious organisation and the exploitation of all the personal contacts built earlier. Previously it could run matters as it wished, quietly, unacknowledged, behind the scenes, and without opposition. Ofer openly challenged its position, and to defeat him the forces had to be marshalled and the campaign organised.

Ofer's first step in a campaign to break the power of the machine, and to introduce some of his ideas of democratisation into the Tel Aviv branch was to gain a majority on the Branch Secretariat. Rather than compromise with the Netzer group, he sought to remove it completely from all positions of power in the Tel Aviv branch by holding elections at all levels of the local party. Ofer believed that if he could demonstrate that a party electoral system could work successfully he would have deprived the machine of its most powerful argument – the need for some group to be expert in the making of the complex decisions about appointments and nominations.

Ofer's challenge to the machine suffered from tactical errors. In the main he neglected to pay sufficient attention to precisely that factor in which the dominant group excelled, the importance of the party functionaries and the need to get their support. Ofer wanted to get rid of them all and to replace them in a dynamic process of regular elections. Under the threat of seeing the destruction of the network carefully constructed over the years, Netzer used his power and influence to convince Mapai central authorities of the dangers to Mapai of the steps that Ofer proposed to take. Through his allies and colleagues Aranne and Golda Meir, and with the support of Ben Gurion (then in retirement) and Prime Minister Sharett, Netzer succeeded in having central pressure placed on the Tel Aviv Branch Secretariat, and in having a more amenable secretary nominated over the head of Ofer who was to become deputy secretary. The result of these manoeuvres and the application of this high-powered pressure was to restore control of the majority of the Tel Aviv Secretariat to Netzer, and Ofer resigned.

Netzer won because he succeeded in creating apprehension in the minds of Mapai leaders of an impending split and conflict in the Tel Aviv branch. He had acquired a reputation as an electoral expert and had proved himself in this sphere, whereas Ofer was regarded as inexperienced and untried, despite some success in trade union elections during his short term of office. Moreover, Netzer was known to have the loyalty and support of the many party functionaries and activists, whilst Ofer had not succeeded in developing any contact or rapport with them. Under these conditions and given their relations with Netzer, the easiest solution was to drop Ofer. Once Netzer demonstrated in this manner that he had the support of the party's leading figures, it was as if an official imprimatur had been placed upon his activities. Overall Netzer came out of the conflict much stronger; not only had he won but he had the stamp of official approval, which enabled him to apply increasing pressure from above upon all levels of the party administrative apparatus and upon its representatives in administrative positions outside. This could now operate much more directly than before; the *Gush* had official approval, whilst the example of what had happened to Ofer served as a constant reminder to would-be recalcitrants of the price they might have to pay. As one delegate from Tel Aviv at the 1956 Conference put it: 'In this large branch there are many, including members holding positions, who do not dare to speak what is in their hearts out of fear, and I say this from first-hand knowledge – this applies even to secretaries of trade unions.'[9]

With the removal of Ofer, the *Gush* was openly and unquestioningly in control of the Tel Aviv branch in a manner which extended not only over the institutions and the functionaries but over the rank and file as well. It constantly used the control and dominance that it possessed further to reinforce and maintain itself with the careful and steady application of pressure from above, via the various strata of local party functionaries. The extent of its hold over the rank and file is clearly evident in the fact that at various local and Conference elections it was able to ensure that leading members of the youthful opposition groups were not elected, or that they were elected only when they had the green light from the *Gush*. Similarly it maintained complete control of the branch institutions, nominating successfully all but a few of the fifty-one members of the Secretariat; for example in 1960 it nominated forty-eight candidates all of whom were elected.

Once the *Gush* became openly recognised as the dominant group in Mapai's Tel Aviv branch its control tended to become self-perpetuating. It appointed local officials, ensured for itself the support of those elected locally, organised local elections, and exercised the decisive influence in the choice of the Council and the Secretariat, and thus maintained control of every appointments committee in the local branch. The controlling group used to meet prior to the meeting of the Secretariat to 'prepare the meeting', and decide what was to be done about matters on the agenda. It was therefore in an unchallengable position to parcel out jobs, to decide who was in and who was to go out, who was to be appointed and who was to be prevented from taking appointments.

The Haifa branch machine

The development of the Haifa machine is very much the party and political history of Abba Choushi. Its origins lie in his work as a wharf labourer in the Haifa port in 1926, then and later, the largest single organised place of employment in that city. In the early period, apart from the port, most of the available work was on the roads, and in the building construction industry, and this tended to be both scattered and insecure. Poor economic conditions added to a fairly serious chronic unemployment problem. These conditions

[9] *Report 8th Mapai Conference, 1956*, p. 153.

were perfect for the rise of a populist labour leader, and Abba Choushi seized this opportunity. From the outset he manifested marked organisational abilities combined with a natural ability to get on with men. His rise to power was rapid. In 1926 he worked as a foreman at the docks and soon after this became a militant spokesman for the dock workers. His militancy made him very popular amongst the working population in Haifa, and he was soon elected to the position of Secretary of the Labour Exchange. In 1931 he was elected Secretary of the Haifa Labour Council, a position he held until 1950.

Abba Choushi's power base was built upon the foundations of his position as secretary of the Haifa Labour Council. He used it to wage conflict on a variety of local fronts in the period 1931–48 until he became the undisputed and unchallenged power in both the Haifa Mapai branch and Haifa Histadrut affairs. Over this period he was in conflict on a number of different fronts; with the leading officials and members of the local Mapai branch until he gained control of it in 1938; with the officials of local Histadrut industries, who were, in the main, his opponents in local Mapai branch affairs as well; and with the central bodies of both Mapai and the Histadrut in Tel Aviv. He continually stressed the autonomy and independence of Haifa from central control, and at the same time used central intervention as a focal point of resentment around which he marshalled his supporters and followers. This was a battle between Haifa and Tel Aviv, and in the process Abba Choushi was able to turn the resentment against Tel Aviv in the direction of the local representatives of the central Mapai institutions. He opposed the local Mapai leadership on personal and ideological grounds, in addition to their having been sent to Haifa from Tel Aviv to take over local Histadrut industry, and in his view to run the local branch and keep him in check.

He thus built a power base united in a deep loyalty to him personally, whilst developing a powerful Mapai and Histadrut structure which the party could always call upon. This was, of course, Choushi's guarantee against strong or direct central intervention in Haifa affairs; as long as he controlled Haifa in Mapai's name and delivered it the vote, it would have been foolhardy to have attempted to replace him.

Choushi was not a man for half measures and used para-military formations dressed in blue shirts and known as *Plugot* to break up the political activities of the local Revisionists and communists. They were directly responsible to Abba Choushi himself, and consisted of the tough and able-bodied workers from the Haifa port and elsewhere. His lieutenant in these operations was Yoseph Almogi. Even though Choushi used these *Plugot* to put down political opposition to Mapai, they were not popular with the Mapai central authorities which, in an investigation into Mapai in Haifa, censured their use of physical force. One of the reasons for the central condemnation of these groups was the inherent conflict between their existence and the attempt of the Yishuv to establish a united and disciplined military force in the Hagana.

These open and hidden conflicts, which served to exacerbate even further the tension between Choushi and the central Histadrut and Mapai authorities, reached a peak when Choushi opposed certain Hagana tactics against the British and left the Haifa Hagana High Command (then still a Histadrut-organised military force).

To cap this off Choushi consistently followed a policy of close cooperation with moderate Arab leaders and had even used the *Plugot* in conjunction with them against Arab terrorist gangs. This cooperation displeased many Hagana leaders who believed that an armed conflict with the Arabs was inevitable.

Choushi's populism and informal para-military organisation, which gave him control of the masses in Haifa, rested upon a tightly disciplined and well-organised formal structure. From his Histadrut positions Abba Choushi was ideally placed to develop a personal following. He achieved this by finding work for the unemployed labourers, and later as industry in Haifa progressed he organised a Mapai cell in each workplace. From the beginning the central figure in each factory and workplace was personally chosen by Choushi himself rather than by the workmen; he thus established a system of personal loyalty. He did not follow the usual practice of allowing the local branches of the national trade unions to have close contact with the plants but allocated the largest places of employment to himself as Secretary of the Labour Council. In this way he managed virtually to exclude the Histadrut Trade Union Department in Tel Aviv. Eventually regular Histadrut Workers Committees were organised which served to formalise the power and the legitimacy of his trusted followers, who took over the leading positions in these committees.

Choushi's various conflicts with Tel Aviv, the Histadrut and the Hagana made him seek to become as autonomous and independent of central institutions as possible, while maintaining general loyalty and support for Mapai. He believed that strong central forces aimed to crush him politically, and that some of their allies in Haifa had at one stage intended to liquidate him physically as well. He therefore decided to consolidate and reinforce his local position as an act of self-defence against the external enemy – the central Mapai leadership and its representatives in major institutions in the state and Histadrut.

Thus he built on the combined foundations of the Labour Council and the Mapai party institutions. His team was headed by twelve individuals in the leading positions in these two bodies, led by Yoseph Almogi, who had emerged as Choushi's right-hand man. Around these were assembled a group of forty individuals who between them were responsible for the largest places of employment, and around them was the Council of the Mapai local branch, some 130 individuals together responsible for all organised places of employment. These had direct contact with another 1300 individuals who were the leading Mapai members of the trade union cells and Workers Committees.

This system of ever-widening circles of influence gave Choushi virtual control of the city as well as of the local party, which he held unchallenged until his election to the Knesset in 1950, when he handed over the position of Secretary of the Haifa Labour Council to Yoseph Almogi.

Choushi became mayor in 1951 and this led to the establishment of two rival centres of power in Mapai Haifa as Almogi developed a personal following of his own from his base in the Labour Council. Following the pattern set up earlier by Choushi he developed a network of personal loyalties among various individuals strategically placed in the various Workers Committees and set up an informal organisation of some 300 individuals known as *Moetzet Vaadei Poalim*, the Workers Committees Council. Despite an internal tug of war, from the outside Haifa seemed as solid and united as ever. Both were strong supporters of Ben Gurion, and both knew that neither was liked by central Mapai and Histadrut bodies. Above all was the recognition that unless they remained united Haifa would not exercise the power and influence in the party as befitted the party's largest branch. Thus at Mapai Conferences the Haifa delegates regularly caucused and voted together as a bloc.

Almogi continued in the path of his predecessor and consolidated Mapai's power in the city. Choushi maintained control over the municipality and what went on within it, but control of the Mapai branch was divided by the development of rivalry between him and Almogi. In cases of disagreement, the tendency was not to push the matters to an open rift, but to exercise restraint, and to compartmentalise matters by allowing Almogi to follow his own policies in his own sphere of authority. An important factor in Choushi's reasoning was the tremendously important role of the Haifa Labour Council in establishing the basis of Mapai's power in the city, a role set on a sound foundation by Choushi and greatly expanded by Almogi. To tamper with this by running into open conflict with Almogi would have meant the possibility of undermining Mapai's overall position in the city.

Thus, in 1959, out of eighty-one Workers Committees representing more than 30 000 workers in the largest places of employment, sixty-three were totally Mapai in membership, whilst the other eighteen had decisive Mapai majorities.[10] A similar pattern emerged for the Workers Committees in medium-sized and smaller establishments. This pattern of control was further reinforced by the fact that many former officials of the Labour Council and the Labour Exchange had been appointed to important positions in the management of these firms, particularly in the personnel sphere. This was especially true of the Histadrut industrial complex in Haifa, but it also applied in a lesser measure to private industry.[11] Mapai's position in Haifa labour affairs was further consolidated at the local and neighbourhood level by the organisation of the Haifa Labour Council. In general, because of the

[10] S. Tevet, 'A Strong Hand over Haifa', *Haaretz*, 20.2.1959.   [11] Ibid.

extremely close nature of relations between the Haifa municipality and the Labour Council under the combined leadership of Choushi and Almogi, the Labour Council, the more directly and openly political of the two, was able to undertake a much wider range of activities than were usually undertaken by such bodies, thus enabling the party controlling these activities, particularly those connected with the allocation of instrumental benefits and material rewards, to derive direct and immediate political advantages from them. The Haifa Labour Council was divided into fourteen areas subdivided into fifty-seven neighbourhoods. These were serviced by forty-seven part-time secretaries, of whom, in 1959, forty-six were trusted members of Mapai. The secretary acted as the major figure in the neighbourhood committee and represented it in Histadrut affairs and in Histadrut institutions. He was approached by the residents of the neighbourhood with regard to many problems that in countries with electoral constituencies might be put before the local M.P. He was asked to deal with many matters including housing, connection to the electricity supply, educational facilities for children and adult education classes. He assisted with the placing of relatives in the Histadrut institutions for the aged, arranged loans or credit in the local Histadrut co-operative supermarket, and through his connection with Workers Committees helped workers be promoted in employment by having them sent to Histadrut training courses.[12]

This was a party machine and organisation that was both of major significance in the party itself, and at the same time cohesive enough to restrain the two leading individuals in it from pushing their disagreements too far and threatening its downfall. One of the things that united Almogi and Choushi was their dedication and support of Ben Gurion in broader party affairs and in security and foreign policy, despite the fact that both had had serious past disagreements with him; Choushi from 1933 to 1951 and Almogi in 1957 over the Ata strike. Their support was clearly evident in the Lavon Affair, when Haifa unanimously voted for Lavon's ouster at the Mapai Central Committee. Almogi's removal to the national scene after 1959 and his appointment as a Cabinet Minister in 1961 meant that effective control of the branch reverted increasingly into Choushi's hands, despite Almogi's maintenance of close contact with local branch affairs and with his trusted followers in Haifa. (Even when a minister he continued to live in Haifa and regularly spent at least one day a week dealing with matters of local concern.)

It is interesting to note that in the Rafi split in 1965, Almogi was one of the foremost followers of Ben Gurion, and it was hoped by Rafi and feared by Mapai that he would succeed in leading the whole united, cohesive Haifa branch out of the party into the Ben Gurion camp. At the early stage of the Ben Gurion–Eshkol conflict, Choushi together with Almogi supported Ben Gurion, but the issue was such that branch unity could not continue to be

[12] Ibid.

maintained. The Eshkol forces were led by Choushi's son-in-law, Amnon Lin, a leading member of the *Zeirim*, who together with many Tel Aviv *Zeirim* had opted for Eshkol. As it became more and more apparent that a split in the party was inevitable, Choushi began to occupy a middle-of-the-road compromise position. When Ben Gurion led his followers out of the party, Choushi refused to follow, dramatically announcing that the Haifa branch would not cooperate in splitting the party. Even more significant was the reasoning that impelled Choushi to remain within Mapai, because it is characteristic of the man and of his role in Haifa. Choushi realised that if Haifa went with Ben Gurion, control of the Haifa branch of the new party, and probably of Haifa, would pass out of his hands to Almogi who by this stage was much closer to Ben Gurion. To Choushi, control of Haifa had always been the leitmotif of his political activity in, and on behalf of, Mapai, and he therefore gambled on Mapai retaining control of Haifa if he stayed in it, thus leaving him in undisputed control of the city. Moreover, his devotion to Mapai as such did not allow him to join in a split. His gamble proved correct and in the 1965 Histadrut and Knesset and municipal elections Mapai in Haifa scored a resounding success.

The Gush as national party machine

A Mapai tradition developed in the Yishuv and carried over into the new state was for the choice of representatives and delegates to internal and external bodies to be effected via appointment committees. Such an arrangement could work smoothly if based upon mutual agreement, but not in a highly competitive situation, unless the sides were prepared to accept both the method and its results. The Mapai leaders who came to power in 1948 had united to defeat the ideological and leadership challenge of *Siya Bet*. Moreover, they were also united by common background prior to this struggle. Despite some differences and rivalries, they were knit by a marked degree of homogeneity of origins, approach and experience. The long experience of working together, the face to face relationships, the informal contact, the common understandings and values, the unwritten rules of conduct and behaviour, and above all, the welding power of the common struggle for independence, rendered this Mapai leadership cohesive and capable of making party decisions among themselves on the basis of mutual agreement and without formal elections. The growth and diversification of the party focused a different light upon these arrangements. First, many more positions had to be filled. Coupled with this was growing pressure for democratisation, as part of a movement towards formalisation and universalism. One such pressure upon the party was for the introduction of democratic elections through which all members of the party could have an equal say in the choice of representatives, delegates and leaders.

The *Gush* as a national machine developed in the mid-1950s as an attempt by a particular group to retain the power positions within the party gained by the pre-state methods against the challenge of the demand for democratic electoral methods. This machine was not set up by the party's top leaders – they had graduated to more important state positions – but by a group of second-string leaders who believed that they were carrying on the traditions of the party, and who sought to provide the top leaders with secure and loyal support for their measures and policies. Secure support necessitated the creation of a structure that represented many groups and sections of the party. Thus the *Gush* became national and diversified and spread itself from its Tel Aviv base to enable it to control most key party appointments.

The establishment of the *Gush* as a national machine was facilitated and furthered by the organisation of the *Zeirim* from about 1951 onwards as a distinct opposition group within the party with specific reforming aims and goals. But the organisation of the *Zeirim* did not create the *Gush*, although it later suited the *Gush* to use this as a justification for its existence and methods of control by claiming that it protected the party from the dire consequences which would arise if the *Zeirim* came to power. Thus while the *Zeirim* acted as a catalyst in the national development of the *Gush*, basic and inherent features of the Mapai organisational structure created the circumstances and conditions under which the *Gush* arose. These were the tradition of making appointments by cooptation and by committees, and not by elections, and the rapid diversification of the party, both of which demanded that the party have 'appointment experts' who could weigh up the advantages and qualifications of all the candidates, and skilfully place them in all kinds of bureaucratic and representative positions. In other words, the *Gush* arose because of the absence of other electoral methods and structures for fulfilling these functions. The party could have done this in some electoral fashion, and this is precisely what the *Zeirim* demanded. And it is precisely at this point that the *Gush* had to further its organisation to oppose them, because their demands represented a challenge to the power base that they had already built up and operated successfully on the lines of mutual agreement. This agreement and set of common understandings were under fire and they banded together to protect them. Once they had done so the process became self-perpetuating; in power they had to take certain measures to maintain and protect the power resources they had already gained, and one of the ways of doing this was continuously to strive after more. Groups of men in power rarely, if ever, voluntarily abdicate it or give it away; they may have it taken from them or lose it in a struggle, but rarely do they simply hand it to their opponents.

The essence of the *Gush* lay in organisation. The first stage in this process was to obtain some degree of organisational spread and coverage. This it did by supporting the decentralising organisational changes of the early 1950s.

On the surface, the *Gush's* support for decentralisation seems incongruous with seeking control of the party machine, as centralisation seems to provide greater opportunities for gaining the control it wanted. In point of fact it believed that its chances were greater the less the degree of centralisation, as in the past this had led to too great a concentration upon a few leading and central individuals. Greatly concentrated power would attract the interest not only of leading party members with whom they were not in a position to compete, but also of possible rivals needing only to gain control of a centralised machine. Decentralisation implied a greater amount of dull organisational work, of coordination, and of regional and local activity, which would effectively exclude the top leaders. It was also a form of insurance policy that would make it more difficult for a rival group to oust it. The *Gush* and its followers were characterised by their willingness to undertake mundane and routine organisational activity in the branches and regions, which the party's top leaders and the *Zeirim* eschewed as dull and uninteresting, and it was here that the foundation of their success lay. In this day to day activity they made the contact with the local activists whose loyalty they won by willingness to assist in all phases of local activity.

A similar tendency was revealed in the *Gush's* continuous support for the principle of special trade union elections whereby the Mapai member would cast two votes for the Conference; the first would achieve the election of 60 per cent of the candidates in the branches and the second the election of the other 40 per cent in trade union cells. The *Gush* favoured this because it too facilitated and consolidated its power base and control. It was already strongly entrenched in the trade union segment of the party. It would have been almost impossible for others to challenge this control from the outside, whilst from inside it would have taken long and patient work on workers committees, trade union branches and so forth, and the development of a social framework and network of relations that the *Gush* had built up in the previous ten to twenty years. What is more, the *Zeirim*, its main rival group, were young, had not had trade union experience, were more likely to be professionals, civil servants, etcetera, completely uninvolved in the blue collar trade union world where the mass of these members were concentrated. And even in the white collar unions where they were members, they were not active in union activities and were outvoted by the lower-level employees who were closer to the *Gush*.

The actual personal membership of the top leadership of the *Gush* demonstrates the way in which this national machine was founded and formed and how these tendencies came together to give it sufficient strength to gain control of the party's decision making institutions from about 1955 to 1965. The basis of its power was, of course, Tel Aviv and from here it spread out in a number of different directions. It eventually encompassed Jerusalem, Petach Tikva, Ramat Gan, many moshavot, notably Kfar Saba, a section of Tnuat

Hamoshavim, and many of the oriental immigrant groups and their leaders. Over a period of time it also developed ties with, and gained the loyalty of, party branches in the development areas. This spread is seen in the actual membership of the *Gush's* top leadership.[13]

An analysis of the membership of this top leadership group reveals two outstanding features. The first is that a number of leading ethnic politicians (Yeshayahu, M.K., Zar, M.K., Menachem Cohen, M.K.) formed an important element of its leadership. In general the strenuous effort to include them stemmed from two sources. For the ethnic groups, becoming attached to the powerful party machine meant opportunities for advancement and benefits for members of the group; in short, it signified a speedy way of integration into the party and participation in its decision making processes, and a quick method of ensuring representation, which, as we saw in earlier chapters, was so important to them. The *Gush* needed their support, both for the votes they provided and for the support it gave their claims of being able to provide the party with balanced representation on decision making bodies.

Second, the leadership of the *Gush* consisted essentially of 'grey' men, of party branch and trade union activists, of secretaries of local Labour Councils and mayors of smaller towns and cities, of devoted party workers, but not of leading and prominent political personalities well known to the public. That they were 'grey' men was part of the secret of their success that they exploited to great effect; they understood that they could wield the degree of organisational power they did as long as they remained in the background, and did not challenge the party's leaders or try to use the *Gush* as a springboard to public prominence. Because they were 'grey' men doing dull and routine party tasks, who served the party with devotion, taking work that no one else was prepared to do, they were left alone to build up this powerful party machine. But they were not without powerful friends and sympathisers. Some of the party's leading figures were, if not privy to their inner discussions,

---

[13] It consisted of Mr Netzer, and from Tel Aviv, Messrs Rabinowitz of the Histadrut's Cooperative Supermarket Union (after 1959 deputy mayor of Tel Aviv), Zev Weiner, director of *Mishan*, a Histadrut network of social services, including individual loan funds, homes for children and the aged, Uri Alpert, Meir Zilberman, Menachem Cohen, M.K. and Eliyahu Ben Yitzchak, of the Tel Aviv Labour Council, Raphael Bash, Secretary-General of Mapai at the time of the formation of the *Gush* as a national machine, and later closely involved in Tel Aviv branch activities, M. Shavit, also closely involved in central party organisational affairs, Yisrael Yeshayahu, M.K.; from Jerusalem, M. Ish Shalom, mayor of the city, M. Baram, M.K., formerly secretary of the Jerusalem Labour Council, Mordechai Zar, M.K., closely associated with it, Ariel Arieli, a senior civil servant in the economic sphere; from Ramat Gan, Uriel Abramovitz, secretary of the Labour Council; from Petach Tikva, Yisrael Feinberg, mayor; from Kfar Saba, Yisrael Surkis, mayor and chairman of *Merkaz Hashilton Hamekomi*, a coordinating body of all local government bodies in Israel; representing other moshavot in general was Yitzchak Shapira, the secretary of the Histadrut's Agricultural Centre, which coordinated all the Histadrut's agricultural activity, and Yitzchak Korn, secretary-general of Tnuat Hamoshavim. These were the main leadership of the *Gush* which met once weekly, but they were not the whole *Gush*.

informed of their decisions and quite close to them. Thus party leaders like Namir, Mrs Meir, Aranne, Becker, Govrin, Naftali, and Haring were quite favourably inclined towards them, while a number of others slightly less so were Sharett, Sapir, Eshkol, and Lavon. But the most important aspect of this leadership attitude was that it made it almost impossible for them to be turned out from the top: the powerful support of these leaders granted them ample space within which to carry on their organisational activities.

The *Gush* concentrated its efforts on gaining control of the party's decision making institutions, and of key administrative and organisational departments of both the Histadrut and the party. It began to organise in earnest early in the 1950s and came into public prominence at the 1956 Conference. It had organised earlier within the framework of the Central Committee and Secretariat and had utilised these bodies and party leaders against the threat of the *Zeirim* in Tel Aviv. It gained majorities on the Standing Committee of the 1956 Conference, and the Constitutional Committee set up by the Secretariat to draft the new constitution that was passed by the 1956 Conference. It was also well organised for the 1956 Conference elections in both local and Trade Union branches which gave it close to half of the delegates at that Conference.

On the Central Committee elected at the 1956 Conference the *Gush* enjoyed a majority and it was thus able to elect a Secretariat which also had a *Gush* majority, despite the attempts of Secretary-General Yosephtal to get around it by using an Inner Secretariat (see above). This control gave it a majority in all the party's various appointments committees. Control of these bodies in this manner led to *Gush* control of all aspects of the 1959 Conference and of branch elections for delegates to the Conference, and thus of the Central Committee. The circle had been closed.

Control of the decision making institutions was complemented by the capture of key organisational posts at the middle level. The *Gush* aimed not for the very top positions, but for those closely related to personnel work just below them. It made sure that one of its loyal and trusted members always headed the Organisation Department which kept in contact with all local branches and officials, supervised local elections and was generally in a position to know what was going on in Mapai branches throughout the country. Similarly, it kept a close hold on the Municipal Department, the ethnic Departments, the Department for Artisans and Members of Cooperatives, and when it existed for a short time in 1957–9, the Personnel Department, which specialised in finding Mapai members for representative and official positions in various institutions throughout the country. Within the Histadrut it kept in particularly close contact with the Organisation and Trade Union departments, whilst other leading members were strategically placed throughout the Histadrut's administrative structure. Eventually it came to enjoy the loyalty and support of about two-thirds of the Histadrut's administrative apparatus. Generally speaking, the support and cooperation of the Mapai Secretary-General was also helpful, as in the period when Almogi occupied this post. But this was not essential as can be seen when Yosephtal challenged the *Gush*, and was beaten on many counts. Although the *Gush* could not literally force a party Secretary-General to do what it wanted, it could certainly impress upon him the value of cooperation by making things extremely difficult both for him and his departmental heads.

The control of these departments by those loyal to the *Gush* placed it in a strategically impregnable position. It was directly in contact with the local Histadrut and municipal administrations, and with the local Mapai branches, and with the central party and Histadrut bureaucracies. It was not difficult to find potential allies amongst the locally powerful and, in winning them over, to gain entire branches and branch institutions and representation. It had the power to reward its friends and the capacity to punish its enemies, as those who opposed it locally could be and were removed from positions of power. Its central connections also put it in a position to perform services for local supporters, via its contacts with ministers, civil servants, Histadrut bureaucrats, the directors of Histadrut industry and so forth, and success in these activities strengthened the local positions of its supporters. Local politicians benefited by supporting the *Gush* loyally as it not only made available greater benefits for their constituents than they might otherwise have been able to procure alone, but it also strengthened immensely their local power base. Strong local supporters were essential to the *Gush* because through them it could maintain the network of loyal Conference delegates via the local activists' ability to control the local election scene.

To see the *Gush* in proper perspective, however, it is necessary to examine what it did with the control that it exercised. The *Gush* was not interested in the content and substance of policy in the party, but in the who of policy makers and appointees of all kinds. One would be very hard put to find an instance where any substantive aspect of policy was decided by the *Gush*, or was even discussed by it and a decision taken guiding its members' vote on the matter. This goes generally for foreign affairs, economic matters, and agricultural policy, in fact for the whole range of policies that confronted the party in the Cabinet, the Knesset and the Histadrut. With its strong Histadrut base one might have expected that at the very least it would get involved in the process of wages policy for blue collar industrial workers and for professionals which attracted the involvement of most sections of the party. But even here the *Gush* made no contribution as a group, leaving it to its individual members to vote as they pleased. What the *Gush* was interested in, and on what it met and took decisions according to which its leaders and loyal supporters were expected to act, were internal organisational arrangements, constitutional discussions and changes, internal power relationships of all kinds and, above all, appointments made by the party to the various bodies on which the party was represented or over which it had control. Its power and energy were conserved for these issues. Within them it carved out a province of its own, in which it wished to be recognised as the expert and the master, and here it brought the full impact of its power to bear to decide who would be appointed to which position, in the party, in the Histadrut, in the local Labour Councils, the municipalities, the Jewish Agency, the civil service (in lesser degree), right down to local trade union activists and workers committee representatives. The area where it exercised the least influence, again partly out of self-restraint, was that of the Knesset and the Ministry, although at least a quarter of the membership of the Mapai Knesset faction, if we take the fourth Knesset elected in 1959 as an example, were either members of the Gush or closely associated with it. It has also been asserted that Mr Govrin's appointment to the Ministry in the early 1960s was under pressure from the Gush, but the case, if true, is more interesting as the exception rather than as the rule.

This raises the rather difficult question of why the Gush built up this powerful machine. Why this power, and on what basis, if not on policy considerations and on attitudes towards particular issues, did the Gush decide the suitability of individuals to occupy the positions which it entrusted to them? There is no easy answer to this question. It saw itself as the protector of the founding generation of Mapai, as the regulator of the party's appointments system, and as the balance wheel that would ensure that all deserving would be rewarded in the face of the assault by the Zeirim. The criteria of fitness and the test which had to be passed by prospective candidates for appointment was simple, the approval of the Gush. And this it gave to those whom it believed were loyal to the party, had experience in party work over a long time developed from the grass roots as its leaders had, the willingness to start at the bottom, and unlikelihood to challenge the Gush head on.

One of the major conditions, if not the major condition, for the success of the Gush lay in an unwritten division of authority between it and Ben Gurion and the party leaders. The Gush and its leaders in particular were undividedly loyal to Ben Gurion and completely under the sway of his charisma. The Gush was quite prepared to leave important matters of policy to Ben Gurion and the Ministry, and believed that its task was constantly to give him majority support for what he wanted in order to make it easier for him to govern. Its function, as it saw it, was to keep the party in order and leave the governing to those who knew best. In return, Ben Gurion came increasingly to neglect the inner affairs of Mapai as a party. This suited him ideally, as he concerned himself mainly with the most important defence and security issues, leading the nation, charting its course through rough seas, and sketching its goals for the future, but it also relieved him of a burdensome task of being involved himself in mundane party matters. Often when such matters were brought to his attention he referred the individual to Netzer, thus giving the latter an unquestioned imprimatur which he could and did use most successfully. It soon became common among Netzer's opponents to refer to him as *Sar Hamiflaga*, the 'Minister for Party Affairs'. Ben Gurion gave the *Gush* a free hand and for a long time had little idea what it did with it, trusting to the loyalty of its members and their devotion to the party; what he intended was that they would be the servants of the party; what their opponents claimed was that they had become its masters.

The degree of control which the *Gush* had over the party and its institutions until 1965 was accompanied by a self-image in which it saw itself not only as the protector of the party and the guardian of its honour, but as the party itself. As one of its spokesmen put it, '[i]n short the *Gush* is nothing but the party itself, with all the good and all the bad in it, and the men of the *Gush* are nothing but the walls of that house, which must protect it from capture and from domination'.[14]

If the *Gush* was the party then all who were not part of it were some kind of 'foreign invader' to be fought off at all costs and against whom all methods might be used to ensure their exclusion. One of the key methods was control of Mapai's internal electoral system, constructed in such a way as to make it relatively easy for a group like the *Gush* to control and produce the results it required, even if this did not quite fit in with the demands of democratic organisation. We turn now to Mapai's internal electoral processes.

Mapai's internal elections

Almost the only way in which the *Gush* could have been overthrown would have been for it to lose its majority at Conference. From there the whole carefully woven net could have been undone: it would lose its majority at the Central Committee and following that its control of the Secretariat, and finally would lose its decisive influence in all appointments committees and those personnel matters that were handled outside formal committees. The *Gush* therefore needed the support of local leaders to ensure a majority of loyal and disciplined Conference delegates. The greater the degree of unity within a local Conference delegation, the greater the bargaining power of its leaders who could deliver that vote. Thus the interests of the *Gush* and the local leaders converged on the electoral process; both were dependent upon success in the local and Conference elections to ensure their dominance and supremacy.

The evidence of Mapai Conference and local elections in 1956, 1959 and 1964 suggests that such control was obtained, not in every branch of the party, but in Tel Aviv and in enough other branches to ensure the *Gush* its control. Technical factors assisted these groups to obtain the results they

[14] Y. Yeshayahu, '"The Men of the *Gush*" Against the Attackers', *Davar*, 1.8.1963.

desired. On voting day each elector in the areas of large Histadrut concentration had to vote four times, twice for the Conference and twice for the branch institutions, with the vote on each occasion being divided in the proportion of 60 per cent to the branch list and 40 per cent to the trade union list. The process was made even more complicated and time consuming by the method used; the voter was not expected to choose one or two candidates out of a small list in a particular region or section of the branch, but to vote for all candidates simultaneously. Thus each voter had to select the specified number of names, usually at least thirty, on each of four separate lists.[15]

This created a number of technical problems, mainly of time and space for fitting in ballots on normal working days, and of being able to remember the names of over thirty candidates in each section of the elections. Various methods adopted to assist the voter also facilitated machine control. Official lists of candidates identical to those used on voting day were sent home, could be filled out there, exchanged for the blank received at the polling booth and placed in the ballot box. This enabled interested parties to mark the ballot in members' homes. For voters whom the campaigners were not able to reach at home there were other opportunities to assist the voter. No closed booths were provided and all the voting was done in the open. Activists were permitted to be present in the hall during the proceedings, and were available to assist voters with their ballot papers. Not only could voters seek such assistance, but activists were also in a position to see precisely what the voter did, or if he altered the ballot already filled out for him at home. Candidates and other activists who were permitted to be present mostly held key Histadrut and municipal positions and often were the voters' employers or superiors. In short, the democratic demand of secrecy was seriously brought into question, if not destroyed, by this method, which gave individuals and groups the power and capacity to control how others voted. Thus the two conditions specified by Banfield and Wilson – that voters place a lower value on their votes than on what the machine can do in exchange, and ability to control internal party elections, were both clearly present.

Such power was further reinforced by the party's provision for branch supervision of the elections and their administration, which was left entirely in the hands of the retiring Secretariat via an Elections Committee. The Elections Committee exercised far-reaching control over all aspects of the elections in which it was directly involved. It could decide on any method that suited its interests best and whichever method was most suitable for neutralising and dispersing any opposition. The committee was also responsible for transferring the votes from the ballot places in the workplaces to the branch headquarters and for the counting of all votes. Doubts were often cast

[15] Length and complexity of election process have always favoured political machines; thus a classic reform tactic has been to propose a short ballot. See Banfield and Wilson, pp. 138–9.

upon the committees with regard to the transfer of envelopes from the work-places to the branch, and with regard to the actual counting of the votes themselves. Not only was it possible for interested groups to control Mapai internal elections, but tremendous advantages were conferred on those already in power in the branch and local institutions. This power was often demonstrated in many branches but perhaps most starkly by the success of the *Gush* in Tel Aviv in preventing the election of a number of leading *Zeirim* as Tel Aviv delegates to the Conference in 1959.

The *Gush* could thus control the Conference by carefully picking its branches and ensuring itself a regular majority. It therefore vehemently defended the system with all its inherent deficiencies. In the main its members and supporters were local activists, in the workplaces, in the branches, in the local municipal, Histadrut, and trade union settings. In control of these resources under Mapai's non-secret methods, it exercised more than an undue influence over the average Mapai voter in internal elections.[16]

Another aspect of Mapai's internal election processes that facilitated and reinforced the power of the *Gush* was the method of choosing those party institutions above the Branch Councils and the Conference. Those that gained control of the Conference and its Appointments Committee could effectively veto individuals from being elected to higher positions, as well as ensuring that those they wanted were elected. Thus the Conference delegates from each branch chose its delegates on the Central Committee; and a small Appointments Committee chose the one-third on the central list. With *Gush* control of both, its opponents and those who did not have its imprimatur as loyal and trustworthy were often kept off party decision making institutions.

Second, the en bloc procedure prevented delegates from expressing any vote of confidence or no confidence in any particular individuals or candidates. The en bloc procedure demanded that an Appointments Committee present a list of candidates to be ratified. The Appointments Committee and later the Standing Committee of the Conference presented the list to the Conference, and all it could do was to accept the whole list or reject it. Similarly, the out-going Secretariat would set up an Appointments Committee to choose a list of candidates for the Secretariat and all that the Central Committee could do was to ratify the whole list or vote against it. For all other committees the same occurred; a committee chose an Appointments Committee, which selected a list of candidates and these were approved en bloc. It was rare for a list to be rejected, although on a number of occasions requests were made for a number of individuals to be added, which was usually done without remov-ing any from the en bloc list. It was even rarer for more candidates than the required number to stand for election and for the electing body to choose

---

[16] For critiques and evidence on which the foregoing has been based see *Davar*, 31.10.1958, 14.11.1958, 22.2.1963, 22.10.1963; *Haaretz*, 2.1.1959, 16.1.1959. *Reports of Party Control Commission*, 1956–1960, 1960–1964; *Hapoel Hatzair*, 9.6.1964.

between them. Mapai rarely had fixed numbers for bodies, and if the pressure was strong enough the numbers were simply increased to cope with the additional demand. The whole procedure was much more akin to one of cooptation than of election.

The use of appointments committees placed their members under pressure to produce a list that would not be rejected outright, that would be sufficiently representative of the party's social and interest diversity to gain en bloc ratification and work reasonably effectively, so as to obviate the need for some form of individual election to determine this. Opposition and minority groups, under this form of cooptation, were more prone to be under-represented. In particular, individuals were not able to campaign on their merits and personal qualities and attributes, they were more prone to dis-qualification because the controlling group did not support their candidature, and, in addition, there was no way of their being able personally to prove themselves or be elected. And just as this veto system kept individuals out it was efficient in working in reverse; at any time individuals could be, and were coopted without having to go through a process of formal election. This may have been flexibility, but it was far from the concept of democratic election.

Appointments Committees and en bloc elections were also used widely in the branches to choose branch secretariats and branch candidates for key local institutional positions. They were consistently supported by the *Gush* as the only way in which the party could achieve a balance between its diverse and conflicting forces. This would ensure that all who should be would be repre-sented. Such an argument was based upon a number of questionable assump-tions. Democratic election systems demand that those seeking representation put themselves to a popular test and leave it to the party membership and its decision making bodies to decide this in a voting procedure which would be responsive to and reflective of the views of the voters. They demand that candidates do what the *Gush* was not prepared to allow to happen – be pre-pared to take a chance on the outcome. The *Gush* argued that this would mean that some groups would not be sufficiently represented. The democratic election assumption was that the only test of whether a group deserved representation was whether it could gain it in a fair democratic election. The assumption of Mapai-style elections and their defenders was that there were some who must be elected, and that they knew who these were and why they had to be elected. Many who were not prepared to trust their chances to an open election lent their support to these assumptions.

The top decision makers in Mapai were elected by a process of sifting which left them many removes away from the rank and file of the party. This con-trasts with the primary system where candidates for office in a constituency are chosen by the members of the branches within the constituency. Thus it was theoretically possible for branches directly to elect their delegates to the Central Committee, rather than have them chosen by the delegates they elected to the Conference. Similarly, the Conference could vote directly for the central list rather than through the Appointments Committee and the en bloc procedure. The Secretariat, too, could be elected by a vote of the party rank and file at the Conference, or in the branches. Instead the rank and file chose the Conference delegates who chose the Central Committee, which chose a committee which chose the Secretariat which chose a committee which chose the Leadership Bureau which chose a committee approved by the Secretariat, which chose the Knesset candidates. Thus, rank and file members were at least seven removes away from the Knesset candidates and the Leadership Bureau, the party's top policy making body and the wielder of effective power.

Mapai's internal election system and the machines that controlled it owed much to the degree of politicisation existing in Israeli society at the centre of which was Mapai. Politicisation in this context meant that the party was not simply a collection of individuals and rank and file members united by common loyalty to ideals and goals and willing to organise in order to pursue them. This was only partly true in the case of Mapai. Mapai was also a federation of interest groups, a meeting point for diverse and conflicting groups, organisations and institutional complexes with demands to make, interests to pursue, policies to be formulated and put into practice, and economic resources and political power to protect and increase. Whereas individuals can be assessed, judged, and either accepted or rejected via the strict numerical and mechanical calculations of the ballot box, interests are not subject in the same way to exact arithmetical calculation or decision. Groups, institutions and interests may be more important than their mere numerical strength and enjoy greater significance than they would achieve were they to attempt to gain representation only on these lines. Mapai, as a party responsible for making far-reaching decisions, adopted the view that it was best for its decision making capacity to incorporate as many of these groups as possible within the party framework so that it could integrate their activities with those of the party and allow its representatives to control their resources and policies from within. It worked from the assumption that common party loyalty will, as a rule, induce men to forgo certain interests in order to protect those of the party as an organisation. As Pendleton Herring once put it: 'Common loyalty to an organization is no small factor in bringing men of contrary interests together. This straddle presumably can stretch only so far; but before the breaking point is reached concessions are often made out of loyalty to the organization which both sides value.'[17] But for this concession making to take place the groups must be represented on the party decision making institutions and must be reasonably happy with their degree of representation.

[17] Quoted in Neil A. McDonald, 'Party Perspectives: A Survey of Writings', in H. Eckstein and D. Apter, eds., *Comparative Politics: A Reader* (New York, 1963), p. 342.

The sociological effects of Mapai's election procedures

Max Weber distinguished between two types of individuals active in politics:
there were those for whom politics was a vocation, who lived off politics; and
another group for whom it was an avocation, who lived for politics. By and
large, the latter were more likely to produce innovative political leadership
receptive to new ideas and to change, precisely because they were independent
of the party and its vested interests, and were not bound to it economically
in their personal occupation. Men of independent means were more likely to
possess political character and charisma, to lay claim to the leadership by
taking a public and independent stand. Thus a generous sprinkling of such
politicians, was, in Weber's view, useful for giving vitality to a system of
legal domination.[18]

An analysis of the Mapai decision making institutions reveals, perhaps not
surprisingly in view of the foregoing analysis, that they were controlled
almost in their entirety by individuals who lived off politics. Mapai's leadership structure was composed almost entirely of officials and others in either
the direct or indirect employ of the party. Few had independent means or
professions that would enable them to survive economically with ease outside
the party. In other words, they were nearly all totally dependent upon the
party for their livelihoods.

While the effects of the concentration of party officials and men who lived
off politics in the party's decision making bodies and amongst its activists
may be subject to differing interpretation, the facts of the situation are not,
as Tables 8.1 and 8.2 and 8.3 demonstrate.

Table 8.1. *Employment distribution of members of Mapai Central Committee, 1954**

Employment	%
Members of Knesset	22.0
Histadrut	34.0
Labour settlement	18.4
Party administration	11.0
Civil servants	4.4
National institutions (Jewish Agency)	5.1
Municipal mayors	2.2
Free professions	1.5
Army	0.7
Private employment	0.7

* Source: S. Rolbant, *Davar*, 6.8.1954.

[18] Max Weber, 'Politics as a Vocation', in H. Gerth and C. W. Mills, eds., *From Max Weber* (London, 1947), pp. 77–128.

Table 8.2. *Source of income of 390 leading party activists, 1956**

Source of Income	%
Histadrut institution	19
Histadrut industry	7
Government	19
Party institution	13
Independent, member of cooperative, or other collective body (including moshav)	12
Kibbutz	10
Municipal institution	9
Other public body	7
Retired	2
Private employment	1

* Source: *Report of Institute of Applied Social Research* (commissioned by Mapai) Jerusalem, 1956 (mimeo).

One interesting fact that emerges out of the comparison of the 1954 with the 1965 figures is the degree to which power has been dispersed locally. This appears most obviously in the municipal segment and less obviously in the proportion of Histadrut institutions. Approximately 30 per cent of those in that sector represent local Labour Council officials. Greater local representation was facilitated by the increase in the size of the Central Committee. Thus, on the other hand, while the number of members of Knesset on that body was numerically the same (twenty-nine and thirty respectively) the proportion became smaller because of the increase in the absolute size of the Central Committee. It should also be noted that the figures for the Labour Settlements

Table 8.3. *Employment of members of Mapai Central Committee, 1965**

Employment	%
Members of Knesset	12.1
Histadrut institutions	34.6
Histadrut industry	5.9
Labour settlement	10.0
Party administration	7.0
Civil servants	8.3
National institutions	3.3
Municipal mayors	13.6
Municipal employees	2.0
Professions	2.5

* Source: analysis of data provided to the author by the Organisation Department of Mapai, December 1965. Although over 300 were elected to the Central Committee in February 1965, data were available on 240 only. The majority of those from whom there was no data had left with the Rafi split. There is no way of knowing exactly how they differed from those that stayed. Impressionistic evidence suggest they differed little, if at all, in this regard.

are in both cases not exactly representative of their position; in 1954 another thirteen members were counted in their Knesset and Histadrut capacities, whilst in 1965 some half a dozen members of the Labour Settlements were counted in other capacities. This does not, however, mask an absolute decline in their membership from thirty-eight to about thirty.

Conclusion

We have so far shown how the machine developed and was consciously furthered by its leaders and supporters. We must now briefly assess its role in relation to our major theoretical concerns, as elaborated in chapter one.

Perhaps the most striking aspect of the national Mapai machine known as the *Gush* was the conscious dichotomy between policy making and the personnel taking decisions. Of course in the long run the two are interwoven: by determining who can have a say in the making of policy decisions one influences the content of those decisions. But this is clearly different from influence and control arising from actual participation in the decision making process. As we pointed out above, the *Gush* did not seek to direct personnel in policy making in important spheres outside the party. It did, on the other hand, follow a consistent approach to party constitutional and election policies, because here lay the foundations of its power.

Clearly, we can say that Mapai's internal election processes were controlled by a cohesive group, but its effects are hard to assess. For example, the machine strove valiantly to achieve widespread representation of the diverse social forces in the party. At the same time, it centralised internal political power which it put at the disposal of the top levels of the party leadership, and thereby could be said to promote efficiency. In other words, it saved party leaders the task of having to fight for policies within party institutions, because in many instances it provided them with a majority of loyal support. But the price paid was the exclusion of dissenting groups and views, their under-representation, or their inclusion and cooptation with the agreement of the machine, and the granting of a high degree of autonomy in intra-party affairs to the machine.

This places our previous analysis of the formal institutional structure and processes into proper perspective. We must distinguish at least three separate situations that describe the relations between the machine and the formal institutions. In cases of intra-party constitutional issues, the *Gush* controlled and directed these institutions in support of the policies it wanted. In many other cases, the *Gush* put its majority support at the disposal of the party leadership to carry out policies they favoured – a classic example was the Lavon Affair, but one could point to many others. A third type of case was where the *Gush* withdrew and issues were debated and compromises reached within party institutions as if the *Gush* did not exist, for example, wages policy. Most aspects of parliamentary policy also clearly fit into this last category.

This leads to a general point: we must separate how individuals were elected to party positions, and the way in which decisions were made in institutions, and the modes and manner of participation of these and other individuals in them. Similarly there were limits to the machine's power in personnel selection. Generally we can say, the higher the body to be elected, the less the degree of control exercised by the *Gush*. Again, its power was greater in cases where it sought to keep individuals out, rather than have them put in.

None of these reservations, however, can detract from the fact that the machine arose and in a self-perpetuating process became strengthened, because the party failed to develop other mechanisms for fulfilling the important elective and appointive functions, and for maintaining contact with the diverse social groups incorporated in the party. Under conditions of lack of alertness of party members and in the absence of concerted efforts to find other methods, the machine, consisting of those doing the essential day to day party work, in contact with the members, able to influence them, and to control their votes, was able to perform functions that formal party institutions might otherwise have performed had they been called on to do so and given the tools with which to perform them.

9. LEADERSHIP SELECTION AND DIRECTION OF
PARLIAMENTARY AND HISTADRUT
INSTITUTIONS

Mapai's continued political success was dependent upon its performance in
the Knesset and the Histadrut. No Israeli government could succeed without
steady cooperation from the Histadrut, whilst its steadfast opposition and
obstruction could, without doubt, prevent effective government. The foundation of Mapai's power lay in its simultaneous control of the government and
the Histadrut. This both prevented the development of strong disagreements
between them, and facilitated the growth of strong cooperative relations.
These developments occurred within Mapai as a party which chose members
and leaders to represent its interests in these institutions. This meant that in
internal Mapai policy deliberations, the representatives of these separate
institutions participated as party members seeking solutions to particular
problems for which they and the party were jointly responsible, and not as
the representatives of separate institutions with specific interests meeting in
a consultative or bargaining framework. Thus, the overarching consensus of
common party membership had important consequences for policy making.
It made the decision making process easier by avoiding the direct confrontation of opposing political parties and their interests, and by utilising common
party loyalty to promote compromise and agreement.

  As we pointed out in our theoretical analysis in chapter one, leadership
selection is one of the most crucial political party functions. The governing
party, through its internal processes of leadership selection, ensures party and
governmental leadership succession. Leadership positions confer greater ability
to influence the allocation of scarce resources, and a major say in policy making
decisions and the selection of other key party personnel. They are a symbolic
indicator of worth, provide psychological gratification and accord prestige.
They are, thus, both a form and an avenue of social mobility. The overall
composition of the leadership group may also indicate the strength of various
groups within the party, and the degree of integration of diverse social forces.
They provide opportunities for interest articulation and can be used as a
mechanism of interest aggregation. Leadership confers responsibility for the

direction of government and for its policy making and policy application. Leadership selection and behaviour also directly affect internal cohesion.

The choice of Knesset candidates

It has often been observed that the use of proportional representation in conjunction with a national list system as exists in Israel tends to emphasise the importance of party as opposed to individuals, and of programme and policy as opposed to political leaders.[1] This form of voting system, it has also been claimed, strengthens the hands of the party leadership and is the source of extra-parliamentary party control over the parliamentary representatives.[2] The argument is based upon the fact that the list form of proportional representation necessitates party procedures to select and rank the party's candidates. It thus effectively determines who will enter parliament, because in a multi-party list system only a certain number of places have realistic chances of success. Individuals must therefore appeal to the party and cannot publicly prove themselves as successful vote earners. Thus Schattschneider has maintained, that 'a party must make nominations if it is to be regarded as a party at all. By observing the party processes at this point, one may hope to discover the locus of power within the party, for he who has power to make the nominations owns the party.'[3]

A number of factors operated to minimise the extent to which this generalisation was true of Mapai. Its nominating bodies, known as appointments committees, were themselves ad hoc bodies elected before each parliamentary election, and dissolved immediately afterwards. While this did not prevent them from considering the parliamentary performances of party representatives in deciding on renomination, it did prevent them from influencing or dictating their parliamentary behaviour. There is no evidence to suggest that Mapai parliamentarians were dropped because they offended members of appointments committees; most were dropped for reasons of age or unsatisfactory parliamentary performance or because groups recognised as having a right to nominate candidates for 'safe' places decided to alternate these among their leading members. Nor is there a great deal of evidence of extra-parliamentary control in the choice of parliamentarians. A feature of the Mapai nominating process was the regular presence of the Prime Minister and other leading ministers and parliamentarians on the appointments committees. Parliamentary performance, then, was judged by those in the best position to do so. On the other hand, the appointments committees were set up by, and responsible to, the central party institutions thereby preventing

[1] The classic statement is by F. A. Hermens, 'Democracy or Anarchy', in Eckstein and Apter, eds., p. 263.
[2] Regarding Israel this point has been made cogently in N. Safran, The United States and Israel (Cambridge: Mass., 1963), pp. 115–17.
[3] Quoted in McDonald, p. 342.

the parliamentary party from becoming a self-perpetuating oligarchy, and enabling the representatives of the party rank and file to exercise some influence in the choice of the party's parliamentary representatives.

Mapai began its parliamentary career with an ideology that raised party to the highest level of value in the pursuit of elevated human and social goals, and therefore regarded its representatives as delegates of the party, bearing its views and beliefs, and subject to the instructions of the legitimate party institutions. The existence of appointments committees and extra-parliamentary control derived from the ideology of the primacy of party over its delegates. In this context it meant the primacy of the party institutions, rather than of the rank and file directly. But in practice a marked degree of independence was granted to its parliamentarians, and the degree of control by extra-parliamentary institutions was accordingly narrowed.

For the elections to the First Knesset in January 1949 Mapai compiled its list of candidates and ranked them according to the procedure which it had practised before 1948. The Central Committee elected an Appointments Committee on the recommendation of the executive bodies, chaired by party Secretary-General Aranne. It consisted of thirteen members of diverse social composition, which is indicative of a conscious effort to obtain a broad and varied parliamentary representation. In addition to seeking expertise the committee strove to include representatives of cities, moshavot, regions, women, agricultural settlements, ethnic groups, new arrivals, workers, free professions, veterans, younger members, Histadrut activists, Jewish Agency activists, and leading party personalities.

When the list was placed before the Central Committee complaints were made by some groups that their particular section of the party was under-represented. On the other hand, Lavon (Secretary-General of the Histadrut) had refused to participate in the active work of the committee because too little attention was paid to the needs of the parliament as an institution and too much to satisfying demands for representation. The Central Committee returned the list to the Appointments Committee with instructions to take these criticisms into account in drawing up the final list.[4] In actual fact this was left to party Secretary-General Aranne.

The procedure adopted here with regard to the First Knesset set the pattern for the future. The Central Committee's power to ratify meant, in effect, that a report had to be given it on the work of the Appointments Committee and that, by and large, it had to pass this in toto. It influenced the decision only to the extent that the Appointments Committee was prepared to listen to criticism and to make changes. Over the years various minor changes were made, for example individuals were moved into more realistic positions if sufficient outcry was raised at the Central Committee, but overall the Central Committee did not make major alterations. This stemmed from the logic of

4 *Minutes Mapai Central Committee*, 4.1.1949.

using an appointments committee. To alter its recommendations in detail might upset the social and interest balance achieved by it. Thus the multi-member Central Committee could either reconstitute the list itself, or return it to the committee for reconstitution, or appoint another committee. None of these alternatives ever occurred, partly because the Central Committee was too big to get directly involved and partly because the appointments committees, both in their composition and in their choice of candidates, took note of the pressures within the party. While in their nature not the most democratic they proved to be adept in balancing conflicting needs.

With the sudden elections following a coalition crisis in June 1951 the Mapai executive bodies decided upon a new tactic in constituting the Appointments Committee. Rather than seek diversity of interest representation on the committee they sought to get the most prestigious and authoritative committee possible. Increasing pressures had been applied on various committees of this kind in the past, which one member described as 'the sheer hell of pressures'. It was therefore agreed to establish an appointments committee which would be strong enough to resist these pressures and stand up against those whom another speaker described as 'the hundreds of voluntary advisers' that attach themselves to these committees. The committee consisted of the Prime Minister, Ben Gurion, and the Foreign Minister, Sharett, and Lavon, formerly Histadrut Secretary-General, and at the time Minister of Agriculture.

According to Mr Sharett the committee met 'with innumerable delegations and received an endless stream of letters and notes' from 'all sorts of sections, ethnic groups, localities, cities, regions and organisations' who altogether suggested twice as many names as could be placed on the list. He emphasised that this Appointments Committee, like its predecessor, had striven to find the middle road between supplying an informed and capable parliamentary party and one which would reflect the party's diverse membership. The Central Committee discussion followed the usual pattern of complaints from various groups that their representation was not adequate with some of these later being remedied by the committee.[5]

Two things stand out about the result of these procedures in 1951. The first was greater emphasis than before upon the needs of the parliament as an institution. The second was greatly increased representation of non-European ethnic groups in realistic places.

For the elections to the Third Knesset in 1955 the familiar pattern was again followed. Three points about it are deserving of particular comment. A lengthy debate ensued in the Central Committee on the Secretariat recommendation that an appointments committee of nineteen be approved. Despite its size various groups and interests complained that they were not sufficiently represented on this suggested committee. It was finally decided to reject this

[5] Ibid. 7.6.1951, 20.6.1951.

Leadership selection and direction   167

recommendation and to elect a committee of five. Those chosen were Ben Gurion, then Minister of Defence, Sharett, Prime Minister and Foreign Minister, Mrs Meir, Minister of Labour, Namir, Secretary-General of the Histadrut, and Kesse, Secretary-General of Mapai. The committee was subjected even more than its predecessor to pressure from various delegations, some of which returned four or five times to press their case. This led to a strong attack upon the whole procedure by Ben Gurion. He criticised it as destructive of democracy and as a major factor in changing a party with an ideology and historic vision into a federation of interested groups.[6] A new element in the process was that some of the party's regions and organisations held elections to choose the candidates that their delegations were to place before the Appointments Committee.

Increasing pressure for rank and file participation and Mapai's support for single member constituencies led to suggestions for change. The matter was debated at length at the 2nd session of the 8th Conference in 1958. The Standing Committee's majority proposal was that the list should be divided into the first fifty 'realistic' places, and the last seventy places. Half of the candidates in each of these sections were to be chosen in the branches, and half centrally through an Appointments Committee. The rank ordering of individuals from both the branches and the central list in both sections of the list would be determined by the Appointments Committee. It was also proposed to let the Central Committee work out how the branch elections would be conducted. A minority proposal on this latter point called for rank and file elections in the branches. A major alternative proposed by a minority of the Standing Committee was to retain the status quo. The third major proposal, again of a minority of the Standing Committee, was much more far-reaching; this was the proposal of the *Zeirim* to elect all 120 candidates in the branches by a process of rank and file elections, but even this proposal left it to some form of committee to rank the candidates on the list.[7]

The debate revealed the line-up of forces in the party and the reasoning employed by the various groups in support of the different proposals. The majority proposal of the Standing Committee had the support of both the *Gush* and the Haifa branch and made its adoption a foregone conclusion as by this time the *Gush* was nationally organised. The *Gush* supported the proposal – it might be even more correct to say that it was basically its proposal – because in reality it changed nothing. It retained the central position of the Appointments Committee, so crucial in *Gush* attitudes and behaviour. Nor did it fear branch selection, because here too it exercised effective control. As against this the far-reaching proposal of the *Zeirim* to elect all candidates by rank and file election in the branches was intended to demonstrate that the party meant what it said in its proposal for constituency elections, by first making similar internal changes. They could find no justification for opposing

[6] *Ibid.* 9.6.1955.   [7] *Report 8th Mapai Conference, 2nd Session, 1958*, pp. 167–77.

this; either candidates were afraid to place themselves before the public for re-election and pass such a popular test, or they had little faith in the public's ability to choose the right candidates. Neither of these could be defended in a democratic regime.[8] The problem with this step, however, as their opponents pointed out in a telling manner, was that it would have had the paradoxical effect of strengthening central control by the Appointments Committee which would have to rank the candidates, and to this the *Zeirim* had no answer.[9]

Predictably the voting showed overwhelming support for the Standing Committee's proposal. The suggestion of the *Zeirim* was rejected in favour of the proposal to choose half locally and half centrally (633:59), whilst the proposal that there be no change was also overwhelmingly defeated.[10] It was left to the incoming Central Committee to decide the exact procedures to be adopted in implementing these changes.[11]

The Central Committee divided the list into two sections, the first with fifty candidates and the second with seventy, both of which were to be chosen half by the Central Committee and half in the branches. The number of candidates from each locality was to be determined by dividing the party into nine regions (including the kibbutzim and moshavim each as separate ones) and alloting their number of candidates according to a fairly complicated numerical formula. Special consideration was given to the agricultural settlement movements above and beyond their numbers. The 'fitting representation' for women and Oriental ethnic groups also laid down by the Conference was to be put into practice both locally and centrally. Elections in these regions were carried out in their institutions, and not by their rank and file. The Appointments Committee was also instructed by the Central Committee to follow closely the rank order of candidates as selected in the Regions.[12] This resulted in the following distribution among the twenty-five realistic places available to the branches: Tel Aviv received five places, Haifa four, Jerusalem two, Sharon-Shomron two, the Galil one, Negev-South two, Central Region four, Moshavim three and Kibbutzim two.[13]

The Central Committee was first presented with a recommended Appointments Committee of eighteen, again diverse and representative in composition. After discussion the Central Committee referred it back to the Secretariat, which chose a committee of seven. This in turn selected a committee of three to prepare a recommendation for the full committee. Its members were Dayan, Namir, and Netzer. The composition is significant because it marks the first time that the *Zeirim* participated in such committees. It worked closely with Ben Gurion in drawing up the list and also travelled around the country holding discussions with the various local branches. While the committee decided not to seek to have leading central figures chosen in the branches,

[8] *Ibid.* pp. 176–7.   [9] *Ibid.* p. 246.   [10] *Ibid.* p. 245.   [11] *Ibid.* p. 283.
[12] *Minutes Mapai Central Committee*, 11.8.1959; *Haaretz*, 12.8.1959.
[13] *Haaretz*, 27.8.1959.

their discussions revealed that some branches were planning to do this anyhow. Thus four ministers, Golda Meir, Eshkol, Sapir, and Shitreet, and Argov, Chairman of the Knesset's Foreign Affairs and Security Committee, were all chosen on local lists.[14]

The complete list was drawn up by the three-man committee and ratified by the full committee before being brought to the Central Committee for final ratification by Ben Gurion on behalf of the full Appointments Committee. He pointed out that in the first fifty-two places, 35 per cent appeared for the first time, 18 per cent were of non-European origin, 25 per cent belonged to various forms of agricultural settlement, and 10 per cent were women.[15] It is interesting to note that only one of the leading *Zeirim* was chosen by the branches – Gideon Ben Yisrael, formerly Secretary of the Beer Sheba Labour Council, elected in the Negev. Dayan, Peres, Eban, were elected on the central list and Amos Degani by Tnuat Hamoshavim. The existence of the central list helped to increase the representation of members of kibbutzim and moshavim by virtue of the fact that a number of ministers and leading Knesset figures belonging to agricultural settlements were elected on this list. It served also to guarantee representation to groups not greatly represented on the local lists, such as women, members of non-European ethnic groups and youth. The central list therefore not only looked after the interests of the Knesset as an institution by catering for ministers and leading parliamentarians, but also helped to balance out the list in terms of representativeness.

For the Fifth Knesset in 1961 Mapai did not choose a new list since the existing Knesset list was less than two years old. It simply nominated the same candidates as before in the same order with the exception of Lavon and Professor Rottenstreich, a leading Lavon supporter, who both declined to appear on the Mapai list. Aron Becker, the new Secretary-General of the Histadrut, took the place of his predecessor.

In 1965, however, following the split and the Alignment with Achdut Haavoda, the party reverted to the procedure of nomination by a central Appointments Committee. There were two basic reasons for this. First the party branches were in a rather chaotic state, and in many it was unclear who was staying in Mapai and who was joining the Rafi list led by Ben Gurion. At the same time Regions had been abandoned as a form of organisation, and no new rules had been drawn up to govern the choice of candidates. Moreover, the final listing was made in a joint committee set up by Mapai and Achdut Haavoda.

The choice of Prime Minister

Mapai as the party with the most votes in all the Knesset elections was always called upon to form a government and to fill the post of Prime Minister.

[14] *Ibid.* 31.8.1959.   [15] *Minutes Mapai Central Committee*, 6.9.1959.

Theoretically the party could have done this by a vote of the parliamentary party, as is the case with the British and Australian Labour parties, or by some form of party convention, as is the American case. In keeping with the ideology and practice of the primacy of party over representatives Mapai placed this choice in the hands of its legitimate internal party institutions.

At first there was no clear decision as to how this choice should be exercised, nor was there any need for one. Mapai had a Prime Minister even before it had a method of choosing one, and there was no necessity to devise a method because there was little likelihood that anyone in the party would challenge him for the position. Ben Gurion was head of the Jewish Agency Executive from the middle of the 1930s, and when the new government was formed after the establishment of the state combining the Jewish Agency Executive and the National Council, it was obvious that he would be the head of the new government. By virtue of his position in the Jewish Agency he was the leader of Mapai without having been formally elected to that position. Despite the obviousness of the choice the Mapai executive bodies did not simply acknowledge the fact that he was going to be Prime Minister. The Secretariat elected a committee of three to nominate its candidates for the ministerial positions that Mapai was to receive in the new government, including that of Prime Minister. This committee chose the candidates with Ben Gurion as Prime Minister, and these were brought to the Central Committee for approval.[16]

Having been Prime Minister in the Provisional Government, Ben Gurion headed Mapai's list for the First Knesset elections, making it clear that he was the party's candidate for Prime Minister. There was, however, no formal election of any kind, and no explicit mention of this fact. It was simply taken for granted that Ben Gurion would be its candidate without facing election or needing any confirmation. Similarly in 1951 he was automatically placed at the head of the list.

The first time a question arose in Mapai as to who would be Prime Minister was when Ben Gurion resigned in 1953. At that stage the Political Committee chose a committee consisting of the party Secretary-General Argov, the chairman of the Parliamentary Party, Govrin, and the Secretary-General of the Histadrut, Namir, to discuss this position with the two persons in the running, the Foreign Minister, Sharett, and the Minister of Finance, Eshkol. Ben Gurion, it seems, preferred Eshkol, but he declined, and thus the committee unanimously recommended to the Central Committee that Sharett be ratified as Prime Minister.[17]

In 1955 Ben Gurion was again automatically placed at the head of the party's Knesset list, and he remained Prime Minister until June 1963. Ben Gurion retired suddenly in 1963 despite his intentions having been known for some months to party leaders who had sought to dissuade him. Ben Gurion

---

[16] *Minutes Mapai Central Committee*, 6.3.1948.   [17] *Ibid.* 25.11.1953.

would not accede to their demands, and informed Mapai's ministers, the Cabinet and the President, in that order, of his decision to retire. Mapai leaders were apprehensive of any delay in governmental continuity caused by possible coalition complications and a new Prime Minister and acted quickly to 'uproot...the confusion that had been created' in both party and nation.[18] The night that Ben Gurion made his sudden announcement Mapai leaders met at the official residence of Mrs Meir, the Foreign Minister. Although the various reports do not make it clear exactly who was present, it seems that the meeting consisted of the Leadership Bureau together with other leading Mapai ministers – Aranne, Meir, Sapir, leaders of the Parliamentary Party, Govrin and Argov, and possibly a few others, for example Namir. They first asked Ben Gurion to remain, but were unsuccessful. Next day the Secretariat met together with the Executive of the Parliamentary Party and were informed of the events of the previous night. The meeting unanimously chose Levi Eshkol as Mapai's candidate for Prime Minister. The Central Committee which met to ratify this choice was also told that Ben Gurion approved of the choice of Eshkol, which was in fact a mild way of stating that Ben Gurion had recommended Eshkol to succeed him. The Secretariat also requested the Leadership Bureau to establish a committee to assist Eshkol in the allocation of Mapai portfolios, and in the negotiations with other parties, and instructed him to form the coalition in accord with the coalition agreement which had been concluded by Ben Gurion at the end of 1961. The Leadership Bureau decided to do this itself and coopted Meir, Aranne, Govrin, Argov, Namir, Idelson, and Shitreet, plus a representative of the Labour Settlements to assist it and this was approved by the Secretariat. All these decisions were approved unanimously by the Central Committee.[19]

This was the last occasion on which Mapai chose a candidate for Prime Minister without any internal constitutional provisions specifying the method to be used. While in the past there had been no need to decide on a method because there had never been more than one candidate, nevertheless it had to plan for the future. Thus the Central Committee was in 1963 empowered by the Conference to decide this. It amended the constitution as follows: 'The party Central Committee and the Parliamentary Party shall in a joint sitting elect the party's candidate for the position of Prime Minister.'[20] Although not specifically mentioned, it seems fairly obvious that this was to take place before the elections and even before the Mapai list for the elections was approved by the Central Committee, although it could also apply in cases of mid-term resignations. Most important of all, it made provision for deciding the Prime Ministership where there was competition between candidates, as could occur in the future. Once the charisma of a Ben Gurion had gone, and

[18] Mr Barkat, Party Secretary-General, addressing the Central Committee, quoted in *Hapoel Hatzair*, 25.6.1963.
[19] *Ibid.*   [20] *Mapai 1956 Constitution* (amended), ch. 5, clause 1.

ministers had acquired experience it was likely that a number of candidates might stand for this office and that the informal processes of reaching consensus in small groups would not suffice.

This procedure was used prior to the 1965 elections, when there were in fact two candidates, Eshkol and Ben Gurion. The election took place at the Central Committee at the height of the conflict within Mapai between the pro-Eshkol and pro-Ben Gurion forces. The Eshkol group had won a majority on all party institutions following the Conference, and the Secretariat put forward Eshkol as candidate for Prime Minister, whilst the minority put forward Ben Gurion. Because of the internal strife the election within Mapai was held at the beginning of June (the Knesset elections were not till November) in order to try and set things straight before Mapai had to face the electorate. Mr Eshkol won 179:103.[21]

The selection of Mapai ministers

From the very establishment of independent government in Israel it was commonly accepted within Mapai that the Prime Minister should have wide powers in the selection of ministers and in their removal from office if he should so desire. This is somewhat in conflict with the practices embodying the doctrine of the primacy of party which render party representatives, including ministers, the party's delegates. But in the case of the selection of ministers this doctrine was not pressed very far. The party exercised its authority over the ministers, not in their choice, but through the actual decision making processes. Although formally chosen by the Prime Minister, the ministers were nevertheless regarded as the party's delegates in parliament and therefore subject to control. The notion was that while the Prime Minister ought to be more or less free to choose those with whom he wished to work, and to allocate portfolios among them, the party institutions could make suggestions to him and fill places left open by him. The ministry as a whole was also expected to work in close cooperation with the legitimate party institutions and in certain situations was obliged to take decisions jointly after consultation.

In the arrangements which Mapai made regarding its participation in the Provisional Government in 1948, the selection of Mapai's ministers was made initially by a committee of three established by the Secretariat. While it is clear from Ben Gurion's remarks at the Central Committee when the decision was brought for ratification that he had the major say in their selection,[22] he was nevertheless unable to convince the party to choose one candidate for the Ministry whom he proposed, Mrs Meir.

In the two governments which Mapai established under Ben Gurion's

[21] *Haaretz*, 4.6.1965 (this will be dealt with in greater detail in chapter 12).
[22] *Minutes Mapai Central Committee*, 6.3.1948.

leadership in 1949 and 1951 the ministry was chosen by Ben Gurion himself with no formal participation of party institutions. In 1952, however, when Kaplan relinquished the post of Minister of Finance, it was the subject of long and intensive discussions between the Political Committee and the Executive of the Parliamentary Party. In this instance, too, Eshkol was not initially favoured by Ben Gurion, but was chosen by the party, and was readily accepted by Ben Gurion.[23] Thus the basic pattern which evolved was that it was up to these two bodies to ratify and approve the choices of the Prime Minister, except in the two particular instances cited. Here, it seems, Ben Gurion willingly accepted both the idea and fact of party institutions not abiding by his preferences. By not insisting on his candidates, he enabled them to make these decisions.

In the government established in 1955, a committee was set up by the Political Committee to assist the Prime Minister in the strenuous coalition negotiations with the other parties, and it seems that he also used it to advise him in the allocation of the lesser portfolios among Mapai ministers. When the matter was brought to the Central Committee for ratification they came as the Prime Minister's proposals. At the Central Committee eight names were proposed for nine positions, and it was left to the committee to fill the vacancy.[24] In 1959 the decision clearly rested with the Prime Minister alone, and although a committee was set up to deal with coalition negotiations it did not participate in any formal discussions about the distribution of portfolios amongst Mapai ministers.[25] The Prime Minister took the final decisions himself, although it is also clear that he was under pressure from various sections of the party about the allocation of specific portfolios, e.g. kibbutzim and moshavim. But the choice of the Zeirim, Dayan, Eban, and Yosephtal, as ministers, and Peres, as deputy minister, against the opposition of forces connected with the Gush, with Lavon (Secretary-General of the Histadrut) and of Mrs Meir, Foreign Minister (in the case of Peres), clearly reveals the Prime Minister's power to insist upon his personal preferences and his ability to include them. Little change was made in the Mapai personnel in the 1961 Cabinet except for the inclusion of Almogi, again a personal choice of Ben Gurion.

The establishment of the Eshkol government was significant for the fact that the Secretariat formally and officially set up a committee to assist the Prime Minister not only in the process of negotiating with prospective coalition partners but also with regard to the allocation of the position of Minister of Defence. In Israel's security situation this was the key ministry after that of Prime Minister, and had been held jointly by Ben Gurion. Dayan, the former chief of staff and military hero, made it publicly known that he did not wish to continue as Minister of Agriculture, and that he sought another position, which was commonly believed to be that of Defence

[23] Ibid. 26.6.1952.   [24] Haaretz, 31.10.1955.   [25] Ibid. 12.11.1959.

Minister. The committee devoted a number of meetings to this problem and to that of the return of Aranne as Minister of Education. The end result of these discussions was Dayan's agreement to remain on as Minister of Agriculture, the assumption of the Defence portfolio by Eshkol, together with the Prime Ministership, the appointment of Aranne as Minister of Education and of Eban as Deputy Prime Minister.[26] These decisions were brought to a joint meeting of the Central Committee and the Parliamentary Party where they were unanimously approved, despite strong criticism from a spokesman of the *Zeirim* that the Central Committee was presented with a fait accompli by meeting only an hour before the government was due to be presented in the Knesset.[27]

These various practices were finally given formal status early in 1964. The constitution specified that the candidate for Prime Minister should bring the list of Mapai ministers to the Secretariat for its ratification and decision, in conjunction with the Executive of the Parliamentary Party. Following this the Central Committee and the Parliamentary Party should be summoned to a joint sitting, where the decision of the Secretariat and the Executive of the Parliamentary Party would be brought to their attention.[28] In this state of affairs the Central Committee had little say whatsoever; it was to be merely informed of a decision already taken elsewhere. The Secretariat's function was mainly advisory, although it did have the formal power to approve or refuse to approve a list placed before it. While no formal provision was made for its participation at an earlier stage, this formal power could act as a constraint upon Prime Ministers who must anticipate their reactions. Similarly the Prime Minister must take the factors of representativeness, party support, past service, and ability, and prominent achievement into consideration, thus also restricting freedom of choice. Thus he was free to choose anyone he wished within these constraints. In so doing he could call on the advice or assistance of anyone he wished, or it could be given without being asked for.

The removal of ministers was usually carried out quietly at the end of a term and the minister was simply not included in a new ministry. Ministers either retired or were given an opportunity to resign gracefully. (The only exception was the case of Dov Yoseph in 1965 who was dropped by Eshkol without prior notice when it was generally assumed that he would retain his Cabinet place. His first inkling that this was not so came when the list was placed before party institutions.) On the other hand, there were various changes during a coalition's term of office. In one case, Aranne resigned from Cabinet over the high-school teachers' wages problems because Cabinet did not accept his proposals. In another, Lavon resigned in the aftermath of an enquiry in 1954 which did not at that time unequivocally clear him of responsibility for a security mishap, and after Prime Minister Sharett refused to

[26] *Davar*, 17–22.6.1963.   [27] *Hapoel Hatzair*, 2.7.1963.
[28] *Mapai 1956 Constitution* (amended), ch. 5, clause 1(b).

sanction changes in the Ministry of Defence and in the General Staff that Lavon had proposed.

In two other well-known instances the Prime Minister more or less forced ministers to resign. The first was that of Sharett in 1956 which deeply shocked a large section of Mapai. Sharett was a former Prime Minister, the country's only Foreign Minister since the establishment of the state and highly popular with most of the party. The background to the resignation was the fact that the Ministry of Defence under Ben Gurion was following an activist line, whilst the Foreign Ministry promoted a much more moderate, even passive, policy. This led to increasingly bitter conflict between the ministries and between Sharett and Ben Gurion themselves, and finally to Sharett's resignation when Ben Gurion applied the pressure.

The matter was brought to the Central Committee for discussion together with the question of a replacement. Sharett announced his resignation to the Central Committee and was followed by Secretary-General Kesse who suggested that the matter ought not be debated by the Central Committee as a whole, but that it should appoint a committee to consider it. This was passed 99:30 and a committee of sixteen was appointed. It heard both Ben Gurion and Sharett, and decided 'that Sharett's announcement is not open to change. In this governmental and state matter it would not be advisable for the Central Committee to discuss it.' The Central Committee decided 35:7 with forty-seven abstentions to take cognisance of the announcement of the chairman of the sub-committee. The wording of the statement suggests that it was not satisfied with the explanations it received, nor was the Central Committee, judging from the number of abstentions. Also significant was Ben Gurion's statement after the vote had been taken that the committee had not been given full details but only general explanations and reasons. It was subsequently made fairly clear that the issue before the sub-committee had not been the substantive question of defence and foreign policy but rather of a separate constitutional policy question – the right of a Prime Minister to force the resignation of a minister because they disagreed.[29] Moreover Ben Gurion in earlier discussions in the Political Committee before the matter was brought to the Central Committee put the issue in terms of either Sharett or himself, and under those conditions there was no doubt which way Mapai's institutions would turn.

The other major case of a Prime Minister asking for a resignation occurred in 1965 during the height of the conflict between the Ben Gurion and the Eshkol supporters. After Ben Gurion had increased his personal attacks on Eshkol and publicly proclaimed that he did not think him fit to be the Prime Minister, Eshkol called upon Ben Gurion's supporters in the Cabinet, Almogi and Peres, to resign if they held the same opinion of him as did Ben Gurion. After some initial hesitation and after some public discussion of the question

[29] Minutes Mapai Central Committee, 17.6.1956.

of whether a Prime Minister had the right to ask ministers to resign because they disagreed with him on intra-party matters, both did so.

The Mapai Parliamentary Party

Mapai before 1948 had developed a set of relationships connecting the party to its delegates, which we have termed the primacy of party. The party chose the delegates to represent it in the institutions of the Yishuv and through them controlled these bodies. It also had the final say over their policies, and the right of the party to overrule them was unquestioned. On the other hand their leadership role consisted in getting the party institutions to adopt their policy proposals, although they often left it up to the party institutions to decide which policies they should follow.

Independent statehood and the establishment of a parliamentary and cabinet system necessitated some changes in these practices. The theory of a parliamentary–Cabinet system demands that both parliamentarians and ministers free themselves somewhat from the dictates of the extra-parliamentary party. Even apart from the fact that it would be both difficult and highly inefficient for party institutions to act as a constant check on, and director of, ministerial and parliamentary activities, the theory of a parliamentary–Cabinet system does not readily admit constant or consistent extra-parliamentary control. The latter tends to cut across the obligations of Cabinet to parliament and of parliamentarians to the electorate, both of which are more widely based than particularistic party interests.

In Israel, the extra-parliamentary party institutions derive additional strength from the historical role of parties in the Yishuv reinforced by the system of proportional representation. The experience of Mapai was to strike some middle course between party control and parliamentary independence, and in doing so, party control was lessened and parliamentary independence increased as compared with the pre-1948 period. This was partly because the sheer weight of legislation made it impossible for the extra-parliamentary bodies to get involved in detail. Thus many matters were left to the ministry and the parliamentarians. More importantly these changes were consciously sought after by the party's leaders and legitimate institutions.

Two general factors heavily influenced the operation of the Mapai Parliamentary Party. The first was its size. In the first five parliaments Mapai's membership fluctuated between forty and forty-seven. The forty-two members of the Fifth Knesset were composed of nine ministers and two deputy ministers, the Knesset Speaker, the chairman of the Jewish Agency Executive, the Secretary-General of the Histadrut, the mayor of Tel Aviv, and Ben Gurion (none of whom served on Knesset committees). If we add to these the four Mapai chairmen of Knesset committees and two deputy speakers, making a total of twenty-two, this leaves only twenty backbenchers. Of these another seven were members of the Parliamentary Party Executive (*Hanhalat Hasiya*). Thus the Parliamentary Party was almost evenly divided between those occupying important official positions and those not. Moreover, the latter were less prominent members of the party and less powerful in its inner councils. Small numbers also limited the amount of legislative activity that could be undertaken by the parliamentary backbenchers.

The second general factor influencing the operations of the Parliamentary Party was Mapai's leading role in the government after 1948. Backbenchers were expected to defend and support Cabinet policies, and to ensure that they passed smoothly through the legislative mill. Their opportunities for independent action and thought were therefore severely limited, as were their opportunities for criticism. Thus in the First Knesset Mapai members did not even think that it would be right for them to ask parliamentary questions (but did so from the Second onwards). Nowhere was their freedom of thought and action more severely curtailed than in the initial formulation of policy. Whereas opposition parties could meet together to hammer out policy on proposed legislation and were free to criticise in the House, Mapai backbenchers had ready-made Cabinet policies placed before them from which they had little opportunity for public comment or dissent. This led to feelings of political inefficacy and insignificance on the part of some backbenchers.[30] Nevertheless, despite these structural problems, Mapai parliamentarians managed to exercise a more significant influence over the process of legislative decision making than might have been expected.

Mapai constitutional provisions governing the operation of the Parliamentary Party date back to 1951. Initially they stated that the Parliamentary Party 'discusses and decides the current questions of the Knesset'. On the other hand, 'basic questions. . .shall be brought for discussion and decision at the Central Committee with the participation of the members of Knesset, or to the Political Committee with the participation of the Parliamentary Party Executive'.[31] The constitution did not, however, lay down whether the Parliamentary Party or the party institutions should initiate such discussions, and until 1956 the latter generally did so, and the Parliamentary Party willingly cooperated. The 1956 constitution continued the same basic pattern with further specification. Thus the 'Parliamentary Party discusses and decides fundamental problems and basic questions of policy in the Knesset – in the spheres of the economy, the budget, and of the Basic Laws, etc.'. It also laid down that 'on the demand of the Secretariat, these questions shall be brought before the party's authoritative institutions'. It followed the earlier provisions regarding the participation of either the Parliamentary

---

[30] For example, see the remarks of Shlomo Hillel, M.K., *Minutes Mapai Central Committee*, 19.9.1957. Not long after this Hillel resigned to take up a position in the diplomatic service. He returned to the Knesset in 1969 and became Minister of Police.
[31] *Mapai 1951 Constitution*, ch. 2.

Party Executive or the full Parliamentary Party in these discussions, leaving it to the relevant party institutions to decide whether Knesset members could vote. A number of new provisions were also introduced. The Parliamentary Party was made 'responsible for all its activities to the Central Committee'. It was also expected to elect an Executive which was to report on the Parliamentary Party's activities to the Central Committee once in six months. Before debates in the Knesset on foreign affairs and defence, the Parliamentary Party was to discuss these topics. Finally, a disciplinary clause was inserted which obliged Mapai parliamentarians to vote according to the decision of the Parliamentary Party and of other party institutions, except in cases where it would be decided otherwise.[32]

These new constitutional provisions simultaneously increased and limited the power and independence of the Parliamentary Party. The range of questions it was to discuss was broadened in scope. On the other hand, the power of the Secretariat to intervene was made more explicit, and the Parliamentary Party became responsible to the Central Committee. Thus a division of power had taken place along two different axes. To cope efficiently with the demands of regular parliamentary activity, the Parliamentary Party was granted a marked degree of independence in operation and in taking decisions in accord with its own view of the parliamentary situation. Nevertheless, the doctrine of the primacy of party was served by constitutionally making the Parliamentary Party subordinate to other internal party institutions. In point of fact, the changes in the constitution had little effect upon the operation of the Parliamentary Party, and the norms and practices which had developed over time as Mapai gained parliamentary experience continued more or less unchanged.

The Parliamentary Party Executive was elected by the members of the Parliamentary Party, and on the average numbered about seven members including its chairman, who was also elected by the Parliamentary Party, but on the recommendation of the party's executive bodies. The Chairman of the Parliamentary Party Executive was also the Chairman of the Coalition Executive which coordinated the activities of all parliamentarians in the coalition parties, and ensured the presence of a majority for legislation proposed by Cabinet. It also acted on occasion to iron out minor party differences on legislation, particularly at the committee stage. The Chairman of the Parliamentary Party Executive was usually a prominent Mapai politician; thus both Aranne and Argov occupied this position for a time whilst they were party Secretary-General, which in no small measure contributed to smooth relations between the two bodies during their terms of office. Both resigned, however, to become Chairman of the Knesset's Foreign Affairs and Security Committee, a prestigious and widely sought after appointment, which suggests that the former had lower status than the latter.

Allotment to the various Knesset committees was done in a number of

[32] *Mapai 1956 Constitution*, ch. 4, clauses 1–6.

different ways. The predominant method was to elect a committee to decide the placing of Mapai Knesset members. On some occasions Mapai M.K.s were asked to state their preferences, which were used as a guide for the committee making the arrangements. On others, this was done without asking the M.K.s, and, on yet others, it was done by the Parliamentary Party Executive. In all cases consideration was given to members who had 'special' claims to particular positions deriving from experience, interest or other factors. The chairmanships of the various committees were, in the main, decided jointly by the Parliamentary Party Executive and the party's executive institutions.

A clear and significant pattern developed in the representation of Mapai members on the Knesset's committees, which served as important arenas within which Mapai members could press their particular interests. These committees receive legislation after the First Reading, discuss it thoroughly and amend it as they see fit after hearing the Minister and the civil servants responsible for the particular bill. Thus Mapai members with particular interests to promote sought to be represented on those committees which dealt most directly with them, where they stood a greater chance of success than they had in the Parliamentary Party at large. A determined specialist committee can have many opportunities to insert amendments in detailed legislation, which, however minor in general, may be of great significance to a particular group. Put in general terms, Mapai members sought representation on these committees to use them as additional pressure levers against Mapai ministers, in particular, who were likely to accept amendments at the committee stage in order not to hold up a whole bill, or in exchange for support on other aspects of the bill. Ministers usually attempted to gain a majority of the committee via the use of coalition discipline, but this was facilitated by some mutual compromise.

Four committees impinged directly on the economic interests of the various groups in Mapai: the Finance Committee, the Economic Committee, the Labour Committee, and the Public Services Committee. A fifth committee, the Education and Culture Committee, impinged indirectly upon the economic interests of the groups within Mapai, and directly upon some of the major interests of non-European immigrants in Israel. The Mapai membership of these committees from 1949 to 1965 reveals an interesting pattern of membership distribution best described as interest and functional specialisation. Taking the Fourth Knesset as a characteristic example, the following distribution emerges. On the Finance Committee it had two kibbutz members, two moshav members, one involved in the Histadrut Agricultural Centre which coordinated all Histadrut agricultural activities, and three of Histadrut labour background. On the Economic Committee there were three of Histadrut labour background including one of non-European origin, two from moshavim, also including one of non-European origin, one kibbutz member, and one artisan. On the Labour Committee there were six of Histadrut labour background including two women, and one ethnic activist. On the Public Services Committee there were three ethnic activists, three women and one artisan. The Education and Culture Committee was also divided along similar lines with three ethnic activists, two women and one literary figure.

The Parliamentary Party itself and its Executive met, on the average, at least once weekly. The major task performed by the Parliamentary Party Executive was to act as an intermediary. Often its chairman participated in the discussions of *Chaveireinu* and *Sareinu*, thus enabling him to request that particular issues or policies be brought to the full Parliamentary Party for discussion. Or, a Mapai M.K. after committee discussion might ask for a Parliamentary Party meeting to clarify points of disagreement, or aspects he sought to amend. The usual procedure was for the Mapai members of the particular committee to meet the Parliamentary Party Executive and the relevant Minister in an attempt to reach a compromise. If this did not occur, or if the matter was of general importance, then it was discussed by the whole Parliamentary Party. The Minister would usually lecture on the proposed legislation and explain its aims and their implementation. Often he would be accompanied by leading civil servants from his department, and it was not unusual for the Mapai Parliamentary Party to be addressed by leading members of the bureaucracy in such circumstances.

There was no general rule as to when matters came to the Parliamentary Party for consideration. Some legislative proposals simply never came before it for consideration. Others reached it before they had been decided upon by Cabinet, that is to say, at an intermediate stage between preparation in the responsible ministry and the Cabinet approval which was necessary before a bill could be placed on the table of the Knesset for First Reading. On other occasions they were considered after Cabinet approval had been given but before the First Reading. And on yet other occasions they were brought to the Parliamentary Party only after the bill had reached the Committee stage. In all these cases the usual procedure was for the Minister to lecture on the bill followed by a general discussion which enabled Knesset members to promote their particular 'constituency' interests or to suggest changes.

The influence of the Parliamentary Party in all these discussions varied. Much depended on whether the discussion remained general or whether it got involved in specifics. It also depended on the degree of insistence of members of the Parliamentary Party. If they were adamant in support of particular amendments it was common for Mapai ministers to give way. On the other hand, where the Minister disagreed strongly with suggested amendments or regarded an issue as fundamental or one of principle, the Parliamentary Party usually gave way. On occasion the Prime Minister was asked to settle such differences. Examples of these methods of compromise were common in many different legislative situations.

These discussions took place within the context of Mapai ministers' and backbenchers' shared policy aims and intentions which created an important disposition towards reaching policy agreement. Because of this both sides were ready to be convinced by the other, and the process operated successfully because generally they were able to reach agreement among themselves. Thus there were no formal rules covering cases of persistent disagreement, nor any method of determining which view should prevail in such cases. The Parliamentary Party did not have the power to coerce a minister to abide by its will, although it could put considerable pressure upon him. There are no examples of issues which found a united ministry ranged against a defiant Parliamentary Party or even a significant proportion of it. To the contrary, disagreements divided both the ministers and the Parliamentary Party, rather than opposing them to each other. One reason for this stemmed from the practice of the primacy of party over parliamentarians and ministers alike, which ensured that matters of fundamental importance or those arousing strongly felt disagreements were taken out of the parliamentary sphere into the realm of the extra-parliamentary party institutions, and it was here that matters were thrashed out and policy decided. Mapai parliamentarians knew each other well and operated as a small cohesive group able to make decisions based upon compromise and consensus in the general interests of the party. Similarly, parliamentarians were also leading members of internal party institutions, and came to them in a similar spirit, knowing other leading party members well and seeking agreement. Thus in these intra-party discussions it was not unusual for ministers to oppose each other and the Prime Minister, for ministers to oppose parliamentarians and vice versa, and for parliamentarians to oppose each other. When matters came to party institutions, notions of Cabinet responsibility and parliamentary discipline did not apply and the situation was fluid and flexible. Emphasis was upon reaching a decision, and upon enabling the party to adopt a policy despite the plethora of contending interests and views, and consequently a premium was placed upon compromise and the formation of a consensus that could evoke maximum agreement. Sometimes ministers' views were upheld, in other cases they were amended or rejected, and this was accepted by them as part of the political game as played within Mapai.

Thus the Parliamentary Party acted as a vehicle for the mobilisation of pressure upon Mapai ministers in pursuit of the particular interests of specific groups within the party. It was most successful and effective in the economic, social, fiscal and financial spheres, where many distinct interest groups were represented within the Parliamentary Party, each seeking to protect, defend, and promote its particular interests. Second, these legislative proposals were easily given to compromise to satisfy such demands. Taxes could be cut slightly, duties lifted, subsidies increased somewhat, or reductions in them withdrawn and so on, without seriously affecting the overall intent of a policy or its total impact.

The other major set of relationships were those between the Parliamentary Party and the party institutions. Above we examined the constitutional provisions governing them. Now we turn to the realities of the situation which are best examined in their historical development. The first period, from 1948 to the mid-1950s, was marked by steady contact, close relations and general satisfaction on both sides. A number of structural factors assisted in their successful cooperation. Matters brought to the party institutions were discussed initially by the Political Committee, which, as we noted above, contained all Mapai's ministers, all its members on the Knesset's Foreign Affairs and Security Committee, and one or two other Knesset members. When specific parliamentary matters were discussed, the Parliamentary Party Executive was present. Overall, parliamentarians constituted a majority on the Political Committee, and it included a significant number of non-ministers. Second, the Parliamentary Party and its Executive were highly conscious of the problems facing European socialist parties in which there existed a continual struggle between two centres of power, between the parliamentary party and the party institutions. They were therefore determined to avoid their typical pattern of ideological and organisational conflict. The Parliamentary Party's basic response was to curtail its own power, and to exercise self-restraint in order not to develop into a second and competing centre of power.[33] It therefore willingly handed over difficult decisions to the party institutions for final decision.

A change in relations took place as the 1950s passed, which was directly related to the internal structural changes in the party and the growth of informal decision making bodies exercising effective power. The demise of the Political Committee and the growth of *Chaveireinu* and *Sareinu*, and later the replacement of these informal bodies as exercisers of effective power by the Secretariat, directly affected the role of the Parliamentary Party and its Executive. Despite the participation of the Chairman of the Parliamentary Party Executive in the meetings of *Chaveireinu*, the position of the Parliamentary Party weakened. Very few backbench parliamentarians were represented in the Secretariat between 1956 and 1960. On the other hand, most of the party's various interest groups were represented, and after 1959 so too were all ministers and deputy ministers. This resulted in an increased tendency for matters to be decided in the Secretariat without a separate Parliamentary Party discussion at any stage, because all ministers were present and were able to reach an authoritative decision there without having to go through the same process in an extra body – the Parliamentary Party. The second point of contention was an increasing tendency for ministers to bring matters to the Parliamentary Party after firm decisions had been taken.

These problems came to a head at the end of 1962 with the resignation of Akiva Govrin, the Chairman of the Parliamentary Party Executive since

[33] *Minutes Mapai Central Committee, 23.9.1952.*

1952, in protest against the non-fulfilment of the constitutional requirements involving the Parliamentary Party in the decision making process. It raised once more the general question of the divisions of function and degree of cooperation between the Parliamentary Party and the Secretariat. Mr Govrin also gave voice to the growing complaints within the Parliamentary Party at the creation of legislative faits accomplis by Mapai ministers. Often, he maintained, ministers decided matters amongst themselves, or together with the Secretariat, and brought their decisions to the Parliamentary Party for the purposes of information only, and, what is more, on some issues it had not even been given information. A joint committee of the Parliamentary Party Executive and the Secretariat was established to set guidelines for the coordination of the Parliamentary Party, the ministry, and the Secretariat. It recommended that the work of the Parliamentary Party should be based upon cooperation and strong connections between the Parliamentary Party, the Mapai ministers and the party Secretariat. Subjects to be discussed in the Knesset, should, if the Parliamentary Party or its executive so decided, be preceded by a discussion in the Parliamentary Party, its executive or one of its committees, in consultation with the relevant minister and with his participation in the discussion. Questions likely to involve the Parliamentary Party in an obligatory vote in the Knesset should be discussed in the Parliamentary Party, its Executive or the relevant committee, in coordination with the Secretariat. Mapai ministers were expected to participate in Parliamentary Party discussions. It was also thought desirable for the party Secretary-General to participate in the discussions of both the Parliamentary Party and the Executive, particularly on matters of fundamental importance.[34]

After Govrin's resignation and under the chairmanship of Yisrael Kargman, these principles, carefully implemented by the chairman together with greater readiness of ministers to participate, led to a return to the relationships of the earlier period. In short, the general recommendations had worked and enabled the Parliamentary Party to participate more in policy dialogues and discussion with ministers, who came not only when called upon to report, but often simply as participants like everyone else. In this the lead given by Prime Minister Eshkol, who participated in Parliamentary Party meetings more frequently than Ben Gurion, was of some significance.

The central Histadrut institutions

We turn now to a brief examination of the role of Mapai in the decision making processes of the central Histadrut institutions and in the selection of leading Histadrut personnel. Before doing so, however, it is necessary briefly to clarify the major differences between the parliamentary and Histadrut spheres. In many countries trade union movements and labour parties are

[34] The resignation and its aftermath are reported in *Haaretz*, 1.11.1962, 6.11.1962, 7.11.1962, 25.11.1962; *Davar*, 1.11.1962; *Hapoel Hatzair*, 13.11.1962, 27.11.1962.

closely interwoven. In Britain, for example, the trade union created the political party as a weapon in the struggle for better working conditions. The trade unions exist independently of the political party, and maintain an autonomous federation or congress seeking to further and promote general trade union aims and interests. One method is continued support of the Labour Party, by recruiting members and parliamentarians, and by contributing funds. The trade union movement thus constitutes a major section of the party, and through almost automatic membership represents the largest bloc of votes at Labour Party conferences. In a sense, the trade union movement is the independent variable, and the political party the dependent variable. When a British Labour leader or Prime Minister comes to a Trade Union Congress to fight for his wages policies, as did Prime Minister Harold Wilson in 1968, he comes as a relative outsider who must plead with the delegates to support his policies. If he cannot convince them he has no institutional means within the party of getting them to follow his point of view or even of working out a compromise.

In Israel the situation is reversed, and it is the trade union movement which is dependent upon the political party. The Histadrut was brought into existence by the agreement of a number of political parties; conflict and competition within it is along political party lines; thus elections in all its bodies are contested by political parties. Whereas in Britain trade union leaders are elected individually by the rank and file on union or industrial policy platforms, in the Histadrut they are nominated by political parties and elected in accordance with the amount of support that the *party* receives in the elections. In short, the political parties control the Histadrut and, to be more exact, Mapai, because of the consistent majority it received in those elections until 1965, controlled the Histadrut.

Party control is hardly questioned in the Histadrut, and manifests itself in various ways. In general the interests of party are quite obvious in all facets of its decision making. In the appointment of bureaucratic personnel, for example, a strict party key is applied. Similarly, at the top level of policy making, considerations of what benefits the party and what serves to maintain its control have been of crucial significance. Thus, for example, an argument often advanced by some Mapai leaders for not nationalising the Histadrut health services, Kupat Cholim, has been that it was the major factor in Histadrut recruitment, and Histadrut members are more readily available for Mapai leadership, influence, and recruitment. Or again, trade union elections and national Histadrut elections have simply been postponed because it was disadvantageous to Mapai to hold them at the ordained time. Similarly, in the consideration of wages policy in which the Histadrut has such a significant say, a major consideration of Mapai Histadrut leaders has been what kind of policy is politically popular.

Moreover, Mapai maintained an absolute majority in the Histadrut, whereas in the Knesset it was dependent upon coalition support. Thus its freedom of action in the Histadrut was considerably wider than in parliament where it had to pay close heed to the views of its coalition partners. This absolute majority control in the Histadrut served to reinforce the predominance of party control and the application of criteria of party benefit.

Technically, too, there are significant differences between parliamentary and Histadrut institutions. The Central Executive Committee (*Vaada Meracezet*) met at least weekly, but in the 1960s had only seventeen members, of whom just over half were from Mapai (in the 1950s it had even less) whilst the Executive Committee (*Vaad Hapoel*) met monthly. The number of decisions taken, their scope and importance, and the amount of time and energy demanded of its members do not rank with those of the Knesset with its thrice-weekly meetings, detailed committee deliberations, and decisions and legislation upon matters of the gravest national importance in all spheres. This had two consequences. First, more was left to the executive members of the Histadrut nominated by Mapai. Second, it was far easier for the party to intervene and direct Histadrut affairs, as questions of Cabinet secrecy and parliamentary responsibility did not arise. Histadrut executive members, although not constantly directed in practice, were certainly more open to direction than Cabinet ministers, and more of their decisions and policies were thoroughly aired in party bodies. On many issues they simply left it up to the party to decide, although on others they made their preferences clear.

The types of Histadrut matters that were regularly discussed in the Secretariat and the Central Committee were: (a) wages policy, and economic policy in general; (b) major reorganisation in the Histadrut, for example, the splitting up of Solel Boneh, one of the major economic enterprises of the Histadrut; and the handing over of the Histadrut's Labour Exchanges to the state; (c) the timing of Histadrut elections; (d) trade union matters such as major strikes, elections, and general aspects of organisation; (e) major personnel decisions for the Mapai members of the leading Histadrut bodies, particularly the Central Executive Committee, and executive positions in the key Histadrut industrial enterprises, and institutions such as Kupat Cholim; (f) local trade union or Labour Council crises that attracted more than local attention. All in all one might suggest that Mapai institutions became involved in decisions of the Histadrut's central institutional hierarchy in so far as they affected Mapai as a political party and its standing as such in the vast network of Histadrut institutions. Any issue, however minor it might have seemed, was discussed in Mapai decision making bodies if it impinged upon this sphere.

A vast myriad of decisions, on the other hand, never reached the party's institutional hierarchy. Under the system of political appointments operating in the Histadrut the leading executive, administrative and bureaucratic posts and many minor ones too, were filled according to a political key, determined by the proportion of votes each party received in the previous election. The top posts went to the nominees of the dominant party – Mapai. The leading party-nominated Histadrut officials could then fill the remaining posts available to the party. With an administrative hierarchy staffed by party men many decisions could be taken by them and executed without ever having to be brought to the party institutions. Thus within the Histadrut's structure the party could rely upon the bureaucratic authority of the top officials to have their decisions carried out.

Those matters that needed party consideration were brought to the party institutions by the relevant officials, or at the instigation of the party bodies themselves. They were covered by general provisions in the party constitution (similar to those relating to the Parliamentary Party) providing for the discussion of 'fundamental matters' on the agenda of the Executive Committee to be brought to the Mapai Secretariat for decision with the participation as voting members of the Mapai faction in the Executive Committee[35] (some sixty members out of a total of just over 100 in the period 1959–65). Although the Executive Committee is the top executive body of the Histadrut according to its constitution, effective power lies in the hands of the Central Executive Committee. Matters brought before the Executive Committee for decision have usually been thoroughly discussed and a course of action decided upon in the Central Executive Committee; the Executive Committee's decision was mainly a ratification, and a pro forma one in view of Mapai's majority in both bodies. There was no provision for consultation of members of the Central Executive Committee with the Secretariat, but in actuality this took place quite regularly due to the presence of at least three members of the Central Executive Committee on the Mapai Secretariat, including the Secretary-General of the Histadrut, and the head of the Trade Union Department. These members could bring matters on to the agenda of the Secretariat and discuss them as they arose. Most of the initiative lay with the members of the Central Executive Committee so that often they came to the Secretariat with clear policy decisions, for which they wanted Secretariat approval. In others, the Secretariat made policy for them, sometimes even against their preferences. In this much depended upon the personality of the Secretary-General of the Histadrut. Lavon, as Secretary-General, was a personally powerful figure, and one of the conditions he made in agreeing to reaccept this office in 1956 was that he and the Mapai members of the Central Executive Committee and the Executive Committee be authorised to decide on the policy and the activity of Mapai in the Histadrut and to direct its affairs pretty much on their own initiative, a condition which was agreed to. Nevertheless even he had to consult the Secretariat on major matters if only to have it ratify his views.[36] His successor, Aron Becker, was more in the habit of consulting with the Secretariat.

The pressures to have Knesset candidates elected by the rank and file never

[35] *Mapai 1956 Constitution*, ch. 10.   [36] *Haaretz*, 28.10.1958.

manifested themselves in relation to the Histadrut institutions. All Mapai representatives to the various Histadrut bodies were chosen by the usual Mapai method of an appointments committee. Even the Mapai delegation to the Histadrut Conference meeeting every five years was chosen by a centrally elected appointments committee of the Mapai Secretariat, and on many occasions Mr Netzer was its chairman. After 1956 60 per cent of the places on the list went to locally nominated candidates, and 40 per cent to the central list. Prior to that date it was customary for the whole list to be drawn up centrally. The same practice was followed to find the 123 Mapai delegates to the Histadrut Council, meeting approximately annually, and the fifty-eight delegates to the Executive Committee. Mapai's delegation to the Central Executive Committee, comprising the party's top policy makers in the Histadrut, was chosen more directly by Mapai executive bodies, and in this the Secretary-General of the Histadrut had a major say, almost akin to that of the Prime Minister in Cabinet. This was clearly seen in 1960 when three Mapai members of the Central Executive Committee, Barkat, Blass and Mrs Yosephtal, who had run afoul of Lavon were dropped from it. The usual practice was for the Secretariat to elect an appointments committee of fairly top-level Mapai leaders to recommend its members of this body. Thus in 1960 the committee consisted of Eshkol, Minister of Finance, Mrs Meir, Foreign Minister, and Namir, mayor of Tel Aviv, the latter two having served as Secretary-General of the Histadrut in the past. Its recommendation was then brought for ratification to the Central Committee as the Secretariat's choice. This procedure was given constitutional status in 1964 when it was formally decided that 'the composition of Mapai members of the Central Executive Committee. . .shall be suggested by the party Secretariat and be brought for election to the Central Committee with the participation of the faction in the Executive Committee'.[37] In view of the widespread initiative left to the Mapai leadership of the Histadrut and in view of the fact that an intransigent Histadrut leadership could paralyse the government of the country this served to give more than formal notification and reminder of the primacy of the party.

Conclusion

Mapai retained power in the state from its establishment in 1948, which suggests that in the minds of the Israeli electorate at least (and in the view of many outside observers), it had proved to be an effective governing party. As we suggested earlier, the task of adaptation to the role of governing party is by no means an easy one, and the failure rate has been fairly high. One of the explanations for Mapai's success in this sphere, although by no means the only one, can be found in the manner in which it undertook the task of

[37] *Mapai 1956 Constitution* (amended), ch. 5, clause 2.

directing the governmental structures, and coordinating these with the party structure, and other key structures, such as the Histadrut. In this chapter we have analysed some of the major mechanisms, procedures and processes adopted by Mapai in this all-important sphere, and we have particularly focused upon both leadership selection and the knitting together of the operations of leadership groups so as to make possible the efficient direction of various structures and coherent policy making within and between them. We can now attempt to tie some of these aspects together in an interim conclusion, and relate them back to our major theoretical concerns.

The Mapai Parliamentary Party was widely representative of the diverse social forces within the party. Despite the tight *Gush* control of general party nominating processes, and its influence upon those of the Parliamentary Party the demands for representation won out. This was particularly noticeable in the case of the *Zeirim*, who had much more influence in the Parliamentary Party, and in the Ministry, than in the internal party machine. Two factors operated to ensure this. The first was the influence of Ben Gurion over key aspects of the parliamentary and ministerial selection processes, and his commitment to the need for youth and new talent in these areas. The second was a general orientation among a wider section of party leaders (including even the *Gush*) that the party's external representative group in the Knesset should reflect important social forces and trends in the country at large. In particular the new generation of youth which had come to prominence in the post-state period, and which had gained Israel's security, and which appealed to a wide cross-section of youthful voters, had to be represented prominently at the parliamentary level. Similar considerations applied to Oriental ethnic groups.

Mapai's internal methods of leadership selection at the parliamentary and ministerial levels were not highly democratic in any strict sense of rank and file participation. But viewed over the long term, perhaps the most interesting factor relating to Knesset selection was the tendency of increasing democratisation. This came about in two ways. The first were the constitutional changes. The second was the practice of intensive consultation by the appointments committee with all sections of the party. On the other hand, it must be noted that this took place within the limits imposed by the list system demanding the ranking of candidates by a committee, thereby denying possibilities of public or rank and file expressions of confidence or otherwise in their representatives.

The spread of representation clearly facilitated the processes of interest articulation and the party's role in interest aggregation. Not only did this occur because parliamentary representation gave access to ministerial and bureaucratic decisions but it was further promoted by the internal arrangements of the Parliamentary Party. In its own operations and in those of the legislative committees there were ample opportunities to articulate and press interests, and have them catered for, in what was a flexible legislative decision making process. Its flexibility and fluidity was even further advanced by the possibility of pressing such issues through internal party institutions in situations where the parliamentary channels had been exhausted or had not proved successful. Among all the internal party election and selection processes, those that seemed to arouse the least controversy and opposition were in the parliamentary and ministerial sphere. This agreement provided the party's ministerial and parliamentary leadership with an important degree of legitimacy, which facilitated its search for the political support that helped to make it an effective ruling group. Clearly, leaderships that enjoy legitimacy will find it easier to gain support for their policies and actions by consensual means than those which do not.

A crucial element in maintaining such legitimacy and support derived from the practices the party developed in connecting external leaders and representatives with internal party institutions, which we termed the primacy of party. Mapai, as we showed, trod a fine line between parliamentary independence and party control. It avoided conflicting relationships between parliamentarians and ministers, on the one hand, and internal party institutions, on the other. Mapai's relationships in this sphere are interesting examples of consensual power relationships based upon common agreement, compromise and the desire to find mutually agreeable solutions through discussion. In this the party was assisted by the face to face relationships that existed within these leadership groups, which were small in size, and where leaders were well known to each other. But this structural factor should not mask the conscious search for agreement by party leaders based upon the general interests of the party, and its public and parliamentary needs for clear and responsible policies.

Certain practices that it adopted contributed to effective policy making, thereby adding to its control and direction of governmental structures. Conflict between parliamentarians and ministers was generally avoided, mainly because both deferred in the last resort to the internal party institutions – which meant of course the primacy of party. This came through most clearly in the settlement of the Govrin dispute, where the solution adopted in cases of disagreement was precisely that – to turn to internal party bodies as the forum within which solutions would be found.

Moreover, conflict between the Parliamentary Party and internal party institutions was also carefully avoided. On the one hand, parliamentarians and ministers recognised the constitutional supremacy and primacy of party institutions. This was enhanced because the party did not attempt to enforce its supremacy through discipline and control – but, on the contrary, granted wide scope and independence to parliamentarians in pursuit of their responsibilities. There was mutual recognition of the legitimate roles of the other. When disagreements occurred they were generally ironed out collectively and in a spirit of the need for mutual agreement. This process was greatly assisted by a number of structural factors. Many parliamentarians were members of internal party institutions and, in particular, leading parliamentarians and ministers were widely regarded and accepted as key party leaders, which gave them great influence in the intra-party discussions.

10. DECISION MAKING

To date we have been concerned with the incorporation of groups and interests within Mapai, and with the local and central organisational structures which united those interests, represented Mapai in outside bodies and directed them, and made decisions inside and outside the party. We have also examined the organisational developments of Mapai's decision making bodies – the hierarchy of institutions, their shifting power and authority, the growth of informal bodies, the development of the party machine, the pressures for rank and file participation, the problems of coordination, patterns of leadership selection, and the way in which Mapai directed key institutions. But merely to know, for example, that a decision was taken in the Central Committee leaves unanswered a number of important questions. More must be known about the actual decision making process – how the various groups and factions lined up, their arguments, the differences between various policy proposals, the factors influencing the final decision reached, and its relation to the initial proposals. To come to grips with these questions we must look at actual decision making processes as they occurred within the party institutions.

The examination of some key decisions and decision making areas in this and succeeding chapters – wages policies, aspects of economic policy, foreign and defence policy, education, employment and health services, and the Alignment with Achdut Haavoda, are particularly useful for an analysis of some of our major theoretical concerns. We shall view decision making from the point of view of participation, in order to assess who participated, whom they represented, and how responsive they were to their followers, which focuses directly on questions of leadership and power relations. We shall also examine decision making in terms of the various patterns of interest incorporation into Mapai. We suggested above that interest incorporation was crucial to the party because it connected diverse social forces with governing structures, and thereby provided support for policies. But this, of course, was dependent upon the policies themselves. The incorporation of divergent and conflicting interest groups may just as easily create difficulties for decision making. Too many conflicting groups may lead to a form of policy paralysis through inability to chart a clear policy approach between these interests. Mapai, as we argued above, expected that the common straddle of party loyalty would facilitate compromises and that groups would all give in somewhat to promote the common party interest. But there were also limits to this process. By examining the decision making process we can assess the degree of Mapai's success in developing decision making capacity.

We hope to illuminate these theoretical questions in this chapter with an analysis of two major areas of decision making in the governmental and Histadrut spheres: wages policy and key aspects of economic policy, and foreign and defence policy (and also in the decisions analysed in slightly different contexts in later chapters). But it should also be made quite clear at the outset what these case studies are *not* intended to do. Mapai controlled the government after 1948 and in that period many fundamental policies were adopted under its leadership and many key decisions taken in different fields. This analysis is not intended to provide a comprehensive coverage of all those policy decisions. Neither is it intended to represent a substantive assessment of the policies themselves, nor is it concerned with a historical account of the development of particular policies from their origins to their effects after implementation. Our focus is on the *internal* processes within Mapai, and on external factors only in so far as they affected the internal situation. Thus among key aspects of decision making excluded are coalition politics, the policies of the opposition parties, the detailed role of the civil service and legislative committees, and the merits and demerits of competing policy approaches. The major criterion has been those decisions which aroused opposition within the party, which were critical rather than routine, and which, therefore, illuminate the party's internal decision making processes. Thus, for example, many contentious aspects of foreign policy such as German Reparations, relations with West Germany, and early policies towards the Communist Bloc are not examined because Mapai was basically agreed upon its policies, and conflict, discussion and debate took place between parties, not within Mapai. Similarly, many major decisions in other governmental fields are not dealt with here primarily because they, too, were made outside the party sphere, albeit by Mapai politicians. A fair assumption in these cases is that the party was in agreement with what occurred, for if it were not it had the power, the means and the institutions whereby it could express a contrary view, as the following examples clearly demonstrate.

Wages policy

In 1948 the principal method of deciding wages policy rested in the periodic adjustments negotiated between the Manufacturers Association and the Histadrut in accordance with changes in the cost of living as recorded in an official index of consumer prices of basic goods. Once this agreement was negotiated it was expected that all other employers would follow suit as far as minimum wages were concerned. In effect, then, this essentially private arrangement between the largest employers' and employees' representative bodies underwent country-wide adoption. Mapai had a large say in these matters through its control of the Histadrut. Thus just before the establishment of the state the Mapai Secretariat met to deal with the economic situation. Amongst the issues it discussed were ways and means of regulating wages. It handed this over to Mapai's representatives on the Central Executive Committee of the Histadrut and to its own Trade Union Department which were to meet and examine the economic situation and decide upon a policy.[1]

This institutional arrangement meant that the new government was completely left out of the framing of wages policy, despite the fact that the latter was clearly a central aspect of economic policy control and planning. The government might have legislated to take over this function itself, or to have erected a completely new set of institutional arrangements. But this would have deprived the Histadrut of a great deal of its power and authority and might have provoked a confrontation between them. The basic tendency of the government in the very early days, moreover, was to leave as they were things that were operating efficiently. Clearly the Histadrut had to be involved in this sphere; the problem was not how to exclude it, but how to include the government so that it could influence the making of wages policy and align it with its general economic policies. The most obvious way was for this to be done within the framework of Mapai where the leadership of both the Histadrut and the government were represented, and where there existed institutions which could decide between them.

It must be remembered that in 1948 the Histadrut was not equivalent to trade union movements and federations in other countries. At the apex of the labour movement, its political parties, agricultural settlements, industrial undertakings, its network of social, health and educational institutions, and its sponsorship of the Hagana, all gave it enormous prestige and its leaders great authority. Having preceded the state it not only enjoyed the advantages of a high degree of institutionalisation, and the loyalty of its members and constituent parties, but also carried out functions that had to be taken over from it by the state. Thus at the time of the establishment of the state they were potentially greater rivals than subsequently when the state came into its own. While willingly handing over to the state such functions as defence, and later education, Histadrut leaders were on the alert to guard against the complete replacement of the Histadrut and the gradual stripping of its powers. This was particularly the case in the area of trade union matters – the original core and genesis of its activities. In this area the state had no standing whatsoever, and no obvious claim to exercise its authority, and here more than anywhere else Mapai Histadrut leaders were likely to oppose too great a state intervention. Mapai government leaders therefore had to tread rather carefully in attempting to influence decisions which ultimately would have to be

[1] *Hapoel Hatzair*, 13.4.1948.

formalised in an agreement between the Histadrut and the Manufacturers Association. Applying influence was about all they could do, the logical place to do so being within Mapai. In this situation, initiative lay very much in the hands of Mapai Histadrut leaders.

Immediately after 1948 the country passed through a period of austerity in which the Histadrut gave full support to the government's economic measures. Thus in 1949 the Histadrut Conference decided that wage rises would occur only on the basis of individual incentive payments for exceeding set production quotas. In the second and third quarters of 1949 the cost of living index registered two successive declines owing to strict price control, which, according to the principle of automatic adjustment, indicated that wages of workers were to be reduced commensurately. This was done in July 1949 but when the second successive decline took place in October worker opposition was such that an inquiry was instituted to see whether the existing index adequately measured living costs. This led eventually to the development of a more accurate index some two years later.[2] In 1950 the Histadrut further supported the government's efforts to improve the chaotic economic situation. By this time inflation was rapidly increasing, the black market was doing a roaring trade and the cost of living was rising fast. The Histadrut reiterated its view that increases in wages be tied to increases in production, and this decision was accepted by Mapai party institutions without dissent. These attempts to achieve austerity were not wholeheartedly supported by the workers, however, and many local Labour Councils and national unions demanded and received wage rises in direct negotiations with employers. Nevertheless, the Histadrut leadership was determined to hold the line, and the wages policy that it proposed for 1951 (approved by the Mapai Central Committee) included only minor wage rises in a number of limited areas.[3]

Particularly significant at the end of 1950 was the attitude to wages policy adopted by the leadership of the Histadrut Trade Union Department at the Central Committee. Relations between Histadrut and government leaders had not been good during the preceding few years. In particular, the Histadrut was unhappy about the treatment of persons employed in government service, and the intention of the government to exclude the Histadrut from its usual role as representative of labour in disputes relating to government employees, although eventually an accord was reached in 1952 which met the Histadrut's objections.[4] More specifically the Histadrut leadership was disturbed at what it regarded as a lack of cooperation on the part of the government, and its

---

[2] This period is more fully covered in M. Derber, 'National Wage Policy in Israel, 1948–62', *Quarterly Review of Economics and Business*, 3 (1963), 47–9.
[3] *Minutes Mapai Central Committee*, 21.12.1950.
[4] On the later development of this issue see *Minutes Mapai Central Committee*, 10.7.1952.

neglect to consult sufficiently with the Histadrut leadership on economic affairs in general.[5]

The Mapai Histadrut Trade Union Department leadership also served notice that it was neither going to be dictated to by the government in matters of wages policy, nor would it take orders on any matters within its sphere relating to workers, even if these came from Mapai ministers, and in matters directly relevant to their ministries. It sought cooperation and joint activity with the proviso that in cases of disagreement neither the Histadrut nor the Mapai ministers would have the right to make the decision, but that this would be done by the party's decision making institutions. Thus party mediation and decision in matters of wages policy was demanded by both sides. The government supported it because this was an acceptable way for it to try and influence this aspect of economic policy and the most likely to avoid headlong collision with the Histadrut. The Histadrut approved because it recognised the right of the government to a say, albeit not the decisive say, in these matters, and therefore sought a body to decide disagreements in which the Histadrut would be well represented and on which it would have a fair chance of having its views prevail. In general, both attitudes fitted in neatly with previous Mapai practices and views of the primacy of the party over its elected delegates and representatives in whichever capacity they served.[6]

The need to put such ideas into action was not long in coming. Early in 1951 a major strike in the crucial metal manufacturing industry secured a wage increase of over 15 per cent and this was followed by strikes in other industries with similar results. At the same time inflationary pressures were spiralling, and black marketeering and tax evasion spreading, leading early in 1952 to the introduction of the New Economic Policy, including a major devaluation and other measures to curb inflation, increase production and encourage investment.[7] Concurrently with the adoption of the new policy the Histadrut framed its wages demands for 1952 which were brought before the Mapai Central Committee late in 1951. The Histadrut again stressed its adherence to the principle of tying wage increases to increased production and profitability, to be accomplished by extending the adoption of production quotas and premiums throughout the economy. The cost of living principle was to be maintained, but its ceiling was raised significantly, and a new index instituted. It also recommended that wages be increased by 10 to 15 per cent for workers who had not benefited from the increases gained in the earlier strikes. At the Central Committee the first two aspects were readily accepted, but the last was opposed by all Mapai ministers except one, Mr Eshkol, the

[5] Ibid. 21.12.1950.   [6] Ibid.
[7] On the economic conditions 1949–51 see Don Patinkin, The Israel Economy: the First Decade (Falk Project, Fourth Report 1957 and 1958, Jerusalem, 1959), pp. 108–11. For a brief analysis of the New Economic Policy see Eisenstadt, Israeli Society, pp. 115–16.

Minister of Finance. Prior to its meeting there had been long and vigorous discussion in a special Economic Committee set up by the Secretariat in 1951 to assist in the overall economic policy planning, which eventuated in the New Economic Policy, and wages policy was intended to form part of this overall economic plan. Represented on the committee were Mapai ministers, Histadrut officials, and leading Mapai members of the Knesset's Finance and Economic Committees. One issue on which no agreement was reached was that of a wage increase and it was for this reason that it had to be decided by the Central Committee. The Central Committee meeting witnessed the participation of many leading Mapai activists in more important trade unions and larger Workers Committees, who, during the course of the debate, placed considerable pressure upon the delegates in support of the wage rises. When the vote was taken all of Mr Becker's recommendations on behalf of the Trade Union Department were accepted; the controversial wage rise passed narrowly 26:23, out of a possible 150 voting members of the Central Committee.[8]

The wages policy for 1953–5 (inclusive) was marked by the Histadrut's stringent efforts to maintain a policy of wage restraint, that is to say, no rise in wage levels. Cost of living payments and premiums, on the other hand, were continued, there being seven increases in the cost of living adjustment, and in 1954 the ceiling was raised significantly to take account of the wage rises of the previous two years. Within the party a definite pattern had begun to emerge in the making of wages policy. It was first discussed among Mapai's members of the Trade Union Department of the Histadrut and after a policy had been roughly worked out it was brought to the relevant party institutions – its trade union section and Secretariat – for discussion and final decision. Intra-party wages policy deliberations for 1954 were carried out even more systematically. On this occasion they took place in the Political Committee, in the party trade union section, and in a joint committee of Mapai ministers and members of the Central Executive Committee, the end result being a continuation of the previous policy.[9]

During 1954 increasing pressure was brought to bear on the Histadrut by the minority parties, Achdut Haavoda and Mapam, to raise wage levels by about 15 per cent. Mapai's Histadrut leaders were not at all disposed to accede to these demands but the nature of the political pressure made it imperative that action be taken to ensure Mapai rank and file support for any policy of wage restraint and the maintenance of the system of production premiums and cost of living adjustments. The first step was to establish a small committee of the Secretariat to draw up such a policy, which gained the support of both the Mapai ministers and the Histadrut leadership. An extensive campaign to gain support for the policy was launched among activists in party

[8] *Haaretz*, 30.12.1951; *Report of Mapai Headquarters to 8th Conference, 1956*, p. 14.
[9] *Minutes Mapai Central Committee*, 22.11.1953.

branches, local Labour Councils, party representatives on large Workers Committees, and the leaders of the national unions. Only after this was the wage freeze policy brought to the Central Committee for final decision. There the suggestion of activists, who sought to match the opposition parties' suggested wages rise of 15 per cent, received no support. The Mapai Histadrut leaders argued that increased wages would lead to inflation, affecting workers worse than others. Although some twenty-three members of the Central Committee abstained when the vote was taken no one voted against.[10]

The debate over the 1956 wages policy was more protracted and complex than any preceding it. During 1955 professionals had become extremely restive and serious strikes had broken out. As a result the Guri Committee was set up to examine professional salaries, and it decided to increase them by about 15 per cent. Non-professional workers, spurred on by the success of the professionals and by the general improvement in economic conditions in Israel, pressed for similar increases. In October 1955 a committee established by the Mapai Secretariat to look into the matter recommended a general wage increase of between 5 and 15 per cent, over the opposition of Mr Eshkol, the Minister of Finance, who believed that a general increase was too inflationary. Towards the end of 1955 his arguments were given added weight by the emergency situation created by the Czech–Egyptian arms deal. The Histadrut had also pressed for special measures of income redistribution to ameliorate the economic problems of the very low wage earners. In view of the defence and security problems, and of the strong stand taken by Eshkol, Mapai's Histadrut leadership agreed to reconsider its demands, and to try and frame them within a general emergency policy. Mr Eshkol sought to freeze wages for six months as part of an Emergency Plan, to levy a Defence Tax, and to cut expenses, and initially the Histadrut agreed to these.

The opposition parties maintained constant pressure to increase wages at least 10 per cent, and even an impassioned appeal to them by Ben Gurion to withdraw in view of the security situation went unheeded. The Histadrut leadership and Mapai economic ministers also proposed that the raise of 15 per cent promised to academics and professionals be cut in half, because of the emergency situation. This, needless to say, was unacceptable to them and they pressed for full payment in 1956. The Histadrut was caught under the tremendous cross pressure of the government, on the one hand, and of professional workers, opposition parties, non-professional workers, and many of its own local trade union activists, on the other. The matter was brought to the Mapai Central Committee for decision early in 1956.

Two separate recommendations were brought to the Central Committee, one of Mr Eshkol for a wage freeze, and another of Mr Becker for salary increases for all workers of between 4 and 10 per cent. When put to the vote Mr Eshkol's recommendation received thirty-six votes as against thirty-seven

[10] Ibid. 2.12.1954; Haaretz, 3.12.1954.

votes for Mr Becker's, and in view of the narrow margin it was decided to pass the matter on to the Secretariat to decide in joint consultation with Mapai's ministers and members of the Central Executive Committee, in conjunction with the original wages committee. Under the tremendous pressures outlined above the Secretariat opted for Mr Becker's recommendation which was then sent back to the Central Committee for ratification. This was passed 39:13 with ninety-one abstentions, including that of Mr Eshkol, with the opposition coming mainly from representatives of agricultural settlements. The extraordinary proportion of abstentions gives clear indication of the difficulty of this decision. It was also decided to ask the professionals to accept a compromise whereby only half their promised increase would be paid, but the latter remained adamant, and went out on strike in February. A compromise was later reached to pay them two-thirds of their increase in 1956 and the rest spread over 1957–8. The major factors leading to this decision were the recommendations of a government-appointed inquiry that increases to professionals ought to be paid, supported even by leading officials in the Ministry of Finance opposed to all other salary increases, and rank and file pressure of Mapai trade union activists stirred on by the opposition parties. (Interestingly enough, Haifa Mapai and Labour Council, normally outspoken and activist in these issues, supported a wage freeze.) Thus the end solution was a reduced general increase all across the board spread out over a much longer period of time.[11]

In preparation for the 8th Mapai Conference in 1956 a comprehensive debate on economic policy took place in a committee chaired by Govrin. Originally known as the Committee of Eleven, it became an official subcommittee of the Conference Standing Committee. Represented were Mapai ministers, its Parliamentary Party and Histadrut leaders. One of the more contentious subjects which it considered and brought before the Conference was the cost of living index. At that time the automatic adjustment was calculated every three months and was applied if the index showed a rise in costs of more than three points (3 per cent). The Minister of Finance and Treasury officials were anxious to stem the inflationary tide and one of the methods they suggested was to lengthen this period to six months, in order to reduce the frequency of impact of inflationary pressure. This move was not opposed basically by the Histadrut Trade Union Department leadership who recognised the need for the introduction of some change, but it aroused widespread apprehension among local trade union activists, particularly those from Haifa, that the cost of living adjustment was to be done away with completely. No such suggestion came before the Conference, but it was clear from their speeches that leading Mapai economic ministers, Eshkol and

---

[11] Ibid. 1.12.1955, 15.12.1955, 5.1.1956, 9.1.1956; Davar, 5.1.1956, 8.1.1956, 9.1.1956. See also M. Derber, 'National Wage Policy and Israel's Wage Differential: A Persisting Problem', Midstream, 9 (March 1963), 3–15.

Sapir, believed that inflationary pressures and the country's inability to improve its export position were directly due to the system of cost of living adjustments. Nor would a move at that time to abolish it completely have succeeded, for the Histadrut trade union leadership regarded it as one of the major mechanisms protecting the country's workers from inflation.

Due to these conflicting views the Standing Committee merely recommended to the Conference in the most general terms that changes be introduced into the cost of living adjustment system, and left it to the Central Committee to decide their precise nature – their incidence, structure, and for how long the period would be extended, etc. Govrin also announced that a six-month period was under consideration even though this did not appear in the resolution. The delegates from Haifa led by Almogi opposed any change, even in principle, on the grounds that the changes mentioned would worsen the position of workers. They called for further discussion of the issue by the Central Committee. A third and more radical approach was advocated by Asher Yadlin, one of the more vocal *Zeirim*, and an economist by training. This was to abolish automatic cost of living adjustments and to protect the worker against inflationary pressure and rising prices through the bargaining facilities of the collective agreements made annually, bearing in mind the increase in production, skill, and the state of the particular industry and the plant within the industry. On being put to the vote the recommendation of the Standing Committee received 594 votes, the Haifa amendments 64 votes, and Yadlin's proposal 21 votes.[12]

The new Secretariat appointed a committee consisting of Almogi, Becker, Govrin, Lavon, Namir, Sapir and Shechter to investigate this matter and report back to the Central Committee. It recommended that future cost of living adjustments be made every six months which was passed without any real dissent.[18] This was only the first step in a series of moves to lessen the impact of inflationary pressures. Early in 1957 the Histadrut altered the existing arrangements regarding the Collective Agreements negotiated annually by making them valid in future for a two-year period. The Sinai campaign and the subsequent threat of United States sanctions again produced overall economic planning and the incorporation of wages policy within the Emergency Plan. The Secretariat after meeting with the full Economic Committee appointed a small committee to prepare such a plan, which consisted of Mapai economic ministers, Histadrut and Trade Union Department leaders, representatives of the Parliamentary Party, members of its Finance Committee, and the party Secretary-General. Mr Eshkol suggested a limit to the cost of living adjustment in the event of price increases. The Histadrut representatives, Becker and Lavon, rejected this, claiming that it would hit

[12] *Report 8th Mapai Conference*, 1956, pp. 377–84. See also speeches of Eshkol, pp. 40–56, Becker, pp. 92–6, Sapir, pp. 136–47.
[18] *Haaretz*, 24.9.1956.

workers the hardest. The result was a compromise agreement to institute a
compulsory loan which would effectively remove 7 per cent of the workers'
spending power. Eventually with Israeli withdrawal from Sinai and the
removal of the threat of sanctions this became academic and a return to the
normal conditions of wages policy making was made possible. The 1957 wages
policy therefore included not only changes in the cost of living adjustment,
but raised the ceiling below which cost of living adjustments were paid from
IL125 to IL500 (the average wage at the time being about IL220). Fringe
benefits for the lowest-paid workers were increased and taxes on them reduced. Non-professional workers also demanded that the proportion of the
1956 increase that had been frozen because of the defence crisis (one-third of
the total increase) now be paid to them, which was agreed to, thus putting
them on a par with the professionals.[14]

The economic situation improved rapidly during 1957–8 and inflation was
kept low, thus obviating conflict between the government and the Histadrut
on wages policies. In March 1958 Mapai's Economic Committee decided that
income tax would not in future be paid on the cost of living adjustments and
this was passed through the legislative channels.[15] At the end of 1958, when
policy was made for the next two years, little basic change was made. No
general increases were proposed but provision was made for those industrial
workers who had not received the proportion frozen in 1956 to receive it.
Similarly, increased family allowances were made and various fringe benefits
for a number of specific groups of workers were also achieved.

In July 1960 the cost of living index was examined and it showed a rise of
2.9 per cent, fractionally below the 3 per cent which would have necessitated
an automatic adjustment. The Mapai Secretariat met to discuss this problem
with the Histadrut pressing for payment, despite the statistics, on the grounds
that this would harness demands for wage rises. Opposition came from Mapai
ministers, Eshkol, Sapir, Dayan, and Meir on the usual grounds. A committee
elected by the Secretariat to decide this matter, consisting of Eshkol, Dayan,
Meir, Sapir, Almogi, Becker, Govrin, and Haring, agreed to leave it to the
Central Executive Committee. The Trade Union Department met and recommended to the Central Executive Committee that the increase be paid. In this
instance it was clear to the ministers that the statistics were so close that their
chances of being successful were slight.[16]

In 1960 the Histadrut decided that in future it would base its claims for
wage increases on net national income, and at the end of the year the economic statisticians showed that on this basis for the 1961–2 period an increase
of between 6 and 8 per cent was justified. This proposal was not forcefully
opposed by Mapai ministers during intensive discussions at the Secretariat,
and indirect negotiations between ministers and Histadrut leaders, and was

[14] Ibid. 11.1.1957, 12.2.1957; Davar, 8.2.1957, 10.2.1957, 13.2.1957.
[15] Davar, 24.3.1958.   [16] Haaretz, 22.7.1960, 25.7.1960.

applied to industry. Professionals and those employed in the public service, by way of contrast, got increases of about 12 per cent after a series of strikes, but these were based upon the decreasing differential rather than on the general calculation.[17]

The government announced a major currency devaluation in February 1962 followed by major economic policy changes. The devaluation of 66 per cent sparked off a major conflict in Mapai over the cost of living payment. At the end of 1961 the consumers' price index had risen 2.8 per cent which was below the 3 per cent required for an adjustment. However, immediately after the announcement of the policy changes the index rose over the 3 per cent barrier, and there were demands that an immediate adjustment be made in view of the fact that prices were likely to rise even further in the wake of the devaluation. The opposition parties in the Histadrut pressed these views and more importantly they were adopted by the Histadrut. The matter came before Mapai's decision making institutions, in the first instance to the Economic Committee, which delegated the matter to its Secretariat. Three proposals lay before it. Eshkol, the Minister of Finance, opposed making any payments before they were due on 1 July. Histadrut Secretary-General Becker proposed that all workers be paid as from April in accordance with the then percentage increase in the COL index. Almogi, Minister without Portfolio, suggested a compromise – that the increase be paid in April but only to lower-income groups. Eshkol's approach, based upon the need to keep costs down in order to enable the devaluation to have the desired effects, was strongly supported by the kibbutz and moshav movements, but was defeated 7:3 receiving only the votes of Eshkol, Sapir and Dayan, all ministers. Then the Becker and Almogi alternatives were put to the vote, but were tied 4:4. Supporting Becker were Becker, Meshel and Haring, all leading Histadrut figures, and Govrin, chairman of the Parliamentary Party and a trade union official prior to entering parliament. Support for Almogi's proposal came from Almogi, Dayan, Eshkol and Barkat, the party Secretary-General. In view of the indecisiveness of the voting and the importance of the issue the matter was brought to the Secretariat for decision. There Eshkol received fourteen votes to ten for Becker's proposal. An analysis of the support for each side reveals some interesting sidelights. Eshkol's stand was supported by seven ministers and one deputy minister, three other members of Knesset, including the chairman of the Knesset's Finance Committee, the party Secretary-General, a representative on the Executive of the Jewish Agency, and the delegate of the Ichud. Becker's proposal was supported by eight leading Histadrut officials and two members of Knesset, Govrin and Aranne, both with backgrounds of Histadrut activity. Almogi's suggested compromise was also put to the Secretariat and received only five votes, those of Almogi

---

[17] *Davar*, 21.12.1960; *Minutes Mapai Central Committee*, 19.1.1961; Derber, 'Israel's Wage Differential'.

himself, Baram, M.K., formerly secretary of the Jerusalem Labour Council, Moyal, Secretary of the Beer Sheba Labour Council, Shapira, of the Histadrut's Agricultural Centre, and Yeshayahu, M.K. The distribution of support is significant. Almogi, together with a number of other activists in local Labour Councils had traditionally supported special measures to assist those in the lowest income brackets, and here Baram and Moyal were motivated by the same considerations. Moyal and Yeshayahu were both representatives of non-European ethnic groups which were heavily represented among the lowest income earners. Shapira was in charge of the Histadrut's Agricultural Centre, and in his sphere of influence were included all employed (and unemployed) agricultural labourers, also in the low income brackets. This breakdown of voting on this issue indicates an almost perfectly symmetrical relationship between socio-economic interest and attitude.

Becker announced that he would appeal to the Central Committee against this decision. Before its meeting further discussion took place on the Economic Committee and the Mapai Secretariat, and agreement was reached on the Almogi proposal with one major change. Instead of the advance on the cost of living adjustment due in July being paid by the employers it was suggested that this be paid by the government out of National Insurance funds so as to prevent any subsequent inflationary price rises. This was passed at the Central Committee 148:38 with 61 abstentions. Two factors altered the initial decision of the Secretariat to support the Eshkol position. The first was genuine concern over the situation of the poor who would be relatively most affected by the rising prices as many of these were of essentials. The second was the intense political pressure exerted by the minority parties in the Histadrut, which virtually forced Mapai's Histadrut leadership to obtain some benefits for workers.[18]

Nor was this the end of the post-devaluation cost of living battle within Mapai. In July payments were due to all workers and the statistics indicated that the rise in the index was likely to be in the vicinity of 7 per cent by the end of June. Moreover, it would have to be paid to those in higher income brackets as well. The government, fearful of inflationary pressure, sought ways and means to stabilise the situation. Mr Eshkol and his ministry officials worked out a scheme that half of this be paid in some form of promissory note to be redeemed after the elapse of a sufficient period of time, and thus give the economy a chance to benefit from the new policies. After initial preliminary discussions with the Manufacturers Association to see how they might react to such a scheme, Mr Eshkol brought it to the Secretariat of the Economic Committee. Here complaints were voiced that the matter had been discussed with the Manufacturers Association before Mapai's Histadrut leadership and party institutions had been consulted. During the discussion

---

[18] *Haaretz*, 1.3.1962, 15.3.1962, 30.3.1962; *Davar*, 15–18.3.1962, 23.3.1962; *Hapoel Hatzair*, 20.3.1962, 27.3.1962.

all parties agreed upon the necessity of maintaining the COL adjustment as a basic mechanism of wages policy, but they differed, predictably, in that the Histadrut representatives opposed the move. Discussions here did not manage to move either side from its position, with the result that the Secretariat of the Economic Committee appointed a special committee to examine these proposals and other ways of preventing price rises. The members of this Mapai committee were Mr Eshkol, Mr Becker, Mr Arnon, Director-General of the Ministry of Finance, Mr Cochav, another leading civil servant in the economic planning area, Mr Meshel, head of the Trade Union Department, and Mr David Golomb, Director of the Histadrut's Social and Economic Research Institute. Simultaneously Mr Eshkol raised the matter at a Cabinet meeting from whence it would pass as a matter of course to the Ministerial Committee for Economic Affairs. Here, too, Mr Eshkol was put on the defensive by other non-Mapai ministers who maintained that the matter should have come to Cabinet before being discussed by the Manufacturers Association and the Histadrut. Mr Eshkol, on the other hand, preferred to have some indication of likely reactions to enable him to frame a concrete proposal for Cabinet consideration.

The Ministerial Economic Committee decided against Eshkol's suggestion and came up with another for a Compulsory Savings Loan, which was then worked out in detail by Ministry of Finance officials. It subsequently received the approval of both the Secretariat and the full Economic Committee of Mapai, and only after this of the Cabinet. At the same time the Manufacturers Association agreed to hold prices in line, and in view of the combined nature of the package there was no opposition from the Histadrut.[19]

At the end of 1962 wages policy for the following two years was due to be made, but in the event it was made for 1963 only. At the outset Eshkol and Sapir demanded a wage freeze for two years, but during discussions at the Economic Committee it turned out that they would accept a one-year freeze. The discussions took place in a widened committee, including the acting chairman of the Parliamentary Party, the chairman of the Knesset Finance Committee, party representatives in the Trade Union Department, the secretaries of the Jerusalem, Haifa, Tel Aviv, Ramat Gan, Petach Tikva, and Beer Sheba Labour Councils, as well as some economic experts. It had also become apparent in the discussions that the Histadrut leadership and its Trade Union Department would also agree to a policy of restraint and a wage freeze for one year, despite tremendous pressure from local trade union activists who demanded an increase of 5 per cent in basic wage levels right across the board. But they also sought a guarantee that current price and tax levels would be maintained as a condition of their agreement, and requested that the Compulsory Savings Loan be not reinstituted after it expired in April. The committee accepted this proposal and handed it to a team of economic

19 *Davar*, 24.4.1962, 29.4.1962, 30.4.1962, 2.5.1962, 6.5.1962, 7.5.1962.

experts to work out the details. Before the Economic Committee made a final decision the party Secretariat initiated an intensive grass-roots campaign to explain to trade union activists and rank and file members why the policy of restraint was necessary, and that guarantees would be inserted to safeguard the workers' economic position. Thus over fifty meetings involving Mapai's national union, local Labour Council and party branch activists in the main areas of Histadrut concentration were held in the space of a few weeks. When this was concluded, the Secretariat, with the participation of the full Economic Committee and the Mapai members of the Central Executive Committee, and of the Knesset's Economic Committee 'recommended to the government and the Histadrut' that the policy be accepted. In its major sections the policy adopted was as already agreed upon by Mapai's economic ministers and Histadrut leadership. These included a one-year wage freeze, extended family benefit payments for low income earners tied to a general economic policy of no increases in direct or indirect taxes of both central and municipal governments, no further compulsory savings scheme and increased efforts to keep prices in check.[20]

Again at the end of 1963 wages policy was to be decided for the period 1964–5. At this time the Histadrut leadership based its claims upon exact statistics about the past and the projected growth of net national product, which indicated an increase of 8 to 9 per cent over the two-year period. The Histadrut had already agreed in 1960 to follow this measure closely in making wages policy, but in attempting to do so it met with strong opposition from the Minister of Finance, Sapir, and the leadership of the Mapai Parliamentary Party who warned against disturbing the relative economic stability and opposed any increase in wages. The statistical evidence for the Histadrut's claims made it clear that within Mapai's Economic Committee and Secretariat, the ministers would not be successful despite their dire warnings of economic instability. But their stand, together with that of the parliamentary section, did result in a lessening of the Histadrut demands. The Histadrut leadership now suggested a policy of increasing wages by 3 per cent in 1964 and by a similar amount in 1965 (even though the statistics entitled them to 9 per cent over the two years). In explaining to Histadrut members why it had not pressed for the maximum, the leadership argued that recently granted income tax decreases should also be taken into consideration in assessing the workers' position (the Minister of Finance had claimed that this in itself was sufficient reason for no rise at all), and that calculations showed that wages would rise anyhow another 1½ per cent through above-award payments, promotions and so on. It also pressed for another increase in the ceiling for the payment of COL adjustments to IL700 which would maintain differentials and lighten

[20] *Haaretz*, 19.11.1962; *Hapoel Hatzair*, 20.11.1962, 27.11.1962, 18.12.1962. See also Y. Meshel, *The Histadrut's Wages Policy for 1963/4* (Information Dept., Histadrut, Tel Aviv, 1963), (Hebrew).

pressure from the more restive professionals, white collar workers and skilled industrial workers, and for the payment of a 4.7 per cent increase in the cost of living adjustment as indicated by the index. In addition family allowances for low income earners were further raised. All of these demands were passed easily, first in the Economic Committee, later in the Secretariat with the participation of the Executive of the Mapai Parliamentary Party, the Mapai members of the Central Executive Committee and the Trade Union Department and the members of the Economic Committee, and later at the Central Committee.[21]

This analysis of the development of wages policies and the processes undergone in making them suggests a number of general observations and conclusions about their characteristic features and political implications. Because private employers in Israel are relatively weak in their bargaining positions union leaders are under greater pressure than in countries where employers are strong. In the latter, union leaders can partially resist the inevitable rank and file demands for higher wages and improved conditions by pointing to the strength of the opposition. In Israel the Histadrut leadership must itself shoulder the responsibility for not giving in to pressure. But conversely, union leaders in Israel, in general, and the top Histadrut officials, in particular, owe their positions and offices to political parties, mainly Mapai, thus effectively protecting them from rank and file deposition. Nevertheless this did not eliminate completely the need for the centralised Histadrut leadership to itself withstand rank and file pressure and to explain why it did so. This pressure was strategically reinforced by the awareness that the Histadrut was potentially capable of bringing down the government and able to impose any wages policy that it desired upon the employers and the rest of the country. But the exercise of potential power demands an act of will by those possessing it, and there is no evidence that this was even a remote possibility.

In view of this tremendous power potential one is struck by the sense of self-restraint and responsibility demonstrated by Mapai's Histadrut leadership throughout this period. Yet one familiar with the origins and history of the Histadrut would not be surprised in the least, for from its very outset the Histadrut saw itself as the agent of the national purpose, as the servant of the Jewish people in bringing about the dream of centuries. The over-riding consideration motivating the Histadrut and its leadership was their conception of the national interest, and their concern with the wellbeing of the whole population and the state as a whole.[22] This was reinforced by its widespread membership, which embraced some 65 per cent of the total population. The history of the development of wages policy and the Histadrut's claims in this area reveal that the Histadrut was deeply concerned not only with the

[21] *Haaretz*, 20.12.1963, 16.1.1964; *Davar*, 19.12.1963, 25.12.1963, 16.1.1964, 19.1.1964, 21.3.1964; *Hapoel Hatzair*, 21.1.1964, 28.1.1964.
[22] For a characteristic statement of such views see Meshel, pp. 19–21.

social and economic needs and problems of the workers, but as well with the economic situation and the effects of their demands upon it. In most countries it is the task of the trade union to concern itself only with the former; it is up to the employer to take a stand on the issue of whether it is in the capacity of industry to pay these claims, and up to the government, in many cases, to examine the issue from the point of view of its effects upon the economy at large. What is interesting about the role performed by the Mapai Histadrut leadership, in the absence of strong employer organisation in Israel, is the degree to which the Histadrut considered the objective realities and problems of the economic situation and the effects of their claims upon society at large. Thus from the very outset of wages policy negotiations the parties were not far apart, by virtue of the fact that the Histadrut was little less concerned about the economy than the government and incorporated this into its thinking as a major policy principle. Similarly the government, led by Mapai, was deeply concerned with the fate of the workers, and as a socialist government was sympathetic to their needs and demands. This convergence was the basis for the relatively easy settlement of wages policy.

Whilst such convergence was the foundation upon which the relative ease of decision making in this area rested, the essential condition for bringing this about was the common party membership of the decision makers and common Mapai control of the two major institutions. Negatively, the costs of inability to reach agreement exerted tremendous pressure on the participants to resolve policy differences. This was reinforced by the desire to retain Mapai control of both these institutions, and the power and authority which the party acquired through this dual institutional supremacy. Positively, dual party control simply made it easier to reach decisions. This could be done within the confines of the party's decision making bodies, away from the glare of public controversy, amongst men who knew each other well, had worked together for many years, and shared common goals and aspirations, not least of which was common loyalty to a party in power and a determination to keep it there. One need only compare this with the usual processes of collective bargaining between employer organisations and employee bodies to recognise the advantages and special characteristics of this situation.

The decision making process also contributed to a strengthening of the practices and doctrine of the primacy of party and is in fact a classic example of that doctrine in operation. Where disagreements occurred between the party's representatives in the government and the Histadrut, no matter how powerful and prestigious these individuals were, they had to come to the party and its decision making bodies for settlement of the dispute. In short, the party, as such, decided the country's wages policy. In this context it mattered little that the major contenders were the Mapai ministers and the Histadrut leaders; the significant thing was that the forum that decided the matter was a party one. It was not an ad hoc body of the two sets of leaders meeting independently of all other party bodies, but rather a number of recognised party bodies on which were represented all sections of the party in which the decision was made. This was particularly evident in those instances when the party representatives in the government and the Histadrut were not able to reach prior agreement among themselves in smaller party bodies and the decision had to be made for them in the larger party bodies.

Basically there were two characteristic types of situation in the process of making wages policy decisions. The usual one was for initiative to be taken by the Histadrut, and for it to make claims and demands over the wages policy for future years. The government was then put in a more defensive position, and it had to indicate whether or not it opposed them. In the second situation the government took the initiative and let it be known that it would oppose future wage demands if they were not within certain limits, or that it would act to lessen the impact of cost of living adjustments or wage rises with compulsory loans or taxes. Then the Histadrut was put on the defensive and it either had to accept this or try to have the party bodies reject it. These differences led, in the 1960s, to the practice of informal contact between Mapai government and Histadrut leaders, often within the framework of *Chaveireinu*, where initial soundings were made, and each side was able to formulate its policy on the basis of the projected approach of the other, which was of great assistance to both.

These two situations led to the evolution of a form of decision making characterised by open debate within Mapai's decision making bodies, particularly the Secretariat and the Central Committee, and a body whose task in the two periods of its effective existence (1957–9, 1962–4) was the discussion of wages policy, the Economic Committee. This process was characterised furthermore by hard bargaining and by tremendous emphasis on compromise and flexibility. In fact, it provides a remarkable example of the consensual form of decision making analysed theoretically in chapter one. It is interesting that in these compromises the proposals put by the Histadrut were never defeated in Mapai bodies. That is to say, the government viewpoint was never the final decision. But from this one should not assume that the Histadrut could get its way as it wished and did so, and that the stand taken by the government was never really very important. To the contrary, it was highly significant in forcing the Histadrut to tailor its demands, to follow a policy of restraint and to compromise in the government's favour. Thus matters were usually decided by party institutions only after a great deal of effort in bringing the two sides closer together, and in encouraging mutual compromise.

The essence of the process, then, was that there be agreement between the government and the Histadrut. Once this had been achieved there was little room for any other group, and no scope for any other decision making body to influence policy. To the extent that these two reached agreement it was only rarely that other pressure could be exerted successfully. Thus the Histadrut was constantly under pressure from three different directions. There was first the constraining influence of the realities of the situation and these were represented by the Mapai ministers. There was second the extraneous political pressure of the minority opposition parties in the Histadrut which usually demanded radical wage increases far above those that the Mapai Histadrut leadership was willing to pay. There was no instance in which they demanded less or suggested that the Mapai Histadrut leadership had endangered economic stability by asking for too much. Then there was the pressure for wage increases exerted by Mapai's own local trade union activists and rank and file workers. Generally speaking, for political reasons, the Mapai Histadrut leadership was more vulnerable to the pressure exerted by the opposition parties. Having constantly to keep the political consequences of its wages policy in mind meant that the Mapai Histadrut leadership had to maintain that rank and file worker support which kept it in power in the Histadrut, and enabled it to make these decisions. Strong campaigning by the opposition parties coupled with general worker support for their position often pushed the Mapai Histadrut leadership into going further than it might otherwise have done. There was, of course, the opposite possibility, that the Mapai Histadrut leadership was able to use such opposition pressure to strengthen its case against the views of the Mapai economic ministers, and to give them reason to be more liberal. They, too, having Mapai's political interests at heart and particularly its specific need to retain joint control of the Histadrut and the government, were also vulnerable to strong opposition political pressure, and some critics have argued that this was often to the detriment of sound economic policy considerations.

While seemingly vulnerable to strong opposition party political pressure, the Mapai Histadrut leadership was much more resistant to that of the Mapai local trade union activists. It certainly listened to their views, and on many occasions they participated formally at various stages of the decision making process, including the very early ones when policies had not yet been crystallised. But the leadership rarely, if ever, gave in completely to this political pressure. When faced with pressure the Mapai Histadrut leadership and its party institutions campaigned strenuously in the local areas to explain their point of view. In doing so they were able to use the possible effects of wages policy decisions upon Mapai's political position in government to convince Mapai trade union activists to moderate their demands. To that extent the application of political considerations reinforced the economic justifications for restraint. Second, the local Mapai trade union and Labour Council activists were bureaucratically responsible either directly or indirectly to the Mapai Histadrut leadership and to the party institutions, both of which were therefore able to exert considerable pressure upon local officials to moderate their demands. But perhaps the most significant point of all was the way in which efforts were made to explain policies to the party activists and rank and file and to gain their support by persuasion. This is not surprising in view of the fact that these very individuals would be under the greatest pressure from the opposition parties in the work places and at the grass-roots level, and more than anyone else would have to explain and defend the party's policy.

Conspicuously absent from wages policy discussions were two groups. These were firstly the officials and managers of the vast Histadrut industrial complex who theoretically ought to have viewed the matter from the stand-point of employers. Whilst their views were often much closer to those of the government, they did not press them and thus exercised no independent function at all in the decision making process either within the confines of the Histadrut or within Mapai. In both these bodies, where differences of opinion occurred between the Histadrut's trade union section representing the interests of workers, and its industrial section representing those of employers concerned to maximise profit, the latter were completely subordinated to the former. The only legitimate consideration in this regard were the needs and situation of the workers, and not the effects that their demands would have on Histadrut industry from the employers' viewpoint. Or put in other words, the profitability of Histadrut enterprises was subordinated to the needs of their workers who theoretically owned these enterprises through their control of the Histadrut, their trade union. This subordination derived directly from the view of the Histadrut held by Mapai and by the Israeli labour movement at large, and by all sections of the Histadrut leadership – that in questions of economic priorities the trade union view and needs of workers for which the Histadrut had been established, came first. This preference was also clearly seen in the structural sphere. The Histadrut economic enterprises' leadership was far less prominent and influential than its trade union leadership. Moreover they shared the ideological viewpoint of the trade union leadership. Organisational cohesion was also relevant, for if the Histadrut ever became split and fought an internal capital–labour battle its very strength would be eroded.

The second group was agriculture, the vast network of Mapai-affiliated kibbutzim and moshavim. We have seen above how both of these opposed increased industrial wages and cost of living adjustments on economic and ideological grounds and although they made their stand known in no un-certain terms at party Conferences and when wages policies were discussed, their viewpoint did not have any discernible measure of influence. The point about rising costs and prices was already represented in the outlook of Mapai's economic ministers who were particularly conscious of inflationary pressures, and especially by the Minister of Agriculture. The ideological point was simply ignored.

The non-participation of these groups facilitated some of the flexibility and capacity to compromise that characterised the Mapai decision making process in this area. Not having to cope with many divergent and mutually contradictory interests at one and the same time effectively prevented the development of political immobilism and inability to make clear-cut policy decisions. As it was, the decision making process was not a simple one, but the fact that it was fought out within Mapai between its ministers and Histadrut leadership made it that much easier than it would have been had agriculture, artisans, professionals and the Histadrut industrial complex all taken an active part in the negotiations and discussions and applied heavy pressure on the Mapai decision making bodies.

One last feature of the wages policy decision process is the almost complete non-participation of Ben Gurion who throughout most of the period was Prime Minister. Even during the particularly difficult period immediately after the 1962 devaluation Ben Gurion did not lend public support to the actions of his economic ministers until the very end when his inactivity and the fact that he had gone on holidays immediately after the announcement were roundly criticised in some newspapers. One can look at this in a number of different ways. There is firstly the well-known fact that Ben Gurion was not interested in economic and financial matters, reserving his major energies for other spheres, defence and foreign policy, the need to disperse the population, and the development of the Negev. Or one could take the line that he was quite happy to leave these matters in the hands of his ministers, and by his non-interference demonstrated his faith and confidence in their abilities, as well as a capacity to delegate authority. But the point of the criticism was that the Prime Minister, in times of major economic reformulation and public discussion, and after major changes had come under attack and benefits gained seemed likely to be worn away by claimant groups, ought to have added his unquestioned political authority in support of his ministers and of his government's policy and not simply remained silent.

Professional and academic wage policies

The demands and claims of professional and academic employees for greater recognition contrast significantly with those of industrial workers. As we saw, in the case of industrial workers the Histadrut leadership generally pressed for greater benefits for workers, while the ministers tended to emphasise the objective limits of the country's economy and sought to limit concessions. Here the situation was reversed, as for example in the case of the Secondary Teachers Association's struggle for higher wages and for the right of independent existence. Their claims, like many of those made by professionals in Israel after 1955, were twofold: demands for higher remuneration, and claims for adequate societal recognition of separate status. In this instance the Minister of Education, Mr Zalman Aranne, was caught between the cross pressures of the Secondary Teachers Association, and the General Teachers

Union backed by the Trade Union Department of the Histadrut. The view of the latter was that under no conditions should the existence of a separate Secondary Teachers Association be recognised, nor should it be admitted as a separate party to wage negotiations or be allowed to split off from these bodies and join the Professional Workers Department of the Histadrut. Two major fears prompted this viewpoint. The first was that if such a precedent was allowed in the case of teachers it might encourage splintering in other unions along status and professional lines. Moreover, it challenged the right of the Histadrut central bodies to decide in which section a union belonged, and called into question its wages policy, in particular, its unwillingness to remunerate professionals at the high rates they demanded and so increase the wage differential.

Between 1957 and 1960 the Secondary Teachers Association pressed their views through a series of strikes, and a variety of methods of non-cooperation with the officials of the Ministry, but none of this moved the Histadrut or the General Teachers Union from their declared position. Finally the Minister worked out an arrangement which he felt constituted a reasonable compromise, and which was acceptable to the Secondary Teachers Association. This was that the Histadrut would neither recognise the dissident group nor grant them the status they demanded – the right to represent themselves in their salary and work conditions negotiations – but that the Ministry would grant them de facto recognition. As their employer, the Ministry, Mr Aranne felt, had to come to terms with their claims and deal with them directly, without recognising them as the sole representatives of secondary school teachers. Thus his proposal amounted to the proposition that in matters of concern to secondary teachers the Ministry would deal separately with both the General Teachers Union and the Secondary Teachers Association. This compromise was not acceptable to the Histadrut or the General Teachers Union. When Mr Aranne presented it for Cabinet approval, his colleagues decided to establish a three-man ministerial committee of enquiry. Mr Aranne refused to accept this and resigned.

Eventually a stalemate was reached on the representation issue along the lines of the Aranne compromise, that is de facto recognition by the Ministry of Education. On the wages issue and particularly over the claim of the academically trained secondary teachers to become free of the old link of their salaries with primary teachers in the ratio 6:5, in order to put them on a par with other professional groups, the controversy dragged on three years after Mr Aranne's resignation. It included two public fact-finding and inquiry committees, long and arduous negotiations with governmental and Histadrut officials, rejection of various recommendations of the committees by the secondary teachers, the renunciation of negotiation as futile, and the resort to strike action which closed secondary schools for thirty-two days in 1961, the threat by primary teachers to strike if secondary teachers' demands were met,

and the establishment of another committee whose findings were to be binding on all, together with advance salary increases pending its report. Finally,
all teachers, primary and secondary, took the view that their position was
linked with that of engineers, and that if the latter received a greater increase
than did teachers, this should also be paid to them. The final settlement in
January 1962 of secondary teachers' claims retained the salary link with
primary teachers but gave secondary teachers various extra benefits, such as
sabbatical leave and accepted the link with the as yet undetermined engineers'
wage agreement.

The issue illustrates our general thesis that in professional struggles for
recognition against the Histadrut, Mapai ministers were to be found on the
side of the professionals against the Histadrut ruling bodies, thus reversing
the usual roles. A similar pattern emerged in the case of the Engineers' Strike
in 1962, with the ministry being more willing to come to terms with the
striking professional group and to recognise the legitimacy of its claims.

The development of secondary teachers' demands also sheds important
light upon the inner workings of Mapai and particularly upon the effects on
its decision making processes of a split between its ministers and Histadrut
officials. In such cases the party's own institutions became clogged up and it
seemed almost impossible for it to reach a decision that would be acceptable
to all parties. In point of fact the dispute concerning the secondary school
teachers was also one between the Ministry of Education and the ruling
authorities of the Histadrut, over the question of whether a Mapai minister
could determine the policy of his ministry or whether he was to be subject to
the veto of the Secretary-General and the Central Executive Committee of the
Histadrut. Normally it was to be expected that the central decision making
bodies of Mapai would settle such matters, for in theory it was their responsibility and function to coordinate Mapai's representatives in positions of
authority throughout the state and the Histadrut institutional networks, as it
did in the case of wages policy and cost of living adjustments. But there were
clearly limits to its power of making authoritative decisions, as this case
illustrates. Where ministers and the Histadrut adamantly adopted diametrically opposed stands, the scope of the party's decision making institutions
was limited, unless they were prepared openly to prefer one over the other
and impose their will upon them.

In such circumstances it is little wonder that Mapai was unable to reach
an authoritative decision on policy. In fact, it was precisely this inability of
Mapai which was a major contributory factor to the intense public struggle
which took place between 1957 and 1963 with regard to the claims of secondary school teachers, and to the constant rejection by both sides of the various
suggested solutions. Once it had thrown this problem out into the public
arena for settlement, Mapai simply had to wait for the conflicting parties to
reach a settlement. It is interesting to note that from the very beginning its

approach was one of withdrawal and abdication, and recognition of the limitations on its capacity to solve this problem, a feature which characterised its relation to many of the problems of professional and academic employees in this period. Its ability to reach authoritative solutions as in the case of the Engineers' Strike, came only through its ability to isolate and neutralise the possibilities of direct and irresolvable conflict between Mapai ministers and Histadrut officials. But once this was present there was little it could do except sit back and wait for the parties to reach agreement among themselves, and in the meantime not use its power to impose solutions either over its representatives, or over its members within the dissident group. All it could do was to try and steer a middle course, which satisfied neither side nor served to promote a solution.

Other key aspects of economic policy

To round out the picture portrayed here one must recognise that the processes of decision making involved in making wages policies were not typical of the process of making economic policy in general. With regard to the latter, although the Mapai institutions did not always participate, they were not always excluded either. Much depended on the nature of the issue. For example, the 1962 devaluation was simply announced by the Minister of Finance with absolutely no decision taken in any party body, for obvious reasons. Similarly an increase in indirect taxes for 1960 was accomplished without any party discussion, because of the effects that publicity would have had on the success of the policy. Matters of this nature were left to ministers, the civil service, and the Bank of Israel. Generally the lower the level of policy and the more directly it affected specific groups, for example agriculture, artisans, etcetera, the more likely party discussion. The more global the policy in its effects, the less likely party discussion, particularly if this involved complicated issues of economic planning, or delicate matters of timing. On the other hand, specific policies, for example the imposition of a special Defence Tax in 1956, or the policy of subsidies, did come to party institutions for discussion and even before they were brought to Cabinet and the Ministerial Committee on Economic Affairs. The process was rather a haphazard and irregular one; there were no rules or conventions about which economic matters were brought before which party bodies. There was, for example, no regular discussion in party institutions of proposed budgets to be introduced into the Knesset, as there was in the Parliamentary Party, and the same applied to taxation measures as well. On the other hand, specific economic measures were discussed if there was disagreement over them between the ministers and the Parliamentary Party, or even between ministers. Thus differences of policy in the early 1960s between Mr Sapir as Minister of Trade and Commerce, and Mr Dayan as Minister of Agriculture, over the areas of

jurisdiction of their respective departments and the policies each was responsible for, were brought, after discussion in the Parliamentary Party, to the
party's Economic Committee for decision. Then again many special committees to advise on overall economic planning were set up, as in 1954, 1956
and 1962, but these were concerned with the general guidelines of economic
policy rather than with specific proposals and usually came up with recommendations such as 'increasing productivity', and 'expanding agriculture',
with which no one could disagree.

Defence and foreign policy

The field of defence and foreign policy makes an interesting contrast with that
of wages and economic policy. Whereas in the latter the involvement of party
institutions in making decisions was at a maximum, in the former it was
hardly existent at all. In this the figure of Ben Gurion towered over the rest
of the party and its institutions, and over the government as well. Prior to the
establishment of the state Ben Gurion had been responsible for the Yishuv's
defence effort and was the successful civilian commander-in-chief of the armed
forces that had guaranteed the state's existence after the declaration of independence. Perhaps more than in any other sphere, Ben Gurion left the imprint
of his ideas on the defence structure of the state, and he regarded the defence
and security of the state as his special task, which he carried out for all but
one year in the period 1948–63. It was he who disbanded all competitive
military formations during the War of Independence and integrated them
into the Israel Defence Forces. And it was he who instituted firm civilian
control over the military, made easier by the fact that he was the actual
embodiment of this civilian control.

One of his most cherished aims in the military sphere was to free the
defence structure completely from the politicisation that pervaded many
other aspects of the new state, and he did this thoroughly and successfully.
Party activity and military activity did not go together; to stand for politics
permanent army men had to resign from the armed forces; political party
campaigning at election time in army camps was severely restricted; and all
political tests for military promotion and appointments were done away with.
A corollary of this form of civilian control was that defence and military
matters were never brought to the party for discussion and decision, and
certainly not in the policy planning stages. The rare occasions that these
matters were even partially discussed in the party, and then in very narrow
gatherings, was where they conflicted with foreign policy.

This firm institutionalisation of civilian control over the military and the
depoliticisation of the armed forces fitted in perfectly with, and in part
derived from, Ben Gurion's personal attitude to Israel's security problems and
organisation. It has been said of Ben Gurion that it was his view; 'that in

matters of security he was vested with special, unique, personal, responsibility which in a way was beyond the usual parliamentary or even ministerial responsibility – thus vesting it with a special charismatic aura, which he shared only with those personal assistants of his whom he chose.'[23] It has also been argued that Ben Gurion's great and unchallenged authority in the military and defence spheres was maintained by his policy of non-intervention in economic affairs, which by nature constituted a sphere where antagonisms and conflicts exist and are generated continuously. Whether a political leader either gives in to, or resists the pressures operating there, he cannot avoid the loss of power and authority and the development of political rivals and challenges.[24]

It also complemented another of Ben Gurion's strongly held beliefs, reinforced by the realities of Israel's security situation, that foreign policy must always take second place to Israel's defence and security policy, and that rather than striking out on initiatives of its own, it existed merely to serve the security considerations. He often, and even somewhat contemptuously, contrasted the self-reliance and freedom of action of the army, with the search for powerful friends and diplomatic assurances of the Ministry of Foreign Affairs and its envoys and spokesmen, and of the latters' over-developed fear of the pressure of world public opinion. In his view the defence and security factors determined the lines of foreign policy and it was up to the Foreign Ministry to implement them.[25]

These views brought him into direct conflict with Sharett, the Foreign Minister, which increased in intensity as Israel's defence forces began to follow a more activist policy after Ben Gurion's return to the post of Defence Minister in February 1955. Until that time the general rule within Mapai had been for party institutions to consider foreign policy reports and information provided to them by the Foreign Minister or Prime Minister, but they had absolutely no say in the making of policy, nor was there an opportunity to influence policy after it had been made, as would have occurred if they had needed to ratify it. As the Ben Gurion–Sharett conflict grew some party bodies were brought into the matter, and indirectly were forced to make foreign policy choices. Thus the Political Committee heard a complaint from Sharett at the end of 1955 that the timing of a particular Israeli reprisal raid in Syria had been bad in that he had been in Washington at the time negotiating about the purchase of aircraft, and that the reprisal had proved to be particularly embarrassing. In the event, the Political Committee supported

[23] Eisenstadt, *Israeli Society*, p. 324. Ben Gurion expressed himself quite directly on this topic during the Lavon Affair. 'I never brought security matters to my party... I always accepted a majority decision in the party, in the Histadrut and in the Cabinet, as self-understood...But in security matters as I see them, there exists for me only my own conscience.' *Davar*, 13.1.1961.

[24] S. Avineri, 'Ben-Gurion – The Price of Ruling', *Haaretz*, 17.9.1965.

[25] For example, see *Haaretz*, 22.8.1955.

Ben Gurion's position that the timing was in fact right and that in any case this was his responsibility and his alone.[26] At the same time it set up a committee of three, Ben Gurion, Sharett, and Eshkol to coordinate defence and foreign policy.

This committee did not help matters much and relations deteriorated in 1956 until Sharett announced in June that he felt obliged to hand in his resignation. Here, too, intensive discussions took place in the Political Committee and the Central Committee which culminated in the acceptance of Sharett's resignation. Although in both instances the substantive policy issues dividing Ben Gurion and Sharett were not discussed in any detail, by accepting Sharett's resignation the Mapai institutions were, in effect, making a foreign policy judgement.

The circumstances surrounding Sharett's resignation, or perhaps better put, Ben Gurion's demand and insistence that he resign, give a clear picture of the foreign policy situation at the time. Three major elements stand out: the basic policy approach of Ben Gurion that foreign policy should be completely subordinate to defence policy; the personality conflict between Ben Gurion and Sharett; and despite much sympathy for Sharett, the inability and unwillingness of Mapai institutions to involve themselves directly in the issue without becoming embroiled in the intricacies and details of defence and foreign policy.

When the Mapai institutions discussed Mr Sharett's resignation in June 1956, Israel was already well embarked on the course that took it into Sinai in October of that year. Ben Gurion, on his resumption of the Prime Ministership in 1955, had refused to accept Sharett's offer not to participate in the Cabinet, and insisted that he remain as Foreign Minister. The two men differed radically in policy and personality. Ben Gurion's policy was tough, activist, independent, and emphasised Israel's isolation, and its need to be ready to stand alone, and followed policies of swift retaliation. Basically it rested on the assumption that not only in the last resort but in the immediate short run, Israel was best served by military responses. In this view, foreign policy considerations, talks, diplomacy, negotiations, and so forth, could be and had to be made to serve the needs of defence and military priorities. No foreign policy activity could be allowed to stand in the way of necessary military action.

Sharett was the archetypical diplomat. Suave, polished, a gifted linguist and orator, patient, attentive, conciliatory, receptive of ideas and views, he tended to have faith in the diplomatic task in which he was engaged, and believed that Israel could be aided and assisted in both the short term and the long term by diplomacy. He thus often counselled and fought for such policies in Cabinet, and acted as a moderating influence on Ben Gurion's point of view. To the extent that he got support in Cabinet he exercised influence

[26] *Ibid.* 30.12.1955.

over the course of events. But as Ben Gurion became increasingly scathing, scornful and critical of all diplomatic efforts, as he came increasingly to regard those who believed in them as faint-hearted, not trusting in Israel's own capacity, and too ready to trust others (and foolishly so), and as he became increasingly resentful of the opposition of Sharett and his policies, the issues became deeply and intensely personal. What had begun as differences in policy, style and temperament ended in deep personal animosity. Sharett later felt, for example, that Ben Gurion had asked him to remain in Cabinet, and not accepted his offer of resignation, so that he could personally force him to resign.

The debate in Mapai's institutions aroused consternation and concern. Many felt that it was wrong that the party's two top leaders should publicly part in such a manner, after having served the movement together for over forty years. But there was no alternative but to accept the Ben Gurion position. The discussion within Mapai at no stage examined the substantive defence and foreign policy clashes of the two leaders, and the party was not called on to study policies, and pass a judgement as to which it preferred. The Mapai practice was against substantive defence–foreign policy discussions. These were matters for Cabinet, and the Knesset. Moreover, Ben Gurion framed the issue quite simply: it was a choice between himself and Sharett – one or other had to go. Nor was it ever in doubt that the Prime Minister had the right to ask for a minister's dismissal. Thus the debate in Mapai was over the tactical questions: could peace between the two men be restored in some fashion? Could a compromise be reached, particularly in view of the effects upon the party and the nation at large, in times of grave defence crisis, that such a resignation would have? When it became apparent that Ben Gurion was adamant and that Sharett took the view that his resignation was irrevocable, the Mapai institutions acceded, and as we saw in chapter nine, with a marked degree of displeasure.

After the Sharett resignation there were only two major issues of foreign policy and defence policy that had substantive airing in Mapai decision making bodies, although in both cases the decision of the government and the ministry was overwhelmingly approved. The first was the withdrawal from Sinai and Gaza, and the attendant problems of getting guarantees of free passage for Israeli shipping in the Gulf of Akaba. The other issue was that of military government of the Arabs in Israel.

The Sinai issue early in 1957 was of prime security significance, and of prime economic significance as well. Not only was Israel's shipping involved, but in addition the United States had threatened Israel with sanctions if she did not withdraw, and for quite a time Israel refused to do so demanding better guarantees of her security and freedom of shipping. Whilst the negotiations were carried on by the Cabinet, which met frequently, Mapai institutions were kept fully informed on the matter and held frequent meetings at which information was handed over and free and frank discussions took place. While not influencing policy these institutions were kept fully in the picture, and at the same time approved the government's stand whenever the issue was put to the test. Particularly active in this regard was the party's Security and Foreign Affairs Committee, the successor to the Political Committee, which between January and May of 1957 met some nine times on these matters. The only occasion on which the Cabinet policy was challenged was at a combined meeting of this committee with the Parliamentary Party, after the Cabinet had finally decided to recommend withdrawal on the basis of specific American pledges regarding Israel's security. Six Mapai members of the Knesset demanded that Israel seek further clarification prior to withdrawal, but in a meeting lasting till three in the morning they were easily defeated.[27]

In 1962 a number of private members' bills before the Knesset aimed at abolishing the system of military government received some limited support from a number of Mapai backbenchers, particularly Mr Yona Kesse. The matter was brought to the Secretariat where Ben Gurion made it clear that he was opposed to any change, as was the Cabinet. Kesse's suggestion that Mapai announce in the Knesset that it was seeking ways to abolish it in the future was easily defeated. The matter was then brought to the Parliamentary Party which endorsed the Secretariat's stand and made a vote opposing abolition compulsory for all Mapai M.K.s.[28]

The paucity of debate within Mapai on matters of foreign policy derived directly from the close connections between foreign policy and defence policy, and, as we noted, in the latter sphere party debate was rare. This stemmed not only from the powerful impact and charismatic authority of Ben Gurion's personality in this area, and from the strong desire to keep party out of military affairs and defence whilst maintaining civilian control, but also from the widespread national consensus on goals in this sphere. Most Israelis and their government believed that the very life and existence of the state were permanently at stake and constantly threatened by their Arab neighbours, and that the price of existence was eternal watchfulness and defence preparedness and superiority. The small size of the country reinforced this belief and created a defence posture which demanded that any battles that broke out be fought on Arab territory, for Israel had no hinterland. This brought Israel to the stage where she was in a position to launch retaliatory raids and reprisals whenever she thought fit, and to carry out massive pre-emptive strikes as in 1956 and 1967 when she felt that Arab encirclement and defence arrangements had tightened the knot around her just that bit too tight. This state of affairs was not conducive to any debate on foreign policy, tied as it was to defence considerations. The aim was to keep Israel strong enough to survive, and the methods were to do what was necessary to achieve this condition. About this there could be little debate for there were few options available,

[27] *Davar*, 20.2.1957, 9.4.1957.   [28] *Ibid.* 7.1.1962.

and those that were could not be discussed publicly because they were so intimately tied to security.

One of the major factors curtailing Israel's options was the stand taken towards her by the Soviet Union and its satellites from the early 1950s onwards. Having helped to ease the British out of the Middle East by supporting the establishment of the State of Israel, the Soviet then turned its attention to achieving good relations with the Arab states. One of the major ways it did so was to provide them with arms in an abundant manner. Israel was left with no choice in its relations with East and West: the East clearly did not want her, and it had to do what it could to secure the arms it needed from the West. Gradually it came down fairly much in the position of seeking Western support; few Israelis could see any sense in pursuing better relations with the East.

Conclusion

The foregoing analysis has illuminated a number of aspects of Mapai's decision making processes. The contrast between wages policy decisions and those in the realm of foreign and defence policy suggest two polar extremes, and two very different approaches to decision making. In the former, participation of rank and file, of local activists and sub-leaders, and of party institutions was high. The process as a whole constituted an elaborate bargaining procedure involving not only the party's top sets of leaders in the government and the Histadrut but many other sections as well. In this manner compromise was essential and consensual power relations were well evident. And where these competing sets of leaders agreed to agree, the final decision was taken within the party's legitimate decision making bodies.

Foreign and defence policies, by their nature in the Israeli situation, were not well suited for widespread public discussion, apart from the narrowness of the available range of options. Moreover, the party regarded them as prototypical of the kind of policy decision that belonged within governmental, parliamentary and civil service spheres. They therefore stood at the pole of minimum party involvement, and to the extent that these matters did come to Mapai for discussion it was most likely to be the personal question of who would be responsible for the policy. Perhaps the main feature of the policy area was the imperious figure of Ben Gurion towering above all other participants, and to the degree that he imposed decisions by the strength of his personal authority, decision making based upon consensual power relations was reduced. At the same time it should be recognised that Ben Gurion enjoyed wide public and party support for his policies.

The case of professional wages decisions lies somewhere between these two poles. The formal participation of party institutions was minimised because of differences of opinion between its top leaders in the government and the

Histadrut, and their inability to agree to compromise of some kind. This suggests as a general rule that the role of party institutions was maximised where the contending groups agreed to submit themselves to a consensual decision making process which committed them to compromise and agreement from the outset. Where both groups stood firm, party institutions were either paralysed, or put into the difficult situation where the only other alternative was to impose their will upon unwilling leaders. While this was always a possibility it was rendered highly improbable, if the party itself was divided and could not decide which solution it wished to impose on either or both sets of leaders. Thus solutions in this sphere were taken outside party institutions (admittedly by party leaders) and tended to be ad hoc solutions, mediations and arbitrations rather than policies, which was of course related to the fact that these problems often involved strike action.

The question of 'constituencies' is also relevant. In the foreign policy area the overall national consensus meant that there was one major constituency, with small opposition groups of leaders. But this was not so in the other areas. Here the contrast is instructive. Where Mapai had incorporated and integrated the relevant constituencies, as in the case of industrial wages policies, its chances of success were to that extent increased, both by direct contact with sub-leaders and rank and file, and by the overarching consensus of party loyalty and the over-riding need for organisational cohesion in order to reach agreement. A major problem for Mapai in the professional field was the fact that only a small part of this constituency was within the party, so that decision making had to take place outside it, and was to that extent much more difficult.

In the same context we can assess the flexibility of Mapai's decision makers and their policies, which was furthered by the party's ability to keep interested but opposed groups, not directly involved in the issues, out of them, so as to prevent the clogging up of the decision making processes. In this sense party control of agriculture and large industrial enterprises were instrumental in producing a flexible consensual decision making process. Similarly this flexibility was strengthened by fairly clear divisions of authority between party, state and Histadrut, which Mapai had institutionalised in the early days after the establishment of the state. We have already noted this division on the development of the internal relations between Mapai executive bodies and Cabinet: it is now time to consider these processes of state integration and depoliticisation in greater depth.

11. DEPOLITICISATION AND STATE INTEGRATION

Politicisation

Two different phenomena fall within the concept of politicisation. The first lies on the well-known sociological continuum of particularism–universalism. This refers to the degree to which membership of a particular group is of assistance to individuals in obtaining advantages in the allocation of scarce resources and instrumental benefits. It should be noted that in comparison with other forms, particularism based on political party affiliation lies closer to the universal end of the continuum if membership is open, and if only limited criteria are demanded of prospective joiners. Nevertheless it must be recognised that this continues to disadvantage those without that party membership, even if their achievement is better. To that extent particularism is decisive. This form of particularism is most limited where party membership is regarded as a criterion for securing scarce resources only within the party itself (for example, parliamentary representation), and it increases as it is applied to more and more spheres of society. It is at its most extensive where entry to the most important spheres of society, the polity, and the economy are conditional upon party membership.

The second aspect of politicisation refers to the degree of permeation of other sectors of society by the political, and, in particular, by party. There are few major areas of institutional life that do not have some connection with political processes or are not affected in their activity by political decisions. But while much of society has some relation to the political, not all of it is affected by political parties or can be said to be politicised. Many institutions, groups and individuals, to be sure, are affected by the activity of government but stand in a bargaining relationship to it. Although they make claims upon it and are subject to its decisions they remain relatively independent of it in their internal activities and those that lie closest to the core of their existence. Politicisation in this context is the degree of their dependence upon parties, the extent to which their activities are subject to political control or direction, their leaderships penetrated and their organisations permeated by those loyal to political parties. At one end of the scale is the pluralist, multi-centric model of society in which political parties constitute some of the many competing groups. Here the groups that mediate and intervene between the individual and primary groups and the political system are independent of the control of the political parties that operate and direct the society's political decision making institutions. Interest groups and associations exist in parallel with political parties sometimes attempting to use them in furthering their claims and at others pressing them directly on the legislative and executive bodies. At the other end of the scale is the totalitarian, one-party state model, in which many areas of individual and group life are subject to party direction and control, and all groups and associations are permeated by political party officials. No independent intermediary structures exist.

In between these two ends of the scale there is a wide range of possibilities. In this intermediate stage political parties and interest groups often enjoy extremely close relations and connections. In some cases these connections are temporary, with groups and parties forming alliances in pursuit of specific objects and returning to a state of relative independence after the goal has been achieved. On the other hand, there may be more permanent relationships between parties and interest groups. In certain instances the political party may be merely an extension of the interest group and completely controlled by it. In others the party may have achieved some degree of independence from a particular or single interest group by aggregating the interests of a number of groups. A third situation is one in which the political party permeates and penetrates many groups, associations and interests and controls them from within. The further this extends throughout the society the greater the degree of politicisation, the less the free play of interests and the more difficult it is for parties to be dislodged by electoral methods only. This need not, of course, be totalitarian, in that such control may be competed for and shared by a number of parties. Nevertheless, competition between parties for influence and control over associations and institutions means that the latter may develop marked power and influence within the parties themselves in accordance with the latters' assessment of their importance. Whereas control by one party produces a high degree of politicisation and leaves the other groups relatively powerless, competition for control amongst a number of parties, while not necessarily diminishing the total amount of politicisation, often tends to increase the power of these other groups and institutions vis à vis the political parties. As this occurs the chances of depoliticisation increase. It may come to be regarded as not legitimate for certain functions and activities to be subject to the pressures of competing political parties. Alternatively, those groups subject to the conflict of parties and the inability of any one to gain control, may become relatively independent of parties, wrench themselves free of their control and get themselves into a market or bargaining relationship with them. In this case the group, institutional or professional loyalty may supersede the party affiliation.

Politicisation is intimately connected with the questions of state building and nation building, discussed in chapter one. Nation building itself involves the casting off of various forms of particularism and the integration of the society into a new national unity. Some of the loyalty and support formerly given to particular groups or structures must be gained by those institutions that seek to represent and act for the nation as a whole. In this way legitimacy will be maintained. The more universal the political institutions, the more that they cater for all citizens equally, irrespective of their particular loyalties or group affiliations, the greater the chance of gaining legitimacy and political support, and of successful nation building.

State building is closely connected with bureaucratic structures, effectiveness, differentiation of functions and institutions, and policy direction and coordination. As we argued in the first chapter, the establishment of a single secular rational authority to cope with these tasks depends upon the abandonment of particularism in favour of universalism, ascription in favour of achievement, and the disbanding of competing political structures that claim a legitimate right to use violence or physical coercion. Moreover, the very essence of rational bureaucracy according to Weber is the consistent application of universalistic merit criteria in appointments to the bureaucracy, in relations within the bureaucracy and in relations with clients. How far this can be achieved, and how far it produces negative characteristics such as over-conformity, dampens initiative and creativity, curtails flexibility and improvisation, and does not permit the development of the social support of informal processes, are still matters of debate among political scientists and sociologists. But one thing is clear; a balance must be struck and in the main, rational–legal universalistic authority structures must be established.

Weber himself also allowed for the need for political direction with his emphasis upon the fact that the head of the bureaucratic structure is never a member of the bureaucracy and not subject to its rules and procedures. This is important in all modern political systems where politicians head bureaucracies and take the formal responsibility for their decisions. Ideally also they provide initiative and direction, although in reality these will arise out of the interaction between political party demands and bureaucratic advice.

Thus bureaucracies can never be completely depoliticised, and their workings are dependent upon the interaction between political and bureaucratic criteria. But, on the other hand, there may be a point where too great an emphasis upon the political aspects within bureaucracies will be a liability rather than an asset. If particularistic political party criteria are allowed to influence the recruitment process or the internal bureaucratic decision making process too greatly, the effects may be felt in loss of public support and legitimacy, and in loss of effectiveness. Legitimacy is bound to decline where the public feels that the supposedly universalistic bureaucracy and through it the government of the state serve the interests of particular groups only, or what is worse, certain political party members and supporters only, and not the population as a whole. These political party considerations may also result in a lower calibre of official and in 'bad' policy decisions. These arguments, of course, lie at the basis of the modern democratic state, with its emphasis upon the equality of individual citizens.

In new states, then, either new structures must be established to cope with the political functions involved in political independence, or older structures must be taken over and converted for new tasks. In both cases, these criteria need to be met. While old structures may enjoy the advantages of public support, legitimacy, and a marked degree of institutionalisation, their conversion may be more difficult than the establishment of new structures, because of past practices, traditions and procedures, and the vested interests supporting them. They must therefore be depoliticised, and in that sense, depoliticisation and state and nation building are highly interconnected, if not synonymous. This was precisely the position that Palestine was in on the eve of independence, and we shall examine these processes, and Mapai's part in them in certain key areas: defence, legal system, education, employment, health, certain sectors of the economy, and the bureaucracy. (We have already noted Mapai's contribution to state building in party–Cabinet and party–Parliament relations in earlier chapters.) To see these changes in proper perspective we must begin with a brief analysis of politicisation in the pre-state period.

Politicisation in the Yishuv and its extension with statehood

The life of the Yishuv was highly politicised. Its pioneering social movements either originated as political parties within the Zionist movement or else eventually formed themselves into political parties. Through participation as political parties in the elections for the Yishuv, Jewish Agency and Histadrut institutions the movements gained allocations of scarce resources to aid their various colonisation and settlement efforts. This was true not only of the parties of the Left, but of the Right as well. These political parties as they developed were not contained within the formal structure of an already existing state and forced to tailor their activities to fit in with existing political arrangements, but were more or less free to develop their own independent institutional frameworks and their own autonomous party environments in which the range of functions they could undertake was not determined by already existing structures. Having an ideological approach to life the political parties therefore moved in the direction of undertaking activity in as many fields as possible, and in fields rarely undertaken by political parties in other countries. The major initiating force in this development was the socialist parties of the Left, but the parties of the Right were forced to follow suit in order to survive.

These conditions led to the formation of the Histadrut and its diversification beyond the spheres of trade union activity and organisation and assistance of agricultural colonisation into the fields of defence, labour exchanges, health services, education, literature and culture, sport, housing, and into widespread industrial undertakings. In the latter sphere were included heavy industry, construction, manufacturing of various kinds, banking and insurance, retail shopping, wholesale distribution and supply, internal transport cooperatives, shipping, water supply and so on. And as we pointed out above, the Histadrut with this vast network of institutions was run by its constituent political parties with Mapai in a commanding majority. In Palestine there was no career civil service, no ideal-type bureaucracy in the Weberian sense, and no system of entry based upon formal qualification and achievement. This was performed by political parties according to their own criteria of political loyalty or party benefit. And this was true not only of the officials of these institutions, but was applicable to their many other employees as well.

Overall, politicisation in the sense of party control and direction was widespread; there were few bodies or groups or associations that were not affiliated in some way with political parties or directed by them. Furthermore, not only were political tests used in determining the allocation of scarce resources and of official positions, they were, if not the only criterion, the most important one. In those days, then, politics and party affiliation played an important part in the life of the individual. The parties as social movements aimed to surround and envelop their members in a net of party-directed and party-oriented relationships and activities that would serve constantly to reinforce their party loyalty and stimulate them to be faithful followers. Nor were the parties cadre parties; from the beginning they displayed marked tendencies towards incorporating as many members as possible, and indeed the mark of their success was the number of members they could bring within the party's umbrella.

Immediately after the establishment of the state it was quickly recognised within Mapai, and in broad sections of the society, that the state stood above political party and social movement. It was clear that whereas the latter were sectional and particular, the state was representative of all citizens without exception and was general, and that the old methods of volunteering were unlikely to be successful in the state, and that more suitable methods of task performance had to be found. This approach was often termed *Mamlachtiut*, and one of its leading exponents was Ben Gurion who constantly reiterated this theme in his speeches. The clearest initial institutionalisation of *Mamlachtiut* occurred with the establishment of the armed forces and the judiciary on party-neutral lines within the first few months of the new state.[1] The cause of universality triumphed first in these two spheres, although there was

---

[1] On those processes in these areas see A. Etzioni, 'The Decline of Neo-Feudalism in Israel', in A. Etzioni, *Studies in Social Change* (New York, 1966), pp. 180–97. On the military in particular see Amos Perlmutter, 'The Israeli Army in Politics: The Persistence of the Civilian over the Military', *World Politics*, 20 (1968), 606–43.

opposition from both Right and Left to the disbanding of the politically connected military formations of the Palmach and the Irgun.

Simultaneously with the depoliticisation of the armed forces, proceeded with vigorously by Ben Gurion despite the strong opposition, other major spheres were further politicised. The immigration process, as we have noted above, was in the hands of the Jewish Agency, where a strict party key and agreement was in operation. The agreement specified the number of emissaries from each party paid from the budget of the Agency, whose major task was the organisation of the immigrant camps in Europe and Africa. Their minor role, but that of most importance to the parties, was that of recruiting agencies for party members, and for party-affiliated agricultural settlements. Immigrant absorption in the cities, too, was highly politicised. On arrival immigrants were given three months free membership of the Histadrut which enabled them to register for employment and provided free health services for that period. After that period membership was usually continued. Once in the Histadrut they were subject to the political competition of its constituent parties which effectively limited the opportunities of some of the right-wing parties. The personnel manning the Histadrut labour exchanges, too, were chosen according to a party key. In theory employment was decided on a first come first served basis, but in practice party criteria were widely employed. Housing, too, was often allocated in this manner.

After 1948 politicisation became more general under the onslaught of mass immigration. However, its meaning and implications were now different. Vast numbers of newcomers who were not the self-selected party converts of the Yishuv period were brought into the country and allocated those resources that were necessary to enable their swift and successful absorption. The numbers meant the establishment of many new bureaucratic institutional structures in the areas of immigration, health, employment, housing, education, social services, and so forth, most of which in the early days fell directly into the hands of the parties. It meant the creation of new municipal governments, new Labour Councils, new Kupat Cholim centres, and so forth, throughout the country, which were manned on political lines. Parties were thus able to reward more and more of their faithful and at the same time to recruit new members at a fast rate while assisting and guiding them in the problems of absorption.

The greatest expansion took place with the creation of the civil service to man the government departments and ministries that came into existence overnight. In the absence of a trained career civil service, government civil service positions were given to those trained in the British Civil Service, or in the Histadrut and Jewish Agency bureaucracies, together with the few immigrants who had overseas experience. The bulk of the decisive appointments and certainly those above the middle levels were party appointments, following upon the traditions of the Jewish Agency and the Histadrut. Whole ministries soon became staffed with party faithfuls. Mapai differed from the other parties in this in only one regard: it had the most important and key ministries and the largest reservoir of members from which to draw its officials, which it did without hesitation.

But whilst the extent of politicisation was thus increased following upon the establishment of the state, further processes of depoliticisation were gradually set into motion by Mapai, to which we now turn.

The depoliticisation of the school system

Both for the religious parties and the socialist parties in the Yishuv, education was an important element in the development of their separate enclaves. For the former it was essential for the perpetuation of the religious heritage and for the inculcation of its practices. It enabled the latter to impart their particular ideological outlook to the next generation and to imbue it with the elevated social and national goals of pioneering, national independence, collectivism and so forth. The Mandatory authority left the field of education to the communities themselves and as in so many other spheres the institutional structures that grew up and were developed to cope with these functions were based around political parties. Thus by the end of the Mandate there were four main educational systems, or trends, as they were commonly known: the workers', the general, the Mizrachi, and the Agudat Yisrael trends. The last two were religious, the second was basically right wing and closest to the outlook of the General Zionists whilst the workers' trend was really a cover behind which Mapai and the other two main labour groups each operated their own socialist and pioneer-oriented educational systems, through the administration, and with the financial resources, of the Histadrut.

With the establishment of the state, the government took over responsibility for education. It quickly legislated for compulsory education of all children aged between five and thirteen, but it left the educational trends as they were. Caution in this regard derived from Mapai's dependence upon the religious parties for the maintenance of the coalition, and it was therefore not prepared to establish the unified state educational system which many Mapai leaders desired. There already existed considerable friction over the education of the children of the religiously observant immigrants (mainly from Oriental countries) living in various immigrant camps. The religious parties claimed that they were being forcibly enrolled in non-religious schools against their will and conscience, and in 1951 the coalition fell over this issue.

Education, therefore, was the central issue of the 1951 election campaign, thus forcing Mapai to formulate an overall policy in this sphere. From the outset it was clear that Mapai would have to compromise on the demand for one uniform education system throughout the state. In March 1951, Ben Gurion (on vacation) had written to the Mapai Central Committee proposing changes in the educational structure. In view of the defects, which he believed the system inherited from the Yishuv, this system, he argued, 'must lead to disintegration and endless splitting'.[2]

He therefore recommended the abolition of the rule of parties and the trend system; the establishment of the authority of the state over all schools, that is, state education (but not uniform education); the ordination of teachers and their appointment only by the Ministry of Education; the fixing by the state of a minimum compulsory content in all schools; the right of parents and teachers to add to the minimum programme fixed by the government as long as this did not undermine its basic principles; the guaranteeing to religious parents of a religious type of school that included the minimum compulsory programme, but with the addition of studies and practices to give it a religous tone.[3]

The Central Committee deferred the matter to a special Council. It also decided that the Histadrut's Central Executive Committee should set up a committee representative of all shades of opinion on the educational question to prepare proposals for the Council. Owing to the Cabinet crisis and the sudden election, however, it was never called. But, in view of the importance of the educational question in the election campaign the issue could not be shelved completely and was again given a full airing at the Central Committee during the discussions on the Mapai Election Programme for the 2nd Knesset. Drafted by Ben Gurion, the programme's education proposals were almost identical with his earlier views. Whilst all other clauses were approved by the Central Committee with little alteration, the education section aroused controversy, with some of it being opposed by the leadership of the Histadrut's Education Department.

In particular there was support for continuing the Histadrut's education system together with a general system. The Central Committee again decided to call a special Council after the election, and in the meantime to pass the suggested draft with some omissions. Thus clauses demanding the complete abolition of party connection with schools were omitted. What remained was the minimum upon which agreement could be gained – support for state education for all children and the placing of all primary schools under the authority of the Ministry of Edueation, together with a general acceptance of the right of parents to have special educational demands above and beyond the compulsory minimum, and guarantees of a religious way of life in schools for religious children.[4]

As matters turned out the government did not introduce legislation in this sphere until 1953. The principles were discussed first in a number of special committees and later in a combined meeting of the Central Committee with the Parliamentary Party and Mapai members of the Histadrut's Executive Committee held in February 1953. The religious parties had placed tremendous pressure on Mapai which resulted in a coalition agreement to establish a dual state education system. Within the Ministry of Education there were to be two sections, one for general state education and the other for state–religious education. Each would provide the minimum, but the religious section, to be staffed and administered by religiously observant administrators and teachers, would provide both religious content in the educational programme and a religious way of life and atmosphere in the schools. Parents could choose between two forms of state education. Thus unlike many western countries which have given religious minorities and groups the right to set up independent religious schools which the parents and the communities must pay for themselves, in Israel religious education is financed and administered by the state. In 1963, 29 per cent of children in primary schools were in the religious network.

The aims of state education in Israel as they are laid down in the legislation closely follow the decision of Mapai's Central Committee. The State Education Law of 1953 states that:

The aim of state education is to found primary education in the state upon the values of the culture of Israel and the achievements of science, upon the love of the homeland and loyalty to the state and the people of Israel, upon trust in agricultural labour and craftsmanship, upon chalutzic training, and upon the aspiration to a society built upon freedom, equality, tolerance, mutual assistance and love of one's fellows.[5]

Although general enough to be subscribed to by a large section of the population, they represent the transfer of the labour movement's goals and values to the state. Nor was there any secret about this. One of Mapai's main declared aims in handing over education to the state was 'to instal the movement's basic values in all schools without exception'. Whether they are in fact implemented in practice is an entirely different question beyond the scope of this work. But in terms of its aim of excluding party influence, Mapai as a party successfully removed itself from the education scene and the general system became depoliticised. Nevertheless, important pockets of politicisation still remained. The additional education beyond the minimum requirements enabled the various kibbutz movements which run their own schools under the direction of the Ministry to include a marked degree of political and ideological education. Moreover, the state–religious education system is firmly held in the hands of the National Religious Party.

Before the legislation was finally passed by the Knesset a decision of the Mapai Central Committee about one of its clauses led to the resignation from the government of the General Zionists and to another coalition crisis. The

---

[5] In Y. Dror and E. Gutmann, eds., *The Government of Israel: A Collection of Readings* (Kaplan School, Jerusalem, 1962), p. 563 (Hebrew).

issue was more symbolic than real. In the Yishuv and in the early days of the state it had been the practice in Histadrut schools for the red flag of the workers to be flown together with the Zionist flag, which became that of the state, and for the workers' anthem to be sung, in addition to the Zionist anthem *Hatikva*, which became the national anthem. The future of these practices was first raised in the Mapai Parliamentary Party when the proposed legislation was discussed there. Mapai's ministers proposed that as schools were state institutions, only the symbols of the state should be allowed in them. Some members of the Parliamentary Party, inclined more to the class and workers' viewpoint of the Histadrut, were not satisfied with this and had the matter removed to the Central Committee for decision. There Ben Gurion defended his stand and that of the Mapai ministers. In his view education was not a matter for Cabinet and coalition bargaining, nor was this a division between Mapai ministers and the party, but was one on which party members also were divided. For him two issues were at stake; first, the content and framework of education, about which there was now no debate in the party, and second, the historical strategy and symbolic tactics of a working class that believed in its mission among the people. In his opinion the latter had changed in view of the 'change from class to nation' and he explained to the Central Committee at length the implications of this change. For Ben Gurion, in the final resort, the issue was simple: 'Is there a state or isn't there a state, that is the question?' The Central Committee remained unimpressed with his arguments. It decided 60:21 that it was obligatory to raise the national flag and sing the national anthem, but under certain conditions and on particular days (the 1st of May and the anniversary of the Histadrut) it would be permitted to fly the red flag and to sing the workers' anthem in schools where the vast majority of parents would request this.[6]

Following this decision the four General Zionist ministers who had joined the coalition only five months previously after long and involved negotiations informed Mr Ben Gurion that they felt obliged to resign from the government. To their mind the decision of the Mapai Central Committee had brought to nought all the efforts of the coalition partners to reach an agreed position about state education that was truly state education. They felt they had no other option in view of Ben Gurion's public announcement that he was bound by the decision of the Mapai Central Committee democratically arrived at. This put the matter in a completely different light. Mapai had worked long and hard to create the first coalition with a party of the Right, which it regarded as being of major importance in view of the country's serious economic problems and the need to maintain the confidence of foreign investors, many of whom, it was argued, were frightened off by a socialist coalition government.

The Mapai Political Committee was therefore most anxious to preserve the

[6] *Minutes Mapai Central Committee*, 17.5.1963, 24.5.1953.

coalition almost at all costs. It suggested first to the General Zionists that Mapai would refer the matter to a special Council to be held some four or five months later, without Mapai obliging itself as to the outcome, but the General Zionists refused to accept such a vague undertaking. In the meantime Ben Gurion applied his full weight in Mapai's inner councils to have the Central Committee decision altered in a way that would enable the coalition to be reconstituted with the participation of the General Zionists. The Political Committee therefore recommended to the Central Committee that it hand the matter over to a later Council to be preceded by widespread rank and file discussion in the branches. In the meantime the legislation was to be brought down in the Knesset immediately with no reference at all to the problem of the anthem and the flag. In the event that the Council would decide to ask for the implementation of the previous Central Committee decision a special amendment to the legislation would be made. This was passed easily. It had the effect of enabling the return of the General Zionists to the coalition, without the Central Committee decision being rescinded; it was merely not implemented pending the Council decision. The Council met in November 1953 after discussion in the branches. It decided 108:25 with 225 abstentions that the same practice as was adopted in other state institutions be adopted in schools, that is, the use of national symbols only.[7]

The depoliticisation of employment

During periods of unemployment or of unstable employment the labour exchanges operated by the Histadrut enjoyed marked potential political influence. Following Histadrut practice they were staffed by political appointees according to a party key. Mapai, the dominant majority party in the Histadrut, gained not only the overall majority of positions in all exchanges throughout the country, but the key positions as well. It was therefore able to benefit its members by finding jobs for them more quickly or by assigning them to those which were more likely to be permanent. Other Histadrut parties could do likewise, but in lesser measure. It was in the interests of the state and of Mapai as the governing party to find employment for all as quickly as possible. Thus preference for Mapai members was only marginal or temporary and did not mean the complete exclusion of others.

The control and direction of employment was also a major mechanism of economic planning. Thus by the middle of the 1950s as unemployment declined and as Mapai began to adopt an overall economic planning approach, it seemed logical to transfer employment facilities and the direction of manpower into the centralised hands of the state. This move was incorporated in

[7] Haaretz, 25.5.1953, 26.5.1953, 1.6.1953, 29.11.1953; Davar, 1.6.1953, Minutes Mapai Central Committee, 31.5.1953; Report Mapai Headquarters to 8th Conference, pp. 17–18.

the general economic policy plans adopted by the 1956 Mapai Conference and aroused no dissension or dissent. The approach taken by the Conference was simple and straightforward. The existing labour exchanges were to be taken over by the state and converted into state labour exchanges, and their employees would become civil servants subject to civil service regulations and procedures.[8]

This passed smoothly within Mapai because of Histadrut support. Following the Mapai Conference a committee of the Central Executive Committee meeting together with representatives of the Ministry of Labour (controlled by Mapai) examined this general proposal and approved it. In particular it had the support of Lavon, the Secretary-General of the Histadrut, and of Namir, the Minister of Labour. The matter was then brought to the Mapai Central Committee where it was approved with only two members dissenting, and from there the necessary steps to implement it were taken in the Histadrut and the Knesset resulting in the 1958 Employment Service Law.

From our point of view the major question is: why did Mapai decide to hand over this Histadrut function to the state? We have already indicated that one of the reasons was concern with overall economic planning. A second reason was Mapai's ideological motivation towards Mamlachtiut, and the belief that certain major functions should be carried out by the state, as had occurred in the case of education, the armed forces and the judiciary. But there was also present an important political consideration, that the political benefits derived from Histadrut control of the labour exchanges were outweighed by the political disadvantages perceived in the widespread criticism that political party affiliation and preference were important in gaining employment.

In the early days the Histadrut enjoyed two major advantages in gaining members. The first was Kupat Cholim – the widespread and high standard mutual health services. The second was the system of labour exchanges, it being mandatory for employers with whom the Histadrut had labour agreements to hire workers through them. As these collective labour agreements were widely accepted throughout the country the power of these exchanges and their officials was enhanced.

Mapai was always interested in increased and increasing Histadrut membership. It welcomed any additional support for the labour camp in Palestine and Israel, as opposed to the forces of the Right. Once in the Histadrut, these members formed an important potential membership reservoir for Mapai itself. As the dominant party it stood to gain greatly in membership from them. Within the Histadrut, as we saw, its officials in all positions were potential and actual recruiters on behalf of the party. With the establishment of the state, control of the Histadrut to complement control of the government became even more important.

[8] *Report Mapai 8th Conference*, 1956, p. 374.

After an initial crisis following the influx of immigrants, employment was at a fairly satisfactory level by the middle of the 1950s. The Histadrut's membership, too, was at a more than satisfactory level, having increased both relatively and absolutely since 1948, and it was in a position of unchallenged supremacy as the representative of labour in Israel. There now seemed to be little political advantage or benefit in keeping the labour exchanges in Histadrut and political hands. Mapai came to believe that it suffered more from the widespread belief that it made employment a political matter and determined employment on party lines, and not on a first come first served basis, as was required, than it gained from retaining the exchanges in Histadrut hands. Since such a large proportion of the population belonged to the Histadrut anyhow, and since employment was at a high level, the party was in fact not able to derive political benefit from the situation, yet was roundly criticised for doing so.

This came out clearly in the debate at the Histadrut Council at the end of 1956 when the proposal to hand over the labour exchanges to the state was fully discussed. The representatives of the other parties, for example, N. Almozolino of Achdut Haavoda, accused Mapai and its labour exchange officials of political favouritism in employment.[9] Similarly, Mr Kol, of the Progressive Party labour group, Haoved Hazioni, maintained that at election time it was a common sight to find officials of the labour exchanges in close proximity to the polling booths.[10] What separated Mapai from its left-wing critics was the fact that Mapai was proposing to transfer these functions to the state, while its left-wing critics, despite all their opposition to political party protectionism as applied by Mapai, were arguing in favour of the Histadrut retaining these functions.

In the same debate the Mapai representatives with Lavon at the head, not only did not deny these criticisms but made them one of the basic reasons for handing over control to the state. According to Lavon, 'In the labour exchange there are organic faults. Why have members not paid heed to the fact that perhaps the deep organic reason for the basic faults in the labour exchange is rooted in the cursed fact that a bureaucracy divided according to agreements (percentages) is not able, naturally, to allocate work on a first come first served basis.'[11] He went on to add that it was not worth it for Mapai to continue to bear the disapprobation that these inherent faults brought about.

One reason why it was not worth it was the retention of Kupat Cholim in Histadrut hands. It was not that Mapai members were healed quicker or better, but that whilst it was able to ensure a high level of Histadrut membership by the mere fact that it provided these health services, Mapai could afford to hand over the labour exchanges to the state. But they could

[9] *Report 70th Histadrut Council*, December 1956, p. 114.   [10] *Ibid.* p. 120.
[11] P. Lavon, *Values and Changes* (Tel Aviv, 1960), p. 158 (Hebrew).

hardly afford to hand over health services as well, for to do so would have removed the other major basis of large-scale Histadrut membership, and with it a major source of Mapai support. For this reason, among others, Mapai never agreed to hand over health services, for with them would go one of the major attractions of the Histadrut for potential members.

The continuing politicisation of health services

Politicisation of health services refers only to the control and administration of the health services of Kupat Cholim by the Histadrut. There is no suggestion that its relations with its clients were determined by the criteria of political party affiliation as occurred in the case of employment, or that in its professional decisions and hiring policies political considerations predominated. Kupat Cholim encompasses a network of clinics, laboratories, and hospitals, with large professional staffs of doctors, nurses and laboratory workers where universal and professional standards and criteria apply. Our concern here is only with membership of Kupat Cholim and its administration both of which were determined on political grounds.

Early in the 1950s pressure to depoliticise Kupat Cholim came mainly from the parties of the Right, from Herut and the General Zionists, who demanded the nationalisation of the Histadrut's health services, that is, their transfer to the control of the government. Later it was taken up publicly by some leading members of Mapai itself, usually those associated with the *Zeirim*. In both cases the attempt to depoliticise and nationalise Kupat Cholim was seen as a direct attempt to weaken the Histadrut, in fact as a frontal attack upon the Histadrut itself. For that reason alone the debate never even got off the ground and at no stage during the period did Mapai seriously consider these suggestions.

We have already indicated briefly above that the reason for this was that it was commonly believed by the Mapai leadership that this struck at the Histadrut's ability to maintain its strength, and at its membership attractiveness. The Histadrut's health services, it was argued, provided the very basis of the strength and power of attraction of the Histadrut. Thus to transfer Kupat Cholim to the state, it was feared, would begin a chain reaction that might bring into question the whole network of arrangements and collective agreements that had been so carefully built up over the years. If workers could receive these services from the state why should they join the Histadrut? After all, only 43 per cent of the membership dues they paid to the Histadrut went to Kupat Cholim, yet membership dues represented 76 per cent of the Histadrut's annual income.[12] Clearly one could receive health services more cheaply without having to subsidise the rest of the Histadrut's activities. Such

---

[12] See S. Tevet, 'Control Through Sickness', *Haaretz*, 3.5.1957; see also Y. Kotler, 'Mapai Against National Health', *ibid.* 28.7.1961.

reasoning was reinforced by the knowledge of how membership of the Histadrut was arranged and encouraged among new immigrants, as we saw above. Kupat Cholim thus helped to ensure that there were very few unorganised workers in the country. Knowing that the Histadrut's power would guarantee their enjoyment of the same working conditions as Histadrut members, many workers might have joined another health service, at lower cost.

Mapai as the majority party with the greatest number of officials and activists and the greatest degree of institutional penetration stood to gain more than its rivals from the Histadrut's strength. This was particularly so in view of the more rigid ideological postures of its main left-wing rivals and their more narrowly limited social foundations. It was here that Mapai hoped to develop the popular support that would retain for it control of both the Histadrut and the government. As Mordechai Namir, Secretary-General of the Histadrut, put it in 1955, Kupat Cholim was the secret of the strength of the labour movement in Israel, and he went on to add that if British Labour had this and the Histadrut economic enterprises they would never have gone out of power.[18]

In this light it is interesting to examine the arguments of those Mapai members who continued to argue for the transfer of the Histadrut health services to the state despite all the fears and apprehensions outlined above. The most sustained and searching analysis favouring this viewpoint was put forward in 1961 by Ahuvia Malkin, the director of Bet Berl, the party's training institute for potential political leaders, and at that time active in the *Zeirim*. In his view it was paradoxical that Kupat Cholim, which had been founded on aspirations of human brotherhood and partnership in fate, and upon mutual help and solidarity, and had reached high standards of health care prior to the existence of the state, should, with the establishment of the state, take on a distinct non-egalitarian character. The fact that 30 per cent of the population, some 600 000 souls in all, did not enjoy a satisfactory and comprehensive health coverage should worry the Histadrut which was founded upon concern for the whole population.

He scathingly attacked the argument that it was worth while for the Histadrut to continue to retain its health services because in this manner it strengthened its connections with the mass of members who otherwise might not have joined, and rejected all class and ideological justifications. 'In order to receive health services the Israeli worker should not be obliged to belong to a specific organisation, nor to adopt a particular ideology; his right is to enjoy them as a free citizen.' Moreover membership of the Histadrut motivated solely by a desire to benefit from these services detracted from the very real socio-economic and ideological connections that the worker had (or should have) with the Histadrut. According to Malkin, once 'state health insurance had been made possible (according to those same principles of responsibility

18 *Ibid.* 23.1.1955.

and mutual assistance), the Histadrut was not permitted to prevent this because of its desire to safeguard the power of attraction of Kupat Cholim'.

Finally he saw no sense in the argument sometimes advanced that the Histadrut had to maintain its strength in every possible way to guard against the eventuality that an anti-Histadrut government might be elected, which would dismantle the whole Histadrut structure.[14] Malkin claimed that any action taken against the Histadrut would fall equally upon Kupat Cholim. Moreover, if such a government attempted to nationalise health services the Histadrut would be in an extremely difficult position trying to explain why it, as a socialist movement, opposed nationalisation.[15]

Partial depoliticisation: the civil service

The civil service in Israel has undergone only partial depoliticisation since 1948. This can be seen particularly in the way in which recruitment is carried out, and the extent to which civil servants are permitted to indulge in formal and public party activity.

Immediately after the establishment of the state, recruitment to the new government departments was very much on political lines. Each party regarded the ministries it received as party spoils and distributed offices to loyal party members. As time went on this process was reinforced where the same party continued to control the ministry, but in ministries that changed parties there tended to be a conglomeration of the members of the various parties that had held the office. The processes of depoliticisation that took place were in the main formal and laid down in legislation, but as they applied only to new appointments, they had little effect upon all those political appointments that had been made earlier. The civil service regulations laid down various procedures of merit appointment, the need to make public announcements of openings and the use of independent experts and representatives of the public in the choice of candidates, and circumscribed the power of new ministers to fire officials who had been appointed by predecessors of a different political persuasion. In addition it was agreed that some of the very top posts were to be left as political posts which the ministers could fill almost at their discretion. Civil servants were not allowed to serve on the executive bodies of political parties, to stand for political office, to campaign publicly on behalf of political parties and so forth.

In point of fact, these regulations did not serve to eradicate all traces of politicisation, even in the appointment of officials. Where appointments were made after an internal announcement of a vacancy, especially, and even after a public announcement, it seems to be commonly agreed that party con-

[14] This argument was put in a reply to Malkin by Michael Lotan, 'The Histadrut, Impetus to the Building of an Egalitarian Society', Ovnayim (Bet Berl, 1961), 48–58.
[15] All the citations are from A. Malkin, 'The Histadrut in the State', ibid. 29–47.

siderations were still important in encouraging candidates to apply, in drawing up the precise qualifications and experience being sought and the exact description of the post available so as to fit a party candidate already in mind, or one already employed under the 'special contract' provisions of the legislation, and in deciding between otherwise evenly matched candidates. But it also seems to be true that if the person preferred for party reasons was manifestly less qualified than another candidate, the latter was more likely to get the job. The effect in many cases then was one of negative screening, that is, the choice was made between a number of suitably qualified candidates all of the right party affiliation. The general situation was one of slowly decreasing politicisation in the area of new appointees, coupled with a solid layer of early appointees on the bottom who were party nominees. Moreover as professionalism and commitment to professional standards increased and as civil servants began to regard themselves more as civil servants and less as party men, the slow progress towards depoliticisation was reinforced.[16]

The continuation of party control and influence
The Histadrut

In the Histadrut party control and influence is regarded as entirely legitimate. The basis of Mapai control in the Histadrut was the elections to the Histadrut Conference that are held on the average every five years. It is understood and accepted that the major executive and representative bodies of the Histadrut are to be filled according to the exact proportion of the votes the parties received in the elections. The same rule applies in all other Histadrut bodies as well, be they industrial undertakings, banks, insurance companies, consumer, producer and supplier cooperatives, health schemes, and so on and so forth. Mapai with just over 50 per cent of the votes should receive just over 50 per cent of the executive offices in all of these bodies. But in fact the system did not work quite this way, and Mapai in effect received far more than a mere 50 per cent. In many areas its proportions were greater, but what is more, in *every* area it received the top, most crucial and most influential executive positions and particularly those which enabled it greatly to increase its proportions at the lower levels.

Beginning first with the trade union and organisational aspects of the Histadrut in its role of representing the workers vis à vis their employers we find a predominant Mapai control at all levels. Some of this arose out of the processes of rank and file election, but some also was gained by indirect

---

[16] See Y. Dror, 'Some Aspects of Staff Problems in Israel', *Kaplan School Reprint*, 1960, and 'Public Policy Making in Israel', in *Public Administration in Israel and Abroad* (Jerusalem, 1962), 5–16. G. E. Caiden, 'Prospects for Administrative Reform in Israel', *Public Administration*, 46 (Spring, 1968), 25–44, and N. Raphaeli, 'The Senior Civil Service in Israel: Notes on some Characteristics', *Public Administration*, 48 (Summer, 1970), 169–78.

election (election by the elected), some by party agreement, and some by appointment. The very foundation of this Mapai predominance lay in the workplaces and in the workers' committees. Mapai controlled most of these committees, particularly the bigger ones in the areas of large worker concentration throughout the country. On this foundation was built Mapai's control of the local trade unions and the local Labour Councils, and of the national trade unions. There was not a local Labour Council in the country in the period 1948–65 in which Mapai did not enjoy a majority, and with it, control of the most important executive positions. Similarly there was hardly a national trade union which was not in the same situation, which was further maintained by their very infrequent elections.

The Organisation Department, and the Trade Union Department coordinated and directed the local Labour Councils and the trade unions respectively. They, too, were staffed in accordance with a party key, with the most important positions including that of the head of the department going to Mapai nominees. The Organisation Department's role was to oversee and direct the activities of the local Labour Councils. It approved the choice of secretary of the local Labour Councils, and generally acted as a channel of communication between the central Histadrut executive bodies and the local executive bodies. As the latter were responsible for the whole range of Histadrut activities in their area, directing some and coordinating others (in general they had little say only in Histadrut industrial undertakings in their area) this provided Mapai with immediate and widespread penetration into the local centres of Histadrut organisation from the top as well as from the bottom. On the other hand, the autonomy of these local Labour Councils meant that this did not constitute anything like constant direction or control. Nor was there much need for the latter in so far as local officials were all Mapai party members and had a good idea of what the party demanded of them and what policies they ought to follow. It was more likely to be of use in times of crisis where it gave Mapai another channel of influence in local affairs backed by Histadrut discipline and executive authority.

The Trade Union Department coordinated the activities of all the national unions, and many of their leading officials were also members of the executive committee which decided the Department's policies. We have already seen how crucial the Department was in the process of making wages policy. Here the Mapai connection at all levels of trade union administration and organisation was vitally important in promoting rank and file support for the policies of the Department especially if they involved wage restraint.

Mapai's successful penetration and control of this far-flung Histadrut trade union network was not without shadows and complications that this form of politicisation found it difficult to avoid. These were generally the results of autonomous action by specific unions, or local Labour Councils against the wishes, and without the approval, of the Histadrut. This related mainly to strike action as a means of pressing industrial demands. Thus a local Labour Council strongly supported by the local Mapai branch could hold out for a long time against even the strongest and most authoritative central pressure from Histadrut, Mapai, and government leaders. This happened in the case of the Ata strike in Haifa in 1957, when Almogi, Secretary of the Haifa Labour Council, for months successfully defied the Minister of Labour, the Secretary-General and Central Executive Committee of the Histadrut, and Prime Minister Ben Gurion who attempted to mediate. Under the pressure of threats to call all of Haifa and its essential services out on strike, Almogi succeeded in gaining many of the demands that had been set by the Haifa Labour Council. Similarly, Mapai control of particular unions and their executives did not always prevent them from going out on strike in pursuit of their demands, as was the case most notably with professional unions, such as teachers and engineers. But in the long run Mapai influence, though greatly muted, assisted in settling such disputes, and it is probable that they were settled more quickly than would have been the case had the degree of politicisation been less.

Mapai's political control and influence within the Histadrut was further promoted and consolidated by its hold over the economic enterprises and industrial undertakings of the Histadrut, known as the Labour Economy. These were united under the roof of *Chevrat Ovdim* which directly or in-directly administered all these enterprises and supervised them on behalf of their owners, the membership of the Histadrut. Formally, the Histadrut's Conference, Council, and Executive Committee were identical in person with the same bodies of *Chevrat Ovdim*. The latter's executive organs consisted of a Secretariat and an Executive Committee. Between them they coordinated, supervised and directed the varied industrial and economic activities of the Histadrut.

This is indeed a vast industrial, commercial and financial empire.[17] If we examine *Chevrat Ovdim's* sphere of direct administration, which included the largest Histadrut companies in industry, building, public works, banking, insurance, marketing, and supply, together with the pension and loan funds, a significant pattern emerges. At the highest level, in the Secretariat and the Executive Committee of *Chevrat Ovdim*, the typical Histadrut procedure of allotting places according to the party proportions was closely followed, although if anything, Mapai came off slightly better than its numerical percentage. But in the administrative apparatus of *Chevrat Ovdim* itself, and in the actual executive bodies of these companies together with their bureaucracies, the picture changes rather dramatically. In general the proportion of Mapai members in the boards of directors of these companies was well above the 55 per cent proportion that elections gave it. There are a number of

[17] See the figures in Ze'ev Onn, *Hevrat Ovdim: Israel's Labour Economy*, 76th Council of the Histadrut, April 1964, Tel Aviv.

important qualifications to this general rule. First, the marketing and supply cooperatives, *Tnuva* and *Hamashbir*, which dealt with the agricultural settlements, were constituted according to the proportions of the agricultural settlement movements and federations composing them, and not according to the election proportions, but here Mapai, to which were affiliated about 275 of the 445 Histadrut agricultural settlements, received a minimum of 62 per cent of the places.

The directorates of the other companies were chosen by the executive bodies of *Chevrat Ovdim* according to a much looser party key than in the representative institutions. From here two things emerged at the executive level of these companies. The first was that the Mapai proportion of directors of the companies was usually in the vicinity of 75 to 80 per cent. Moreover, all their general managers were, without exception, Mapai men, as were nearly all of the active directors. In addition the key positions – secretary, treasurer, public relations, financial controller, personnel, workers' representative, were nearly always in Mapai hands. As we move down the administrative ladder to positions just below the top, and down to the middle levels of management, the process snowballs and the proportion of Mapai men in these positions reached 90 per cent. Similarly, in the administrative apparatus of *Chevrat Ovdim* itself, where no party key applied, the proportion of Mapai members was also in the vicinity of 85 per cent. In some important companies this chain of Mapai membership reached down to the level of foreman. Thus as we go down the management line the proportion of Mapai members increased most significantly.

A similar process was evident in the administrative set-up of Kupat Cholim, although not in its professional sphere. The top policy making body of Kupat Cholim was constituted on a party key and approximated the Conference percentages. But at the administrative level below this the Mapai proportions rose dramatically. Thus in 1965 of the fifteen regional directors of Kupat Cholim, fourteen were Mapai men, and of the sixteen administrative heads of Kupat Cholim hospitals, twelve were known to belong to Mapai.

How can we explain this phenomenon of the progressive increase of Mapai power and control in the administration of Histadrut economic enterprises and its social service network? The first and basic factor accounting for this consolidation of control is that Mapai always received the top executive positions together with a majority of the boards of directors. One could very well argue that if it were intended to follow the proportional principle exactly Mapai should have received the top executive positions in only 55 per cent of Histadrut industry, with the rest divided up among the other parties proportionately. As it was, Mapai was able to convert its bare electoral majority into nearly 100 per cent control. Precisely because there was no key system for middle-level appointments Mapai could use its executive control to allocate positions to party men, ideally, suitably qualified. Within the Histadrut most appointments to these positions were on the basis of personal acquaintance rather than of public competition or announcement. It was only natural for a Mapai managing director, or assistant manager, or personnel officer, to find a person from amongst his party acquaintances, or if he hadn't one available, to cast around among his fellow Mapai management officials so that they could help in the quest. In addition, the party was always keenly sensitive to the advantages and opportunities available to it through administrative control and constantly sought to derive maximum benefit from its position in the Histadrut economic empire. Mapai regarded itself as being in control of these institutions (albeit through the Histadrut), and therefore felt free to find positions within them for party members. Then again the suggestion may have come from one of those leading party personalities who specialised in finding posts for the deserving party member. This process became self-generating as those aspiring to such positions often recognised that their chances would be improved by joining the party and did so.

An additional factor facilitating this process were the membership advantages enjoyed by Mapai vis à vis its main rivals in the Histadrut, Mapam and Achdut Haavoda. The latter were kibbutz-based parties with few urban members compared with the 200 000 strong Mapai at the end of 1964. Not only were there more Mapai members available, but, in addition, its membership was much more urban based, and contained more individuals with administrative experience, or with university training which, even in the Histadrut administrative apparatus, was slowly coming to the fore.

The municipal sphere

A similar process of politicisation was operative in the municipal sphere. Here, too, Mapai's electoral success provided the basis. Thus in the 1959 municipal elections Mapai's representatives led the municipal government in twenty out of twenty-four cities, and in forty-seven out of sixty-one towns and rural regions in the Jewish sector. Its control in the sphere of municipal government was therefore close to saturation point, and its political rivals were left far behind. Mapai was always aware of the instrumental and political advantages to be derived from this situation which were reinforced by the tradition of coalition arrangements, and always made sure that it got the most important positions in the municipal administrations for its loyal and trusted party members. In particular, it sought the two key posts in the local government bureaucracies, namely those of secretary and treasurer, as well as heading some other key municipal departments. It sought also to consolidate its rule by gaining a majority of those permanent administrative employees on the highest rungs of the administrative scale. Although there are public advertisements of vacant positions the traditional practice of party division of the posts prevailed and in it Mapai came out on top. It was less interested in lower positions and these were usually filled by the Government Employ-ment Service with no attention to political qualifications. But if a party member wished to be employed in these lower levels there was ample scope for this to be arranged and similarly with the non-administrative jobs. In fact here the process worked more in the other direction; people joined the party in order to get jobs of various kinds or in order to assist their chances of promotion, and only later became loyal, useful and active party members.

The filling of administrative positions on party lines and particularly those involving contact with the public, placed bureaucrats under tremendous pressure from party members seeking the various forms of instrumental benefit that the municipality could confer or deny, in addition to the usual claims of the general public in the same spheres. More often than not these claims and demands would not be made directly by the claimant himself but by a Mapai party or Histadrut official requesting that the particular indi-vidual be assisted in the desired manner.

The Jewish Agency

The Jewish Agency, too, which looked after the process of immigration and settlement, and with whom the immigrants had their first contacts, was, if anything, even more avowedly political in the development of its adminis-trative apparatus. Despite the fact that it was carrying on official, quasi-governmental functions of prime importance, it was staffed on the basis of a party key which was frankly acknowledged. As we noted earlier these officials performed the dual roles of official, and of party recruitment. In many cases Mapai representatives in the Jewish Agency bureaucracy set in motion the party process that operated within the other bureaucracies where Mapai members had been installed. One of the reasons for the frank recognition of the politicisation of the Jewish Agency bureaucracy was the declining public responsiveness and representativeness of the Jewish Agency, as compared with the pre-1948 situation. With the establishment of the state, elections to the Jewish Agency ceased as it radically declined in importance, and as many of its major functions were taken over by the state. The absence of elections meant a decline in public interest and in the Agency's responsiveness to the public in turn, and it came more and more to be regarded as the federation of Zionist political parties which ran its affairs in the absence of elections on the basis of agreement among them. This was a matter for hard bargaining for positions of power, for the distribution of executive positions, lower-level administrative positions and financial and other resources. In this bargaining process the parties agreed on a party key and it was by this key that each party's share was determined.

The effects of politicisation

The overall picture then was one of widespread penetration and permeation by Mapai of Israel's major bureaucratic structures. In this context we should also note the politicisation of various interest groups by Mapai, particularly artisans and small shopkeepers organisations, trade unions, professional associations, agricultural interests, ethnic organisations, *landsmanshaften*, religious groups, students, youth, and women's organisations, all of which were analysed in previous chapters. It is now time to turn to the effects of this widespread politicisation.

This network was used by Mapai in a number of different ways. It was of assistance in the mobilisation of votes and support for the party at election time. This was done within the organisations and groups themselves and within the society at large. In some cases, notably that of Histadrut institutions, this was reinforced by donations to Mapai campaign funds. Where funds were divided up between all Histadrut parties in proportion to their strength, it was done openly, but where large sums were given to Mapai solely (because of its control of these resources) or came from bodies such as Kupat Cholim, it was carried out secretly, and the evidence suggests that this was not an uncommon occurrence.[18]

This network of politicisation also had important effects upon the process of policy formation, as we have seen in a number of different ways in preceding chapters. We have seen how budgetary and tax policy, and, in particular, wages policy, were discussed within the party, and how the fact that these different groups were united by a common party loyalty facilitated the process of decision making. At the same time members of the interested groups gained access to the decision makers. We have also seen how agricultural interests, artisans and craftsmen, and municipal interests used the same network of party loyalty to initiate and pursue policy proposals seeking to satisfy their demands. Mapai ministers, civil servants, municipal, Histadrut and Jewish Agency officials were variously utilised within the framework of the party's decision making institutions, and outside it in their own administrative structures and representative institutions, to answer the needs of the various groups that made up the party. In our view, in almost all cases it was easier for these groups to obtain what they wanted because they were so affiliated with the party, than it would have been had they been outside the party and merely in some bargaining relationship with it. Thus widespread politicisation contributed to the effectiveness of policy making and thereby to the overall strengthening of Mapai's position, and facilitated the taking of policy decisions that would have been much more difficult if not impossible outside the Mapai framework.

Politicisation did not mean constant surveillance and control over the large

[18] E. Gutmann, 'Israel', *Journal of Politics*, 25 (1963), 711.

network of officials and representatives, or day to day direction in their activities. The opposite is probably closer to the truth. In local Histadrut and municipal affairs, as we saw, the Mapai branches rarely gave policy directions to their representatives, leaving it up to them to decide for themselves, and this was even more true of the party members in bureaucratic positions. The expectation was that representatives and officials would know for themselves what the party's general lines of policy and interests were, and that they would be able to operate within them independently of day to day control or direction. It was also expected that where disagreements between them occurred or where matters of basic importance were involved, they would turn to the relevant party institutions for discussion and an authoritative decision. In such a complex network of interests and institutional affiliations it was inevitable that differences would arise and essential that the party institutions be able to settle them and agree on a policy.

The need for the party to be able to make decisions was emphasised by the electoral competition which existed in most of these institutional frameworks, and upon which it built and consolidated this network of politicisation. Because it was under constant threat of the loss of power and position and the demolition of this carefully constructed network of affiliations, the party was under tremendous pressure to make policy decisions efficiently and well. Electoral competition and its attendant publicity, constituting a marked degree of responsiveness to public reaction, also served to minimise the degree, if any, of personal corruption involved in the administration of these various institutional structures. Party members may have been preferred, or found it easier to gain access to decision makers or to secure scarce instrumental benefits or resources, but generally there is little evidence of bribery, of officials lining their own pockets, of the exclusion of members of other parties from available resources to which they were entitled, the avoidance of justice, the pocketing of public funds, the taking of kick-backs, and so on.

Politicisation, as we have described it, served to assist in the incorporation of social forces into the political system and into Mapai. Not only was access available for the articulation of interests and their aggregation, but the positions themselves were open to and used for the placing of individuals from many groups in society in decision making positions at various levels of importance. In certain instances this had a chain effect in that those same individuals were in a position not only to assist in the achievement of group goals, but to help individual members of those groups as well. To the extent that they were able to do so, further support for the party among these groups was likely to be forthcoming.

Politicisation, therefore, by promoting the centralisation of political power in the hands of one party in a divided multi-party system where immobilism was a possible outcome, contributed greatly to the task of state building. It facilitated policy coherence and institutional coordination, and provided some degree of assurance that policy application would not be sabotaged or impeded at lower levels by opposed or competing political interests.

At the same time a balance was struck between the need for centralised political power and the need for universalism which in the Israeli context meant depoliticisation, that is, the relinquishment of control by particularistic political parties over important political and societal functions. Mapai led the movement for the abdication by political parties of these functions and their handing over to the state where universalistic criteria of citizen equality and merit would be better able to apply. In doing so it made a vital contribution to state building: it enabled political power formerly divided among political parties to be centralised in the hands of the state. Moreover it was able to accomplish this without any loss to its own power resources or leadership, while this did entail a loss of power resources by other parties and institutions. By handing over Histadrut power and functions to the state the Histadrut was weakened and the state and nation strengthened, as they were also by the gradual development of depoliticised state bureaucratic structures. Mapai did not lose, because it remained the major force in the Israeli government, and directed the state structures and institutions. From this point of view its position was even strengthened, because it directed these same functions in the name of the state, rather than of the Histadrut. Not only did it have state coercive power at its disposal, it also gained wider public support and legitimacy for itself and for the new system of government through its emphasis upon the universalism of *Mamlachtiut*.

But while its external power capacity may have been strengthened by these forces and policies, it was also dependent upon its internal organisation. Specifically it was dependent upon its own ability to maintain itself organisationally and to retain internal cohesion. Many organisations undergo such tests at various critical times in their history: in Mapai's case the critical issue that was most closely bound up with organisational maintenance and internal cohesion was the question of leadership succession against a background of inter-generational conflict. Interestingly enough from our present context, the degree of commitment to *Mamlachtiut* constituted a critical element in this struggle. It is to these issues that we now turn.

12. LEADERSHIP, SUCCESSION AND ORGANISATIONAL MAINTENANCE: CONFLICT, SPLIT AND REUNIFICATION

The theoretical relationship of organisational maintenance, leadership and succession

In earlier chapters we examined the aggregative and incorporative character of Mapai, the way in which diverse social forces were integrated into the party. We noted then that whilst these groups articulated their particular interests within Mapai, the party sought to aggregate these divergent interest demands into coherent policies and to gain their support for its goals. One characteristic approach of the party was to adopt various patterns of organisational penetration in the belief that incorporating these groups and socialising them would enable it to apply the welding and compromising influence of common party loyalty in the task of policy making. We also focused upon the organisational methods used to further incorporation, to achieve interest aggregation, and make policy decisions. This involved examination of the problems of internal and external institutional coordination, the processes of leadership selection, and the participation of various groups of leaders and party bodies in the making of major policy and personnel decisions. Here, too, we emphasised the straddle of party loyalty as a mechanism of decision making.

These concerns come together in relation to the major problem of this chapter; the problem of organisational cohesion and maintenance. According to Selznick organisations typically undergo a process of increasing institutionalisation.

> As an organization acquires a self, a distinctive identity, it becomes an institution. This involves the taking on of values, ways of acting and believing that are deemed important for their own sake. From then on self-maintenance becomes more than bare organizational survival; it becomes a struggle to preserve the uniqueness of the group in the face of new problems and altered circumstances.[1]

Leadership plays a crucial role in organisational cohesion. Not only must it set goals in relation to effective internal and external demands and continually shape the social structure of the organisation, it must also defend institutional

---

[1] P. Selznick, *Leadership in Administration: A Sociological Interpretation* (New York, 1957), p. 21.

integrity and survival – it must maintain values and distinctive identity. Particularly relevant in this context is the ordering of internal conflict among competing constituent interests. 'This is so because the direction of the enterprise as a whole may be seriously influenced by changes in the internal balance of power.'[2] Nowhere are these more evident than in the question of succession: that is, those policy choices and personnel decisions that refer to the very top leadership of the institution into whose hands the distinctive values, identity, and institutional survival of the organisation are being given.

The question of succession is potentially fraught with danger for organisational cohesion because the stakes are so high: the future direction of the whole organisation itself. Consequently internal conflict between rival leadership succession groups may develop to a point where loyalty to the party no longer acts as a straddle conducive to compromise and consensual decision making; it can stretch only so far and no farther, with the result that internal cohesion is rent. In such struggles, there can be no certainty that an organisation will survive intact. The top leadership group will usually have considerable influence over whether such crises are likely to arise. While the top leadership must give expression to and continually redefine the organisation's key values, it must also guide it in facing internal and external environmental changes. Its responses to these may provoke intense opposition which must be foreseen and taken into consideration. Thus its definition of key values may be challenged by groups seeking to maintain the old, or to promote the new. In selecting successors it may provoke opposition by preferring one set of leaders over another. In its policies towards external groups, it may threaten internal cohesion by making key member and leadership groups feel threatened. Conflicts affecting institutional survival and organisational maintenance thus often involve, at their roots, questions of values, or at the very least will be framed in terms of the organisation's values and goals. Succession is not just a question of personnel but involves the maintenance of distinctive values and identity and is usually fought out in terms of both these aspects, which eventually become inseparable.

In this chapter we shall examine the major internal conflict within Mapai which began not long after the establishment of the state, produced a party split in 1965, and culminated in a wider reunification in 1968. Because of Mapai's dominant position in Israeli society and the state, its internal intergenerational conflict was a struggle for succession which involved not only the direction in which it would develop, but the direction in which the whole society would evolve and develop, and the degree to which it would maintain the institutions and values of the Yishuv era or would seek new goals and new methods of accomplishing them.

Our analysis above indicated that succession was directly linked to organi-

[2] *Ibid.* p. 63.

sational values and goals and to organisational cohesion. Because of the importance of these issues, such conflicts tended to manifest themselves in many aspects of party activity – in conflicts over internal party organisation, democratisation, the role of the party machine, the process of politicisation, ideological formulations and commonly accepted ideological values, the relationship between the state and other major institutions in society, particularly the Histadrut and its leaders, and the methods and tempo of state activity. A major focus of this analysis will be to try and explain why Mapai, which was so successful in mediating, solving and reaching acceptable compromise in many other spheres of conflict and disagreement, was unable to do so in this instance. Why was it that its mechanisms of conflict resolution and decision making, emphasising consensus and agreement, broke down in this instance? Why did the straddle of party loyalty not produce the desired results?

The desire for active participation in party affairs: inter-generational conflict and the struggle for democratisation

What eventually split the party had very simple and even humble origins. After the War of Independence, former leading members of Mapai's Young Guard, *Mishmeret Hatzeira*, met together in youth clubs set up by Mapai in Tel Aviv and Jerusalem. In all they numbered about 400 members in fairly tightly closed circles. Some were party members who had left kibbutzim, others were members of moshavim, whilst a few had already begun bureaucratic and administrative careers. Half the membership was situated in Tel Aviv, whilst about 30 per cent were at the time over thirty years of age.[3] These groups carried on intellectual discussions about the party's policies and activities. They sought to ensure that the party critically discuss and clarify ideas and values, including those commonly accepted and sanctified in the pre-state era. Basic to their whole approach was free and public discussion of all party affairs. Thus their very first public statements and activities tended to be rather critical. They proclaimed the need for the party as a whole to discuss its policies in major areas affected by the achievement of independence – education, *chalutziut*, defence, the economy. In particular they sought after a new type of *chalutzic* pioneering which would be more in tune with the new challenges and problems. They were critical of the fact that decisions were taken from above, and of the absence of rank and file participation in decisions, and even in discussion. They were also critical of state bureaucratic procedures and of the party's internal administration. These themes were combined with a demand for democratisation, which implied the acceptance of internal opposition and differences of opinion, and greater attention to

[3] *Haaretz*, 14.2.1951.

branch discussions. Overall, they called on the party to coordinate its thought and activity better, and to strengthen its authority over its delegates in the executive frameworks of the state and labour movement.

Early in 1951 they called a nation-wide conference to discuss these matters, under the banner of *Hatnua Lehitchadshut Hamiflaga* (Movement for Party Regeneration). But the semblance of national organisational form made the central party institutions apprehensive. They did not want Mapai publicly exposed to harsh internal criticism, which would weaken its public image, and they feared the development of a new faction. The Central Committee finally permitted the proposed meeting to take place on the proviso that it be held out of the limelight in the country at Kfar Hayarok. But the basic attitude of the party institutions was summed up by a spokesman of the elder generation, a moshav founder who asked 'Why doesn't the party youth go to the Negev? What has to be renewed is that our youth should have the desire to live the "beginning". In this way the *chalutzic* renewal can be expressed, and not through discussion at this table.'[5]

The next few years saw the initiation of a number of schemes whereby youth could assist the state in immigrant absorption, and especially in agriculture. Prominent in them was the group known as *Bnei Hamoshavim*, members of the second generation in the moshavim, who left their own farms for a number of years to work among the immigrants as agricultural and social instructors. A number of leading *Zeirim* were involved in this and other similar activities. But it was not long before the inter-generational conflict reappeared, this time in Tel Aviv, where Abraham Ofer, one of the leading *Zeirim*, became the secretary of the Tel Aviv party branch. We have already seen in chapter eight what happened in the Tel Aviv branch, when Ofer attempted to liven up the sub-branches, enable rank and file participation, encourage discussion and exchange of ideas, and carry out democratic elections. This early experience made it clear that to put their ideas into practice, the *Zeirim* would be involved in a direct confrontation with the powerful and dominant party machine. This was no longer a discussion of ideas but a major struggle for power between young and old. Thus to their emphasis on democratisation the *Zeirim* had added a challenge to the prevailing organisational patterns and dominant administrative figures within the party. While the two were not synonomous they were complementary in that democratisation as they understood it would help to bring about organisational reform, which would in turn bring about greater participation and thus strengthen democratic internal life and give meaning to internal elections. At about the same time they also came to recognise that an entrenched administrative machine like the *Gush* could not be unseated, or support gained for democratisation without a degree of permanent organisation, and

---

[4] *Ibid.* 14.12.1950, 9.1.1951; *Davar*, 14.1.1951.
[5] *Minutes Mapai Central Committeee*, 14.1.1951.

we noted above in chapter four how the *Zeirim* unsuccessfully attempted to gain this following the 1955 Knesset elections.

These internal tensions burst out into the open at the 8th Mapai Conference, held in August 1956, the first since 1950. A major item on the agenda arousing intense interest was constitutional reform. The outgoing Secretariat had appointed a constitutional sub-committee, on which the *Gush* had a clear majority, but on which a number of leading *Zeirim* were represented, whose task it was to prepare a draft for the Conference to consider. The stage was set for the conflict by Ben Gurion in a wide-ranging opening address which was concerned with the party and the state in the past and the future. In enumerating past party failures Ben Gurion suggested that one of them had been insufficient attention to giving responsibility to the younger forces in the party, Histadrut, and state activities.[6]

The atmosphere at the Conference was tense and rowdy, when the *Zeirim* unsuccessfully challenged certain aspects of the election of the Standing Committee, which had been managed by the party machine.[7] A major debate also took place over the constitutional provisions governing the election of the Central Committee, which was dealt with in chapter six. In all these issues the *Zeirim* favoured greater rank and file participation, less central control, and immediate rather than delayed implementation of any changes agreed to. They enjoyed the support of the united Haifa bloc of delegates – the only time in their history of conflict with the *Gush* that they did so – and of most of the delegates of the Ichud and of a large section of those of Tnuat Hamoshavim. This enabled the *Zeirim* to win a number of narrow victories on the more technical and procedural aspects of elections (on the major issues of the size of the Central Committee, initial victory was turned into defeat by behind the scenes *Gush* pressure, as noted in chapter six. But the key point was that the 8th Conference neither heralded major changes in the party nor served as a turning point in intra-party affairs in the direction of democratisation; it left the power of the entrenched party machine firmly intact, and was little more than a preliminary skirmish in a long-drawn-out battle. Yet in many ways the achievements of the *Zeirim* at this Conference, minor as they were, were to represent their greatest successes in open conflict with the dominant powers in Mapai; on no subsequent occasion did they succeed in having the majority recommendations of the Standing Committee defeated on the floor of the Conference.

The struggle against the party machine

The one major victory that accrued to the *Zeirim* was agreement reached at the Conference to nominate Dr Giora Yosephtal to the position of Secretary-General of Mapai (see chapter seven). His election focused for the first

[6] *Report 8th Mapai Conference, 1956*, p. 21.   [7] *Ibid.* p. 36.

time a strain of thinking amongst the *Zeirim* which, as the ensuing years passed, became steadily more important in their battle against the *Vatikim*; the conflict between abstract ideological theorising tied to the sacred values of the past, and the emphasis upon getting things done efficiently, and in the interests of the state, whatever their effects upon the values of the past and the institutions to which these gave rise. This was the conflict over what became known as '*Bitzuism*', from the Hebrew word, '*bitzua*' meaning implementation or putting into effect. Their opponents claimed that those who were guilty of '*Bitzuism*' were pragmatists and technocrats concerned only with performance and with what was attainable; they were not interested in relating it to the sacred values of the movement, and were only too ready to give in too easily if it was thought that what they wanted was unattainable.

Yosephtal's election shifted the focus of the conflict directly on to the central executive institutions of the party itself, and it took on the new dimension of a headlong organisational confrontation. It was, in short, a struggle for power within the party's major decision making bodies. Yosephtal sought to introduce into party work younger members who had outside administrative experience, and in this he succeeded for a short time, except for the Organisation Department where Netzer and the *Gush* blocked the appointment of their old rival, Ofer. In general, party organisation and administration from 1956 until about the end of 1958 was characterised by widespread conflict between the party Secretary-General and the *Gush*. Yosephtal's view was that for the sake of the future the party had to allow and even encourage its younger members to become active and to take on leading positions of participation at all levels, including the most central ones. This would integrate the generations, bring about active cooperation, and enable the leadership of the young generation to share in responsibility and activity.[8] For the *Gush*, this generational integration was being achieved, not by adding to what was existing and to the leadership and activists of the older generation, but by removing the older generation.[9]

The *Zeirim* were at a disadvantage in this attempt to gain a footing in the party administration because they were not prepared to work their way up the party ladder from the bottom. Often over-trained for such positions, they were unable to build a power base from which to topple their rivals. Even the top levels of party administration were not particularly appealing to them, and certainly not as appealing as the higher levels of the civil service, the Knesset, the diplomatic corps and so forth. Work in the party and in many areas of the Histadrut, from whence came control of Mapai party institutions, was not to their taste. The *Zeirim* were not prepared to serve this kind of long and almost interminable apprenticeship, or to go to the development towns, the Negev and other outlying areas, where, it was constantly pointed out to

[8] *Report 8th Mapai Conference, 2nd Session, 1958*, p. 30.   [9] R. Bash, *ibid.* p. 143.

them, their talents were most needed. And they could not help but feel cynical about the advice to go to such distant places, when it was preached in the name of pioneering by those who held many of the more centrally placed positions of power.

The support for democratisation reappeared briefly at the second session of the 8th Conference held in May 1958, over the choice of Knesset candidates. As noted in chapter nine the *Zeirim* proposed that the branch section of the Knesset list be chosen by a rank and file ballot, and not by the branch institutions, as was favoured by the majority of the Standing Committee.[10] It was argued that this would serve to create a closer connection within Mapai between the elector and the elected, and would give meaning to the notion of representation.[11] When put to the vote, this motion was easily lost 633:59.[12]

Critique of the Histadrut and old-style pioneering: Mamlachtiut

About the middle of 1958 this situation altered radically and dramatically with the entry into politics of the retiring Chief of Staff of the Israeli Defence Forces, General Moshe Dayan. At the same time it became known that Shimon Peres, Director-General of the Ministry of Defence, Abba Eban, Israel's Ambassador to Washington and the U.N., and Dr Yosephtal, would all seek election to the Knesset in the 1959 elections. It was commonly believed that all four would occupy prominent places in Mapai's Knesset list because of their expected attractiveness to the country at large, and to the youth in particular. All were known to be on good terms with Ben Gurion, if not protégés. But it was the entry into Mapai affairs of Dayan, more than of the others, that changed the picture. This was in part chronological – Dayan became involved earlier – but it was also related to his personality, achievements, position in Israeli society, and his views.

Immediately upon entering political life Dayan became associated with the *Zeirim* and was commonly regarded as their unofficial leader and spokesman; most of his public political statements were made in their forums. This represented an important qualitative change in the very basis of the *Zeirim's* challenge to the dominant group. For the first time they had a national political personality of the first order. Dayan had been Chief of Staff for five years, and had been the spectacular, dashing hero-architect of Israel's military successes in Sinai in 1956. In his term Israel's defence forces had been built up to their highest peak of efficiency and professional skill, and their technological and weapons systems improved out of sight. Simultaneously, the place of defence and security in Israel's overall planning and world view, as well as in its foreign policy were higher than ever before. Not only was Dayan a dashing military hero, more importantly he was recognised as a military policy maker as well, and in this sphere was known to enjoy Ben Gurion's

[10] A. Remez, *ibid.* p. 176.,   [11] *Ibid.* p. 177 and p. 192.   [12] *Ibid.* p. 247.

close cooperation and confidence. Nor was he a stranger to Mapai: he was the
son of Shmuel Dayan M.K., one of the founders of the moshav movement,
and had been born on a kibbutz and grown up on a Mapai-affiliated moshav,
in Mapai youth movements, and later the Palmach.

On leaving the army in the middle of 1958 he was immediately besieged
with speaking engagements, many of which he accepted, and his outspoken
comments on a number of matters encountered widespread public reaction,
and strong opposition from the dominant group in Mapai. He shifted the
focus of the *Zeirim*'s criticism from intra-party affairs and democratisation to
the general sphere of Israeli society; in particular, he began to question in-
sistently, loudly and publicly, certain of the given assumptions and values
of the pre-1948 period regarding the labour movement as a whole, and the
role of the Histadrut in particular. His views attracted wide public interest
because of his own status, because it was rare for a leading Mapai figure to be
outspokenly critical of such matters, and because he was regarded as the voice
of the new generation coming into political power, expressing its opinion
about the future development of the whole society. In a sense then, his views
were thought to be a portent of what the future had in store for the country
and the labour movement.

Dayan's major criticisms were directed against the Histadrut's trade union
policies. He attacked them for protecting inefficient labour and came out in
favour of management's right to dismiss inefficient employees, which struck
at the very root of Histadrut labour organisation, and the role of the workers
committees. He was also critical of inefficiency in the civil service and Histadrut sectors in particular, and opposed the Histadrut's plans to improve
workers' social conditions. In his view productivity had to be increased and
costs lowered, so as to decrease Israel's economic dependence and he favoured
strong measures even if this entailed temporary unemployment. He coupled
this critique with demands for a new type of *chalutziut*, and the suggestion
that the old-style *chalutziut* was outmoded, and that under the conditions of
the independent state the Yishuv form of *chalutziut* was inefficient. This was
taken to be a critique of the whole kibbutzic movement and way of life,
which, if not widely practised, still stood at the apex of the socio-political
values in Mapai. Thus on many occasions he proposed a new definition of
pioneering, state pioneering, *Chalutziut Mamlachtit*.[18] Overall, the state
occupied a central position in his thinking coupled with a critique of the
inadequacies of the Histadrut. This soon developed into a conflict along these
lines, of the state versus the Histadrut, or more correctly, of Histadrut leaders
versus some Mapai ministers and others, stressing *Mamlachtiut*.

Dayan's views fitted in well with those of the *Zeirim*, who also proclaimed
the ideology of *Mamlachtiut*, opposed sectionalism and did not sanctify

[18] In an interview with the *Jewish Observer and Middle East Review*, 7.11.1958; see also
ibid. 13.6.1958, 19.12.1958.

physical labour, and placed their faith in scientific development and technological expertise and efficiency.[14] But in our view at this stage the ideological
conflict, though publicly emphasised at the time, was probably less significant
than the institutional conflict and the personal rivalries involved. The
tendency to emphasise the ideological aspects is more a comment on the
conventions of public debate in Israeli society than a reflection of reality.
There were few important Mapai leaders who did not recognise the importance
of the state and were not committed to *Mamlachtiut*, and all that it implied,
including the extensive use of state bureaucratic mechanisms to get things
done, rather than to rely upon voluntary and personal pioneering. In fact
Mapai ministers and Histadrut leaders of the older generation were every bit
as pragmatic as their younger critics and rivals. The differences between them
were more those of temperament and style of activity, and the accusation of
the younger that all those who did not go about things in their way were
inefficient. They stemmed also from a long-standing personal conflict between
Dayan and Peres, on the one hand, and Lavon, Secretary-General of the
Histadrut, on the other, which was known within the party, but became
public knowledge only some years later. These differences took on the appear-
ance of ideological conflict about the boundaries of Histadrut and state action;
the proponents of *Mamlachtiut* supported further extensions of depoliticisation and the takeover of more Histadrut functions, for example, Kupat
Cholim, by the state; the 'defenders of sacred values' depicted this as a
violation of the most cherished values of the movement and the beginning of
an attempt to dismember the whole Histadrut structure in the interests of a
leviathan state. In our view, this conflict was marginal in the perspective of
the cooperation between the state and the Histadrut in the past, and in view
of the recognition by both sides of the necessity for this cooperation to be
maintained in the future.

Lavon opposed them not only because of their ideology or out of loyalty to
his institutional position, but also because of a personal conflict which
originated in 1954 when he was Minister of Defence, Dayan the Chief of
Staff, and Peres Director-General of the Ministry. Lavon's personal relations
with both Dayan and Peres then were bad, although they were all activists
in defence policy. Nor did he maintain good relations with Sharett, the Prime
Minister, who was a moderate in defence and foreign policy, or in point of
fact with the other key Mapai Ministers, Eshkol, Aranne, and Meir. Not
having been cleared by an investigation committee of the responsibility for a
security mishap in 1954 and having lost the confidence of most of his fellow
Mapai ministers, Lavon resigned under a cloud in 1955, and occupied no office
on behalf of Mapai until he became Secretary-General of the Histadrut in
1956.

By the middle of 1958 Lavon had been reinstated at the top level of the

14 See *Haaretz*, 13.5.1958 and 19.12.1958.

Mapai leadership and had got its support in his efforts to reorganise the Histadrut industrial complex. A brilliant orator, he was a possible candidate one day to become Prime Minister, his chances of which would be improved considerably if he could clear himself of the responsibility for the security mishap. But at the same time his erstwhile opponents and enemies were making their voices heard and laying their claims to participate in the top Mapai leadership, by attacking and criticising the Histadrut institutions of which he was the head, as part of a general attitude towards *Mamlachtiut*. Their incorporation in the Mapai leadership group would not only make things difficult for him and for the party in terms of personal relations, it would also add a powerful counterweight and opposition to his claims. At precisely this point the interests of Lavon and the party machine led by Netzer converged: both were interested in limiting the participation of the *Zeirim* in the top leadership of Mapai, but for different reasons. This background of bitter personal conflict between Dayan and Peres, and Lavon, was known only to a small and intimate circle within the upper levels of the Mapai leadership; until 1960 the public knew nothing of it except that Lavon had resigned under a cloud.

Unsuccessful attempts at peace making

These matters were brought to a head at the end of 1958 at two special meetings of the Secretariat (to which a number of leading *Zeirim* were invited) held to discuss intra-party affairs, and particularly relations between the *Gush* and the *Zeirim*. This was noteworthy because for the first time the fact of the *Gush*'s existence was publicly discussed in Mapai, and because of the frank exchange of views and accusations which occurred.

Ben Gurion pleaded ignorance, claiming 'that I don't know very well what has been going on inside the party except for what I read in the newspapers' – yet roundly criticised the *Gush*. Although recognising its great party loyalty and devotion, he castigated it for the way in which it dominated Mapai institutions on personnel decisions. He also urged greater opportunities of participation for the *Zeirim*.

The members and leaders of the *Gush* defended themselves against the combined attacks of Ben Gurion and the *Zeirim* with their usual arguments. They merely protected the authority of the legitimate party institutions; Yosephtal's organisational methods had threatened elementary party democracy; the *Gush* had saved the 8th Conference from breaking up in complete chaos; balanced representation had to be achieved by the *Gush* and its leaders who were specially qualified and experienced in striking such balances; and that it was not a faction. They were also somewhat critical of Ben Gurion for his inactivity in intra-party affairs and for his patronage of the *Zeirim*. Thus Netzer himself complained that:

Now there are Ben Gurion's lads who fly to the Knesset and the Cabinet on an aeroplane. Take it slowly, for there may be a stoppage on the way. The movement will not allow such speed. . .I beg you, Ben Gurion, to look around you, in that strange sector of the party. You do important work in matters of security and therefore I have not bothered you and have not told you many things, because I am not interested in quarrelling. But what bothers us, Ben Gurion, is that you stood far away from the affairs of the party. You must return, lower the authority of *Chaveireinu*, and live with us through the affairs of the party. And then through discussion we shall define what *Chaveireinu* is, what the Inner Secretariat is, what the Central Committee is.[15]

Members of the older group in Mapai, such as Mrs Meir, Eshkol, and Aranne, and one or two others were more moderately opposed to the *Zeirim*. Eshkol felt that Ben Gurion had been too soft with them; that they had overstepped the limit in their public criticism of the party and that this should have been condemned from the highest 'pedestal'. While recognising that the *Gush* had given the party a marked degree of stability in the past he preferred the party to work directly through elected institutions without its form of pre-organisation. In general, he favoured greater participation of the younger generation, but also called upon them to demonstrate greater *chalutzic* spirit and action. Mrs Meir felt that too great an emphasis upon the factor of age as a criterion of evaluation did not enable a correct and objective assessment of the situation or increase the prestige of the individuals concerned. The most outspoken of the three was Aranne:

What is the *Zeirim*'s struggle about? Is the struggle about the fact that they are not allowed to be members of workers committees, labour councils, trade unions or to guide youth? Instead of preaching and demanding of the *Zeirim* that they go and reinforce the foundation, the house, and the house is first of all, the whole mass of workers, they have created confusion by claiming that there are *Vatikim* who do not allow them to reach ruling positions. . .not in the party nor the Histadrut, but in the Knesset.[16]

The *Zeirim*, Dayan and Peres in particular, defended themselves strongly, and from their speeches we can see how the themes we identified above – participation in party affairs and democratisation, *Mamlachtiut*, the generational gap in spirit and tempo, and the history of poor relations with Lavon – were all closely inter-twined at the very base of their struggle. According to Peres the young generation in general had developed an attitude of 'apathy, lack of confidence, boredom and lack of identification with party activities in general'. To overcome this he favoured getting the party branches working via discussions, leadership visits and meaningful voting decisions. With regard to the latter, the voting system had to be altered to avoid the almost private,

[15] *Minutes Mapai Secretariat Special Meeting, Kfar Hayarok, 29.11.1958.*
[16] *Ibid.*

intimate atmosphere created by elections fixed beforehand by appointments. He also emphasised, in contrast to this, the commitment to *Mamlachtiut*. 'Since the establishment of the state there has been a striving for *Mamlachtiut* among all of us, for preferring law over intimate personal relationships, for preferring an objective method that gives an opportunity to everybody over the accepted method of fixing things in the dark, and unobserved.' Finally he suggested that the problem was much wider than simply providing high offices for certain *Zeirim*. It was not 'putting *Zeirim* in the Knesset or the Cabinet. That problem is one for those *Zeirim*. The problem is Mapai's, of how to incorporate a whole generation of *Zeirim* whose style is different, whose language is different and whose whole way of thinking is different.'[17]

Dayan was characteristically frank, forthright and open. The fact that Lavon complained that a 'Dreyfusade' had been organised against him, implying that this was done by Dayan and Peres, made the question of their participation in party affairs extremely delicate. Thus others 'were forced either not to believe us, or not to believe Lavon'. In his view the real problem was one of participation in decisions and elections; that the party 'had not found a way to allow the public entering it, if not to influence, at least to elect or to refuse to elect individuals, to vote for and against'. Under the system of appointments committees he could see no reason why anyone should join the party. Finally, he firmly rejected any notion of apprenticeship as it were, prior to joining the top ranks of the party, in either the party or the Histadrut, 'the house', in which one had to grow up before one aspired to leadership:

I do not accept this. The concept house does not begin and does not end either with the party or the Histadrut. Every field of public life in the state if it is positive, is part of the house, and there is no obligation to grow up on the lap of the Histadrut or of the party branch or of the Central Committee. It is possible to be in any positive sector and from there to enter the Cabinet or the Central Committee.[18]

This conference partly fulfilled its purpose of bringing internal peace prior to the public election campaign, by leading to a temporary armistice between the *Zeirim* and the *Gush*, or at least those *Zeirim* pushed and supported by Ben Gurion. In the Knesset list prepared in August 1959, Dayan served together with Netzer on the three-man appointments committee compiling the list, whilst he, together with Eban, Yosephtal and Peres, all occupied prominent places towards the top of the list. The word had come down from Ben Gurion that these were potential ministerial material, and when the Cabinet was formed in November 1959, Dayan, Eban and Yosephtal were made ministers and Peres Deputy Minister of Defence to Ben Gurion. Moreover, the *Gush* as 'election experts' realised the enormous drawing power and attraction of these individuals, as their election meetings demonstrated, and

[17] *Ibid.*   [18] *Ibid.*

it has been argued that they were largely responsible for Mapai's resounding
success in gaining seven new seats.

Intensified criticism of the Histadrut and its leadership

Early in 1959 the focus of the conflict shifted to the Histadrut. Lavon, hither-
to silent in public regarding Dayan's criticisms of the Histadrut and its trade
union policies, took up the cudgels with a blistering attack. He accused
Dayan of 'irresponsibility', and the *Zeirim* of 'infantilism'. He poured scorn
on those who likened the *Zeirim* and their attitudes to the Fabians; in his
view the *Zeirim* had none of the distinguishing features of the Fabians, who
had demonstrated high intellectual capacity, and been loyal democrats and
had shown no great desire to rule. By way of contrast, among the *Zeirim*

> There is no true desire or ability to jointly examine the basic problems of
> our existence. There is no understanding of the fundamental questions of
> the mass of the workers. Is it not necessary to reach the conclusion that the
> only thing that unites these men under one flag is the will, legitimate
> enough in itself, to capture positions of power and by storm, and not in an
> organic manner through hard work, to enter the highest reaches of the
> leadership of the state.[19]

For the next two years the relationship of the state to the Histadrut was
the most controversial matter in party affairs. We have already noted in
chapter seven that relations between Lavon and the rest of the Mapai leadership worsened when Dayan *et al.* joined the top councils of the party, that
Lavon left *Chaveireinu* in 1959, and that during the middle of 1960 intensive
discussions took place at the Secretariat level (on which quite a few *Zeirim*
were now represented) as to which forum should settle differences of opinion
between the Histadrut and the state. There were also a number of sharp disagreements between ministers and Lavon over economic issues. In general it
is clear that marked changes had taken place in relations between the Mapai
ministers and the leadership of the Histadrut which prevented them from
settling matters informally and in the previously successful manner.

It was commonly believed that Ben Gurion stood firmly behind Dayan and
Peres in their continuing sharp attacks upon the Histadrut and their demand,
amongst others, to transfer Kupat Cholim to the state. The Histadrut leadership viewed this as being motivated solely by the desire to weaken the
Histadrut itself and thereby strengthen its would-be rival, the state. Ben
Gurion himself had often given voice to sentiments which could be interpreted
in that way. Thus he had told the 1960 Mapai Conference, 'our movement
will not tire or become weary of demanding day and night the unity of
Israeli workers, just as it will not be deterred from preferring the good of the

[19] *Davar*, 4.1.1959.

state and its needs over the good of any particular organisation, even if it is the possessor of the greatest rights in the state, like the Histadrut.'[20]

What Ben Gurion said generally and obliquely, his followers among the *Zeirim* made explicit and direct. Probably the most outspoken of these attacks was one by Peres in August 1960. For him the one common factor in Israel which had many classes and *Edot*, and was overladen with parties, was the new generation which had been born and was yet to be born. He criticised the trade unionist tendencies that had recently seemed to overcome the Histadrut. In his view 'our responsibility as workers is first of all to the state and only after that to ourselves. The special quality of the Histadrut was always that it denied the pure principle of the trade union. The Histadrut always maintained a general and state view. Its present problem is not only the relationship of the state to the Histadrut, but also the relationship of the Histadrut to itself.' He bitingly questioned 'why there was a need for political party football', or why it 'was necessary to heal the sick in a Histadrut manner'.[21]

These attacks were too much for both the *Gush* and the Histadrut leadership to take without a suitable response. The *Gush* suggested to the Mapai Secretariat that the ideological circles of the *Zeirim* be disbanded because they had become a faction. In this the *Zeirim* were defended by Ben Gurion who suggested that Mapai was a democratic party in which everyone was free to express his opinion and that this was of benefit to the party as a whole. He did not regard the *Zeirim* as a faction, but as an ideological discussion circle.[22]

The spokesmen for the Histadrut attacked not only the *Zeirim*, but also Ben Gurion. The most outspoken was Zev Haring, a member of the Central Executive Committee. His response is important not only because it provides a good indication of the high feelings that had been aroused, but also because it represents the Histadrut leadership's ideological position. In the ensuing months Histadrut spokesmen kept returning to the same themes in defending its interests as an institution against the encroachment of *Mamlachtiut*, which Lavon later described as '*etatism*'. In Haring's view what the party needed were *Zeirim* who were prepared to carry out missions and 'not *Zeirim* of patronage'. He went on:

The true revolution in our lives is in changing the foundations of society in order that it shall be a free labouring society, creating and existing in its own right and not a dependent society, reliant upon the state. . .But there

[20] *Report 9th Mapai Conference, 2nd Session*, 1960, p. 100. It is interesting to note that the printed report of the Conference omits the words 'the Histadrut' from the text of Ben Gurion's speech. We have included them not because his intention is clear but because they appear on p. 110 of the same report in a speech by Dayan in which he read the text of Ben Gurion's speech (from the stenogramic record taken on the spot) and included them at the end of the sentence we have cited. Clearly what Mapai's editors have omitted in order not to strain relations has escaped notice here.

[21] *Davar*, 1.9.1960.   [22] *Ibid.* 8.9.1960.

are those who for some reason look grudgingly upon the independent and praiseworthy initiative of public bodies – like the Histadrut – and are of the opinion that their progress must be retarded and that they must be brought under the wings of the all-powerful administrative machine, as it were. There are none loyal to the state and her economic and security needs like the Histadrut and it doesn't need a certificate attesting to this loyalty. But precisely that loyalty to the state demands that it utterly reject the pure theory of administrative *Mamlachtiut* – the meaning of which is to cut down the social branch upon which the young state rests. . .The state is not an end in itself but an instrument for promoting the affairs of man and society.[23]

The official spokesmen of the Histadrut also accused those *Zeirim* who were bound by parliamentary discipline and Cabinet responsibility of having breached these by supporting and publicly demanding policies for Kupat Cholim which went directly against the official party policy of maintaining the existing sick funds.[24]

It is also instructive to take brief note of the attitude of the young group within the Ichud kibbutzim, known as *Zeirei Haichud*. As members of kibbutzim and pioneers, they, more than any other section of the party, should have been found among the 'defenders of the sacred values'. However, the guarded and limited support which they gave to the *Zeirim*, reinforces the interpretation that this was not a struggle between conflicting and irreconcilable ideologies, but was basically an inter-generational conflict which manifested itself in organisational, institutional, interest, and power dimensions, in differences in the style, tempo, mood and general outlooks of the pre- and post-state generations, and in the different value preferences and demands for change in institutions and methods of achieving ends, which some tended to cast in ideological terms.

The Ichud youth, according to their leading spokesman Aharon Yadlin, 'saw in the circles of the *Zeirim* a social-intellectual framework that brings together in its midst a wide and varied group of activists who belong to the *continuing generation* and not to the *founding generation* in Mapai'. Their discussion circles fulfilled two major aims: to overcome political apathy among the youth of their generation and to encourage them to become active in politics; and to enable deep and often bold examination of basic ideas, and thus to fight against superficiality. On some matters their opinions differed. Many of the leading *Zeirim* had left kibbutzim in the past, they disagreed about the role of personal *chalutziut*, and over the size of the wage differential. Moreover, Yadlin continued, 'we did not accept the theory of omnipotent *Mamlachtiut*, and we didn't turn the state into a supreme value – but we did not negate the approach of *Mamlachtiut*, nor did we observe any contradiction between personal *chalutziut* and a *chalutzic* regime. On the con-

[23] *Ibid.* 1.9.1960.   [24] *Ibid.* 9.9.1960.

trary we regarded the state as a new and important partner, obliged to join its efforts to those of the *chalutzic* movement in realising the national tasks.' Finally the Ichud youth:

> did not turn a blind eye to the excessive ambition and to impatience regarding positions of power and leadership, nor to manifestations of undue aggressiveness on the part of *Zeirim* in intra-party affairs. On the other hand attention was paid to the fact that the party and its *Vatikim* did not make sufficient efforts to give *Zeirim* responsibility and the feeling of a home.[25]

The Lavon Affair 1960–1

A whole book can be written, and many have,[26] on the intricate and hotly disputed details of the Lavon Affair. It is not our purpose to record these here but briefly to trace its outlines so that it may be seen in the light of the succession struggle and inter-generational conflict in Mapai.

In 1960, Lavon, on the basis of new evidence and documents, sought rehabilitation from Ben Gurion, that is, a statement to the effect that Ben Gurion cleared him of responsibility for giving the order that led to the security mishap. Although Ben Gurion set up various investigating bodies, he eventually refused to make a personal statement rehabilitating Lavon, because he claimed that this was tantamount to accusing another individual, that he was not a judge or investigator, and therefore could not decide between two individuals. Lavon pressed him, relations between them became strained, and eventually broken. The matter was taken to the Knesset Foreign Affairs and Security Committee to get it out of the press via the use of parliamentary privilege, a move which failed because its proceedings were leaked. At this committee accusation and counter-accusation were made, and allegations affecting Dayan and Peres, officers sympathetic to them and sections of the Ministry of Defence, were freely made. Mapai was in consternation, and the party leadership was split over the issue. Moreover, as the issue directly related to security, the party initially was hesitant about intervening. Cabinet eventually set up a Ministerial Committee of Enquiry which did not enjoy the full backing of Ben Gurion, who wanted a judicial enquiry. Cabinet lost his support completely when the Ministerial Committee reached a conclusion exonerating Lavon. Ben Gurion claimed that it had gone beyond its terms of reference and had wrongly arrogated to itself judicial functions. He declared that he could have no part in any Cabinet that did these things and resigned. Other Mapai ministers too, particularly Meir and Sapir, were on the point of

[25] *Iggeret*, 7.11.1956 (emphasis in original).
[26] See E. Chassin and D. Horowitz, *The Affair* (Tel Aviv, 1961) (Hebrew); Y. Arieli, *The Conspiracy* (Tel Aviv, 1965) (Hebrew); D. Ben Gurion, *Things As They Are* (Tel Aviv, 1965) (Hebrew).

resigning, in protest against Ben Gurion's violent attacks on the members of the Ministerial Committee.

Within Mapai, a major crisis developed, and the main question was how to settle the issue, and particularly how to get Ben Gurion back as Prime Minister. This was not easy as Lavon enjoyed powerful support, and many believed he had been badly wronged in 1954, and in 1960 by Ben Gurion both by implication and in direct public and intra-party attacks. Nor did Lavon withhold from publicly attacking Ben Gurion and the leading *Zeirim*, Dayan and Peres. Eventually, after many harrowing meetings, attempted investigations and suggested compromises, Eshkol, who had strongly supported the Ministerial Committee and had been a member of it, emerged as the intra-party conflict resolver. Despite some sympathy for Lavon, he was forced to come to the conclusion, as was being widely canvassed by Ben Gurion supporters, that Lavon had to be removed from his position as Secretary-General of the Histadrut. He shepherded this through the Secretariat and the Central Committee, the main grounds being that Lavon could not continue in view of his public behaviour damaging to Mapai and denigratory of the army and the Defence Ministry, and in view of the impossibility under these conditions of normal relations between Mapai's state and Histadrut leaders, particularly in such bodies as *Chaveireinu*. At the Central Committee, the vote was 159:96 in favour of Lavon's deposition, which indicates the strength of Lavon's support, given the fact that it was widely assumed that this was a pre-condition for Ben Gurion's return to the Prime Ministership. Many in fact regarded it as a moral victory for Lavon.

What were the immediate consequences of this Affair? Externally it resulted in a severe loss of prestige both for Mapai as a party and for Ben Gurion as a political leader. Ben Gurion's prestige declined because there existed marked scepticism over his motives, and about the purity of his commitment to legality, which was strengthened and reinforced when it became apparent that he had become a party in the Affair, and was aligned solidly and bitterly against Lavon. It declined even further among those who believed that he virtually dictated Lavon's dismissal for having opposed him. Following his attacks upon the Cabinet findings it proved impossible to re-establish a coalition. In the ensuing elections Mapai lost five seats. With the establishment of a new coalition, the Affair was effectively buried: the coalition agreement made no mention of it, nor was there any indication that Ben Gurion was given a free hand to uncover the truth through judicial proceedings.

Within the party the Lavon Affair and its aftermath produced some contradictory results. In one sense it contributed to party unity; the differences between the *Zeirim* and the *Gush* were temporarily settled as they found themselves joined together as allies and supporters of Ben Gurion against Lavon. In a very real sense the only victors in the struggle were Dayan and

Peres. Lavon as a political rival and contender for the succession was finished, but had he been successful or even remained in a position of power within the party they would have remained under constant challenge and attack, and the legitimacy of their claims to leadership in the party would have been constantly in question, for their involvement, however slight, in the un-savoury aspects of the 1954–5 period.

It should also be pointed out that there was no evidence, nor did Lavon suggest, that Dayan and Peres were directly involved in the forgeries and false evidence before the 1955 Enquiry Committee. The most that was ever maintained in this direction by Lavon was 'that there were individuals who, when the cart began to move, began to jump aboard it', that is to say, they stood to gain directly from these acts. Thus Dayan, who had been in the United States at the time of the security mishap, and Peres, had both given evidence damaging to Lavon at the 1955 Enquiry Committee. Similarly Lavon's removal facilitated the reestablishment of satisfactory working relationships within the party institutions, such as *Chaveireinu* and *Sareinu*, which was assisted by the pressure of the need to fight an external election. Faced with such a challenge the party was more or less forced to pull together.

This was true of all groups except the sworn and devoted supporters of Lavon, who created an internal opposition group with its own journal, both of which went under the title of *Min Hayesod* (From the Foundation). These were mainly members of kibbutzim and intellectuals, academics and students, who campaigned during the 1961 elections for the placing of blank papers in the ballot box as a sign of protest. The limited extent of their success can be gauged from the fact that Mapai lost just under 750 votes in the Ichud kibbutzim in 1961 as compared with 1959. But their impact was not in num-bers but in the fact that they constituted a bitter and talented opposition group within the party, and were a constant reminder to the public of the problems and difficulties aroused during the Lavon Affair, and of the fact that the wounds had not healed.

Reemergence of Gush–Zeirim conflict: organisational power and democratisation

Following Lavon's deposition relative quiet reigned in relations between the Zeirim and the Gush. But a rivalry and conflict as deep-seated as that between the Gush and the Zeirim could not be expected to disappear permanently, and some of the old problems slowly resurfaced. But these soon paled as it became clear that the real issue was that of party leadership and succession to state leadership.

This was most apparent during the Secretariat's major debate on the young generation's organisational activities in January 1963. For *Zeirim* like Smilanski, Peres and Dayan, all members of Knesset, it was essential that the party provide the younger generation with freedom of expression to discuss party affairs, to propose new solutions, goals and methods, to establish a democratised internal regime, so as to accord it real influence within the party and encourage it to accept responsibility. They rejected the continuing notion of the *Vatikim* that the younger generation had a special responsibility to realise the Zionist–Socialist goals of pioneering, and to serve the party in outlying areas.

Leading *Vatikim* in the debate again criticised the *Zeirim* for neglecting the old values of agricultural settlement, productive labour, cooperative activity and voluntary party work. But in a sense these were the issues of the past. It was Zalman Aranne who put the issue in terms of the present and the future by raising the question of succession. The *Vatikim* had never before directly addressed themselves publicly to this problem. Their usual response had been that there was plenty of time, and that the turn of the *Zeirim* had not yet arrived. But it had never been doubted that their turn would one day arrive. Here, for the first time, Aranne suggested that, in fact, it might not arrive at all. He served notice that the *Zeirim* were not indispensable and that there was another possible future leadership group. While not immediately perceived at the time, his views take on significance if seen in the context of the preliminary discussions Mapai had just begun with Achdut Haavoda over the possibility of unity between them. Thus Aranne suggested that the question of the *Zeirim* was of their *right* to succession:

> This interests me from the point of view of the inheritor. Who will inherit this whole thing which is called the state with all that this implies?... What will be the image of this inheritor? I spoke about this with Bar Yehuda some two years ago before the appearance of Ben Aharon's article.[27] When I talked of the chances of unity between the party and Achdut Haavoda I said that it is the function of a group that lives in this world to prepare its successor.[28]

Ben Gurion's retirement: the advent of Eshkol

The struggle for succession began in earnest with Ben Gurion's retirement in June 1963. In the past, by his identification with, and support for the leading *Zeirim*, Ben Gurion had acted as a balance between the *Zeirim* and *Vatikim*, and as a leadership figure around whom both these conflicting groups could unite. Till then most of the conflict was between the *Gush*, the second rank leaders among the *Vatikim*, and the *Zeirim*, rather than between the *Vatikim* group as a whole and the *Zeirim*, or between the leading *Vatikim* and the leading *Zeirim*. While not exactly enamoured of the *Zeirim*, leading *Vatikim* like Eshkol, Namir, Meir, Aranne, and Sapir managed to cooperate with them

---

[27] Bar Yehuda and Ben Aharon were Achdut Haavoda leaders.
[28] *The Zeirim and the Party* (Mapai Secretariat Discussion on the Young Generation), (Tel Aviv, 1963), p. 49 (Hebrew).

under the umbrella of Ben Gurion's leadership. Similarly the *Zeirim* could not launch an all-out attack on the party leadership without in some way implicating Ben Gurion in the deficiencies they criticised. Ben Gurion's departure, therefore, paved the way for an open confrontation between the *Vatikim* as a group, and especially its top leaders, and the *Zeirim*, for control of the party, and with it the power to decide the question of succession. When Ben Gurion retired and leadership passed to Eshkol, it remained within the generational group to which Ben Gurion himself belonged. The basic question then focused on the issue of who would inherit the leadership after Eshkol.

The battle began with Ben Gurion's announcement of an irrevocable intention to resign. He designated Eshkol as his successor, but remained aloof from all further activities relating to the establishment of the Eshkol government. Immediately, the 'heads of Mapai' met at the house of Mrs Meir, in an informal gathering of the members of the Leadership Bureau and a number of other leading *Vatikim*, but with no *Zeirim* present. They set up a committee of leading *Vatikim* to assist Eshkol in establishing a new coalition and in distributing the Mapai ministerial portfolios. Not a single member of the *Zeirim* was on this committee, which is indicative of the evolution of a collective Mapai leadership around Eshkol, consisting only of *Vatikim*. A challenge to this collective leadership came almost immediately from Dayan, who announced that he would not continue to serve as Minister of Agriculture under Eshkol and that he was interested in another portfolio, commonly believed to be Defence. Eshkol, shored up by his advisory committee, decided to take it himself, carrying on the past practice. When the new government was established Dayan agreed temporarily to retain his Agriculture portfolio providing that he received a greater all-round say in Cabinet: after some months of public dissatisfaction with, and criticism of the Prime Minister, Dayan finally agreed in September 1963 to remain in Cabinet. He was given a greater voice in defence matters, and jurisdictional disagreements in the economic sphere between himself and Sapir (Minister of Trade and Commerce) were cleared up to his satisfaction.[29]

The formation of the committee to assist Eshkol and the method of establishing the Eshkol government provoked sharp attacks and criticism from some of the *Zeirim*. Such critiques led to regular public reference by the *Zeirim* to 'Golda's kitchen' as the centre of decision making in Mapai. At the same time it became clear that the major conflict was now between Dayan and Peres supported by the *Zeirim*, and the leading ministerial supporters of Eshkol among the *Vatikim*, Meir, Sapir and Aranne, whom the press and their opponents dubbed the 'Troika'. With the support of the *Gush* they defended themselves and Eshkol against the *Zeirim*.

Nor was this notion of a 'Troika' pure fantasy, for both Sapir and Aranne

[29] *Davar*,19.6.1963, 20.6.1963, 30.6.1963, 14.7.1963, 26.7.1963, 10.9.1963; *Haaretz*, 3.7.1963, 14.7.1963, 6.9.1963.

had publicly made their positions obvious. Thus the country was treated to the strange spectacle in a Cabinet system with collective responsibility, of ministers publicly criticising and attacking each other. As time went on this public debate and criticism intensified. Aranne publicly rejected any imputation that the Eshkol Cabinet was 'a government of old people' foisted upon the party by the 'Troika'. In addition to rejecting this 'biological attack', he also denied that party democracy had been perverted as had been claimed by the *Zeirim*. He continued:

> There is no intelligent person in Israel who thinks that with the resignation of D. Ben Gurion his 'identity card' has passed on to comrades S. Peres and M. Dayan, with all their importance. All the party's Cabinet members recognise the capabilities of M. Dayan, and desire his membership in it, but they do not recognise, to paraphrase Orwell, 'that all members of Mapai in the Cabinet are equal, except for Moshe Dayan who is more equal'.[30]

But the real problem for Aranne was not the exact or present status of Dayan, but the place of his whole generation in the party and in the state:

> One does not conquer a 'generation that is going' like a military target. And if it 'goes' slowly, it is good that it 'goes' slowly; I am certain that the whole nation holds it in awe, has trust in it and desires it, whilst its strength is retained; for this leadership generation will never recur. It studied in most of the 'faculties' of the academy for the resurrection of the Jewish people, in the Diaspora and in Palestine, during the period of vision alone, and during the period of realisation. What it learnt and taught – cannot be acquired by grabbing.[31]

For Mr Sapir the matter was even simpler, 'someone is in a hurry, and he stands with watch in hand'.[32]

The alignment with Achdut Haavoda

After Eshkol and Dayan had agreed in September 1963 upon the conditions under which Dayan would remain in the Cabinet the focus of this intergenerational conflict shifted away from the personal demands of the leading *Zeirim* to the negotiations which were proceeding for an electoral alignment between Mapai and Achdut Haavoda. In March 1963, and the date is significant because it was before Ben Gurion's resignation, the Mapai Secretariat formally decided to proceed with these discussions to clarify 'the possibilities of a union – complete or partial – of the labour movement'.[33] Mapai pursued the course of unity with Achdut Haavoda for a number of different reasons.

There was firstly the ideological motivation. Mapai had long been committed to the unity of labour in Israel. Since its inception it had cherished the ideal of one united labour party in Israel. Its leaders thus welcomed the opportunity that presented itself when a call for unity was made by one of

[30] *Davar*, 26.7.1963.   [31] *Ibid.*   [32] *Ibid.* 4.8.1963.   [33] *Ibid.* 10.3.1963.

the leaders of Achdut Haavoda, which indicated that the minority labour parties were more prepared than in the past seriously to consider this eventuality.

There were also sound practical and electoral reasons why Mapai sought labour unity. Its majority in the Histadrut had steadily decreased from over 80 per cent in the 1930s to 55.4 per cent in 1960, and with Histadrut elections due in 1964 there was no guarantee that Mapai would again win a majority. Loss of control of the Histadrut and a coalition arrangement there would have seriously weakened not only Mapai's position in that body, but also its overall political power in the state, which to a large extent rested on its dual control of the government and the Histadrut. Union with Achdut Haavoda or even an electoral alignment would ensure its continued Histadrut control.

Similarly in the Knesset sphere Mapai had long tired of the difficulties and uncertainties of coalition rule, and had sought ways and means of introducing a constituency electoral system which would give it the possibility of being able to form a majority government, which was practically, if not theoretically impossible under proportional representation. Unity of the labour movement was an obvious alternative to this proposal. Mapai together with Achdut Haavoda and Mapam in 1963 controlled fifty-nine of the 120 seats in the Knesset, and in the 4th Knesset had controlled sixty-three seats between them. This suggested that even under proportional representation they had a good chance of gaining an absolute majority if united. Mapai's efforts in the past to secure the agreement of other parties for the establishment of a constituency system had come to nought. Labour unity looked like a reasonable and realistic alternative solution to a problem that had long concerned Mapai's leaders.

Unity with Achdut Haavoda also promised deep emotional satisfaction and gratification to Mapai's leaders. Having been committed to the ideal and dream of unity throughout their activity in Mapai, they had suffered intensely from the split in their own party that had produced Achdut Haavoda. This was for them a nightmare made even more harrowing by bitter divisions within the kibbutz movement which had followed the party split. The latter not only hurt personally through the loss of a whole generation of younger party members, it also stood as a living monument that constantly belied their talk of unity. Unity then would be proof of their faith in their ideals, and at the same time would enable the return of 'rebellious sons' to their home with all the emotional satisfaction that that would engender.

The return of Achdut Haavoda would also serve as a reinforcement to the party's leadership group. Although Mapai itself had successfully developed younger leaders of national stature, it could only gain from the infusion of men of experience and political stature represented by individuals like Yisrael Galili, Yigal Allon, and Yitzchak Ben Aharon, all of whom had been ministers in the past. As a generational group they fitted in neatly between the over-sixty group of the *Vatikim*, and the *Zeirim*, who were mostly in their forties and younger, so that they represented a leadership addition not only for the present but also for the future. And in this context they differed somewhat from the *Zeirim*. Although in many ways similar (for example in terms of the military backgrounds and exploits of some of their leading members), they differed from them ideologically on a number of important issues. They were more closely attuned to the old values of the Yishuv, to pioneering, and the Histadrut, and even less enamoured of *Mamlachtiut* than the *Vatikim* in Mapai, whom they had been criticising for years for rejecting these same values and for overcommitment to pragmatism. On an ideological continuum they stood to the left of the *Vatikim* who were in the centre with the *Zeirim* on their right.

It was precisely on the personal, succession, and ideological aspects of the proposed Alignment with Achdut Haavoda that the *Zeirim* and its leadership focused their opposition. At first, while Ben Gurion was still Prime Minister, they supported the idea of union enthusiastically and accused the Mapai leadership of dragging its feet. But after his retirement, and when the process of Alignment negotiations began seriously, the *Zeirim* saw the Alignment as a move by the *Vatikim* to settle accounts with the *Zeirim* once and for all, by bringing into the party an alternative leadership group more closely attuned to them ideologically and to whom they would then pass on the mantle of leadership, thus bypassing the rightful heirs and successors, the *Zeirim*. In other words the *Zeirim* saw this, at worst, as a move to dispossess them, and, at best, as a tactic to establish a rival leadership group that would neutralise their influence and with whom they would have to share power. There was also a marked element of self-fulfilling prophecy in this claim: the stronger the *Zeirim's* opposition to the Alignment and to the party leadership, the more appealing the Alignment must have appeared to the latter.

In pursuing their opposition to the Alignment, the *Zeirim* became deeply involved in the moral and personal crusades launched by Ben Gurion. Whereas the leading *Zeirim* were at first mainly interested in the succession question and the ideological direction involved in the Alignment, and benefited from Ben Gurion's support on this question, they had no alternative but to go along with Ben Gurion in his moral crusade on the Lavon Affair, despite the fact that there was on this issue a clear conflict of interest between them and Ben Gurion. They went along at first because they were committed to him personally and emotionally, and because it was tactically sound to do so. But more importantly as conflict in Mapai developed, and as the *Vatikim* became crystallised as a distinctive leadership group, they felt that they needed Ben Gurion on their side as a major weapon in their struggle, in the hope that he could still swing the majority of the party behind him, as he had always done in the past. Eventually they sought his return as Prime Minister, because this appeared to them to be the only way in which they could secure their future in the party, and their right to succession. In effect what happened in Mapai was a complex intertwining of the *Zeirim–Vatikim* conflict around the separate issues of the Alignment, the Affair, and the increasingly bitter personal conflict between Ben Gurion and Eshkol (supported by the *Vatikim*) as they took diametrically opposed views on the two former issues. Thus the struggle for eventual succession quickly became an immediate fight for the leadership, and with the victor, presumably, went the determining say on the future succession question.

The origins of the Ben Gurion–Eshkol conflict

Concurrent with growing *Zeirim* opposition to the Alignment, Eshkol came into direct conflict with Ben Gurion over his attempts to heal the rift with *Min Hayesod*, which was on the point of leaving Mapai. Early in 1964 *Min Hayesod* put increasing pressure on the Mapai leadership to do something about Lavon's status, so as to enable him and his supporters to return to active party participation, and to right the wrong which had, in their view, been done to him. Whilst Ben Gurion retained his leadership there had been no chance of doing anything in this direction. But now that Eshkol had taken over it was felt that it was now fitting and opportune to heal Mapai's internal dissension. This was strongly reinforced by the movement towards labour unity; in the early negotiations on the Alignment, Achdut Haavoda suggested the return of *Min Hayesod* as one of two preconditions to their entering the Alignment (the other was an attempt to include Mapam in the Alignment, but this fell through very quickly). Achdut Haavoda was motivated partly by Ben Gurion's bitter attacks upon them for their particularly strong support of Lavon in 1960–1, and for their active participation in the Ministerial Committee. Nor were they averse to causing embarrassment to Ben Gurion with whom they had a long list of political accounts to settle, and to the *Zeirim* with whom they would have to contend in the future. It also served tactically to give them some indication of how far the incumbent *Vatikim* leadership behind Eshkol was prepared to go in seeking to cement the Alignment, and how far they would turn their backs on Ben Gurion and the *Zeirim*. To Ben Gurion this looked like public renunciation by Mapai of the cause of justice which he had fought since 1960–1 and with which he was still deeply concerned, and a public acknowledgement that Mapai had been wrong in its course of action at that time in seeking to meet Ben Gurion's wishes. To the leading *Zeirim* any rapprochement with *Min Hayesod* added further opposition weight against them, whilst again appearing to compromise them politically in their leadership struggle as it had threatened to do once before. But perhaps most ominous of all, it seemed to indicate to them just how far the *Vatikim* leadership was prepared to go to reach agreement with Achdut Haavoda, which did not augur at all well for the future.

Mr Eshkol after a series of meetings with the leaders of *Min Hayesod* sent a personal letter to the *Min Hayesod* conference at Kibbutz Chulda at which its future course of action was being considered. In it he intimated that he no longer personally believed that the Central Committee decision against Lavon was still binding, and he invited them to return to active party work, which they had refused to do since 1961. Ben Gurion, living in retirement at Sde Boker, was incensed by Eshkol's action. He demanded to know which party institution had given Eshkol and his supporters the authority to negotiate with this faction, and unilaterally to declare that Lavon's disqualification had ceased to have effect. But Eshkol had not acted unilaterally. He acted in close cooperation with leading Mapai ministers (Aranne, Sapir and Meir) and with leading party officials throughout the country, in informal gatherings rather than in formal institutional contexts. In particular, he proceeded only after the *Gush* had supported his move.

Despite attempts by Eshkol to placate him Ben Gurion remained outspokenly opposed, and was quickly joined by some of his most important supporters, particularly the Haifa and Tel Aviv party branches, which also led the *Gush* to have serious second thoughts. Needless to say his attitude reinforced the position of the leading *Zeirim* in their generalised opposition to Eshkol and the *Vatikim*. The party was now deeply embarrassed publicly; its two leading figures were openly at loggerheads and its two most important party branches had repudiated the Prime Minister's action. This was especially embarrassing to Eshkol who was depicted as having bypassed legitimate party bodies, and of having personally attempted to undo an authoritative decision of the Central Committee.

The party institutions were now placed in the extraordinarily difficult position of having to take a decision which would avoid making a choice between Ben Gurion and Eshkol, and after days of frantic meetings the Secretariat, at the suggestion of the Leadership Bureau, came to a compromise solution. It took note of a statement made before it by the Prime Minister explaining his actions, in which he specified that the letter was sent personally and did not contradict the decision of any authoritative party institution. It then immediately passed on to its normal agenda without any discussion at all. The Secretary-General of Mapai in summing up the debate stressed that 'the Secretariat neither ratified nor rejected anything, but merely listened to the Prime Minister's statement'.[34]

The debates over the Alignment

The immediate short-term effect of Eshkol's letter was to set Ben Gurion and Eshkol on a collision course which gradually spread over many fronts. At first it was centred around the problem of labour unity and the Alignment.

[34] See *Davar*, 29.4.1964–5.5.1964; *Hapoel Hatzair*, 5.5.1964.

The closer agreement between Mapai and Achdut Haavoda appeared to be, the greater the intensity of the opposition of the *Zeirim*, and Ben Gurion. Thus from early 1964 leading *Zeirim* began to speak out more and more openly against the proposed Alignment. Dayan and Peres, for example, complained that the leadership of Achdut Haavoda was using its bargaining position to oppose certain individuals in Mapai, and to suggest that Mapai would have to remove them. They criticised the Mapai leadership for giving in to ultimata set down by Achdut Haavoda on the question of electoral change, and this, together with the question of the organisation of the Alignment in the Histadrut, became the focus of the opposition.

In mid-July 1964 Achdut Haavoda made it a non-negotiable condition of its agreement to establish the Alignment that for the period of its existence both parties would agree not to attempt to establish a majority electoral system. In effect this bound only Mapai, which had campaigned in the 1955, 1959 and 1961 Knesset elections on the need to introduce the constituency system, and had unsuccessfully attempted to legislate in this direction. Ben Gurion and the *Zeirim*, in particular, had invested this proposal with high hopes. Now, however, Mapai was for the first time faced with an alternative approach which meant freezing the possibilities of electoral change for four years. For Achdut Haavoda, this was an insurance policy; should the union not work out as planned it would, under the proportional representation system, be able to maintain its independent existence. Ben Gurion and the *Zeirim* attacked Mapai's suggested agreement to this proposal and to certain others relating to the organisation of the Alignment in the Histadrut after its elections, in such a way as to make it clear that they were opposed to the Alignment in general rather than to its conditions.

Undaunted, Eshkol with majority support of the Secretariat, proceeded to cement the Alignment on conditions agreed to between himself and Galili, approved by the Mapai negotiating team, and finally ratified by the Mapai Secretariat. However, before the motion agreeing to proceed with the Alignment was put to the Central Committee Dayan resigned from the Cabinet in order to gain a much freer hand in fighting internal party battles. But his resignation had no effect on the outcome of the debate at the Central Committee which decided 182:8 with 25 abstentions, 'that there exists a basis for the Alignment'. In protest against this decision Ben Gurion resigned from the Central Committee.[35]

The rekindling of the Lavon Affair

Just before the Secretariat reached a decision on the Alignment, matters became more complicated by the rekindling of the Lavon Affair. On the basis

[35] *Davar*, especially 13.7.1964, 15.7.1964, 19.7.1964, 24.7.1964, 18.8.1964, 1.9.1964, 13.9.1964, 15.10.1964, 25.10.1964, 26.10.1964, 27.10.1964, 8.11.1964, 12.11.1964.

of information which he had gathered Ben Gurion specifically requested an enquiry of Supreme Court judges to investigate the Government's handling of the Affair in 1960. In view of Eshkol's leading role in the Ministerial Committee in 1960 his request was interpreted by many in the light of his current campaign against Eshkol and his policies. After considerable hesitation and under immense pressure from both sides, Eshkol refused to agree to any form of investigation, despite a compromise recommendation from the Minister of Justice that the 1954 Affair be investigated.

After many other attempts at compromise failed, the Mapai Secretariat met to decide how to proceed. Eshkol argued that the existing Cabinet coalition would not be maintained if it was decided to reopen the Affair. He therefore requested the Secretariat to give the Mapai ministers the authority and freedom to vote on this matter according to their conscience. Dayan, on the other hand, wanted the Central Committee to express its opinion *prior* to the decisive Cabinet decision, but without binding ministers. In his view, a prior Cabinet decision would preclude free internal debate. Torn in these conflicting directions the Secretariat took no policy decision, and handed the matter on to the Central Committee.

At the next day's meeting of the Central Committee these arguments were reiterated. The Central Committee debated the matter at length but adjourned without reaching a decision. Before it reconvened, however, Eshkol announced his resignation, and with it that of the whole Cabinet. He thus brought to a head the issue of party and state leadership which was implicit in the conflict between himself and Ben Gurion. His move made it clear that for Ben Gurion to succeed in his present campaign he would need to be prepared once more to take over the reins of government. Ben Gurion, at this stage, was not ready to do so. Moreover, Eshkol in this way avoided the question of whether the Central Committee had the power to instruct the Mapai ministers. He also prevented a vote at the Central Committee, which in all probability he would have won, but with only a narrow margin. Instead, he was unanimously called upon by the Secretariat and the Executive of the Parliamentary Party to reestablish the same coalition, and it was simultaneously decided that ministers would be free to decide whether a judicial enquiry would be held. On December 18 the Central Committee unanimously endorsed Eshkol's candidature as Prime Minister together with the same team of ministers. It voted 124:61 in favour of a free vote for the ministers regarding a judicial enquiry, and against a recommendation to look into the events of 1954. On 27 December the Cabinet met and decided without a formal vote not to establish a judicial enquiry into the Affair, with only two ministers, Almogi and Yoseph, favouring this course of action.[86]

[86] *Davar*, 23.10.1964, 4.12.1964, 7.12.1964, 11.12.1964, 13.12.1964, 14.12.1964, 15.12.1964, 17.12.1964, 18.12.1964, 28.12.1964.

The Tenth Mapai Conference: conflict on all fronts

This was not, as might be expected, the end of the matter. Elections to the 10th Mapai Conference had taken place in June of 1964 and the Conference itself was long overdue, having been postponed as a result of the state of affairs in the party, and the conflicts over the Alignment and the Affair. Thus the Conference became the focus of an intense struggle over the two particular issues of the Alignment and the Affair, around which the struggle for leadership and succession was taking place. Only Conference could overturn the previous decisions. To defeat the Alignment would have meant an important victory for the *Zeirim* and their guaranteeing of the right to succession, but would not necessarily have toppled Eshkol. On the other hand, a decision to reopen the Affair would probably have had this effect. Thus in preparation for the Conference the party was organised around two distinct groups with campaign and administrative personnel of their own. The first, led by Eshkol, favoured the Alignment and opposed the reopening of the Affair. The second, organised by Almogi and the *Zeirim* on behalf of Ben Gurion, opposed the Alignment and supported the reopening of the Affair. Ben Gurion and Eshkol followed each other around the country addressing rank and file party meetings and campaigned strenuously among activists and delegates to the Conference to secure their votes on the two major issues. On Ben Gurion's side were to be found most of the *Zeirim* (although some who had been prominent in the past now came out for Eshkol, namely Arye Eliav, Abraham Ofer, Asher Yadlin, Aharon Yadlin,) most of the Haifa branch, including both its major figures, Almogi and Choushi, and large minorities in the kibbutz and moshav movements, together with about two-thirds of the Tel Aviv branch led by Netzer. Ben Gurion also let it be known that if his view on the Affair was rejected he would not allow his name to appear on the Mapai electoral lists for the Knesset and the Histadrut which he had traditionally headed, which would have amounted to a public declaration of opposition.

On the eve of the Conference the President of the State, Shazar, intervened in an attempt to mediate and bring Ben Gurion and Eshkol together, but this availed nothing. The Conference itself was tense, dramatic, emotional, and completely dominated by the debate over the Affair and the Alignment, but no new issues were raised. Its highlights were Ben Gurion's fiery address, Eshkol's dramatic request to him 'to give him credit for four years' to carry out his policies, and concerted and bitter attacks upon Ben Gurion led by Sharett (at the time incurably ill and confined to a wheel chair), Meir, Shitreet, and Aranne, followed by many others from both the older and younger generations. In terms of the realities of power the significance of the Conference undoubtedly lay in its decisions on the two major issues, as well as in the personnel distribution of the new Central Committee. A secret ballot was held on both controversial issues; a resolution put forward by the *Zeirim* that the Conference agree in principle to Ben Gurion's claims was defeated 1206:848 (59 per cent opposed); the resolution favouring the Alignment was passed 1306:770 (62.9 per cent in favour). These steady proportions led to the crystallisation of two blocs in the party, the Eshkol supporters with about 60 per cent, called the majority, and the Ben Gurion supporters with about 40 per cent, the minority. This distribution was also maintained in the new Central Committee elected at the Conference, following intense bargaining between these two groups on the Appointments Committee.

The party split

The Conference might have served as the final stage in this conflict. We argued in the first chapter that, in general, party conferences serve an important function as the locus of final sovereignty, provided that the contending groups regard their decision as final. But the minority was not prepared to regard this as the end of the road; it began a concerted campaign to replace Prime Minister Eshkol by Ben Gurion, unless Eshkol acceded to its demands. Whilst previously it had fought on the issues, now they were pushed into the background. This became particularly important to the leading *Zeirim* who began to feel that only Ben Gurion in power would be able personally to guarantee their places in the leadership and the mantle of succession.

But the minority got nowhere, and in point of fact the pattern was one of decreasing influence and continuous loss of institutional power. The majority was prepared to let it have no more than 35 per cent of the places on the Secretariat and Leadership Bureau, as against the 40 per cent the minority demanded. After Ben Gurion publicly announced that 'Eshkol was not fit to lead the state',[37] Eshkol publicly called for, and gained the resignation of the Mapai ministers (Almogi and Peres) who shared Ben Gurion's views of him. Ben Gurion retaliated by agreeing to head the Mapai list and to establish a government after the elections, and the minority concentrated all its efforts in this direction.

The majority forced the issue immediately and brought the question of Mapai's candidate for Prime Minister to the party institutions in June, five months before the elections. A specially convened Central Committee meeting supported Eshkol for Prime Minister against Ben Gurion 179 votes (63.5 per cent) to 103 votes.

Following this decision the minority itself now became divided, as the question of a split loomed on the horizon. Some leading members like Abba Choushi, and Uzi Feinerman of Tnuat Hamoshavim favoured remaining within the party and were not prepared to split it; on the other hand, Almogi and many *Zeirim* strongly supported the idea of a separate list. But the key to

[37] *Haaretz*, 13.5.1965.

their future action lay in the hands of Ben Gurion and Dayan, without whom, it was believed, a separate list would have little chance of success. Ben Gurion himself strongly favoured a separate list, because Mapai was 'not fit to lead the state', to 'keep Mapai's real character', and because Mapai was characterised by 'a regime of fear and deceit'. Dayan at first remained uncommitted.

As a split became more imminent the minority began to lose previously secure support. Not only did Abba Choushi personally oppose a split, more significantly, he organised at the grass roots level in Haifa, gained the support of most of its largest Workers Committees and through this a majority on the branch institutions, leaving Almogi isolated with the support of only a small minority centred around the Port. Similarly in Tel Aviv, the *Gush*, led by Netzer, quickly gathered together a majority of the branch institutions against a split, and even some of those who had only a month earlier actively sought to install Ben Gurion as Prime Minister supported Eshkol. To cap this off, Dayan let it be known that he, too, was opposed to the minority establishing a separate list, on the grounds that it did not have a realistic chance of success. In his view it did not have a broad enough policy programme of change for the state, and had neglected its original goals of *Mamlachtiut*. Instead it was too closely allied to the problem of the Affair and to the question of Ben Gurion as a personality. He preferred to continue to fight within Mapai for the *Mamlachti* approach as against the narrow sectarian and class approach being imposed upon it by Achdut Haavoda, and therefore he would not support a separate list. But if the majority went ahead he would temporarily retire from politics, rather than remain a Mapai M.K.

This combined opposition was widely thought to have averted a split, but the relief was premature, and did not take into account the stubborn insistence of Ben Gurion who simply announced the formation of a separate electoral list called Rafi (Israel Workers List) and invited his supporters to join him. This effectively split the party although the formal split did not come until about six weeks later when after a most acrimonious hearing by the party's internal adjudicative bodies those members who established the new list were expelled.

Rafi appeared at both the Knesset and Histadrut elections on an intensely anti-Mapai and anti-Eshkol platform, combined with a programme of extensive change focused especially on the Histadrut. This helped it eventually to win the active support of Dayan, who, early in September, agreed to join its Knesset list. But neither its personalities nor its policies provided it with the success that it sought. In particular it failed in its short-run political goals of preventing the Alignment from gaining a majority in the Histadrut, and preventing Eshkol from forming a coalition. It hoped by the latter either to prevent Mapai from governing, or to extract its favourite demands from it. The Alignment stood up surprisingly well under the competition; it gained 50.88 per cent as against 12.13 per cent for Rafi in the Histadrut elections, and 36.7 per cent in the Knesset as against 7.9 per cent for Rafi. (In the 1961 Knesset elections, Mapai had 34.7 per cent and Achdut Haavoda 6.6 per cent.)

Rafi enjoyed the support of sizeable minorities in Ichud kibbutzim (15.7 per cent in the Knesset elections) and Tnuat Hamoshavim (22.2 per cent), but these were somewhat different groups. In the Ichud they included leading members of the older kibbutzim and were led by well known *Vatikim* such as Arye Bahir, Yoseph Yizreeli and others. In the moshavim they consisted mainly of non-European members of the newer settlements, and were joined by very few of the leading *Vatikim*. Common to both were a large section of those born in the country, who had been associated with the *Zeirim* in their past struggles and who saw the split in terms of *Mamlachtiut*, the question of succession and their strong antipathy to Achdut Haavoda. On the other hand, although Rafi enjoyed the support of minorities in branches throughout the country it did not succeed in capturing any branch as a whole, and the party organisational structure remained loyal to Eshkol.

Most significantly the formation of Rafi broke up the *Zeirim*. Only a section of the *Zeirim* supported Ben Gurion, although this included its leading figures – Dayan, Peres, Smilanski, Degani, and Ben Israel, all of whom had been Knesset members, as well as others from the second rank – Bareli, Avizohar, Aviad, Yaacobi, and Ben Porat. Eshkol and the majority were supported by Asher Yadlin, Aharon Yadlin, Arye Eliav, Abraham Ofer, Ahuvia Malkin, and many other active *Zeirim*.

Except for the *Zeirim*, most of those who chose Rafi did so out of loyalty to Ben Gurion, out of an intense belief in him as a charismatic leader who had always been right in the past, and whose political judgement had to be followed. This was particularly true of those of his own generation who followed him out of the party. The others of his generation, despite grave misgivings and even guilt on the part of some, chose the party over the individual, its unity over loyalty to Ben Gurion, the institution over the charismatic personality. Among the younger generation, many supported Ben Gurion for the same reasons; but others saw Rafi as embodying their commitment to *Mamlachtiut*, and as espousing the ideological viewpoint that the *Zeirim* had propounded since the mid-1950s. Above all support for Ben Gurion in opposition to the Alignment, and to the leadership group that had crystallised around Eshkol was important in their struggle for succession. On the other hand those *Zeirim* who supported Eshkol did so out of profound disagreement with their former colleagues over the significance of personal loyalty to Ben Gurion, and on the pragmatic premise that the ideas of the *Zeirim* were more likely to be put into practice by Mapai of the Alignment than by Rafi in the wilderness. Moreover, they, too, were moved by notions of party unity.

The split also brought about the decline of the *Gush* as the party's dominant organisational force because its membership and leadership were torn between conflicting loyalties to Eshkol as party leader and the authority of its legitimate institutions and decisions on the one hand, and their intense personal loyalty to Ben Gurion on the other. Moreover, there were structural reasons for its decline. For the first time in its history since 1948, a Mapai Prime Minister had become party leader. Ben Gurion, as Prime Minister, had not been active in intra-party affairs; and the effect had been the delegation of an enormous amount of power to the *Gush* within Mapai, with Netzer as 'Minister for Party Affairs'. Eshkol, always closely connected to party matters and less anxious than his predecessor to confine himself to dealing with the great affairs of state, became deeply and directly involved in the party's internal problems. When eventually the party became divided into the pro-Eshkol and pro-Ben Gurion groups, the *Gush* was relegated to a position of support rather than being able to exercise dominance or control. Loyalty to the *Gush* ceased to be relevant; it was either loyalty to Ben Gurion, or to Eshkol. When eventually it gave most of its support to Eshkol it had considerably weakened its position with the majority by sitting on the fence for so long, and by having supported Ben Gurion for a considerable distance.

An evaluation of the split of 1965

One can examine the Mapai–Rafi split as it stood in November 1965 from three separate points of view; the failure of Mapai to contain a major internal conflict; the external electoral success of Mapai despite this failure; and the position of Rafi and its leaders in Israel's party politics, and the effects that their political miscalculation was likely to have for their future succession prospects.

A consistent theme of our previous analysis has been that a major strength of Mapai was the manner in which it managed to incorporate many diverse social groups into the party by providing for their ideal, material and symbolic interests. In particular, it was argued that this was reinforced by the party's decision making processes, which used the straddle of party loyalty to weld together competing groups, and to produce decisions and policies based upon acceptable compromise and consensus. The party thus emphasised the paramount importance of party unity, of maintaining organisational cohesion in order to face the external battle, and above all to ensure its continued hold over the central power positions in the state. Yet in this instance Mapai failed to reach such a compromise, and endangered its whole position of dominance in Israel's politics. In the light of its successes in the past in avoiding such situations, this failure demands explanation.

Perhaps the first and basic reason is that the stakes were so high, and the issues so diffuse and generalised that compromise could not easily be achieved. This contrasts with economic or intra-party organisational decisions which by their nature were relatively specific and limited in scope, and therefore more easily given to compromise. Thus in 1964–5 there was bitter personal and policy conflict between the two top leaders of the party: one Prime Minister and active head of the party; the other, the charismatic founder of the state Prime Minister for nearly fifteen years, and the party's mentor, spiritual guide and inspiration. Before it could assert its independence and demonstrate its political capabilities, the post-Ben Gurion collective *Vatikim* leadership came into conflict with the *Zeirim* who sought to stake their claim to the succession in the future. The issues at stake between them were diffuse; they involved long-standing differences in personality, temperament, style, ideology and values, and to these were added the questions of immediate power and future succession and with these the future identity and distinctive values of both the party and the state. Ben Gurion further injected into the conflict the issue of morality; these were questions of 'truth', 'justice', 'incorruptibility' and 'purity' over which it was extremely difficult to compromise.

In the last resort, of course, the choice was up to the minority. No party is infinitely united and capable of containing opposition, if the latter does not wish to cooperate. A dissatisfied minority always has the option of leaving the party. In this case the minority had four alternatives; giving in to the majority decisions and maintaining active party participation; remaining in the party in a more inactive capacity; leaving the party and retiring from politics; and leaving the party and forming an active opposition. Such a choice is generally one that only the minority can make. The majority may make its choice easier by compromise of various kinds. In our case the incumbent Mapai leadership did not do so; it gambled on being able to include Achdut Haavoda and to contain the internal opposition. It did not believe that a split was inevitable, and therefore did not face the alternatives of either the Alignment or a split until *after* the Alignment had been agreed to, when compromise was nigh impossible. The minority for its part made compromise difficult by putting its demands in terms that made it look as if the majority was being dictated to by the minority.

The record for Mapai was mixed. It failed to contain an internal conflict and the result was a party split, and the exit of Ben Gurion and top future leaders like Dayan and Peres. On the other side it formed an Alignment with Achdut Haavoda which meant steady cooperation with other top leaders such as Allon, Ben Aharon, Carmel and Galili, and the possibility, if not probability, of full union in the near future. The Alignment at the 1965 Knesset elections, however, polled nearly 5 per cent less votes than its two constituents did in 1961 (a bad year for Mapai), and 8 per cent less than in 1959. Nevertheless Mapai retained its position of political dominance in the Histadrut and the state. By and large it also maintained the basic organisational framework intact. The split demonstrated the strength of the party's organisational and institutional framework in the hands of the majority and led by the individual who was both Prime Minister and formal party leader. Thus not one single party branch fell to the control of the minority. Mapai's performance is evidence of its high degree of institutionalisation, which enabled it to withstand a challenge from its most charismatic leader and the illustrious founder of the state. Organisation triumphed over charisma and institutional power over prophetic morality. It showed how Mapai's political power rested upon its incorporation of diverse social forces, on its long-term institutional and organisational penetration and control and on the structures and processes it had developed over the years to weld these diverse forces together. It also demonstrated conclusively the small degree to which power in Mapai was personalised and individual.

At the same time, the split and the conflict surrounding it highlighted a weakness of the Mapai institutional and organisational structure – the absence of formal constitutional methods of leadership selection. This was particularly apparent in the use of appointments committees, and in the absence of direct, secret, rank and file ballots, and made it possible for the legitimacy of the institutions so chosen to be called into question. Secondly, it meant that in leadership struggles the *Zeirim* were at the mercy of such methods, and that there was no avenue of direct appeal for support to the party membership, or to the electorate. Thus while organisational strength was an advantage for Mapai, tight control by a small group neither directly chosen by, nor responsible to the rank and file was a serious disadvantage because it intensified internal opposition that might have been muted by the existence of party bodies enjoying the unquestioned legitimacy of rank and file electoral choice and support.

A complex combination of motives led Rafi out of Mapai: an inexorable sequence of political events which provided no acceptable alternative; personal loyalty and devotion to Ben Gurion; the attraction of a new programme and policy platform embodying all the ideas and ideals of *Mamlachtiut*. After the split its political strategy was designed to weaken Mapai by keeping it out of office completely, or by being in a strong enough position to extract concessions from it. It thus hoped to obtain externally what it had failed to achieve internally. As it turned out, this proved to be a bad political miscalculation, and they failed to take sufficient votes away from Mapai to achieve either of these goals. The immediate result of its poor performance was that Almogi, Dayan and Peres, previously near the centre of power and ministers, were now in a minor opposition party, and much further removed from the succession than had they remained within the Alignment. Thus while the Rafi split and its aftermath settled the internal issues for Mapai, and pointed in a particular direction in regard to the succession question, it did not settle it for the ex-Mapai Rafi leaders. It merely delayed it.

The situation, then, at the end of 1965 was that leadership succession had passed from one to another within the *Vatikim* generation, but had not yet passed out the hands of that generation. The events of 1965 had not only not settled the problems of succession that the *Zeirim* had raised and fought for, they had accentuated them even further. With the existence of Rafi, the succession issue, formerly an internal Mapai question, became an inter-party and public question which the public might eventually become involved in deciding at the polls. Thus the question became whether this issue would continue to be the subject of inter-party conflict to be settled by electoral means, or whether the possibility still remained of healing the breach, of maximising leadership strength and capabilities within the one party, and of solving the problem from within.

The reunification process

In the event, the latter alternative was adopted, and less than three years after the Rafi split a new enlarged Israeli Labour Party (*Mifleget Haavoda Hayisraelit*) uniting Mapai, Achdut Haavoda and Rafi and also including *Min Hayesod* was established. This signified the end of Mapai as an independent political party under that name. Our task here is to analyse and assess the critical factors in bringing reunification to successful fruition. This process falls neatly into three clear chronological periods in which different factors were operative: the period between November 1965 and May 1967; the last two weeks in May 1967, culminating in the Six Day War in June 1967; and the aftermath of the Six Day War from June 1967 until January 1968.

November 1965–May 1967

A number of features stand out clearly in this period. The Alignment between Mapai and Achdut Haavoda underwent steady consolidation and institutionalisation, and marked cooperation and convergence of views and behaviour were manifest everywhere. They were particularly noticeable in the Cabinet, parliamentary, Histadrut and municipal spheres, in all of which joint bodies of consultation and decision were quickly established and operated successfully. Thus, despite separate party organisational frameworks and decision making bodies, the tendency was for important decisions to be taken in jointly constituted bodies by majority decision of those present, rather than on party lines. This had two effects. Party differences on issues, for example in the Histadrut and economic policy spheres, became blurred, and were often replaced by the usual institutional differences. Thus Mapai and Achdut Haavoda ministers sided with each other against Mapai and Achdut Haavoda Histadrut leaders. Secondly, party organisational decision making bodies declined in importance and conscious efforts were made to avoid their use in contentious situations so as to maximise the degree of inter-party cooperation, and the blurring of party lines, and to prevent the freezing of decisions according to party stands where Mapai would then have to use its majority power. This cooperation was particularly evident in the parliamentary sphere where it was decided against meetings of the separate party factors. Instead these would meet as one faction, voting on individual lines and electing its own executive bodies. Similarly in the Histadrut sphere where despite Achdut Haavoda's long history of thorny opposition to Mapai, its members on the Central Executive Committee became part of the weekly meeting of *Chaveireinu*, which met before the Central Executive Committee meeting, and Mapai members did not hold separate faction meetings.

In the inter-party sphere other methods of cooperation were successfully adopted. Formally at the head of the Alignment stood a six man Alignment executive, equally constituted from each party. In the economic policy making sphere, an Economic Secretariat combining ministerial, parliamentary and local and central Histadrut leaders of both parties was set up on approximately a 7:3 ratio in favour of Mapai. Its task was mainly that undertaken by Mapai's former Economic Committee (see chapter ten), that is wages policy, cost of living adjustments, and general economic policy discussions, and the emphasis was upon reaching unified policy agreement based on joint consultation and discussion and not on inter-party bargaining. Thus individual Mapai decision making bodies specifically kept out of such discussions whilst they were taking place in the joint bodies, and they became involved only to ratify agreements already reached in the Economic Secretariat. Similarly, a joint National Alignment Municipal Committee was established to co-ordinate municipal policies in the sixty municipal coalitions that the Alignment controlled, which covered 73 per cent of the country's population.

But above all these important manifestations of institutional cooperation, policy consultation and leadership integration stood the considerable degree of agreement and unity between the top ministerial and party leaders on both sides. There was a marked unanimity of interest and view between Eshkol supported by Sapir (Minister of Finance), Aranne (Minister of Education), Eban (Foreign Minister), and Mrs Meir (Party Secretary-General), and leading Achdut Haavoda figures Galili, Allon and Carmel. It was the agreement and cooperation at this level which gave the whole Alignment its motive power and its ultimate embodiment.

But despite all these manifestations of cooperation, convergence and the submergence of independent party institutions, complete union between the parties, although talked about considerably, did not seem to be an immediate possibility. Mapai and its leadership supported the idea wholeheartedly and generally put pressure on Achdut Haavoda towards this end. In their view, this was the logical culmination of the Alignment. In these considerations Rafi, in absentia, played an important role. Those in Mapai most strongly opposed to Rafi favoured quick union with Achdut Haavoda to consolidate the anti-Rafi forces, and to try and settle the succession issue by keeping Rafi away from the centres of institutional power. Those in Mapai who still had hopes of reintegrating the Rafi group preferred an eventual three-way union to an immediate two-way union which might in the long run preclude the chances of the three-way union. But the main stumbling block for complete union was the unwillingness of Achdut Haavoda. Some of its leaders, notably Allon, who in terms of succession stood to gain most from complete union, supported it unequivocally and immediately. But many others still had reservations about their fate in Mapai. They were worried that they would be completely swallowed up in the much larger unit, whilst in the Alignment they got the best of both worlds; distinctive identity and a secure share of power. This was especially true of the important kibbutz element in the party. Many in Achdut Haavoda, while not opposed to complete union, were equally not wildly enthusiastic about it and were not likely to support it if the only tangible benefit they could see was to improve Allon's chances of succession. Directly contributing to this hesitancy and reluctance was a marked degree of disappointment in Eshkol's performance (see below). Thus in response to constant Mapai pressure to set a date for the complete union, and to the internal pressure from Allon and many younger members who had found a common voice with many younger Mapai members, an Achdut Haavoda Council delayed taking a decision and put it off for a party Conference to be held three months later in June. The basic argument was that union was not simply a question of dates but of completing the integration process. In the event, the Conference was never held, as the Six Day War intervened.

The second key aspect of this period were the relations between Mapai and Rafi, and Rafi's general political situation. After the elections Rafi found itself in the political wilderness and many of its political leaders who for so long had fully participated in key institutional power positions and decisions were for the first time in their political careers in opposition and without the immense resources, support and influence afforded by being in power. They thus felt the full impact of their failure in the 1965 elections. Their major task therefore was to prepare for an indefinite future in opposition by organising the party from the grass roots upward to complement and support the leadership group that already existed. By the end of this period they managed to gather together about 25 000 members. A brief sociological breakdown reveals the emphasis on youth; 60 per cent were aged below thirty-five years. About 18 per cent were in labour settlements, about 24 per cent in Tel Aviv, Haifa and Jerusalem and 23 per cent in development areas.[38] These figures indicate the emphasis in Rafi on youth and ethnic groups (development towns) and the general lack of success among established metropolitan urban groups where it clearly lacked the kind of administrative resources necessary for that degree of institutional penetration that in the labour sector of Israel's society facilitates membership incorporation. Nor did its popularity seem to be increas-

[38] *Davar*, 12.5.1966.

ing. In Tnuat Hamoshavim, for example, its popularity underwent a steady decline; in the Histadrut elections in September 1965 it received 27 per cent of the votes: in the Knesset elections in November 1965, 22 per cent of the votes, and in the elections to the internal decision making bodies of Tnuat Hamoshavim in May 1966, 14 per cent of the votes.[39] The other major factor in Rafi's search for organisational consolidation is that, not surprisingly, its organisational framework was an almost exact replica of that of Mapai, despite all its proclamations that it was new, innovative and completely different from the old 'establishment'.

Its external political stance was strongly and bitterly anti-Mapai, and anti-Eshkol, and there was a general increase in the intensity of its personal attacks upon Eshkol. This was particularly true in the defence sphere where (led by Ben Gurion) they constantly reiterated what they regarded to be his complete weakness and lack of ability and publicly accused him of making disastrous errors in the field of defence planning and strategy. Ben Gurion, in particular, supported by other Rafi leaders, constantly maintained a barrage of public criticism aimed at undermining public confidence in Eshkol by declaring him to be totally unfit to be Prime Minister in every possible way.

Simultaneously there were attempts to try and bridge the Mapai–Rafi cleavage, whether on the basis of a dual union or on the basis of a tripartite union including Achdut Haavoda. These were initiated by Mapai and Rafi activists in the Ichud and Tnuat Hamoshavim. Both feared greatly for the future unity and integrity of these closely-knit settlement movements. Although they had until that time successfully isolated the conflict in various ways and prevented the political differences from affecting the wholeness of their settlements, they were apprehensive of their future ability to do this, and were fully mindful of the tremendous consequences of the split in the kibbutz movement in the late 1940s. Despite the absence of clear ideological differences at that stage, they could not be sure that these would not develop in the future; nor could they continue to rely on the sense of self-restraint that had characterised their political behaviour until then. As we pointed out in chapter two, these settlement movements were politically incorporated into Mapai on the basis of non-competitive institutional penetration and control. Internal political competition might mean the division of settlements, the breaking up of friendships, and the tearing asunder of families. Under these conditions the unity of the settlements came first, and they therefore sought to avert such potential disasters by healing the political rift.

Mapai at first opposed these moves as being premature, but eventually came around to supporting them, so long as these discussions were on the basis of party decisions already taken (for example about the Alignment, and the Affair). In this it had nothing to lose, because talks under these conditions implied Rafi capitulation. Rafi at first supported the talks because it felt that

[39] Ibid.

they were embarrassing to Mapai, but it quickly came to oppose them for sound internal political reasons. All its energies and resources were being used to build up an independent political organisation of its own: talk of unity and return to Mapai led many rank and file followers to ask why the need for such independent organisational efforts at such great cost if unity was in the offing. Rafi leaders therefore opposed any talk of unity because they realised that without a sound independent organisational base any discussions with Mapai on return would be on the basis of weakness rather than strength, and would not help to extract concessions from it.

But the factor which overshadowed these complicated political relationships was the enormous decline in Eshkol's prestige as Prime Minister, and the crisis in morale and spirit that overcame the whole country during 1966. In many ways this was the severest crisis in morale that the state had undergone since 1948. The main factor was the economic situation. Inflation gave way to economic policies of tightening the belt and to austerity. Where previously there had been a rising standard of living, increasing consumption, and full employment, there was now unemployment which at times reached about 100 000 persons, a very high figure in terms of Israel's labour force. There were spontaneous (and politically organised) hunger strikes, demonstrations and various other manifestations of anomic behaviour derived from economic dissatisfaction. Morale in the country was at its lowest ebb, and the emigration rate reached an all-time high, particularly among the middle classes, native born and professionals. In the context of Israel's Zionist policies of ingathering the exiles and demands for the immigration of Jews everywhere this was doubly demoralising. A famous cartoon sadly showed a long queue of people leaving, with the caption, 'would the last person please turn out the lights'.

Eshkol had always been regarded as the financial and economic expert, the man of compromise and negotiation, the man able to find agreed solutions to the most complex problems. Now he bore the full weight of public disappointment and anger at the inevitable result of about ten years of steady inflation for which he himself was not solely responsible. (If anything it was the over-extended consumption demands and standard of living expectations of the Israeli citizen, combined with the latter's low productivity which were to blame.) He was now regarded as a ditherer, a man unable to make up his mind, as incapable of making decisions, a man who did not lead, but followed, or was simply drawn along by the rush of events. Books of jokes about Eshkol emphasising these points made the rounds. Where previously they were sympathetic and pleasant, and reflected affection and indulgence, now they were antagonistic and bitter, and reflected hostility and complete lack of patience and loss of confidence. A favourite joke was, that when asked in a cafe whether he wanted tea or coffee, Eshkol replied, 'half and half'.

These feelings were not only widely felt among the populace, they were constantly hammered home by Rafi leaders and were reiterated at every opportunity by leading and influential sections of the Press, with the influential *Haaretz* in the vanguard. Even coalition partners publicly expressed disquiet: at the end of 1966 Moshe Kol, a Minister in Eshkol's government, called for an enlargement of the coalition to include the opposition parties so as to restore public confidence by the establishment of a National Coalition Government. And Press reports indicated that this view was supported by the National Religious Party, and that there was also some support for it in influential Mapai circles. The rumours and pressures were so strong that both Eshkol and the Mapai Leadership Bureau were forced to deny publicly that any negotiations to widen the coalition had taken place, and placed the blame squarely on Rafi as being responsible for all these rumours as part of its campaign of personal vengeance against Eshkol by lowering Mapai's and Israel's prestige throughout the world.[40]

There was certainly disquiet within Mapai which expressed itself more in the defence sphere. The political elite centred around the Defence establishment and particularly those in Mapai came to believe that Eshkol indeed lacked ability to make firm decisions in this sphere, that he was drawn along by, and too dependent upon, his advisers in this sphere, and that in actual fact the Chief of Staff was really the Minister of Defence. This dissatisfaction was symbolised at the end of 1966 when four leading members of Mapai's Secretariat and Central Committee formally requested Mrs Meir, the Party Secretary-General, to institute moves to have Eshkol replaced. The particular issue that had brought their dissatisfaction to a head and which led to such radical action on their part was a particular security and intelligence mishap that had occurred. It was not that they believed that Eshkol was either involved in, or responsible for it, but that he had neither established lines of communication which would have enabled him to become aware of, and prevent, such ill-advised actions by those under his authority as Minister of Defence, nor did he seem able to make up his mind what to do when the mishap and its international ramifications were brought to his attention. They believed that in this instance certain personnel dismissals were absolutely essential, yet Eshkol refused to make a decision. In the objective absence of a possible successor this move got nowhere, but from our point of view what is most significant is the move itself rather than its effects.

14 May–1 June 1967

This lack of confidence in Eshkol, and the depth of the decline in public morale and spirit came to a head between 14 May and 1 June 1967, the crucial period prior to the Six Day War. During this short space of time there was an incredible and complex succession of political events in Israel and throughout

[40] *Davar*, 12.12.1966, 13.1.1967; *Haaretz*, 11.12.1966.

the world, which together with the actual happenings of the war itself have given rise to a complete literature of their own, seeking to recreate and reconstruct every action, every moment, every thought of this dramatic time.[41] In terms of the concerns of this book the most significant aspects were the appointment of Moshe Dayan as Defence Minister, thereby relieving the Prime Minister of this portfolio, and the entry into a National Unity Government of Rafi and Gahal.

When it became apparent in May 1967 that Israel was in a situation that made war likely, it was quickly agreed at the top level of Mapai and the Alignment that the leading opposition parties, Rafi and Gahal, should be kept fully informed and consulted on defence matters, so as to maximise and emphasise national unity. It was therefore proposed that representatives of these parties should for the time of the emergency become members of the Ministerial Defence Committee, but without joining the ministry and the coalition.

Rafi with its defence expertise strongly expressed the view to many Mapai leaders that the government as then constituted was not capable of dealing with the crisis, and sought an official meeting with Mapai to discuss the issue. While Israel's success a few weeks later make such views strange, it was widely believed that war would be much more costly than in 1956. Not only would there be more military casualties, but there were fears of immense civilian casualties, and the figure of 40 000 was commonly given. While the military did not share this view, how could they prove their claim that war would be short, and that there would be few civilian casualties? And at that time diplomacy had not been tried. Eban convinced the government to try it first, and was on his way to Paris, London and Washington to see if the crisis could be averted diplomatically. But diplomacy, even if successful, is normally a slow process, and neither the Israeli population nor the army was patient. Many felt it would certainly fail, that war was inevitable and that the longer Israel waited, the greater the number of Israeli casualties. Above all waiting was attributed to an indecisive government, not in control of the situation, but simply pulled here and there by events. It seemed to lack leadership, a sense of purpose and direction, an idea of what was needed.

At this stage, one of the strangest things in the history of Israeli politics occurred. Begin, the leader of Gahal, proposed Ben Gurion, his arch-rival and bitter political enemy, as Prime Minister. In combined talks between Gahal, Rafi, and the National Religious Party (a member of Eshkol's coalition), it was proposed by Mr M. H. Shapira, the leader of the NRP, that Ben Gurion become Defence Minister. Although they clearly lacked confidence in Eshkol as Defence Minister, as a member of the coalition, they did not wish to depose Eshkol or to undermine his position. After much pressure from Peres, Ben

41 See, for example, W. Laqueur, The Road to War (Harmondsworth, England, 1968) (Penguin); S. Nakdimon, Towards the Zero Hour (Tel Aviv, 1968) (Hebrew).

Gurion finally agreed to serve under Eshkol, despite all that he had said about him in the previous two years.

This combined tactic therefore was two-pronged: to have the coalition widened to establish a National Unity Government by including Rafi and Gahal, and to have Ben Gurion included in it. There were many attempts by Rafi to influence key Mapai individuals and sections to support this, for example Choushi and Haifa, and Netzer, Tel Aviv and the *Gush*. Mr Shapira, the leader of the NRP and Minister of the Interior, had the unhappy task of putting this plan to Eshkol, who refused adamantly to countenance the inclusion of Ben Gurion as Defence Minister, or to be relieved of the portfolio himself in any way. If, on the other hand, his colleagues wanted Ben Gurion, then he would depart. By implication he rejected the need to establish a National Unity Government by widening the coalition to include Rafi and Gahal, while at the same time recognising the need to keep these parties fully informed of events and plans in some consultative way.

A new element then entered the situation. A meeting of Mapai and Rafi leaders in the Ichud jointly urged the establishment of a National Unity Government, but suggested that they would prefer to see Moshe Dayan included in it in preference to Ben Gurion. This was both to make it easier for Eshkol, on the one hand, and with an eye to the future on the other, apart from the immediate goal of reestablishing public confidence and morale with regard to defence and security. Further crucial support for the establishment of a National Unity Government quickly developed when the National Religious Party formally decided to press for the widening of the coalition to include Gahal and Rafi. A second coalition partner, the Independent Liberals, also took the same line.

The official Mapai institutions, the Leadership Bureau, the Secretariat, and the Alignment Political Committee, led by Eshkol and Meir, and strongly supported by Aranne and Sapir, opposed changes or additions to Cabinet, and sought to protect and maintain Eshkol's status. Although agreeing to meet Rafi as requested they accused the latter of trying to demoralise the nation by seeking, not additions to the Cabinet, but a complete change of personnel. To agree to Rafi's demands would be tantamount to an admission of all the charges and denunciations made by Rafi in the previous eighteen months about security deficiencies'. Despite the official Mapai and Alignment view, pressure began to grow within the party. Choushi met Eshkol and told him that the Haifa Mapai branch supported a National Unity Government to include both Dayan and Begin, the leader of Gahal. Support for a National Unity Government also came from Netzer.

These feverish negotiations had all taken place in the space of a few days, following Nasser's closure of the Straits of Tiran. The Israeli military advised immediate attack. The army was fully mobilised, the country was prepared for war, but nothing happened, whilst Eban was on a diplomatic mission.

Public confidence declined as tension rose, and political indecision and in-ability to agree seemed to be the explanation. The more that this attitude developed the greater was the pressure to take dramatic internal political steps to reassure the populace by making personnel changes at the top levels of Cabinet defence decision making. Yet the Mapai leadership refrained from doing so, partly because it was waiting to see if diplomacy would work, partly because it did not want to appear to have been pushed into making decisions that were unpalatable, involved considerable loss of prestige, and could be con-strued as admission of serious error, default, and lack of capacity, and partly, as in the particular case of Mrs Meir, by complete confidence in the ability of Israel's defence forces to win whenever war occurred. Thus she was widely reported to have told the Mapai Secretariat, 'We need no partners for victory'.[42] Yet whatever the reason, the longer they waited, the greater the pressure grew.

Suggestions were then made that Yigal Allon should be made either Minister or Deputy Minister of Defence, but Eshkol rejected this. The issue of a National Unity Government became critical when it was made clear that constitutionally it was not possible to participate in the Ministerial Com-mittee on Defence without being ministers. Thus the Alignment was forced to concede this issue – that is, the establishment of a National Unity Govern-ment by widening the coalition. The question then became the terms for a new coalition agreement, the identity of the new partners and in particular of their ministers. Thus while conceding this point to Begin, leader of Gahal, the Alignment would not agree to his demand for Dayan as Defence Minister, which needless to say was now also supported by Rafi despite Ben Gurion's opposition to its entry into Cabinet as a party. In order to soften the blow for Mapai, and again with an eye to future succession prospects, Peres, Rafi Secretary-General, indicated to Mapai leaders that if they demanded it as a condition of Dayan's becoming Minister of Defence, Rafi would 'return to Mapai without conditions'.

This was the situation on Eban's return when he went straight into a Cabinet meeting that had already been in progress for a long period of time and the results of which were anxiously awaited by the whole country. On the basis of his discussions in Washington, Eban counselled against war and that Israel should for the next two weeks rely on diplomacy, rather than be branded the aggressor by attacking in Sinai. His views led to acrimonious exchanges, first in Cabinet and later with the army. Those opposed to him took the view that there was no sense in waiting and no reason to be patient, there was nothing the Great Powers could or would do.

At a first Cabinet meeting, a trial vote ended in a clear division, nine for war, nine against. Among the Ministers of the Alignment those favouring

---

[42] Quoted in Laqueur, p. 170. Mrs Meir later denied the statement attributed to her, see Nakdimon, p. 153.

military action were Allon, Gvati, Galili, Yeshayahu, Carmel, Yaacov Shapira, Sharef, Sasson, and Eshkol. No ministers of any other party took this view. Against military action on the Alignment side were Eban, Aranne and Sapir, together with three NRP ministers, two Mapam ministers and one Independent Liberal Minister. Eshkol later said that 'I know that if I would have pressed them I would have received the support of the majority...had I banged the table and insisted, no one would have resigned from the government. I did not do that.'[43] Following the meeting Eshkol received emphatic and strong diplomatic notes from President Johnson and U.S. Secretary of State Rusk, advising Israel to refrain from military action, and warning of grave consequences if she did not. In the light of these notes Cabinet decided the next day by a large majority to enter a further waiting period.

Eshkol now had to explain this decision to the nation which had waited anxiously for days for signs of governmental initiative and action, and to the country's military leadership which strongly supported immediate action. His broadcast to the nation was live, and the statement itself briefly and precisely explained the government's decision to wait, whilst affirming its belief in Israel's right and capacity to defend itself in the face of Egyptian aggression. But Eshkol's delivery and presentation were catastrophic: where strong words, morale-boosting, the creation of confidence, and the welding of national determination were badly needed, what resulted was a heightening of national loss of confidence bordering on hysteria and panic. Eshkol was never an orator; his speech on this occasion, probably the most important of his career, was marred by stammering, stuttering, groans and sighs, was almost inaudible and hardly comprehensible to the listeners throughout the nation glued to their radio sets. What is more, at one stage he halted for a few minutes in the middle, unable to read a hand-written amendment in the hastily composed text – and the nation heard him whispering to his aides, 'What's this?' His abject failure to inspire symbolised public loss of confidence in him, and dramatically heightened the political pressure upon him to hand over the defence responsibility, and to broaden the coalition. This was even more marked in the political elite which quickly became aware of the fact that immediately after the broadcast his meeting with the military General Staff was bitter and acrimonious, that he put up a poor show in attempting to defend the government's policy against the generals who warned that army morale was ebbing, that the military could not wait indefinitely, that waiting strengthened the Egyptians' hands, and above all that the government publicly demonstrated that it lacked faith in the armed forces. It was little wonder that the leading independent newspaper *Haaretz* in its editorial next morning expressed complete lack of confidence in Eshkol's ability to lead the nation at this critical time. Nevertheless a meeting of Mapai

---

[43] Quoted in Laqueur, p. 162.

ministers held immediately after the discussions with the General Staff brought no change in their opposition to Dayan as Defence Minister.

Pressure upon Eshkol mounted inexorably in every possible direction. Some favoured Allon, and in response Eshkol agreed to have him as an unofficial Defence adviser, without any public announcement of his status, as he did not wish to appear merely as a rubber stamp. The NRP increased its pressure for Dayan and a National Unity Government. Leading defence officials met many top-level Alignment members to inform them of the low level of morale in the army. But the first real break came from within the younger generation of the Alignment. Three of its leading members, Arye Eliav, Aharon Yadlin (Deputy Minister of Education) and Gabi Cohen of Achdut Haavoda agreed that Dayan must be included in some way or other in the government in a defence capacity, either as Minister or joint deputy minister with Allon, and began to seek support for this within the Alignment. This was followed by a meeting of the Alignment Knesset faction attended by Eshkol at which many members including loyal Eshkol supporters of the *Vatikim* generation, as well as the more youthful members, openly supported Dayan and a National Unity Coalition. For all of them national morale was crucial, and this seemed to demand Dayan. Eshkol's political secretary later wrote that here for the first time was Eshkol made fully aware of the gap between the Ministry and the Alignment parliamentarians, and of the breadth of the demand for a National Unity Government and Dayan.[44]

But Eshkol and his close supporters were not easily to be moved, and the Alignment Political Committee therefore proposed on 31 May that Yigal Allon be appointed Defence Minister. This was of course a tremendous blow to Eshkol who had till that time steadfastly refused to be pushed into relinquishing the Defence Portfolio. But it seemed the lesser of two evils. If it could be achieved it would keep this key portfolio within the Alignment, and could prevent the widening of the governmental coalition to include Rafi and Gahal. What is more it would have profound implications for the future succession issue, just as the appointment of Dayan would have these in a different direction.

But Mr Shapira of the NRP (at that time working in unison with the Independent Liberals to achieve a National Unity Government and Dayan as Defence Minister) refused to agree to this. He argued that if Eshkol was now finally resigned to separating the Defence portfolio from the Prime Minister-ship, there was no reason why it should not be given to Dayan. Similarly Shapira opposed Eshkol's attempt to have Dayan take a key army position when he refused an offer to be Deputy Prime Minister, because it would have meant that neither Rafi and Gahal who were both committed to Dayan would join the coalition. He therefore demanded a Cabinet meeting to discuss this whole matter, to which Eshkol agreed.

[44] *Nakdimon*, p. 170.

The Mapai Secretariat and Cabinet met simultaneously, which meant that Eshkol was not present at the Secretariat. The Secretariat met and in a most bitter and acrimonious meeting, Mrs Meir as Party Secretary-General had the task of defending the Eshkol position and was the key figure. Despite her adamant opposition the Secretariat decided that all changes in Cabinet had first to be brought before it for ratification. This was clearly intended to prevent Cabinet agreeing to Allon in preference to Dayan. But here the Secretariat need not have worried because at Cabinet Shapira of the NRP threatened his party's resignation from the coalition if Allon were appointed, even though Eshkol was now prepared to agree to the inclusion of Rafi and Gahal. Thus the Cabinet meeting ended inconclusively.

At a continued meeting of the Mapai Secretariat next day overwhelming support for Dayan was expressed, it having been made clear to it that Dayan had agreed to take a leading position in the army only because the Ministry of Defence was not being offered to him, but that he clearly preferred the latter. The strong feelings of the Mapai Secretariat were brought to Eshkol's attention, and almost simultaneously Gahal and the Independent Liberals placed increasing pressure upon him. With no other option available to him, Eshkol invited Dayan to accept the Defence portfolio, at about the same time as Allon, aware of the general developments, but not aware of Eshkol's decision, removed his own candidature. Eshkol explained that it had been made clear to him 'that there was no Rafi without Dayan, and no Gahal without Rafi. And without these the government is in a shaky situation, because of its complete paralysis by the NRP. Dayan wants only the Defence portfolio, and there is no escape from this.'[45]

Eshkol was thus forced to acquiesce to Dayan's appointment, and it was this 'situation without escape' that he often later referred to as a 'putsch'. Eshkol's lack of alternatives came from a number of factors – public loss of confidence and opposition pressure, on the one hand, culminating in a gradual erosion of internal Mapai support and in the tremendous pressure of Eshkol's NRP coalition partner. Within Mapai the loss of support affected not only the younger generation but also Haifa and the *Gush*, it overtook the parliamentary faction of the Alignment, the Alignment Political Committee, and above all the Mapai Secretariat. Particularly prominent in the erosion of confidence in Eshkol and the demands for Dayan were the previously undividedly loyal veteran Eshkol supporters. By the time Eshkol was faced with ultimata from the Mapai Secretariat and Cabinet, his only undividedly loyal supporters were Mrs Meir and Aranne (Sapir was in America).

Thus under the pressure of impending war and national crisis, the internal succession question had been turned on its head. Rafi and Dayan, the outsiders, were now well and truly established at the centre of power and major decisions. Achdut Haavoda, the insiders and the preferred successors, had been

45 *Nakdimon*, p. 247.

rudely shouldered aside. Eshkol and the veteran Mapai leadership had suffered a serious loss of prestige and erosion of public confidence, which was only partially reinstated by the swift and spellbinding Israeli victory in which all the national leaders shared. The major long-term consideration was Mapai's response to this change in political fortunes in relation to the succession question. It now had to decide whether to press for a two-part union with Achdut Haavoda as had been foreshadowed before the war, or to seek to capitalise on Rafi's seeming willingness to return to Mapai now that Dayan was Minister of Defence. Reunion with Rafi could be achieved in a three-part arrangement including Achdut Haavoda, or it could also occur in a two-part agreement excluding the latter and putting an end to the Alignment. This was the problem that faced not only Mapai but the other two parties as well: which arrangement suited their interests the best, which gave them the greatest leverage for the future and for succession, and what were the best terms that they could hope to extract from Mapai?

June 1967–January 1968

The period between the Six Day War of June 1967 and the formation of the Israeli Labour Party in January 1968 witnessed intense bargaining and negotiations between Mapai, Achdut Haavoda and Rafi. As we saw above, the war and its prelude completely altered relations between the parties. It now seemed that Rafi was on the way up both in terms of public confidence, and in terms of the considerable support within Mapai for Dayan in preference to Allon. It was therefore able to envisage a secure future for itself in a new party uniting all three groups. This was both symbolised and embodied in Dayan's position as Minister of Defence. Provided that he retained this position he was now a logical and strong candidate for the succession. In any such contest he could expect to attract considerable support within Mapai, where large sections were more sympathetic to him than to Allon, and regarded him as basically Mapai.

On the other hand, it was believed that if Rafi did not unite with Mapai, Dayan would eventually be forced to relinquish his position. This made Rafi even more sensitive than before to the advantages of institutional power, and of being in government rather than in opposition. As we noted above, a constant theme in its short history had been the choice between capturing power from without in electoral competition, and working within Mapai despite its establishment and party machine which it criticised. In such calculations Dayan's position of power was a crucial element. In this regard there was also the subsidiary question of whether it was possible to swallow its pride and work together in one party with Eshkol and Mrs Meir, after its two years of bitter attack, criticism and complete negation of Mapai's leadership capabilities, and moral deficiencies. And once inside, could it realistically hope to gain Mapai support for the ideological and institutional changes and innovations which it sought? These questions posed a serious dilemma for Rafi.

In response to these questions Rafi argued that the war and all that went before it, and in particular the need for national unity in the face of the new defence and security situation after it, demanded and necessitated as great a degree of Rafi influence in governmental policies and decisions as possible. This was now an explosive and contentious defence and security situation of a permanent nature that opened up both possibilities and dangers for long-term peace in the Middle East about which Israel had to be united. Rafi's view was that it had special ability and expertise in these fields and, as well, a particular policy approach.

Achdut Haavoda's dilemma was of a very different kind. Its weakness as a suitor had been clearly demonstrated. Despite leadership integration and close relationships at the very top level during the Alignment, the Mapai middle level leaders and rank and file seemed to be much more sympathetic to Rafi, to the extent that a reunification between Rafi and Mapai was likely even if Achdut Haavoda decided not to proceed. Thus to protect its influence on the top state leadership, and to keep its options alive on the question of succession, Achdut Haavoda had little choice but to go along with whatever Mapai offered it. The most it could hope for was to extract for itself from Mapai the greatest degree of protection of its special interests in the new party. It had already seen the drawing power and popular attraction of Dayan and Rafi; while these were in the ascendancy its prestige and power position seemed to be in decline. Yet not to participate in the new party would be self-defeating and retrogressive; it would completely exclude it from power and succession, and would return it to the relative obscurity of a splinter opposition party that it had occupied until 1965. All the benefits of the Alignment would be lost. On the other hand, there was a new element pressing for unification. A large section of the kibbutz federation of Achdut Haavoda, previously opposed to the Alignment and to union with Mapai, now looked with favour on Rafi because they shared activist security policies and maximalist views regarding the future of the Arab territories that had fallen into Israel's hands during the war. They thus actively sought a tri-partite reunification to strengthen their combined influence against the strong 'dovish' section in Mapai.

Tactically Mapai was in a strong position, potentially able to play off one suitor against the other to get the kind of union it wanted, and in a general sense this is what happened, except that it took time and considerable negotiation to get there. The main reason was that Mapai itself was not quite united over the kind of union it wanted and how to go about it. The veteran Mapai leadership headed by Eshkol and Mrs Meir were bitter about Rafi, over all that had passed between them after 1965, and particularly during the period preceding the Six Day War. They believed that Rafi had set out to undermine national morale and to destroy public confidence in the Alignment, and to force the overthrow of the government and the replacement of Eshkol. That Rafi had not achieved this did not assuage their hurt, because its pressure had succeeded in compelling a very unwilling Eshkol to relinquish his position of Minister of Defence in favour of Dayan, and to widen the coalition. In terms of prestige and power Mapai and Eshkol had taken a severe beating, and Rafi and Dayan had won a glorious victory. To the veteran Mapai leadership the whole episode seemed like a 'putsch' and they publicly described it as such. To reunify with Rafi under these conditions would be yet another victory for Rafi. Dayan had demonstrated his influence on Mapai while outside; his inclusion in the party would be full of danger for the future. It would not be beyond him openly to challenge Eshkol for the leadership and to win it from within, if the party continued to be split, and if the kind of party machine that had in the past ensured majority support for incumbent leaders remained broken and divided in loyalty. Nevertheless, Dayan outside the party was also a danger. Not only was a major ministry, for the first time, outside Mapai's control, which posed problems of inter-party policy coordination; this also gave Dayan a broad and powerful base from which to seek to convert Rafi into the major coalition partner, if not to take over the government. It was, however, clear that it would not be advisable for Eshkol to attempt to break up the National Unity Government and relieve Dayan of his portfolio (despite Rafi's fears of this) given the security situation, and the internal Mapai support for Dayan as Defence Minister.

This latter factor was crucial. There was a clear split between Eshkol, Meir and the supporters of the veteran leadership, and many of the middle level leaders, and rank and file, who not only did not oppose reunification with Rafi but actively supported it. Thus the tactic for Eshkol and the veteran leadership was publicly to support tripartite reunification, but at the same time to work towards a prior union with Achdut Haavoda, which would give the combined party greater leverage and force Rafi to accept reunification on whatever conditions were offered to it. There was also the faint possibility that prior union with Achdut Haavoda might have the effect of forestalling and preventing the tripartite unification by making conditions so unattractive for Rafi that it would be left with no alternative but to withdraw from negotiations. This would probably have been the most appealing to the veteran Mapai leadership, but it reckoned without the majority support for Dayan and Rafi within the Mapai institutions, which circumvented and nullified this strategy.

Immediately after the war, Peres, Secretary-General of Rafi, formally wrote to Mapai reiterating that Rafi was prepared to return to Mapai 'without conditions'. He was supported in this by a majority of the Rafi Secretariat to whom he explained that Rafi ought not give up its influence over key political decisions, that it had to be concerned with the future, and that it could only do this within Mapai. He emphasised that for him the past had finished on 5 June. He also supported the unification of Achdut Haavoda with Mapai. Those opposing unification took the view that there should be no return to Mapai unless it made leadership changes. Rafi's Central Committee ratified this decision, but took account of the opposition to unification by stipulating that 'the united party will decide anew on its institutions and on its representatives in the state leadership'.[46] The implication was clear: immediately after the formation of the new party all institutions were to be reconstituted and all ministers, including the Prime Minister, would need new mandates (or be replaced).

The veteran Mapai leadership together with Achdut Haavoda quickly sought to achieve full union between Mapai and Achdut Haavoda before any agreement could be reached with Rafi, despite considerable support within Mapai for simultaneous negotiations with Achdut Haavoda and Rafi. The Mapai Secretariat paid lip service to the latter notion by establishing two separate committees to negotiate simultaneously but separately with the two parties. The two committees, predictably, worked at different speeds and in different directions. The negotiating committee with Achdut Haavoda finished its work very quickly; that with Rafi took much longer, and what is more the latter settled on arrangements directly contradictory to those previously reached with Achdut Haavoda.

The agreement with Achdut Haavoda represented that party's basic position and sought to protect its interests as a distinctive unit within the new party, and to give it the option of independent existence outside the new party should the union not work well. Thus it was agreed that there was to be no discussion of changes in the country's electoral system until just before the Seventh Knesset Elections, due in 1969, and that any change decided upon would not be implemented until after the Eighth Knesset Elections in 1973. The first elected Conference of the new party would not take place till after the Seventh Knesset Elections and until then all internal party institutions would be divided up between the groups according to their proportions in the Histadrut – 60 per cent to Mapai, 22 per cent to Achdut Haavoda and 18 per cent to Rafi. Similarly the new party's list of candidates for Knesset, Histadrut and municipal elections in 1969 would be fixed in accordance with their proportions in those bodies at the time of the union. It thus sought to avoid all forms of internal competition and election for as long as possible, and to have the party operate on the basis of federative agreements. This would ensure leadership stability and prevent Rafi gaining in internal conflict and open elections, and thus stop it from capitalising on the public and intra-party popularity of its leaders.

Rafi's basic position, in addition to the leadership clause mentioned above,

[46] *Davar*, 11.6.1967, 15.6.1967, 16.6.1967, 20.6.1967.

was to discuss changing the country's electoral system as soon as possible, even during the Sixth Knesset, and to hold secret, direct, personal intra-party elections within one year for the Conference, which would then enable the election of new party institutions by direct personal elections. Rafi thus sought to open up the new party as much as possible and to maximise internal electoral competition. This stemmed not only from the long-standing commitments of Rafi and the *Zeirim* to democratic elections, and against appointments committees and a high degree of internal administrative direction, it also made sense in terms of their immediate and long-term political position. Such arrangements would enable them to increase their strength within Mapai and gain a greater say in its leadership and decisions by exploiting their electoral attractiveness. Similarly, a form of constituency elections in the state was supported not only because they had for a long time been ideologically committed to this, but also because it would decrease their dependence on central party administration and appointments committees, and, in fact, increase the party's electoral dependence on them, as popular national figures.

Mapai therefore had to try and bridge the gap between these two conflicting positions and some four to five months were spent in negotiations to do so. It is not necessary to go into involved detail of every move and countermove in reaching the final agreement. What is important is that the attempt by the veteran Mapai leadership to reach prior agreement with Achdut Haavoda was consistently forestalled at the Mapai institutions by a coalition consisting of Abba Choushi and the Haifa branch (in close cooperation with Almogi), Netzer and most of the *Gush* and the Tel Aviv branch, the representatives of the Ichud Kibbutzim and Tnuat Hamoshavim who feared for the unity of their settlements, and many of the *Zeirim* still in Mapai, led by Arye Eliav. This group together had the support of over two-thirds of the membership of the Mapai Secretariat and Central Committee. The issue was never put to the vote directly but each time the question of prior agreement with Achdut Haavoda came up this coalition swung its support behind moves which ensured the simultaneity of negotiations and equality of status for Rafi and Achdut Haavoda. When it became apparent that the Mapai institutions would not allow preferred status for Achdut Haavoda, Eshkol reluctantly 'resigned' himself, as he put it, to the inevitability of a three-part union.[47] He was preceded in this by Mr Pinchas Sapir, Minister of Finance, who recognising the realities of the situation, became extremely active in negotiations and eventually chaired the joint tripartite negotiating committee that hammered out the final agreement. (He also became the first Secretary-General of the new party, resigning as Finance Minister to do so.)

The final agreement reached by Mapai, Achdut Haavoda and Rafi contained only two substantive clauses, each representing compromise by the

[47] *Davar*. 20.8.1967.

various parties. On the question of state leadership, on which Mapai was adamant, Rafi accepted a formula that 'just prior to the elections for the seven Knesset the authoritative institutions of the united party would choose its intended representatives for the state institutions'.[48] Thus stability of leadership was ensured until just before the Knesset elections, it being understood that the leadership question would not be raised until then, and that when the party chose leaders prior to elections, their mandate normally extended for the whole Knesset term of four years. On the question of electoral change, Mapai and Achdut Haavoda were bound by the Alignment agreement not to do anything about this during the duration of the Sixth Knesset, while Rafi wanted immediate action of some kind. A compromise was reached which removed the timetable set by Achdut Haavoda, yet made it clear that no action would be taken during the Sixth Knesset. This was to establish a committee 'to search out the most desirable electoral system for the state'.[49] It satisfied Achdut Haavoda because it did not specifically demand electoral change as an immediate goal, and Rafi because it did not ban electoral change, nor put off the possibility until the distant future. It was also agreed that a party Conference should be held about eight to twelve months before the Knesset elections in 1969, but how it was to be constituted (elected or by party agreement), and how other party institutions were to be constituted (elected or by party agreement), and how lists for the Knesset, Histadrut and municipal elections were to be selected, were all left for the new party to decide after its establishment. A tripartite committee was also set up to work out how party institutions were to be constituted until new ones were elected, the proviso being that Achdut Haavoda and Rafi be given equal representation. This committee finally settled on 57.3 per cent for Mapai, and 21.35 per cent for each of the other partners,[50] which was achieved by Mapai giving up about 3 per cent of its entitlement.

The final agreement was almost unanimously supported by Achdut Haavoda. Rafi, on the other hand, split over the issue: about 58 per cent of its Conference supported the tripartite union and 40 per cent supported continued independent existence (with 2 per cent abstaining). In the end, the majority of Rafi, including the top leadership, joined the new party: only Ben Gurion, who could not bring himself to join but did not actively oppose the ratification, and a few of his supporters stayed outside it. Their view was that there was no hope of change within Mapai, that the party machine would always be too strong, and that even with Dayan in Mapai they would never be in the majority.

Perhaps more important for the question of succession and the future was the note on which Dayan and Peres agreed to join the new party. For Peres, this was clearly not a return to Mapai but the establishment of a new party,

[48] Davar, 11.7.1967, 13.7.1967, 30.10.1967.
[49] Davar, 12.9.1967.   [50] Davar, 14.1.1968.

through which the desired and necessary social and economic changes in the state would be accomplished.[51] Dayan entered the new party in an extremely aggressive mood:

If I go to 110 Hayarkon Street, [Mapai headquarters] I go in order to fight, in order to suggest that the Prime Minister should not be Levi Eshkol, and the Finance Minister should not be Pinchas Sapir. I go in order to struggle for a change in the electoral system, and for a dismantling of the 'machinism' that dominates the state. I do not go to support, but to fight and to oppose.

The Mapai leadership can be replaced only within Mapai. We must decide, either we are an alternative to Mapai, or we oppose only the Mapai leadership. With only ten seats in the Knesset, it is impossible to be an alternative government in Israel.[52]

The new party, the Israeli Labour Party, was formally and ceremonially brought into being on 21 January 1968. On that date Mapai, founded in 1930, ceased formally to exist as an independent entity. But the formation of the Israeli Labour Party did not settle the country's outstanding problems. It did not even settle the succession question. As is clear from Dayan's remarks above, he returned to Mapai mainly to stake his claim to the succession, and so too did his party. But events did not turn out this way. When Eshkol died suddenly in February 1969, and the Prime Ministership was open, within a few days it had been passed on without any competitive election to Mrs Golda Meir, another of the Ben Gurion and Eshkol generation. What had happened in the interim was that Mr Sapir had become Secretary-General of the party and had welded together a central party majority around the Mapai base. It was so strong that Dayan did not allow his name to be put forward, despite his opposition to Mrs Meir's candidacy. As he put it, he did not wish to act as a Don Quixote.[53]

Mapai may have ceased to exist formally, but in actuality it continued to exist as the key and dominant factor in the Israeli Labour Party. Gradually it reasserted the characteristic methods and processes, and reconstructed the distinctive institutions and structures that have concerned us throughout this book. How it did so is another story. What is significant at this stage is that at the time of writing, leadership of the state and the dominant party had not yet passed out of the hands of the veteran founding generation, the *Vatikim*, into those of the younger successor generation, the *Zeirim*. The *Zeirim* began a succession struggle in the early 1950s, taking youth as their leitmotif. In the early 1970s, Mrs Meir, the most redoubtable of the veterans, was firmly in control at the age of seventy-three, and the *Zeirim* are no longer young. Dayan at the age of fifty-six had still not succeeded to the Prime Ministership. Nor did it appear certain that he would.

[51] *Davar*, 5.11.1967.   [52] *Davar*, 14.12.1967.
[53] N. Yanai, *Split in the Top Leadership* (Tel Aviv, 1969), p. 325 (Hebrew).

13. CONCLUSION: POLITICAL ORGANISATION AND POLITICAL SUCCESS

Our study began by seeking to explain how Mapai, the governing party, coped with the problems confronting the new state, the social changes that followed independence, and with the general functions and roles of political parties, so as to retain its position of dominance and leadership. In particular, we undertook to explain how the party's organisational framework dealt with the various political, social, and internal challenges that it encountered. It is now time to try and draw together some of the main themes of the preceding analysis.

Of the fact of Mapai's dominance in Israeli politics there can be no doubt. It won most seats at every national election from 1948 to 1965, formed and led the governmental coalition, and held all the key Cabinet posts. Its leaders and ministers were the best known, most popular and most influential political figures in the country. It held an absolute majority in all central and local Histadrut bodies, and ruled either in its own right or with coalition support in most of the local government authorities, including the major municipalities. And in 1968, it successfully broadened its base and increased its dominance through bringing about greater unity within the labour sector in Israel and forming the Israeli Labour Party.

If the main aim of political parties in competitive political systems is to win power in elections and to retain it, then Mapai was clearly a highly successful political party, and dwarfed all others in Israel, without blanketing them completely. We must therefore explain Mapai's success in this sphere. (It should be noted, of course, that there may be other criteria of success: one may examine the policies adopted and implemented, and attempt to assess their correctness or value in relation to various normative criteria, or in relation to other possible alternatives. One might then argue that according to these criteria the party was not successful despite continued electoral victory. Throughout our analysis we have not been concerned with this type of question, nor shall we attempt to do this now. Our concern is to explain an objectively measurable criterion of political success.)

At a very simple level we could say that Mapai retained its dominant position because it gained and retained the support of the population, because its organisational framework proved conducive to the direction of other major political institutions, and because it was able to perpetuate and maintain itself as an ongoing organisation. But this is at such a simple level as to be trite and almost tautologous. Our analysis has attempted to go deeper and explain *how* Mapai gained the support of the population, *how* it went about the task of directing government, and *how* it maintained itself.

Nor is it satisfactory merely to argue that Mapai retained its dominant position because it was the leading party at the time of independence, or because Ben Gurion, as the only individual charismatic leader, was the party's choice for Prime Minister, and that people supported Mapai because of their belief in him. While there is some truth in both of these positions – neither is sufficient explanation. Other parties that have led independence struggles elsewhere have been defeated, or have fallen prey to internal disunity. Other charismatic leaders have led their parties in the direction of personal rule, rather than in the direction of firmly established competitive democratic procedures as occurred in the case of Ben Gurion and Israel.

The basis of Mapai's continuing ability to gain and retain public support lay in its aggregative and integrative character. Mapai was the opposite of the exclusive political party: it went out of its way to incorporate diverse social forces, however opposed to each other in interest and goal these were. As a result of its aggregative policies Mapai as a party combined such different elements as close-knit communities, functional groups, economic interest groups, and primordial groups as well as individuals. To integrate these diverse elements into the party a combination of approaches was utilised: ideological appeals and commitments, policy promises and rewards, and various methods of institutional and organisational penetration and control. Welding these groups into one large inclusive party enabled Mapai to avoid two major problems that might have arisen: class polarisation and ethnic polarisation. By cutting across class and ethnic boundaries Mapai muted the force and bitterness of these cleavages, and in doing so facilitated the solution of basic socio-economic and ethnic problems.

Analysed from another viewpoint, Mapai recruited and socialised supporters, members and leaders who were instrumental in maintaining the organisation as an ongoing system. By openly seeking to recruit new members from almost all spheres of society Mapai made itself available as a focus of interest articulation among the various groups. Not only did they themselves view Mapai in this light because of its power, Mapai actively encouraged them to do so. It must be remembered that Israeli society underwent rapid and far-reaching changes after 1948. Making itself available to the new groups and social forces thrown up by these changes was one way in which Mapai sought to adapt to them. But adaptation to social change for Mapai as a governing party involved more than this. It meant coping with the new challenges, and more importantly, directing them and channelling them and the forces they created. Thus for Mapai adaptation to change had two facets. Mapai adapted to newly arisen groups like ethnic groups, professionals and

artisans by acknowledging that its historic membership and social structure
were too narrowly constructed, and that room had to be made for these
groups within the party if it was to succeed in gaining their political support.
By incorporating them a degree of control and direction over their activities
was also sought. Adaptation to these and other changes such as increasing
technological complexity and sophistication, economic modernisation and
independent political sovereignty also took another form, of attempted control and direction by Mapai. It had to make the policies, choices and decisions
which would affect the way in which these challenges would be met, and
in which these changes would develop. Adaptation in this sense meant
capacity to channel and direct change, and a degree of control over its consequences rather than blind or helpless dependence.

Mapai's approach to interest incorporation was to include as many groups
as it could within the party in the hope that the straddle of common party
loyalty would render decision making easier than if it took place in the competitive public political arena. Our analysis suggested that this assumption
proved correct in those areas where decision making took place within the
party. But it also showed that many decisions never reached party bodies,
and that others were not so successfully handled within the party. Nevertheless, even here in most cases they were handled by Mapai representatives
and leaders acting in ministerial, bureaucratic and arbitratory capacities.
Furthermore the incorporation of many diverse groups within the party
increased the autonomy[1] of the party as a decision making structure in that
no one group was strong enough to control proceedings, and the result was
often an elaborate bargaining and discussion process. The party was thus left
as final referee, arbitrator or decision maker. On the other hand, the attempt
to incorporate a new leadership group through the Alignment, and the many
implications this had for party identity and succession stretched the straddle
of party loyalty too far and led to a split. In the short view this weakened
Mapai, but in the longer term, a new, united, stronger party in which Mapai
was dominant eventuated. The formation of the Israeli Labour Party in 1968,
despite all the problems and vicissitudes that it encountered, must therefore be
seen as a vindication of the policies and processes of incorporating diverse
social forces, and as aggregating them into a stronger, more autonomous
amalgam.

Incorporating social forces, adapting to change, enabling the articulation
and aggregation of interests, on the one hand, and directing governmental
structures, on the other, were connected together by the party's organisational
and decision making framework. It was here that choices had to be made,
policies decided, and coordination of far-flung activities undertaken. It was
here that there was established the nexus between the party's internal and

[1] On the concept of autonomy in relation to strength of institutions and structures see
Huntington, *Political Order*, pp. 20–2.

external operations. Groups are not incorporated in a vacuum – but through organisational frameworks. It is through internal party organisation that interests may be pressed, leaders selected, and representation gained, and the manner and pattern in which these occur are of fundamental importance. In short, concern with participation, representation, responsiveness, internal constitutional arrangements, patterns of institutional coordination, and internal processes of decision making complemented our analysis of the incorporation of social forces. What is more, how the internal organisation works will to a large extent determine the success of the policies of incorporation and aggregation, and how the party organises internally will, in general, greatly affect the way in which it performs all its other political functions.

In the internal sphere we noted that Mapai did not succeed as well as in the external sphere. Its internal operations were flawed by insufficient attention to formal and universalistic criteria, particularly with regard to elections, which cast doubts upon the legitimacy of its electoral processes, aroused intense internal dissent and made it possible for certain groups to impair the participation of others. On the other hand, these same processes were able to produce results that were highly representative in terms of the party's social diversity, even if there was a marked degree of control over the exact identity of personnel making up this representative group, which may not have been a true reflection of membership views. Similarly, lack of concern with constitutional formality led to centralisation of control in the hands of narrower executive bodies, and the inevitable lessening of the influence of the wider representative bodies. But at the same time, such centralisation also provided the party with a degree of flexibility and capacity for improvisation, and prevented decision making processes from becoming clogged up. Moreover, centralisation facilitated the process of coordinating the various institutions which the party controlled, in so far as these narrow party bodies (however chosen) included in their memberships the leading personnel in these institutions.

Thus formal and constitutional processes were aided and assisted by various informal processes. One of these which we just noted was the growth of non-constitutionally recognised top executive bodies wielding effective power. Another was the growth of the party machine which developed to fill the void in the performance of key political functions where formal processes either did not exist or were not so well suited to the task. (And to the extent that the machine stepped in, it later made it more difficult for constitutional procedures to be established.) The machine provided loyal and undivided support for party leadership, and won its trust by being basically devoid of external political ambition. It thereby provided a degree of coherence and centralisation which the leadership was able to use, thus enabling it to concentrate upon important state matters. Similarly the machine served as an interest broker; it aggregated interests, and represented them successfully at various bureaucratic levels, and greatly aided the party in incorporating claimant groups. It was thus a key mechanism for meeting interest demands, for selecting leadership at various levels, for providing symbolic and psychological gratification. But precisely because it arose on the basis of procedures and conditions that lacked legitimacy, it became the focus of intensive internal conflict that threatened internal cohesion and engendered severe problems of organisational maintenance. Whatever its positive contributions, its undemocratic character and influence brought with it serious negative consequences which sowed marked internal disunity.

The internal decision making process as we have analysed it provides impressive evidence against Michels' theory of political party organisation and in favour of the counter-theory which has been elaborated elsewhere.[2] It shows clearly that there were many centres of decision making within Mapai, that various groups exercised power, and that there were different publics interested in, participating in and affected by decisions in different spheres. Generally speaking the processes that we analysed were based upon consensual power relations: the views of many groups were put forward or taken into consideration, and bargaining and mutual compromise characterised the discussions. (This of course excludes the area of personnel selection dealt with above.)

Mapai as a party provided coherence and facilitated coordination among these many decision making publics, and in this two elements were crucial. The first was the presence on the main party decision making bodies of Mapai ministers, parliamentarians, civil servants, Histadrut and municipal leaders and functionaries, and machine politicians who worked together to find mutually agreeable decisions. In cooperating in this manner they emphasised the practices and doctrines that we termed the primacy of party – the agreement to be bound by party decisions where differences of opinion occurred between them, based upon the recognition that the party took precedence over its individual representatives and leaders. This was reinforced by allowing leaders a wide latitude in conducting the affairs of the institutions which they ran on behalf of the party – they were rarely given orders, directed or shadowed, so that the party made decisions for them only when they came to it for decisions or when they agreed to such action. The primacy of party was therefore enhanced by the rarity of its implementation and by the agreement of those concerned.

From the political point of view Mapai's position was strengthened by the practices and norms which it evolved to govern relations between the party and the state. There was firstly the historical factor – Mapai preceded the state, and it had experience both in wielding power and in sharing power. It had also gained experience in connecting party to external administrative and political structures. Moreover, Mapai was committed to universalistic and

[2] Medding, 'A Framework for the Analysis of Power in Political Parties', pp. 8–17.

democratic norms of behaviour, and its leaders were aware of their operation in other societies. Despite the fact that the party preceded the state historically, its members and leaders always deferred to the idea and actuality of the state. While valuing the party highly they regarded it as a means to gaining power in the state and governing it; although of great significance, the party and its interests took second place behind those of the state. But at the same time the state was not glorified or magnified in a manner that threatened the independent existence and value of all other institutions in society, including the party. The state, too, was seen by Mapai in the context of the Zionist–Socialist movement, not as an end in itself but as a means to the fulfilment of elevated human and social goals, and was to be judged by its contribution towards them. In this sense the state was on a par with, if not secondary to, the party which embodied these goals and ideals through its leadership of the Zionist–Socialist movement.

This ideological relationship of party and state was given expression in Mapai practices. Mapai established a careful balance between party and state. It elevated party above the individuals in it, and the state above the party, while simultaneously elevating the majority party view of what was good for the state over any other view of what was in the state's interest.

In institutional form these relationships were established not long after independence in the way in which relations developed between the party institutions, Mapai's Cabinet ministers, its Parliamentary Party, and the bureaucracy. They were to be seen also in the manner in which Mapai handed over key functions to the state or took action to ensure state control of them. Its commitment to citizen equality and universality are clearly to be seen in the establishment of civilian control over the military, of an independent judiciary, and of a state educational system and employment service. More generally they are to be seen in the commitment to, and gradual establishment of a neutral bureaucracy.

Crucial to Mapai's success in handing over these functions to the state was the fact that independence brought about a vast expansion in the amount of political power available for distribution. The general extension of governmental activities led to a vast expansion of the party's power and roles, and it was thus able to hand over these particular functions without seriously weakening its own position. In fact, we argued above that in giving up these functions it strengthened itself through increasing its legitimacy and that of the system, whilst retaining its direction and control of these governmental structures and their functions, on behalf of and with the assistance of state power.

All this was achieved while maintaining an interest in the party's continued existence with the implied need to take into consideration the effects upon internal cohesion of various activities. Mapai developed a strong sense of organisational identity and the need for self-maintenance, a marked desire for institutional survival. This derived partly from the organisation's inbuilt imperative for survival and partly from the key role that the party played in the state. For the party to fail, to split, or to lose power would in the view of Mapai and its members create irreparable harm for the state with which it was closely involved in so many spheres of activity. Thus the party, as we noted in the last chapter, successfully withstood a major challenge to its unity and internal cohesion because it had inculcated in its members and leaders the paramount interest of the party, and its need to survive and to retain institutional identity. And in this context it is interesting to recall that the challenge to the party, its leadership, and its authoritative decision making institutions came from the party's only truly charismatic leader, who placed his will above that of the party, and who claimed that he did so in the name of the greater good of the state, and for the sake of the greatest human goals of justice and morality. The strength of the party as an institution can be gauged from the manner in which it successfully withstood this challenge.

To all these factors must be added the depth of Mapai penetration and control and its institutionalised form. It was not merely the political party as a collection of individuals which connected the population with the government and provided the latter with support. Nor was it a party of individuals together with a number of supporting interests such as trade unions which connected society and government. Mapai stood at the apex of a whole inter-connected network of organisations and institutions which it controlled and directed from within. Thus it not only controlled the key governmental structures but many of the secondary associations that filled the social space between individuals and their government, and it harnessed these to the party's cause. In some cases it set them up, in others it gained control of established structures – but in every instance it brought their organisational strength to bear in support of the party and its policies. Thus its channels of communication to the population were mediated and reinforced by con-nection with bodies and institutions that provided some of the population's most basic needs and interests. And it was recognition of the depth and scope of this institutional penetration, interconnection and control, above all, which forced Rafi to recognise that its leaders could come to power only within Mapai, not outside it.

This form of institutionalised penetration stretching from the centre right down to the local level facilitated institutional coordination, made it possible to satisfy interests immediately and locally, made support for the party secure, and made any change of government seem not only unlikely but also rather dangerous and foreboding, because it involved so much more than just the government. This situation was neatly described by a party official addressing the 1956 Mapai conference:

I once came to a Region Council, and spoke on a particular subject. A member got up and asked: Why is there no doctor here? I said to him: I come from Mapai headquarters, and not from Kupat Cholim headquarters. He answered me: 'Everything is Mapai...' For this member and many like him there is only one address. He sees the party at the head of the government, at the head of the Histadrut, at the head of the municipal authorities, at the head of the local government authorities, at the head of Kupat Cholim, at the head of Solel Boneh, at the head of the Labour Exchanges, and before him there is drawn an image of a party, that can do everything, and therefore he directs all his demands to it, and rightly so.[8]

A key external and situational factor must also be considered in assessing Mapai's success in retaining political dominance in Israel, and eventually in 1968 consolidating it even further by establishing the Israeli Labour Party. This relates to the logic of a multi-party coalition system. Mapai was by far the major power in every coalition. No government could be formed without it, and it was surrounded by a large number of smaller parties from among whom it could choose coalition partners. In this situation of one large party with at least one-third of the votes and usually more, and many other small parties, the large party will always do better than might be expected on the basis of its numerical proportions. This is particularly the case where, as in Israel, the largest party is close to the centre of the political spectrum, thus making it difficult, if not impossible, for extreme left and right parties to form a viable alternative coalition. In fact, it will often do better than a party with a majority in a two-party system which is subject to regular changes of government and periods in opposition. The major party in a coalition of the Israeli type can consolidate its power precisely because it does not have a majority, and shares power with other parties. This arises firstly because there exists less fear of absolute power in a coalition situation, and secondly because it can exercise some degree of choice over its partners. This becomes reinforced the longer the party retains its dominance, and the more it is able to perpetuate its hold over key power positions. It was precisely in recognition of this factor that Achdut Haavoda was attracted to the Alignment, and Rafi back to Mapai. Both realised that outside the major party access to and influence over key decisions and power structures were severely limited, and full-scale succession a virtual impossibility.

But by the same token it must not be assumed that such a situation is permanent. While it is difficult, or even unlikely, that other parties will be able to reduce such dominance and themselves become the largest party, it is not impossible. Whilst dominance rests on open electoral competition, while public moods may change, while there is the ever-present possibility that the party's internal cohesion will suffer and the organisation will be rent asunder, while technological and social changes continue, other parties may come to power. They may face difficult tasks in capturing this power and in unravelling the web of dominance built up by Mapai and succeeded to by the Israeli

[8] *Report 8th Mapai Conference*, 1956, p. 262.

Labour Party, particularly as their forces are spread across a number of other parties. Yet the opportunity is nevertheless there, and the social and institutional areas within which they must seek to displace the Israeli Labour Party clearly defined. Thus it cannot be taken for granted that a particular dominant party like the Israeli Labour Party will remain in power for ever. But this, after all, is the stuff of democratic and competitive politics.

SELECTED BIBLIOGRAPHY

OFFICIAL PARTY DOCUMENTS AND RECORDS

Mapai Central Committee, *Constitution, 1951.*
  Constitution, 1956.
  Constitution, 1956 (amended).
  Electoral Constitution, 1964.
  From Conference to Conference: A Review of the Activities of Mapai Head-quarters and Departments for 10th Mapai Conference, 1965.
  Minutes, 1948–61.
  Report 8th Mapai Conference, 26–30 August 1956.
  Report 8th Mapai Conference, 2nd Session, 13–16 May 1958.
  Report 9th Mapai Conference, 2nd Session, 23–25 March 1960.
  Report 9th Mapai Conference, 3rd Session, 15 October 1963.
  Minutes 10th Mapai Conference, 16–19 February 1965, mimeo.
  Report on Party Activities, October 1942–December 1943, presented to Mapai Council, January 1944.
  Report to 8th Mapai Conference, August 1956.
  Towards the Unity of the Labour Movement in Israel: Fundamentals of the Alignment between Mapai and Achdut Haavoda, 1965.
Mapai Control Commission, *Report on Control Commission Activities, 1950–1956.*
  Report to 9th Mapai Conference (for the period 1956–1960).
  Report to Mapai Central Committee (for the period 1960–1961).
  Report to 10th Mapai Conference (for the period 1960–1964).
Department for Artisans, *Internal Report on Departmental Activities, 1963–4* (mimeo).
Department of Information, *The Zeirim and the Party: Mapai Secretariat Discussions on Activity among the Young Generation, Jan–Feb. 1963.*
  Towards the 8th Conference, no. 1, 1956.
  Guide for Branch Secretaries, 1960.
Organisation Department, 'Lessons for the 1965 Election Year' (mimeo), n.d.
All the above publications are in Hebrew.

OTHER OFFICIAL PUBLICATIONS
Bank of Israel, *Annual Report, 1961.*
Central Bureau of Statistics, *Statistical Abstract of Israel,* 16 (1965).

Government Printer, *Israel Government Yearbook*, 1951–64.
Histadrut Executive Committee, *Shnaton Hahistadrut*, Vols. 1–5, 1962–8.
Knesset, *Divrei Haknesset*, 1949–60.

NEWSPAPERS AND PERIODICALS

Ashmoret, 1948–9, Tel Aviv (Hebrew).
Bterem, 1946–54, Tel Aviv (Hebrew).
Davar, 1948–68, Tel Aviv (Hebrew).
Haaretz, 1948–68, Tel Aviv (Hebrew).
Haboker, 1957–61, Tel Aviv (Hebrew).
Hador, 1949–52, Tel Aviv (Hebrew).
Hapoel Hatzair, 1945–68, Tel Aviv (Hebrew).
Iggeret, 1951–68, Ichud Hakibbutzim, Tel Aviv (Hebrew).
Israel Seen From Within, 1959–64, Tel Aviv.
Jerusalem Post, 1948–65, Jerusalem.
Jewish Observer and Middle East Review, 1956–62, London.
Maariv, 1958–68, Tel Aviv (Hebrew).
Mabat Chadash, 1965, Tel Aviv (Hebrew).
Min Hayesod, 1962–3, Tel Aviv (Hebrew).
Niv Hakvutza, 1948–68, Ichud Hakibbutzim, Tel Aviv (Hebrew).
Tlamim, 1950–68, Tnuat Hamoshavim, Tel Aviv (Hebrew).

BOOKS AND ARTICLES

C. Ake, *A Theory of Political Integration* (Homewood, Ill., 1967).
B. Akzin, 'The Role of Parties in Israeli Democracy', *Journal of Politics*, 17
    (1955), 507–15.
    'The Knesset', *International Social Science Journal*, 13 (1961), 567–82.
B. Akzin and Y. Dror, *Israel: High-Pressure Planning* (Syracuse, 1966).
G. A. Almond, 'A Comparative Study of Interest Groups and the Political
    Process', in Eckstein and Apter, 397–408.
G. A. Almond and J. Coleman, eds., *The Politics of the Developing Areas*
    (Princeton, 1959).
G. A. Almond and G. B. Powell Jr., *Comparative Politics: A Developmental
    Approach* (Boston, 1966).
A. Antonovsky, 'Ideology and Class in Israel', *Ammot* 2 (June 1963), 11–22
    (Hebrew).
D. E. Apter, *The Politics of Modernization* (Chicago, 1966).
A. Arian, *Ideological Change in Israel* (Cleveland, 1968).
Y. Arieli, *The Conspiracy* (Tel Aviv, 1965) (Hebrew).
S. Avineri, 'Localism in Reality – and its Dangers', *Ammot*, 2 (April 1964),
    52–5 (Hebrew).

E. Banfield and J. Q. Wilson, *City Politics* (Cambridge, Mass., 1963).

R. Bar Yoseph and D. Padan, 'The Oriental Communities in the Class Structure of Israel', *Molad*, 195-6 (1964), 504-16 (Hebrew).

A. Becker, *Our Path in the Histadrut* (Tel Aviv, 1965) (Hebrew).

S. H. Beer, *Modern British Politics* (London, 1965).

J. Ben-David, ed., *Agricultural Planning and Village Community in Israel* (Unesco, 1964).

J. Ben-David, 'Professionals and Unions in Israel', *Industrial Relations*, 5 (October 1965), 48-66.

D. Ben Gurion, 'In Defence of Messianism', *Midstream* 12 (March 1966), 64-5.

Things As They Are (Tel Aviv, 1965) (Hebrew).

M. H. Bernstein, 'Israel's Capacity to Govern', *World Politics*, 11 (1959), 399-417.

The Politics of Israel (Princeton, 1957).

Y. Braslavski, *The Jewish Workers' Movement in Palestine* (Tel Aviv, 1959-1963), 4 vols. (Hebrew).

M. Burstein, *Self-Government of the Jews in Palestine Since 1900* (Tel Aviv, 1934).

G. Caiden, 'Prospects for Administrative Reform in Israel', *Public Administration*, 46 (1968), 25-44.

Zev Carmi, *Trade Unionism in Israel and Among the Nations* (Tel Aviv, 1959) (Hebrew).

C. W. Cassinelli, 'The Law of Oligarchy', *American Political Science Review*, 47 (1953), 770-9.

E. Chassin and D. Horowitz, *The Affair* (Tel Aviv, 1961) (Hebrew).

M. Clawson, 'Israel Agriculture in Recent Years', *Agricultural History*, 29 (1955), 49-65.

'Man and Land in Israel', *Agricultural History*, 35 (1961), 189-92.

E. Cohen, L. Shamgar and Y. Levi, *Research on Immigrant Absorption in Development Towns* (Jerusalem, 1962) (Hebrew) (mimeo).

P. Cohen, 'Ethnic Group Differences in Israel', *Race*, 9 (1968), 303-10.

'Alignments and Allegiances in the Community of Shaarayim in Israel', *The Jewish Journal of Sociology*, 4 (1962), 14-38.

R. A. Dahl, 'A Critique of the Ruling Elite Model', *American Political Science Review*, 52 (1958), 463-9.

H. Dan, *In an Unpaved Path: The Story of Solel Boneh* (Jerusalem, 1963) (Hebrew).

H. Darin-Drabkin, *The Other Society* (London, 1962).

M. Derber, 'Israel's Wage Differential: A Persisting Problem', *Midstream*, 9 (March 1963), 3-15.

'National Wage Policy in Israel, 1948-62', *Quarterly Review of Economics and Business*, 3 (1963), 47-60.

Y. Dror, 'Nine Main Characteristics of Governmental Administration in Israel', *Public Administration in Israel and Abroad* (1964), 6–17.

'Public Policy Making in Israel', *Public Administration in Israel and Abroad* (1961), 5–16.

'Some Aspects of Staff Problems in Israel', *Kaplan School Reprint* (Jerusalem, 1962), 1–29.

Y. Dror and E. Gutmann, eds., *The Government of Israel: A Collection of Readings* (Jerusalem, 1962) (Hebrew).

M. Duverger, *Political Parties* (New York, 1963).

H. Eckstein and D. Apter, *Comparative Politics: A Reader* (New York, 1963).

S. N. Eisenstadt, *The Absorption of Immigrants* (London, 1954).

'Channels of Social Mobility', *Ammot* 2 (April 1964), 55–7 (Hebrew).

'Israel' in A. M. Rose, ed., *The Institution of Advanced Societies* (Minneapolis, 1958), 384–444.

Israeli Society (London, 1968).

'Patterns of Leadership and Social Homogeneity in Israel', *Social Science Bulletin*, 8 (1956), 37–41.

'The Sociological Structure of the Jewish Community in Palestine', *Jewish Social Studies*, 10 (January 1948), 3–10.

S. N. Eisenstadt, H. Adler, R. Bar-Yoseph and R. Kahana, eds., *The Social Structure of Israel: A Collection of Readings and Research* (Jerusalem, 1966) (Hebrew).

S. J. Eldersveld, *Political Parties: A Behavioral Analysis* (Chicago, 1964).

A. Etzioni, 'Agrarianism in Israel's Party System', *Canadian Journal of Economics and Political Science*, 23 (1957), 363–75.

'Alternative Ways to Democracy: The Example of Israel', *Political Science Quarterly*, 74 (1959), 196–214.

A Comparative Analysis of Complex Organisations (New York, 1961).

'The Decline of Neo-Feudalism in Israel', in *Studies in Social Change*, 180–97.

Studies in Social Change (New York, 1966).

Falk Project, *Fourth Report*, 1957 and 1958 (Jerusalem, 1959).

Fifth Report, 1959 and 1960 (Jerusalem, 1961).

L. Fein, *Politics in Israel* (Boston, 1967).

A. Friedman, *Workers Committee Research* (Tel Aviv, 1963) (Hebrew).

C. J. Friedrich, *Man and His Government: an Empirical Theory of Politics* (New York, 1963).

C. Geertz, ed., *Old Societies and New States: The Quest for Modernity in Asia and Africa* (New York, 1963).

'The Integrative Revolution: Primordial Sentiments and Civil Politics in New States', in Geertz, ed., 105–57.

H. H. Gerth and C. W. Mills, eds., *From Max Weber: Essays in Sociology* (London, 1947).

E. Gutmann, 'Citizen Participation in Political Life: Israel', *International Social Science Journal*, 12 (1960), 53–62.

'Israel', *Journal of Politics*, 25 (1963), 703–17.

'Some Observations on Politics and Parties in Israel', *India Quarterly*, 17 (1961), 1–27.

F. A. Hermens, 'The Dynamics of Proportional Representation' in Eckstein and Apter, 254–81.

A. Hertzberg, ed., *The Zionist Idea* (New York, 1960).

D. Horowitz, 'The Differences Between a Chalutzic Society and a Normal Society', *Molad*, 146–7 (October 1960) (Hebrew).

S. P. Huntington, *Political Order in Changing Societies* (New Haven, 1968).

O. Janowsky, *The Foundations of Israel* (New York, 1959).

Scott Johnson, 'Major Party Politics in a Multi-Party System: The Mapai Party of Israel', *Il Politico*, 30 (1965), 331–46.

R. Kahana and A. Einhorn, *The Social Structure of Israel: A Statistical Collection* (Jerusalem, 1966) (Hebrew).

E. Kanovsky, *The Economy of the Israeli Kibbutz* (Cambridge, Mass., 1963).

Y. Katan, 'At the Beginning of the Process of Integration', *Ammot*, 2 (April 1964), 57–61 (Hebrew).

E. Katz and S. N. Eisenstadt, 'Some Sociological Observations on the Response of Israeli Organizations to New Immigrants', in S. N. Eisenstadt, *Essays on Comparative Institutions* (New York, 1965), 251–71.

S. Koenig, 'The Crisis in Israel's Collective Settlements', *Jewish Social Studies*, 14 (1952), 145–66.

Y. Korn, *The Ingathering of the Exiles and Their Settlement: Towards a History of Immigrant Moshavim in Israel* (Tel Aviv, 1964) (Hebrew).

O. Kraines, *Government and Politics in Israel* (Boston, 1962).

R. Lane, *Political Life* (Glencoe, Ill., 1959).

J. LaPalombara, ed., *Bureaucracy and Political Development* (Princeton, 1963).

J. LaPalombara and M. Weiner, eds., *Political Parties and Political Development* (Princeton, 1966).

W. Laqueur, *The Road to War* (Harmondsworth, England, 1968) (Penguin).

P. Lavon, *Values and Changes* (Tel Aviv, 1960) (Hebrew).

D. Lerner, *The Passing of Traditional Society: Modernizing The Middle East* (New York, 1958).

S. M. Lipset, M. A. Trow and J. S. Coleman, *Union Democracy* (New York, 1962).

M. Lissak, 'Geographic Localism, Sectoral Particularism and Societal Democracy', *Ammot*, 2 (April 1964), 61–3 (Hebrew).

M. Lissak, 'Patterns of Change in Ideology and Class Structure in Israel', *The Jewish Journal of Sociology*, 7 (1964), 46–62.

M. Lotan, 'The Histadrut, Impetus to the Building of an Egalitarian Society', *Ovnayim* (1961), 48–58 (Hebrew).

A Malkin, 'The Histadrut in the State', *Ovnayim* (1961), 29–47 (Hebrew).

N. Malkosh, *Histadrut in Israel: Its Aims and Achievements* (Tel Aviv, 1958).

J. Matras, *Social Change in Israel* (Chicago, 1965).

J. D. May, 'Democracy, Organisation, Michels', *American Political Review*, 59 (1965), 414–29.

Neil A. McDonald, 'Party Perspectives: A Survey of Writings', in Eckstein and Apter, 332–51.

R. T. McKenzie, *British Political Parties* (London, 1955).

P. Y. Medding, 'A Framework for the Analysis of Power in Political Parties', *Political Studies*, 18 (1970), 1–17.

J. H. Meisel, *The Myth of the Ruling Class* (Ann Arbor, 1958).

R. K. Merton, *Social Theory and Social Structure* (Glencoe, Ill., 1957).

Y. Meshel, *The Histadrut's Wages Policy for 1963/4* (Tel Aviv, 1963) (Hebrew).

R. Michels, *First Lectures in Political Sociology* (Minneapolis, 1949).

Political Parties (Glencoe, Ill., 1958).

S. Nakdimon, *Towards the Zero Hour* (Tel Aviv, 1968) (Hebrew).

S. Neumann, 'Towards a Comparative Study of Political Parties', in S. Neumann, ed., *Modern Political Parties* (Chicago, 1956), 395–421.

Z. Onn, *Hevrat Ovdim, Israel's Labour Economy* (Tel Aviv, 1964).

M. Ostrogorski, *Democracy and the Organisation of Political Parties*, S. M. Lipset, ed. (2 vols., New York, 1964).

T. Parsons, 'On the Concept of Political Power', in S. M. Lipset and R. H. Bendix, eds., *Class, Status, and Power* (New York, 1968), 240–65.

Structure and Process in Modern Societies (Glencoe, Ill., 1960).

R. Patai, *Israel Between East and West* (Philadelphia, 1953).

A. Perlmutter, 'The Institutionalization of Civil-Military Relations in Israel: The Ben Gurion Legacy and Its Challengers (1953–1967)', *Middle East Journal*, 22 (1968), 415–31.

'The Israeli Army in Politics: The Persistence of the Civilian over the Military', *World Politics*, 20 (1968), 606–43.

Louis Pincus, 'The Egghead and the Israeli Labour Movement', *Israel Seen from Within* (September 1958), 8.

W. Preuss, *The Labour Movement in Israel* (Jerusalem, 1965).

L. Pye, *Aspects of Political Development* (Boston, 1966).

N. Raphaeli, 'The Senior Civil Service in Israel: Notes on some Characteristics', *Public Administration*, 48 (Summer, 1970), 169–78.

S. Rolbant, *Mapai: The Israel Labour Party* (World Federation of Mapai, Tel Aviv, 1956).

A. Rubner, *The Economy of Israel* (London, 1959).

N. Safran, *The United States and Israel* (Cambridge, Mass., 1963).

G. Sartori, *Democratic Theory* (New York, 1965).

L. Seligman, *Leadership in a New Nation* (New York, 1964).

P. Selznick, *Leadership in Administration: A Sociological Interpretation* (New York, 1957).

E. Shils, *Political Development in the New States* (The Hague, 1962).

Y. Talmon-Garber, 'Social Differentiation in Cooperative Communities', *British Journal of Sociology*, 3 (1952), 339–57.

A. Tartakower, 'The Making of Jewish Statehood in Palestine', *Jewish Social Studies*, 10 (July 1948), 209.

D. B. Truman, *The Governmental Process* (New York, 1952).

H. Viteles, *A History of the Cooperative Movement in Israel* (7 vols., London, 1966–8).

F. Von Der Mehden, *Politics in the Developing Areas* (Englewood Cliffs, N.J., 1964).

M. Weber, *The Theory of Social and Economic Organisation* (New York, 1947).

C. Weil, *Communal Problems in an Immigrant Settlement* (Kaplan School. Hebrew University Researches in Sociology, 2, Jerusalem, 1957) (Hebrew).

M. Weiner, *Party Building in a New Nation: The Indian National Congress* (Chicago, 1967).

'Political Integration and Political Development', *The Annals*, 358 (March 1965), 52–64.

A. Weingrod, 'Immigrants, Localism, and Political Regime', *Ammot*, 2 (February 1964), 15–22 (Hebrew).

Israel: Group Relations in a New Society (London, 1965).

Reluctant Pioneers: Village Development in Israel (Ithaca, 1966).

R. Weitz, 'Family Farms Versus Large Scale Farms in Rural Development (Israel's Case History)', *Artha Vijnana*, 5 (1963), 225–40.

D. Willner, 'Politics and Change in Israel: The Case of Land Settlement', *Human Organisation*, 24 (1965), 65–72.

Y. Yagol, *Changes in the Jewish Labour Movement* (Tel Aviv, 1958) (Hebrew).

N. Yanai, *Split in the Top Leadership* (Tel Aviv, 1969) (Hebrew).

R. Zamir, *Beer Sheba 1958/9: Social Processes in a Development Town* (Kaplan School, Hebrew University Researches in Sociology, 3, Jerusalem, 1964) (Hebrew).

W. P. Zenner, 'Sephardic Communal Organisations in Israel', *Middle East Journal*, 21 (1967), 173–93.

F. Zweig, 'The Jewish Trade Union Movement in Israel', *The Jewish Journal of Sociology*, 1 (1959), 23–42.

UNPUBLISHED

Israel Bureau of Applied Social Research, 'Mapai Activists – An Analysis of Their Social Structure and Attitudes', June 1956 (commissioned by Mapai).

L. J. Fein, 'The Political World of Jerusalem's People: A Study of the Political Orientations and Cultural Backgrounds of Traditional, Transitional and Modern Types in Jerusalem' (unpublished Ph.D. dissertation, Michigan State University, 1962).

A. Perlmutter, 'Ideology and Organization': The Politics of Socialist Parties in Israel 1897–1957' (unpublished Ph.D. dissertation, University of California, Berkeley, 1957).

INDEX

Histadrut Trade Union Department, 237–9
  and wages policy determination, 192–
    213
  and women, 73
Hitachdut Baalei Mlacha, see Artisans
  Association

Ichud Hakvutzot V'hakibbutzim, 22–35
  (Ichud) see also kibbutzim
  economic interests, 26–7
  foundation of, 23–4
  ideological interests, 28
  industrial undertakings of, 26
  organisational relationships with Mapai,
    28–35
  size of, 24
ideological collectivism
  consciously avoided by Mapai kibbut-
    zim, 32
  in non-Mapai kibbutzim, 30, 34
ideological differences, and conflict between kibbutz movements, 23–4
ideology
  intensity of, in some kibbutz move-
    ments, 23
  kibbutz leadership of, in Palestine, 22–3
  strength of, in Palestine, 11–13
immigrant associations, 70
  see also Iraquis, Oriental immigrants
incorporation
  of diverse social forces into Mapai, 19–
    81, 82–3, 191, 301–2
  of artisans, 53–9
  of ethnic groups, 67–72
  of industrial workers, 47–53
  of kibbutzim, 22–35
  of moshavim, 36–45
  of professionals, 59–65
  of religious groups, 75–78
  of women, 72–5
  of youth, 80–1
  assisted by politicisation, 244
  basis of Mapai's political power, 279,
    300
  conscious Mapai policy of, 157
  difficulties of, with regard to collective
    settlements, 33–4
  diverse tactics of, 300
  failure of policy of, during party split,
    277–80, 301
  importance of organisational structure
    in, 83–4
  and institutional autonomy, 301
  leads to control of social forces and
    institutions, 300–1
  policy of, vindicated, 301
industrial interests, 50–1

industrial workers, 47–53
institutionalisation
  and autonomy, 301
  high degree of, in Mapai, 279, 305
interest aggregation
  as major function of political party, 2, 4
  capacity for, basis of Mapai's domin-
    ance, 300
  dependence of leadership selection upon,
    65
  dependence of political recruitment
    upon, 65
  difficulty in regard to diffuse and sym-
    bolic interests, 66–7
  importance of organisational structure
    in, 65, 83, 301–2
  and incorporation of diverse social
    forces, 19–20, 301
  promoted by leadership selection pro-
    cesses, 4, 163–4
  promoted by politicisation, 244
  role of political machine in, 302–3
  shared with other political structures, 4
  various approaches to, 300
interest articulation
  as function of political party, 2
  in interest groups, 4
  in parties, 4
  in party ideological groups' demands, 4
  of oriental ethnic groups, 69–71
  organisational structure in, 83
  and politicisation, 244
  problem of, for moshavim, 35–6
  and representation, 188
Iraquis, and ethnic conflict in Beer Sheba,
  97
  see also Mapai Department of Iraquis
Irgun Imahot Ovdot (Organisation of
  Working Mothers), activities of, 73–5
Iserson, Zev, see Onn, Zev
Israel Defence Forces, 225–6
Israeli Labour Party, 280, 292–8

Jewish Agency
  Executive in Jerusalem, 10, 12
  party key used in, 226, 242
  politicisation during Yishuv, 224
  Settlement Department of, 38–9, 40

Kaplan, Eliezer, 173
Kargman, Yisrael, 183
Katznelson, Berl, 78
Kesse, Yona, 123, 218
kibbutzim, 22–35
  economic interests of, 26–7
  growth of (1922–45), 23–4
  and wages policy, 209

party–Histadrut relations—*cont.*
party control of Histadrut, and legitimacy, 184–5
role of parties in Histadrut, 183–4
Party Machine, Mapai, 134–61
see also *Gush*, Mapai Haifa branch, Mapai Tel Aviv branch
party–state relations, 84–5, 219–20, 303–304
relations of party and government, 116–119, 131–2, 189
state above party, *Mamlachtiut*, 225
via Parliamentary Party, 176–83
Peres, Shimon
appointed to ministry on Ben Gurion's insistence, 173
attacks Histadrut, 258–9
attitude to Israeli Labour Party, 292–298
forced to resign from ministry (1965), 175, 274
enters politics, 80, 252
preselected for Knesset on Central list, 169
strained relations with Lavon, 128, 254–257, 261–3
see also *Rafi, Zeirim*
Plugot, paramilitary force in Haifa, 142
policy application, as function of political party, 2
policy making, 191–220, 301–3
as function of political party, 2
as problem after independence, 3
in Mapai, facilitated by overarching consensus of common party membership, 163, 192, 243
effects of politicisation upon, 243
facilitated by resort to intra-party institutions, 189
made more difficult by conflicting internal interest groups, 20, 191–2
viewed from point of view of participation, 191
Political Committee, Mapai, *see* Mapai Political Committee
political independence, 1–3
and expansion of political power resources, 3, 304
and nation-building, 2–3
and state-building, 3
in Israel, 13; creates problems of coordination for party institutions, 117; and decline of primacy of kibbutz, 24–5; and establishment of new institutional structures, 29–30; and general problems for Mapai, 13–16; immigration after, 14–15; industrialisation

after, 14; social changes following, 13–14
political machines, theory of, 134–6
political parties
central role of, in Palestine, 6–13, 225
connecting link between government and social forces, 1–2
control government, 1–2
distinctive institution of modern politics, 1
legitimacy in, via representative formal electoral process, 133
organiser of mass support, 1
power in, 5, 135, 303
political recruitment, 2
as function of political party, 2
as party membership, 19
of new immigrants, 38–9
of Oriental ethnic groups, 68–9
problems of, without organisational penetration, 81
success of, reason for Mapai's dominance, 300–1
via organisational structures, 83
political socialisation
as function of political party, 2
and incorporation of new social forces, 3
and legitimacy, 3
by other social institutions, 4
Mapai direct channel of, for Oriental ethnic groups, 69
of Orientals, within new moshavim, 37–39
problem of, without organisational penetration, 81
success of, reason for Mapai's dominance, 300–1
via organisational structure, 83
politicisation, 221–4
effects of, 243–5
effects of establishment of state upon, 225–6
continuing politicisation of Jewish Agency, 242
continuing politicisation of Kupat Cholim, 234–6, 240
in Palestine, 224–5
population
of Palestine (1900), 7
of Israel (1948), Jewish, 14
Preparation Committee, Mapai, *see* Mapai Preparation Committee
primacy of the party, 116–19, 165, 189–90, 195, 206–7, 303–5
Prime Minister
Mapai constitution amended to provide for selection of Prime Minister, 171–2

social forces,
  connected to government by political
    parties, 1
  incorporation of, by Mapai, 19–85
  see also incorporation
socialisation see political socialisation
Soviet Union, attitude to Israel, 219
Split, the, 263–80
  Abba Choushi stays in Mapai, 275
  effects on Gush, 276–7
  evaluation of, 276–80
  Netzer stays in Mapai, 275
  Rafi dissidents expelled from Mapai, 275
  Rafi list announced by Ben Gurion, 275
  see also Alignment, Zeirim, Rafi, Lavon
    Affair
state building, 3–4, 222–4, 244–5, 303–5
strikes
  Ata strike in Haifa, 239
  Engineers strike (1962), 64, 212
  in metal manufacturing industry, 195
  amongst professionals (1955), 197
  of Secondary Teachers Association, 211–
    213
sub-branches of Mapai, functions of, 89–
  91
succession
  as function of political party, 2
  conflict over, embraces many aspects,
    248
  ensured by party processes of leadership
    selection, 163
  and organisational cohesion, 246–8
  problematic after independence, 3
  unresolved, 298
  conflict about, in Mapai, 246–98
Succession problem, the, 246–98

Tel Aviv, Mapai branch in, see Mapai Tel
  Aviv branch
Tenth Mapai Conference, see Mapai
  Tenth Conference
Tnuat Hamoshavim
  economic interests of, 39–41
  and interest representation, 42–3
  Mapai, relations with, 35, 43–5
  and Mapai membership, 37
  and pre-1948 settlers, 35–6
  and post-1948 settlers, 37–9
  and religious settlers, 76
  reaction to split (1965), 43–5
  see also moshavim
Trade Union Department, Histadrut, see
  Histadrut Trade Union Department

Trade Union Department, Mapai, see
  Mapai Trade Union Department
Troika, the (Meir, Sapir, Aranne), 265–6

Vatikim, 246–98
  see also Gush, Zeirim
vertical cleavages, 66–7

wages policy decisions, 192–213
Weber, Max, on politicians, 158–9
women, 72, 74–5
Women Workers Council, (Moetzet
  Hapoalot), 73
Women Workers Movement, (Tnuat
  Hapoalot), 72–3
Women's Department, Mapai, see Mapai
  Women's Department
Workers Committees (Vaad Ovdim), 48–
  51

Yadlin, Aharon, 260–1, 273, 290
Yadlin, Asher, 199, 273
Yaffe, Eliezer, 36
Yeshayahu, Yisraeli, 130, 149 and n., 153
Yishuv, 6–13, 224–6
  kibbutzim in, 22–6
  moshavim in, 36–7
  party life in, 86–9
  politicisation in, 224–6
  professionals in, 59–60
  religion in, 75
  see also Palestine
Yizreeli, Yoseph, 139
Yoseph, Dov, 174
Yosephtal, Dr Giora, 124–7, 173, 250–1,
  252
Yosephtal, Mrs Senta, 187
Young Generation Staff (Mateh Dor
  Hatzair), 79
  see also Zeirim
Young Guard (Mishmeret Hatzeira), 78,
  248
  see also Zeirim
youth, 78–81
  see also Zeirim
Youth Department, Mapai, see Mapai
  Youth Department

Zar, Mordechai, M.K., 149 and n.
Zeirei Haichud, 260–1
Zeirim, 78–81, 124–6, 139–41, 147–9, 155,
  234–6, 246–98
  see also Ben Gurion, Dayan, Ofer, Peres,
  Yosephtal, Rafi, Vatikim, Gush

For EU product safety concerns, contact us at Calle de José Abascal, 56–1°,
28003 Madrid, Spain or eugpsr@cambridge.org.

www.ingramcontent.com/pod-product-compliance
Ingram Content Group UK Ltd.
Pitfield, Milton Keynes, MK11 3LW, UK
UKHW042147130625
459647UK00011B/1224